BLACK!
Feminist!
FREE!

BLACK!
Feminist!
FREE!

Selected Writings, Interviews, and Speeches

Beverly Guy-Sheftall

Third World Press
Publishers since 1967
Chicago

 Third World Press is a project of Third World Press Foundation, P.O. Box 19730, Chicago, IL 60619.

First Edition
Printed in the United States of America

ISBN: 978-0-88378-433-4 | Paperback
29 28 27 26 25 1 2 3 4 5

Cover illustration by Nicole Carter
Cover and interior layout and design by Denise Borel Billups

Table of Contents

Preface ix
Acknowledgments xiii
Introductions xvii

Beverly Guy-Sheftall and the Time-Traveling Legacy of Black Feminist Genealogies — Banah Ghadbian xix
For Beverly Guy-Sheftall — Moon Charania xxv

PART I
The Personal is Political

1. Reflections on Forum '85 in Nairobi, Kenya (1986) 3
2. Women's Studies at Spelman College: Reminiscences from the Director (1986) 6
3. Practicing What You Preach: Strategies of an Ex-English Professor (1991) 15
4. Breaking the Silence: A Black Feminist Response to the Thomas/Hill Hearings (1992) 21

PART II
Black Feminism

5. The Evolution of Feminist Consciousness Among African American Women: WORDS OF FIRE (1995) 27
6. Gender Talk, (Introduction with Johnnetta Betsch Cole) (2000) 51
7. African Feminist Discourse: A Review Essay (2003) 62
8. Remembering Our Feminist Forefathers (2006) 70
9. Black Feminist Studies: The Case of Anna Julia Cooper (2009) 82

PART III
Black Studies/Women's Studies

10. The Promise and Challenge of Black Women's Studies: A Report from the Spelman Conference, May 25-26, 1990, with Patricia Bell-Scott and Jacqueline Jones Royster (1991) 93
11. Black Women's Studies: The Interface of Women's Studies and Black Studies (1992) 101
12. Reconstructing a Black Female Intellectual Tradition: Commentary on Harold Cruse's *The Crisis of the Negro Intellectual* (1994) 110

13. Exploring Difference: Racial and Global Perspectives in Graduate Women's Studies (1998) 114
14. Shifting Contexts: Lessons from Integrating Black, Gender, and African Diaspora Studies (2002) 120
15. Conquering the Black Girl Blues (with Lani Valencia Jones) (2015) 128

PART IV
HBCUs

16. Black Women and Higher Education: Spelman and Bennett Colleges Revisited (1982) 145
17. Educating Black Women Students for the Multicultural Future (with Kimberly Wallace Sanders) (1996) 156
18. Shared Governance, Junior Faculty, and HBCUs (2006) 161
19. Audre Lorde and Spelman College (with Johnnetta Betsch Cole) (2014) 168
20. Breaking Silence (with M. Jacqui Alexander) (2019) 170
21. Challenges and Possibilities at HBCUs after the COVID-19 Pandemic Reinvesting in Vital Institutions, with Kimberly M. Jackson (2021) 198
22. Building the House You Want to Live and Teach In - How Women's Studies Nurtured Radical Transformation at Spelman College (2022) 203

PART V
Celebrating Black Women

23. The Women of Bronzeville (1979) 211
24. Warrior Women: Art as Resistance (1996) 224
25. Elizabeth Catlett: Making What You Know Best (2003) 236
26. "Rebel Woman" in *Mickalene Thomas: I Can't See You Without Me* (2018) 243
27. Coretta Scott King: The Beloved Community Revisited (2025) 249
28. Loving bell hooks (2022) 270

Part VI
Friendships

29. Tribute to Rudolph P. Byrd (2011) 277
30. Love Note to Toni (2014) 279
31. Letter to Dr. Levi Watkins, Jr. (2020) 281
32. Remembering Professor Peter Agbor-Tabi (2021) 286
33. Letter to Alice Walker (2021) 289

Part VII
Interviews

34. Whither Black Women's Studies? Interview with Evelynn M. Hammonds (1997) 297
35. Toni Cade Bambara: Black Feminist Foremother (2008) 309
36. The ROOT Interview: Beverly Guy-Sheftall on Black Feminism by Akoto Ofori-Atta (2010) 323
37. What Would Harriet Do? A Legacy of Resistance and Activism: A Conversation with Barbara Smith and Beverly Guy-Sheftall, Moderated by Paula Giddings (2014) 327
38. Feminist Freedom Warriors (Linda E. Carty and Chandra Talpade Mohanty in conversation wth Beverly Guy-Sheftall) (2015) 345
39. *Auburn Avenue* Interview (2016) 368
40. Honoring Beverly Guy-Sheftall, by Moya Bailey (2018) 371

Index 375

Preface

When Haki Madhubuti and Michael Simanga approached me about publishing with Third World Press a body of my writing, which began in 1979 with the publication of *Sturdy Black Bridges: Visions of Black Women in Literature,* I was startled and pleased but remembered that Haki had been making a persuasive argument in this regard for years. I immediately said "yes" this time because I now thought such a book would make it convenient to read in one place what I have been thinking and saying for more than forty years. I also thought it was important to capture the thinking over time of an African American woman, born in the Jim Crow South of the 1940s, who had spent her entire professional career at historically Black colleges, and who had crafted a particular life as a feminist scholar/activist that might be instructive for younger generations.

I have arranged what is included thematically—stand-alone essays, book chapters, introductions, reports, interviews, and personal reflections. I wanted to capture my scholarly self as well as who I am politically and personally. Because Spelman College, the oldest historically Black college for women, has been my home as a teacher over the past 50 years, as well as the place where I began my college days as a sixteen-year-old from Memphis, Tennessee, in 1962, I wanted reflections about my work where I have spent my adult life. So, I asked for introductions from Dr. Banah Ghadbian, whom I taught as a first-year student in my Introduction to Women's Studies class and who recently completed her PhD in Ethnic Studies, and Dr. Moon Charania, a relatively recent colleague with whom I share intellectual and political interests in the field of Women's, Gender, and Sexuality Studies. My instructions to them were simple: Write whatever you like about our connections and what has impacted you as a result.

I begin with how I got here. After two years teaching at Alabama State University, 1969-1971, I began what we could now call my permanent teaching career in the Department of English at Spelman in 1971, where I had graduated in 1966 as an English major. I taught five courses each semester and I did not have a PhD. I had a master's degree from Atlanta University where I wrote a thesis on "Faulkner's Treatment of Women in His Major Novels." I was not only untenured, but not even on the track!! Eight years later, I worked with my department colleague, the late Roseann P. Bell, and later Bettye J. Parker, to publish *Sturdy Black Bridges,* the first anthology of its kind. In addition to the writings, it featured amazing photographs as well as original art by now Dr. Rick

Powell, who was an undergraduate student at Morehouse College and who is now a premier scholar of African American art and a distinguished professor at Duke University. Like much of my subsequent writing, the anthology was a fulfilling, collaborative project. I was not motivated by tenure protocols with respect to co-authored scholarship. In fact, over the course of a long academic career, I have been interested in producing work that advanced the fields of African American and Women's Studies and eventually Black Feminist Studies, so it is not surprising that I was drawn to feminist writing partners, especially Johnnetta Betsch Cole and Rudolph P. Byrd, with whom I produced the most exciting anthologies *Traps: African American Men on Gender and Sexuality* and *I Am Your Sister: Collected and Unpublished Writings of Audre Lorde,* as well as a monograph, *Gender Talk: The Struggle for Women's Equality in African American Communities.* I was pleased as well to work with Professors Stanlie M. James and Frances Smith Foster on the anthology *Still Brave: The Evolution of Black Women's Studies,* in which we were able to celebrate the now iconic first Black Women's Studies anthology, *All The Women Are White, All The Blacks Are Men, But Some of Us Are Brave: Black Women's Studies,* edited by Gloria T. Hull, Patricia Bell Scott, and Barbara Smith.

Roseann and I were motivated by what might seem unusual now. It is perhaps easy to forget now our students' unfamiliarity—like students everywhere at the time—with Black women's rich literary tradition, given the prominence today of such writers as Zora Neale Hurston, Toni Morrison, and Alice Walker, who was a sophomore at Spelman when I was a first-year student. Our editors' note for the collection was bold. Though we didn't have the language then, we were writing against a masculinist literary canon:

> When we consider that it took Ralph Ellison a score of years to write *Invisible Man,* and Alex Haley twelve to write *Roots,* the four years of labor poured into *Sturdy Black Bridges* seem almost insignificant. However, *Sturdy Black Bridges* is a different kind of experience from that of *Roots* or *Invisible Man,* not in quality or even concept, but in its eclectic commitment. That eclecticism, represented in works as diverse as Margaret Walker's classic poem "Lineage" and Mae Jackson's "Cleaning Out the Closet," has been at times frustrating; more often it has led to valuable exposures—encounters with people, places, and ideologies which have enhanced our own and others' lives. (vii)

The volume marked my first encounter with scholar/activist/writer Toni Cade Bambara. I took myself over to her apartment on Simpson Road in Atlanta with a tape recorder that I did not even know how to operate, and I interviewed her with her daughter, Karma, running around. The interview that appeared in *Sturdy Black Bridges,* "Commitment: Toni Cade Bambara Speaks," is among the first, if not the first, published interview with Toni, whose pioneering *The Black Woman: An Anthology,* which had appeared in 1970, is now iconic in Black feminist studies and feminist theory more broadly. As we wrote in *Bridges*:

> The shape of this anthology is incomplete and fluid—all collections are which purport to be fundamental. But the work is generically incomplete, for such are the lives of people, and Black women, among others in the First World, are people, creating and destroying with regular frequency ideas and even dogmas. Hence, the unfinished song of *Sturdy Black Bridges.* (vii)

It was impossible for us to have imagined what *Sturdy Black Bridges* might have set in motion in terms of scholarly output establishing the richness of our Black women's literary tradition that began in the U.S. in the 19th century. In my first published essay, included in the collection, "The Women of Bronzeville," I analyzed Gwendolyn Brooks' poetry and deployed, without realizing it, a Black feminist lens that is now pervasive, the results of which when employed by scholars are now dazzling.

Over the course of a forty-year writing practice, I have moved a long way from *Bridges* in many ways. I have moved away from literary studies for the most part and have spent many years as an archeologist, uncovering and making the case that we also have a very rich Black feminist intellectual tradition, including men, across many disciplines with varying theoretical stances. My work has included tracing the development of Black feminist thought, which began in the early 19th century, and writing about the radical politics of Coretta Scott King, which repositions her and takes her out of the narrow roles of "mother of the civil rights movement" and widow of Martin Luther King Jr. It places her where she belongs—as one of the most progressive figures in the civil rights movement, particularly around LGBTQ issues. On this journey, I discovered Claudia Jones and other Black communist women. I am also now exploring with colleagues the critical role of African American women in the so-called "second-wave" women's liberation movement and moving them from the margins to the center of that history.

My deeper dive into Black women's history also strengthened my scholarly commitments to queering our history. In this regard, I explored the personal papers of Audre Lorde, which are at the Spelman College Archives as a result of her friendship with then President Johnnetta Betsch Cole. I was often frustrated that Audre was not on the syllabus of many African American literature classes or in the broader American literary canon. I discovered that Lorraine Hansberry, the well-known playwright (*A Raisin in the Sun*), had also written anonymous letters to *The Ladder*, the first nationally distributed lesbian magazine. I became especially interested in the politics and power dynamics of gender and sexuality matters in African American communities. I became more interested in our memoirs and journals and letters and became more convinced about the need for Black women to write more revelatory, in-your-face texts so that we might learn more about our intimate, interior lives. This desire motivated me to write more about my own personal life, and I hope to finish my own memoir since I now have the courage to complete it, having been inspired by like-minded comrades who have also penned memoirs.

Unlike *Sturdy Black Bridges*, this collection *Black! Feminist! Free!* is complete in the sense that I am sharing the most important writing and speaking, including interviews, I have done since 1979. At the end of a long, fulfilling academic career at historically Black colleges, I want to remember my mother and father, who had an enormous influence on who I became personally and professionally. Ernestine Varnado Guy graduated from Lane College (in three years) as a math major and worked at Owen College, initially in the business office where my uncle Levi Watkins Sr. was president and brother-in-law; he had married her sister and best friend, Lillian. When my mother died too young in 1980, I remembered that she was the one who had encouraged me to pursue a college teaching career and eventually get a PhD. Her last words to me were about how proud she was of my first book, *Bridges*. When I went through her keepsakes back home, I also discovered her college transcript with all A's, which underscored for me why education for her three daughters had been so important to her.

Walter P. Guy Jr. graduated from LeMoyne College with a major in political science and spent his entire career at Manassas High School teaching art. What I remembered most was his master teaching, since from the sixth grade until I graduated in 1962 my sisters and I had the privilege of observing him in action. Perhaps my love for teaching was inspired by the impact he had on his students for over 40 years. At the end of his life, especially since I rarely went home to Memphis, my father asked me what I did and I simply said, "I'm a teacher, like you." I didn't mention the writing or the books because I suspected it was Beverly the teacher that would have made him proudest. I am sure that if my parents were able to hold this book in their hands, they would be happy and say to themselves that they had done a good job with their often contrary, non-traditional daughter, who was always insistent about how she wanted to live in the world, irrespective of all the race/gender messages she heard.

Acknowledgments

I acknowledge gratefully that the following entries, sometimes in slightly different versions, were published previously. Specifically:

"Reflections on Forum '85 Nairobi Kenya: Voices from the International Women's Studies Community," *Signs*, 11(3).

"Women's Studies at Spelman College: Reminiscences from the Director," *Women's Studies International*, 9(2).

"Practicing What You Preach: Strategies of an Ex-English Professor," *Liberal Education*, 77(1).

"Breaking the Silence: A Black Feminist Response to the Thomas/Hill Hearings," in *Court of Appeal: The Black Community Speaks Out on the Racial Politics of Clarence Thomas vs. Anita Hill*, eds., *The Black Scholar*, Robert Chrisman, and Robert L. Allen. Ballantine Books.

"The Evolution of Feminist Consciousness Among African American Women," in *Words of Fire: An Anthology of African-American Feminist Thought*, ed., Beverly Guy-Sheftall. The New Press.

"Gender Talk,": Introduction, in *Gender Talk: The Struggle for Women's Equality in African American Communities*, eds. Johnnetta Betsch Cole and Beverly Guy-Sheftall. Ballantine Books.

"African Feminist Discourse: A Review Essay," *Agenda*, 17(58).

"Remembering Our Feminist Forefathers," in *Progressive Black Masculinities*, ed., Athena D. Mutua. Routledge.

"Black Feminist Studies: The Case of Anna Julia Cooper," *African American Review*, 43(1).

"The Promise and Challenge of Black Women's Studies: A Report from the Spelman Conference, May 25-26, 1990" (1991). *NWSA Journal*, Spring, 1991, Vol. 3, No. 2 (Spring, 1991).

"Black Women's Studies: The Interface of Women's Studies and Black Studies." *Phylon*, Spring - Summer, 1992, Vol. 49, No. 1, 2.

"Reconstructing a Black Female Intellectual Tradition: Commentary on Harold Cruse's *The Crisis of the Negro Intellectual*," in *Voices of the African Diaspora: The CAAS Research Review*, 9(1).

"Exploring Difference: Racial and Global Perspectives in Graduate Women's Studies Education," *Feminist Studies*, 24(2).

"Shifting Contexts: Lessons from Integrating Black, Gender, and African Diaspora Studies," in *Encompassing Gender: Integrating International Studies and Women's' Studies*, eds., Mary M. Lay, Janice Monk, and Deborah S. Rosenfelt. The Feminist Press.

"Conquering the Black Girl Blues" (with Lani Valencia Jones), *Social Work*, 60(4).

"Black Women and Higher Education: Spelman and Bennett Colleges Revisited." *The Journal of Negro Education*, Summer, 1982, Vol. 51, No. 3.

"Educating Black Women Students for the Multicultural Future" (with Kimberly Wallace Sanders), *Signs*, Vol. 22, No. 1 (August 1996).

"Shared Governance, Junior Faculty, and HBCUS." *Academe*, Nov. - Dec., 2006, Vol. 92, No. 6.

"Audre Lorde and Spelman College" (with Johnnetta Betsch Cole), in *Feminist Wire*, Feb 27, 2014.

"Breaking the Silence" (with M. Jacqui Alexander) in *Building Womanist Coalitions: Writing and Teaching in the Spirit of Love*, ed., Gary L. Lemons University of Illinois Press.

"Challenges and Possibilities at HBCUs after the COVID-19 Pandemic" (with Kimberly Jackson). *Academe*, Spring 2021.

"The Women of Bronzeville," in *Sturdy Black Bridges: Visions of Black Women in Literature*, eds., Roseanne P. Bell, Bettye J. Parker, and Beverly Guy-Sheftall. Doubleday.

"Warrior Women: Art as Resistance," in *Bearing Witness: Contemporary Works by African American Artists*, Jontyle Robinson, 1996.

"Elizabeth Catlett: Making What You Know Best," in Grant Hill, *Something All Our Own: The Grnt Hill Collection of African Art*. 1 ed. Duke University Press, 2003.

In Andrea Barnwell Brownlee, "Deborah Roberts—*The Evolution of Mimi*," Spelman College, Museum of Fine Art, 2018

"Rebel Woman," in *Mickalene Thomas: I Can't See You Without Me,* 2018, Wexner Center for the Arts.

"Love Note to Toni," *Feminist Wire,* October 27, 2014.

"Whither Black Women's Studies?: Interview with Evelynn M. Hammonds," in *Differences: A Journal of Feminist Cultural Studies,* 9(3).

"Toni Cade Bambara: Black Feminist Foremother." In *Savoring the Salt: The Legacy of Toni Cade Bambara,* eds. Linda Janet Holmes and Cheryl A. Wall. Temple University Press.

The ROOT Interview: "Beverly Guy-Sheftall on Black Feminism," November 24, 2010.

"What Would Harriet Do? A Legacy of Resistance and Activism: A Conversation with Barbara Smith, Beverly Guy-Sheftall, Moderated by Paula Giddings." *Meridians,* Vol. 12, No. 2.

Interview with Chandra Talpade Mohanty and Linda Carty, eds.. *Feminist Freedom Warriors: Genealogies, Justice, Politics, and Hope.* Haymarket Books, 2018.

Auburn Avenue Interview. https://www.theauburnavenue.com/beverly-guy-sheftall-interview

Moya Bailey, "Honoring Beverly Guy-Sheftall," moyabailey.com

"Loving bell hooks," Center for Urban Education, University of Pittsburgh.

"Building the House You Want to Live and Teach In," *Public Seminar,* New School Publishing Initiative, April 28, 2022.

INTRODUCTIONS

Beverly Guy-Sheftall and the Time-Traveling Legacy of Black Feminist Genealogies

BANAH GHADBIAN

Everywhere, Black women, femmes, trans, and gender nonconforming queer subjects use their words, bodies, and spiritualities as time travel in order to conjure other realities. These spirits enter the room in Spelman College's Women's Resource and Research Center, in Dr. Beverly Guy-Sheftall's classes, writings, and in her life-changing relationships with her students. In these spaces, Spelman students are invited to read the words of revolutionary Black women who boldly and bravely leave their legacies behind.

Dr. Guy-Sheftall curates the rich and complex intellectual history of Black feminist changemakers for her students to absorb and be transformed by. To be a student of Dr. Beverly Guy-Sheftall means to watch her connect theories of global majority groups around the world and carefully weave together a transnational network of revolutionary consciousness. It means witnessing her and other great thinkers of our time convene and offer space for students. It is to watch her sisterhood with Johnnetta Betsch Cole, Aishah Shahidah Simmons, bell hooks, Alice Walker, Pauli Murray, Angela Davis, Pearl Cleage, Chandra Mohanty, and so many others—to see this Black feminist consciousness in action—steeped in love.

To be a student of Dr. Beverly Guy-Sheftall's means watching her change, watching her dedication to students beyond the classroom and into the world. It means witnessing a commitment to truth seeking and remembering. It means to engage in a libation, a calling in of Black feminist foremothers who came before. Reading litany for survivals on the wall, remembering the labors who made it possible to be in the space, in a community that extends far beyond the walls of the classroom.

A few months before I arrived at Spelman, a revolution broke out in my home country of Syria. My mother and I had just fled the Syrian border where we narrowly escaped being kidnapped by Syrian secret police agents. We were wanted for a ransom of one million dollars each. Shortly thereafter I packed my bags and headed to Spelman. The women and children dying in the streets singing freedom dreams were playing vividly in the back of my mind. This is when I met Dr. Guy-Sheftall. She encouraged me to bring Syria to Spelman. My friends Amoni Thompson-Jones, Olivia La Flamme, Asha Grant, Mamasa Camara, and many others in the large circle of community around the Women's Center made Sisterfire fliers, Feminist Majority Leadership Alliance pamphlets, AFREKETE event posters, and spent late nights slipping them under dorm room doors on campus. I was ignited by the Women's Resource and Research Center and my friends were too.

I took feminist theory with Dr. Guy-Sheftall spring semester of my first year. In this course we did not begin with the dominant white genealogy of feminism so often narrated in academia, which organizes feminism into "waves" beginning with Seneca Falls and the early white suffragists. Instead, we began with Paula Gunn Allen's "Red Roots of White Feminism," in which she describes the way white women borrowed indigenous women's matriarchal governance values from the Iroquois Nation to create the Seneca Falls Declaration of Sentiments. We read Sojourner Truth's "Ain't I a Woman?" in which she brilliantly intervened in white feminist debates by pointing out the intersection of being Black and a woman during the debates on the right to vote. We read Amy Jacques Garvey, Frances Beale, Anna Julia Cooper, Lorraine Hansberry, and so many other visionary Black feminist voices who are often intentionally erased and forgotten in the canon of feminist theory. I think this is the essence of what Dr. Guy-Sheftall does—instead of resigning to the way that dominant histographies of feminism erase Black and Brown labor, she carves out our own spaces, and in doing so, points out that feminism has always been Black and Brown. She exemplifies the living heart of feminism as a political practice—a constant awareness of the Other, and a willingness to transform and grow, to fight for a world where justice is realized.

Dr. Guy-Sheftall invited her radical sister friend Patricia McFadden to our class during a unit on global Third World Black feminisms. Dr. McFadden urged us to wake up every morning and ask, "How can I be more radical today?" The following year, we had the privilege of listening to Alice Walker and Angela Davis speak to us, both touching on Palestine at a time when it felt like the struggle against anti-Zionism still hadn't breached the mainstream left. We met with Dr. Guy-Sheftall while writing our Women against Violence Brigade petition against misogynistic music on Spelman's Campus. The petition emerged after a group of students decided we wanted to curb the many reports of sexual harassment at a weekly campus event called Market Friday and proposed a change of music. We gathered signatures to encourage the administration to invite queer women DJs on campus. The backlash was intense. We were shunned socially and were known as those feminist lesbian bitches who were ruining all the fun. We even got threats sent our way via Morehouse brothers on Twitter, and a few Spelman sisters gave those harassers our phone numbers. At the same time, our allies in Safe Space, the Women's Center, and the radical alum who came before us held us down and some serious changes were made.

We would huddle around the table at the Women's Center during Toni Cade Bambara Scholar Activist Writer's Collective meetings with all kinds of ideas for new protests and joyfully embraced during the opening nights of the momentous annual conference. We stayed late nights at Feminist Majority Leadership and AFREKETE meetings and snuck in food from the newly formed Social Justice Fellows program. We hunched over documents in the Audre Lorde and Toni Cade Bambara archives, tracing their handwriting with our fingertips. Dr. Guy-Sheftall and Dr. Kuumba were the electric forces behind these movements, giving us intellectual and political grounding, encouraging us to root the student activism in a long genealogy of Black feminist resistance. Dr. Guy-Sheftall was the ignition behind the creation of Students for Justice in Palestine, the first ever SJP at a historically Black college. She and Dr. Kuumba sent us to New York to attend the Russel Tribunal on Palestine and to Puerto Rico for the National Women's Studies Association Conference. Her spirit of generosity as a Black feminist anti-colonial praxis exemplifies what bell hooks theorizes in *Teaching to Transgress: Education as a Practice of Freedom.* That a revolutionary teacher cares not only for the student's mind, but for their spirit too. I remember how, upon our founding SJP, she gifted us Spelmanites in Students for Justice in Palestine keffiyehs from the last keffiyeh factory in Al Khalil. I think of the countless times Dr. Guy-Sheftall has showed up for her students, answering their phone calls, staying late into the night at her office hours, once driving out while sick with pneumonia in the rain to attend a poetry reading of mine.

When Toni Cade Bambara visited Vietnam with an anti-imperialist feminist delegation as guests of the Vietnam's Women's Union in 1975, she wrote, "I composed a letter to the Vietnamese women the other night trying to thank them. They gave me back my grandmother...With all those women who kept on keeping on. You're in the presence of Vietnamese women for five minutes, and you recall, yes, Harriet Tubman, Sojourner Truth. They gave me back my grandmother." When I first met Dr. Guy-Sheftall, I saw a kind of elder

I had never seen before in my life, whose work is to uplift the histories so often left behind, whose dreams are of the future, who does not invest in patriarchy but actively fights against it. And in being that elder for so many, she reminds us of all the elders whose spirits come alive in her words.

The African American feminist tradition illuminates life-giving resistance strategies that emerge from surviving the intersections of anti-Blackness and misogyny, classism, homophobia, ableism—systems that exist in every culture and across all regimes. And Black women, femmes, nonbinary, trans, queer, and gender nonconforming people have theorized from their embodied wisdom for centuries. Both Bashar al Assad's regime and the Zionist settler colonial structure that occupies Syria and Palestine operate on patriarchy, anti-Blackness, classism, and white supremacy that devastates rural farm-working people in particular. The Black Palestinian and Black Syrian voices in our community point to the urgency of connecting transnational struggles for joint liberation and the necessity of dismantling anti-Blackness and misogyny that deteriorates humanity.

I write this as my communities in Syria and Palestine are being ethnically cleansed from our lands. I write this as 1500 residents of Silwan, Jersualem, 900 of whom are children, are being forcibly evacuated from their homes so that Zionist settlers can construct a theme park. I write this as 50,000 people are under Assad regime siege in a small Syrian town called Dera'a. Dera'a is a rural area where our revolution began in 2011 when a group of children were tortured for writing the word freedom on their school walls. For the past ten years, settler occupation and patriarchal totalitarianism in Syria and Palestine have reached new heights. Chlorine gas attacks have given my baby cousins leukemia. Family members were forcibly evacuated for their resistance. The Syrian government launched offenses on the secret tunnel activists use to smuggle in food to starved areas. And yet, in the same places, a group of Syrian women who call themselves the Hurras, or Free Women Guardians, have more than 350 mobile art vans and libraries for local kids to draw and play as bombs drop from the sky. They ask children to draw freedom. They ask them to imagine a blue sky with green things. They ask them to think about a world without rubble and gray smoke. In the photos they post on social media, the kids hold onto their drawings, linking arms. They hold on with tiny fists clenched around their revolution dreams. I look up at the stars at night and think of how enslaved West African diasporic women freedom fighters followed their indigenous wisdoms and trusted in the divine flow of liberation, which was a form of time travel. Those moments of deep creativity, rooted in survival, make new futures possible. As Toni Cade Bambara wrote, we must remember "the dances forgotten, the elders, and the ancient wisdoms put aside, the memory of home scattered in the wind. Home in the future. The future here now, developing. Home liberated soon. And the earth would recover. The rain would come. The ancient wisdoms would be revived. The energy released. Home a human place once more." When Dr. Guy-Sheftall carved out the Women's Resource and Research Center as a political and intellectual home, she time traveled into another space, into now, into the future, where Spelman students are given a refuge where the dreams of the ancestors become real.

As Toni Cade Bambara put it, "Suffice to say that I do not take lightly the fact that I am on the earth at this particular time in human history, and am here as a member of a particular soul group and of a particular sex, having this particular adventure as a Pan-Africanist socialist feminist in the United States." And as Anna Julia Cooper wrote in 1892, "To be alive at such an epoch is a privilege, to be a woman then is sublime." I do not take it lightly that I have the honor to share this time and space with the visionary Dr. Beverly Guy-Sheftall. She is a revolutionary dreamer, and beautiful things are born from her mind. I am in perpetual awe at the way she creates spaces where they did not yet exist. The way she labors with a deep love to honor the words of Black and Third World feminist visionaries that are often misplaced, erased, and forgotten. The way she reshapes how history is told and brings back the dead so that we may never, ever forget the work they left behind.

DR. BANAH GHADBIAN is an Assistant Professor of Comparative Women's Studies at Spelman College. They hold a PhD in Ethnic Studies and research the creative strategies Syrian and Palestinian women conjure during revolution and war. Dr. Ghadbian has the distinction of being the first former comparative women's studies major to have secured a tenure-track faculty appointment in the program, effective August 2022.

For Beverly Guy-Sheftall

MOON CHARANIA

"She is a friend of my mind." – Toni Morrison, *Beloved*

It was twenty-five years ago, at a small liberal arts women's college in the South, that a white feminist professor planted Beverly Guy-Sheftall's *Words of Fire* in my hands. I had spent the semester engaged in heated discourse on the absence of black and brown women from the feminist ideas circulating in our classrooms. There was just a small handful of women of color in that class (and at the college in mid 1990s) and we were determined to challenge the prescriptive language of feminism that was being offered to us—a feminism tout court that didn't include our histories, our marginalizations, our onto-epistemologies, our modes of being in the world. While my then-professor couldn't fill the gaping absence of brown women, by handing me Guy-Sheftall's canonical feminist text—a text that quite literally demanded to be read (and taught) as it was and really still is the only book of its kind—she set me on the fiercely unapologetic route of black feminism. This was the first time I sat with Beverly, and I am grateful it was not the last.

Beverly's black feminist thought and practice—her anti-imperialist, anti-racist, transnational commitment—unlocked my own epistemological predicaments and offered me a way into the deeply racialized global histories that circumscribe black and brown women's lives. Reading her expertly written and meticulously researched books (*Gender Talk* is a must!), her articles ("Breaking the Silence: A Black Feminist Response to the Thomas/Hill Hearings" is indisputable!), her interviews (too many to name!), I immersed myself into Beverly's project and practice of feminism. Her tough, savvy, critical posture, the ease of her analytical sleight, her wittingly mined metaphors, her unflinching honesty, and, perhaps most profoundly, her bold refusal to cast aside intra-racial patriarchies for the proliferation of anti-racist grammars empowered me, emboldened me. Beverly's writings were fundamental pedagogical moments in my intellectual genealogy—moments in which I realized the depth of marginalization of black women's voices in the academy, moments in which I realized that my brown diasporic lesbian feminism and her southern black radical feminism weren't anathema to one another, but deeply interlinked modes of thought. My episteme in formation with hers.

So, when I arrived at Spelman College eighteen years after reading *Words of Fire* and Beverly casually extended an invitation to sit on a committee of feminist scholars, I knew in that moment that, just as Maxine Hong Kingston wrote our childhoods are marked by our mother's stories, my feminism was about to be (even more) marked by Beverly. And indeed, every one of our conversations—intimate, humorous, irreverent, and robust—became treasured moments. It was one thing to feel solidarity with Beverly through her writings; it was another thing altogether to intimately realize and experience Beverly's feminist friendship as a reflexive, open, compassionate, and politicized solidarity across our different racialized and gendered modes of being. For her, it was always about the larger feminist project—one that builds steadfast and urgent solidarities among and between black and brown women, from different geographies, of different generations, with different trainings in different modes of inquiry.

What does it mean to think across black and brown feminism, to find solidarity across uneven colonial constructions of race, class, gender, sexuality, and violence, to find in common patriarchal inheritances? As a brown lesbian scholar (of Pakistani descent), I felt a profound resonance with the critique Beverly offered around patriarchy *tout* patriarchy, the absence or refusal to talk about or take seriously violence against women of color, specifically black women, the romanticization of men of color in communities of color (too often by women of color). What appears to be a disparate archive of patriarchies across lands, borders, and oceans was actually rife with resonances that transgressively and repressively held scenes of violence together. These resonances reveal how saturated, overloaded, permeated, inundated the world is with violence against black and brown women. Beverly pushed me to ask out loud and without apology: why the inability to politicize violence against black women in the same or even similar way we politicize violence against black/brown people by the prison or the police or by a stranger? What kind of reading of violence against women of color do we need to guarantee its politicality, its political charge?

Her questions compel a more radical vocabulary and grammar for making sense of how racialization and gendered violence are co-formations and co-occurrences, even as the latter is often left behind. Beverly's questions are a complicated indictment; so too are they extraordinarily precise. Over and over again, through both her scholarly archive and in every speech act, Beverly puts pressure on the project of feminism and on feminists, demanding that we stay actively jarred, shaken, and vexed about how misogyny endures and the deadly specification with which it circumscribes the lives of women of color. Lucid and insightful, she makes alarming that which has become mundane, urgent that which has become ordinary, cacophonous that which has become silent. Beverly is a feminist sage who urges us to do better.

The language of solidarity is difficult to express. We know when it's there, we feel it, we connect with it, are grateful for it. It's a visceral, bodily charge as much as love, as much as the erotic. This kind of solidarity is rare, wild. It gives oneself over to another regardless of self-interest. It is a deeply resonant affinity that requires constant affective labor, constant epistemological undoing. This is the kind of solidarity Beverly practices—not one of oblateness, pity, compassion, forgiveness, or charity—but one of intense allegiance, generous love, abiding and insistent connectivity and collectivity. For Beverly, solidarity is as much an ethic as it is analytic. It demands from its practitioner nuance, capaciousness, porosity, generativeness. Across geopolitically distant yet proximal feminist concerns, sharing a beautiful Malbec and spicy biryani, Beverly taught me how feminist solidarity is formed, firmed, and lived out. Hers was a practice of truth-telling, wisdom-sharing, and space-creating. Sitting with her is an opportunity to sit with and think through the difficult dialogues that have shaped 20th century women of color feminisms and how one feminist committed her life, her time, her energy, her creativity to justice for over five decades.

MOON CHARANIA is an Associate Professor of International Studies at Spelman College and the 2024-25 Anschutz Distinguished Fellow in American Studies at Princeton University. She is the author of two books: Archive of Tongues: An Intimate History of Brownness (Duke University Press, 2023) and Will the Real Pakistani Woman Please Stand Up: Empire, Visual Culture, and the Brown Female Body (McFarland 2015). In addition to her books, Charania's work has also appeared in top journals such as, Meridians, Camera Obscura, Feminist Studies, and Sexualities, and in public forums such as USA Today, NBC, Boston Magazine, Chronicle of Higher Education, among others. She has previously held fellowships at the Emory University Psychoanalytic Society, Emory University James Weldon Johnson Institute for the Study of Race and Difference, and as the Beyer Resident in Queer Studies at St. Lawrence University. Charania is currently working on third book project — a collection of personal essays which double as a portrait of the multiple moving parts of brown diasporic life in contemporary America.

Part I

The **Personal** is Political

1. Reflections on Forum '85 in Nairobi, Kenya (1986)

Forum '85 was particularly significant for the women of African descent who were at the conference. Over one thousand were American Blacks and over seven thousand were from African nations. The high visibility of these and other Third World women was apparent from the very beginning. On July 10, the opening session of the Forum, which was held at the Kenyatta Conference Centre (named after President Jomo Kenyatta), was convened by Dame Nita Barrow of Barbados. Present on the platform with her were Margaret Kenyatta, the daughter of Kenya's first President and leader of the Kenyan delegation, and Leticia Shahani, Secretary-General for the Nairobi Conference, as well as Eddah Gachukia, former member of the Kenyan parliament and chair of the Kenyan forum organizing committee. The meeting was opened by Kenneth Matiba, minister for cultural and social services, who received loud applause when he indicated that he was accustomed to saying, "We women shall overcome." I was reminded of the impact of the civil rights movement in the United States on the women's movement, and it occurred to me that while women had indeed accomplished much over the past decade in their struggle for equality, development, and peace (the three major themes of the decade), there was still, as is the case with Blacks throughout the world, much more to overcome.

While women certainly had not achieved equality with men over the past decade, I was reminded in Nairobi that equality between women, despite the universality of their oppression, was a goal not yet fully realized. As moderator of a panel on "The Integration of Race and Class/Caste into Women's Studies," sponsored by Women's Studies International, I began by emphasizing the critical importance of integrating race, ethnicity, and class into Women's Studies courses and research on women. I argued that Women's Studies was at a crucial stage in its development because it was beginning, after almost a decade of emphasis on white, middle-class, western, urban women, to acknowledge that women of color were in fact in the majority and should therefore be at the center of feminist discourse rather than relegated to footnotes. While women throughout the world share many experiences because of their gender identity, women, because of class and ethnic differences, should not be perceived to be a monolithic group. Certain groups of women also benefit from racial privilege, an important concept, I maintained, for Women's Studies teachers and scholars to acknowledge and analyze.

Since my primary interest at the forum was women with special needs—the elderly, those living under apartheid, refugees, abused women, those in occupied territories, and those who were the victims of racism no matter where they resided—I attended as many sessions as I could (as was the case with hundreds of other participants) on South African women. Their situation was perhaps the clearest example of the significance of the concept of racial privilege in any analysis of gender. I reminded the audience during the panel discussion of "The 'New' Women's Literature: Autobiography, Diaries, Letters," that it was actually illegal in South Africa for Black women to write, even privately, about their experiences under apartheid—keeping a diary could be dangerous.

Spelman College, founded in Atlanta in 1881, is the oldest liberal arts college in the United States devoted exclusively to the education of Black women, and I went to Nairobi in my role as director of its Women's Research and Resource Center and coordinator of the college's Women's Studies minor. Given Spelman's historic commitment to the education of women of African descent—it welcomed students from Africa as early as 1891 and first sent graduates as missionaries to Africa in 1899—it was appropriate that the college send a Spelman delegation to the NonGovernmental Organization (NGO) Forum of the United Nations Decade for Women Conference in Nairobi. Because of the center's close working relationship with the Women and African Development Program of the New York-based African-American Institute (AAI), the Spelman delegation joined the AAI delegation, which included over eighty women, mostly women of color, from throughout the United States. We visited rural health projects, colleges and universities, women's cooperatives, and agricultural extension projects, and we participated in a fund-raising event to support secondary education for girls in Kenya. We also made a special effort to network with university women. In this regard, one of the most heartwarming evenings we spent in Nairobi was at the home of a university dean during which we ate delicious Kenyan food and talked about a wide range of topics: the dating habits of teenagers in Nairobi, male-female relationships among rural Kikuyans, and the problems of urban professional Kenyan women.

The most exciting aspect of this once-in-a-lifetime experience was the opportunity the conference provided to interact and network with so many women from around the world. As I boarded the plane on the evening of July 20, I realized that I probably would never again have the chance to be in the same place for almost two weeks with so many women from diverse cultures who were committed to improving the lives of women, children, indeed, the entire human race.

As we left Nairobi, the group from Spelman felt especially pleased because we had been able to present to the Secretariat a full-tuition scholarship for a Kenyan coed to attend Spelman during the 1986-87 school year. I knew that she would find our Women's Studies offerings exciting and sensitive to her own experience. I was reminded as we left for home that Spelman had maintained its more than one-hundred-year commitment to our sisters in Africa. I hope that the conference held a special meaning for the hundreds of Black American women who traveled to Nairobi. It was an opportunity to embrace their "sisters" and to experience firsthand the conditions under which the majority of women in the world live.

2. Women's Studies at Spelman College: Reminiscences from the Director (1986)

Spelman College, founded in 1881 in the basement of Atlanta, Georgia's Friendship Baptist Church, is the oldest and best-known college for Black women in the world. Because of its historic commitment to the education of women, especially Black women, Spelman has been over the past decade and a half in the forefront of curriculum development in Women's Studies on historically Black college campuses in the U.S.A. In 1981, exactly one hundred years after its founding, the Women's Research and Resource Center, the first of its kind on a Black college campus, was established with a small grant from the Charles Stewart Mott Foundation. A major component of the program was the development of an interdisciplinary Women's Studies minor. Since its inception, the Center has had three major goals: curriculum development in Women's Studies with a particular focus on the intersection of race, class and gender, and cross-cultural perspectives on the female experience; research on Black women; and community outreach, especially to Black women locally and regionally. Within the past two years, the Center broadened its program to include an international component which focuses on Third World women, with special attention to women of African descent. In this regard, Spelman sponsored a delegation of five women, including the Center director, to attend the U.N. Decade Conference in Nairobi this past July.

Though Spelman's involvement in Women's Studies is relatively recent, the College's involvement in sponsoring seminars and conferences on issues relevant to Black women is considerably older. Even as early as 1944, for example, Spelman was the site of a Conference on Current Problems and Programs in the Higher Education of Negro Women during which representatives of several Black colleges focused on directions for the post-war education of Black women. While a number of Women's Studies courses had been developed as *electives* at Spelman since 1969, they remained tangential, for the most part, to the curriculum until the implementation over the past two years of a curriculum development project in Black Women's Studies, which mainstreamed Women's Studies into required core curriculum courses at the College. A chronology of the early development of separate women's studies courses at Spelman follows: Psychology of the Sexes (1969); Psychology of Women (1971); Women in Africa (1972-73), taught for one year by a guest professor, then discontinued; Images of Women in Literature (1973-74), which I designed; Human Sexuality (1974-75); Images of Women in the Media (1976-77), which I designed; and Women, Values, and the Law. Since 1979, the following courses have been designed by various faculty in separate departments: Women of the Bible; Sociology of Women; Woman as Writer; Women in Drama; Women in Management of Organizations; Black Women: Developing Public Leadership Skills; Women in America; Communication and Gender; and Women, Literature, and Identity.

Since 1983, the Center has been involved in a major curriculum development project designed to incorporate Black Women's Studies into the curricula at Spelman and four participating institutions in the Atlanta area—Agnes Scott, Clark, Kennesaw, and Morehouse Colleges. Funded by the Ford Foundation, this project addresses the need for a gender and race balanced core curriculum that is sensitive to the unique experiences of Black women. At Spelman, ten core courses and/or introductory courses in various disciplines were targeted for revision. These included Freshman English, World Literature, World Civilization, Introduction to Sociology, World Religion, and Introduction to Psychology. The Center also played the major leadership role in the establishment of an interdisciplinary Women's Studies minor program at Spelman; it is unique among Women's Studies programs not only because it focuses on minority women but also because it analyzes women's experiences from a cross-cultural perspective. This achievement and others have given national visibility to Spelman College as an institution committed to Women's Studies. In 1982, Spelman was chosen as the major participating institution in a two-year Black Women's Studies Faculty and Curriculum Project at the Wellesley College Center for Research on Women, funded by the Fund for the Improvement of Postsecondary Education (FIPSE). As co-sponsor of the project, the Center hosted workshops for faculty at historically Black colleges. The Center is currently working with Atlanta University, the graduate institution in the Atlanta University Center, on a faculty development project in Africana Women's Studies.

What I will do in the remainder of this essay, which will be more personal in focus, is to trace the development of Spelman's involvement in Women's Studies since my return to my alma mater in 1971 after having completed a master's degree in English at Atlanta University (my thesis was on Faulkner's treatment of women in his major novels) and having taught for two years at Alabama State University, a large public Black institution in the Deep South.

When I returned to Spelman to teach freshman English in the fall of 1971 (after having graduated in 1966), I came with no particular vision about the kind of Black women's college I wanted Spelman to become nor was I particularly aware of the extent of my commitment to feminism or Black Women's Studies (a non-existent concept at that time). I do recall after teaching a couple of years being frustrated about my Black female students' lack of familiarity with Black women's literature, a frustration which was shared by my colleague and friend, Roseann Bell, who was also teaching English. We decided rather abruptly during 1974 that we would assemble a collection of readings which would include positive literary images of Black women and would make them available to our students whom we felt were in desperate need of literary role models and stories about themselves. This was before writers such as Toni Morrison, Paule Marshall, and Alice Walker, to name a few, were being consumed by large numbers of college students. After a cursory review of the literature, which revealed very little, we decided to undertake a more ambitious project which was the compilation of an anthology which would include critical essays on Black women writers, interviews with Black women writers, and literary selections, mainly short fiction and poetry, which included positive/complex images of Black women. After five years of hard work, *Sturdy Black Bridges: Visions of Black Women in Literature* was published in paperback by Doubleday in 1979. By this time, the women's movement was in full swing, and I had begun to immerse myself in feminist theory, women's history, and Black Women's Studies, though I would not have used this term at that point. Since 1976, I had also enrolled in the doctoral program in American Studies at Emory University and was on leave from Spelman pursuing Women's Studies formally and reading everything I could to understand what it meant to be female, especially a Black female, in this place and throughout the world. Occasionally, I would stop and try to understand why I had become so addicted to feminist material, and I began to reflect on my own experience and discovered that I was probably a good case study for the development of a Black feminist academic.

First, I grew up in a female-centered (not matriarchal) household and was raised by a mother who had left her husband's house and moved to her parents' home with three daughters when I was in the eighth grade. Uppermost in my memory is her insistence that we develop the kind of emotional and financial independence that would enable us to survive without men if our marriages did not work. As important was her belief that studying was more important than doing household chores, so that I became a bookworm with limited domestic skills. The extent to which my mother (who died of breast cancer four years ago) was more interested in our intellectual development than our preparation for wifehood was apparent by her regularly excusing us from household duties if we were doing schoolwork and her encouraging me to bypass home economics as a ninth grader and take typing instead. When I graduated from high school at the age of fifteen (she had allowed me to start the first grade early and to complete the second and third grades in one year), she insisted that I leave home and attend Spelman because of its solid academic reputation and because she was convinced that the protective environment that a women's college provided would be the most suitable place for my emotional and intellectual development.

Though I needed a job upon graduation four years later, which probably would have been teaching English in the public school system, she insisted that I take advantage of a fifth year of study at Wellesley College because it would get me out of the segregated South and would "expand my horizons." I am convinced that without the kind of persistent encouragement and support from a mother who had graduated from college (I was to discover her all A's college transcript among other memorabilia tucked neatly away in her dresser drawer after the funeral) and pursued a career but who had not had the opportunity to realize her own dream of becoming a certified public accountant, I would not have found myself back at Spelman in the early 1970s doing the kind of work that was to become an obsession.

My life was also altered in significant ways because of two more trips to New England during the next five years and the impact of both personal and institutional models. While on leave from Spelman at Emory in 1976, a colleague from the English department and I traveled to the Boston area to examine several Women's Studies programs which were in the embryonic stage. This trip turned out to have been a major turning point in my own professional development. When I returned to Spelman in 1981, with all but the dissertation completed, I was firmly convinced, as were others at Spelman, that the College needed a women's center and a Women's Studies program which would be geared to the special educational needs of Black women since the programs which I had seen were white and middle-class in focus. I had also become immersed in the Spelman archives as I prepared to write the College's centennial history during which I became even more convinced of the appropriateness of a focus on Black Women's Studies at this very special place for Black women. Though Spelman had been offering a few Women's Studies courses since the early 1970s, there was no campus-wide program with an explicitly Black feminist perspective which would address such sensitive issues as rape, male/female relationships, incest, violence against women, or abortion, to name only a few topics. As the Center's program evolved, it became more cross-cultural and global in its perspective and began to address such issues as women under apartheid.

When I reflect upon the relative ease with which the Center has been able to carry out its mission of addressing Black feminist issues on the campus and making the Spelman curriculum more sensitive to Women's Studies, it occurs to me that since I happened to have been a Spelman alumna and had been teaching at the College for ten years before getting involved in an open way with "women's issues" I was perceived to be "safe." I was also astute enough at the beginning to avoid the term "feminist" which is frequently perceived to be a dirty word in the Black community even among academics. I remained sensitive to the conservative/traditional setting in which I was working while at the same time working very hard to "feminize" the Spelman environment in ways which were appropriate for a women's center director.

The past four years have not been easy, but not because there has been resistance to what I've tried to accomplish at Spelman and in the broader community, but because of the sheer magnitude of the work. I can barely remember a day when I have not worked, on the campus, at home, or in the community, fewer than twelve hours in a 24-hour period. I seem to be in perpetual motion. The most recent joint project of the Center, the founding of *SAGE: A Scholarly Journal on Black Women,* which was conceived a little over a year ago by me and my friend and colleague Patricia Bell-Scott (who co-edited *All the Women Are White, All the Blacks are Men, But Some of Us Are Brave: Black Women's Studies, Feminist Press,* 1972), has been the most difficult challenge yet.

A second trip to New England in the fall of 1981 turned out to have been the second most important professional decision I was to make. When the Center opened I decided that it was important for me to meet another Black woman who was directing an important minority women's project at a major research center for women, so I returned to Wellesley, after having spent a year there in 1967, to meet and confer with Patricia Bell-Scott, who was the director of a large grant funded by the Women's Educational Equity Act (WEAA) at the Center for Research on Women. Pat and I later became close friends and have worked together, always harmoniously, on several projects within the past few years. This includes our joint editorship of the journal and our most recent codirectorship of a National Endowment for the Humanities seminar for college teachers on Images of Black Women in Literature: A Life Cycle Approach. It occurs to me at this very moment that my work at Spelman might not have taken the direction it did were it not for my association with Pat, who provides constant guidance, as was the case with my mother, even though we remained miles apart.

Though I am proud of what the Center has been able to accomplish in a relatively short time, which would not have been possible without external grants, the work of Professor Jacqueline Royster, and strong administrative support from President Donald Stewart and Dean Barbara Carter, there is much more to be done. I suppose I am happiest about our considerable progress with the community service component, evidenced by an increase in the number of women within the local community, throughout the nation, and from abroad who participate in workshops, seminars, and conferences sponsored or co-sponsored by the Center. These activities offer a diverse group of women intellectual stimulation, support, fellowship, and the opportunity to discuss topics of interest to women. Of special interest in our community outreach activities was the enrichment program for Third World Women sponsored by the Center (and funded by President Stewart) in collaboration with the Continuing Education Division of the college. This program, which involved women from Africa, Asia, India, and the West Indies, was the first of its kind designed by the college specifically for Third World Women, most of whom were non-professionals. The women were enrolled in two courses (Introduction to the Computer and Introduction to Child and Adolescent Psychology) which were taught by members of the Spelman faculty. To accommodate the women who were mothers of small children, the college provided baby-sitting services. Through social activities and informal discussions, the women shared women's experiences across cultural lines and developed a strong sense of cohesiveness as a group of Third World women. This activity, which culminated in a graduation exercise for the women, won the Center and the college many friends among the Third World community in Atlanta.

Because of the Center's involvement in national networking among women and women's centers, Spelman is emerging as a site for national conferences that address critical issues facing women in general and Black women in particular. Already, the Center has been instrumental in bringing to the campus several major conferences which received nation-wide participation. The first conference, held in October 1982 and sponsored by the Center, examined Black Women and Public Policy Issues in the Eighties. The second, held in June 1983, under the auspices of the National Black Women's Network, was the first national Black Women's Health Conference. It attracted more than 1,500 participants and was an historic and unforgettable occasion. It was fitting that a forum for the discussion of Black women's health issues take place at Spelman since the training of health care professionals had been a critical component of the early curriculum of the college. Spelman's nurse training department, which began in 1886, was the first of its kind available to Black women in this country. The forum was the most successful community outreach effort in which the college had been involved over its 103-year history. It was a bittersweet experience. The serious physical and mental health problems that too many Black women suffer were painful to hear about. Yet, the intensity of the commitment ·on the part of hundreds of women to improve the health status of Black women was heartwarming indeed! I was reminded again at the end of it all that Spelman is really a very special place for Black women. For three days it was a perfect haven and provided a brief interlude from the continuing struggle to reclaim good health for Black women. I was thrilled that my work at the Center had brought me in close contact with women like Byllye Avery, who had conceived of the entire project. A year later, the Center co-sponsored a national conference on Southern Granny Midwives with the University of Medicine and Dentistry of New Jersey and Bryant College. This unique conference attracted midwives, scholars, teachers, print and photojournalists, archivists, and women from the Atlanta community. One of its major accomplishments was the establishment of the Association for the Study of Traditional ·African American Midwifery, which will compile a Directory of Resources for the study of the subject. The Center is the clearinghouse for this vital research tool.

Over the past several years, several significant activities and projects have demonstrated the Center's and the College's commitment to research on Black women, a new priority for Spelman. Among them was a photo-documentary exhibition, *Black Women as Healers: A Noble Tradition,* which was a major attraction at the Black Women's Health Conference in 1983 and was prepared by Jacqueline Jones Royster, Director of the Writing Center and past Research Associate of the Center. A first of its kind, the exhibition, which includes a valuable exhibit catalog, has been in demand from various organizations and institutions in the Atlanta area and elsewhere in the nation. It is housed permanently in the Center meeting/reading room. Equally impressive was the selection of the Center, in 1983, for membership in the National Council of Research on Women and my appointment as Vice Chair of the Board of the Council. Only two of the Council's thirty-seven centers are directed by Black women, and Spelman has the distinction of being the only historically Black college represented at the Council.

The fact that the Center is asked to participate in research projects of national significance is further indication of the attention we are receiving as a research center. We are currently involved in a collaborative project with the Center for Research on Women at Memphis State University and the Duke University/University of North Carolina Women's Studies Research Center in the production of a working papers series on "Southern Women: The Intersection of Race. Class and Gender." During 1985-1986, I am the recipient of a distinguished professor's chair by Delta Sigma Theta Sorority and will be engaged in a collaborative project with Sage Women's Educational Press on Black mother/daughter relationships.

I will not consider my work finished at the Center until the Spelman Archives is a reality and a required course in Women's Studies is a part of the core curriculum. I can still remember having left Spelman in 1966 with no understanding of patriarchy or colonialism or apartheid. I did not know the conditions under which the majority of the world's women lived. I did not know what female circumcision or foot-binding or purdah or sati was though I did know about the horrors of the Middle Passage, lynching, and the Holocaust. Though I knew the particular burdens of Black women as a result of my own family history and what I had observed growing up in Memphis, Tennessee, before integration, I did not fully understand the concept of "double jeopardy" as it related to women of color, and I was ill-equipped to handle a class analysis of the plight of Black women. I did not know many of our important Black foremothers—Frances E. W. Harper, Anna J. Cooper, Selena Sloan Butler (a Spelman alumna), Josephine St. Pierre Ruffin, or even Zora Neale Hurston (an unfortunate circumstance which Alice Walker, a fellow student, also bemoans). I had not read Sojourner Truth's now famous "Ain't I A Woman" speech or Du Bois' moving account of the tragedy of Black womanhood in "The Damnation of Women" from *Darkwater* (1920), though I had read his more familiar *The Souls of Black Folk* (1903). I was unaware of the strong Black feminist tradition in the intellectual history of African Americans that had been bequeathed to us by Sojourner Truth, Frederick Douglass, William E. B. Du Bois, and Mary Church Terrell, to name only a few.

It is imperative that our Black female students (and our Black male students for that matter) not leave Spelman's gates at the end of four years with the gaps in their knowledge with which I left nearly twenty years ago. I am concerned about their commitment to improving the lives of women, especially Black women, no matter where they live in the world. They must be concerned about adolescent mothers with inadequate pre-natal care and limited resources; they must be concerned about the rural woman in Kenya and elsewhere who walks miles every day in search of firewood in order to feed her family; they must be concerned about women in South Africa who are virtually imprisoned in "homelands" far away from their husbands who must seek work in urban areas. If all this is accomplished, and more, Spelman will have become the kind of Black women's college that all of us can revere. It will have surpassed the vision of its founders. The Center remains committed and vigilant in its support of the College as it carries out its very special mission of educating Black women who will make this planet a better place for women and men to live.

My mother would have certainly been very proud of her daughter and the Center. I am pleased that at least some of my dreams have been fulfilled.

3. Practicing What You Preach: Strategies of an Ex-English Professor (1991)

In a compelling essay describing her own revolutionary pedagogy, Black feminist theorist and professor bell hooks invokes Miss Annie Mae Moore, her favorite high school teacher, who embodies the idea of the teacher as subversive and whom Hooks reverentially calls her "pedagogical guardian." Miss Moore was "passionate in her teaching, confident that her work in life was a pedagogy of liberation... one that would address and confront our realities as black children growing up... within a white supremacist culture." Miss Moore, hooks adds, "knew that if we were to be fully self-realized, then her work, and the work of all our progressive teachers, was not to teach us solely the knowledge in books, but to teach us an oppositional world view—different from that of our exploiters and oppressors, a world view that would enable us to see ourselves not through the lens of racism or racist stereotypes but one that would enable us to focus clearly and succinctly, to look at ourselves, at the world around us, critically—analytically."[1]

In his introduction to Paulo Freire's *Pedagogy of the Oppressed*, which delineates the concept of "education as 'the practice of freedom,'" Richard Shaull, hooks reminds us, offers a concise definition of revolutionary pedagogy to which Miss Moore might have exclaimed "amen": "Education either functions as an instrument. . . to facilitate the integration of the younger generation into the logic of the present system and bring about conformity to it, or it becomes the practice of freedom, the means by which men and women deal critically and creatively with reality and discover how to participate in the transformation of their world."[2]

My own teaching over the past twenty-one years has struggled against two major problems in the academy. First, much of what goes on reinforces the problematic and erroneous notion that the normative human experience is white, Western, male, Christian, middle class, and heterosexual. A deep sense of alienation is likely to plague students whose own identities are different from what they've been led to believe is the norm by the texts they read and the Eurocentric values they are encouraged to embrace. Students who represent this dominant majority—and they're fast becoming a minority in many educational settings—have difficulty seeing the world and their place in it differently.[3] Second, because students have not been encouraged to feel connected to what they learn, it is no surprise that students feel unattached to the world of real human beings and therefore disinclined to want to change the conditions under which too many people live. As I consider the academy and my own professional career as a professor/activist, these questions intrude:

- Can the university be a site for radical political work?
- Can one be truly radical or subversive as a university professor within one of society's most hierarchical institutions?
- Can we teach in ways that don't reinforce structures of domination, racism, sexism, class exploitation?
- How can we use our power as teachers in ways that are not coercive, punitive, controlling?
- Can we undo the "miseducation" that most students have been subjected to by the time we get them in our college classes?
- Can we undo our own "miseducation," since most of us are also victims of patriarchal, racist, sexist ways of knowing and teaching?
- Are we willing to endure the anger and frustration—even hostility—of students when we challenge their most cherished ways of seeing the world and themselves?

Christopher Columbus, for example, did not "discover" this country in 1492; he invaded indigenous peoples' territory, exploited the people, and began a process of decimation and even genocide. I continue to be haunted by discussions following a video in which a black male was mistakenly perceived by the audience to be a thief when in fact it was a white male who had stolen. How radical it would be for us to teach in a way that all children would know who the real thieves have been throughout history! One gets a hint by visiting museums here and in Europe and seeing artifacts belonging to someone else. How refreshing it would be to know who the real victims have been throughout history and what has been stolen by whom! How radical it would be simply to tell the truth, which would begin with admissions about the annihilation of native peoples here in our own country! It now would be impossible for me to teach an American literature course as I experienced it as an undergraduate English major.

In my own classrooms on the first day of class, I am explicit about what I am attempting to do. I don't present myself as politically neutral, void of a value system and biases. I indicate that much of what I think and believe and value is not consistent with the dominant culture's belief system. I acknowledge that I don't know everything, that I am always in the process of growth and self-evaluation, that I'm not the same teacher that I was ten or fifteen years ago, and that I am not the ultimate authority in the class.

On the first day of Introduction to Women's Studies, which I co-teach with Spelman President Johnnetta Cole, we assign a group of autobiographical texts by non-Western women or women within our own culture who would be considered "other" and tell the students that they will become "experts" on the cultures from which these texts emerge. Later, they will provide insights they've gleaned from their assigned texts and their reading about these cultures as we discuss race/class/ethnicity/gender questions. On that first day, I also introduce myself to the class and have students introduce themselves so they will know that who they are as particular human beings is significant to what transpires in the classroom. I tell them that contrary to what they may have experienced in the curriculum, the majority of the world looks like them—people of color and women. What they have experienced already, therefore, is more representative of the lived experience of the world's population than what they've read about in most of their classes—the experiences of a small group of Western white males. A significant component of my "radical" or "oppositional" pedagogy is to decenter Eurocentric male models and experience and critique the process by which we come to believe that whiteness and maleness are the most valuable commodities humans can possess.

Where one begins is very important. In my literature classes I begin where human civilization began—not with the *Iliad* and *Odyssey*, but with texts from ancient Africa. In our Introduction to Women's Studies class, I begin with the experiences not of middle-class Western white women but of many so-called Third World women who are still agricultural workers, food producers who work very hard and whose very survival depends on, for example, their ability to locate water and find firewood.

A second major pedagogical strategy is making central to my students' learning the idea that knowledge is also experiential. We learn not just by reading books and doing library research, but by getting outside the parameters of conventional classroom instruction. A major assignment in Introduction to Women's Studies requires students to choose a site where gender/race/class issues are played out; students visit their chosen sites not just as objective, unconnected participant observers, but as workers (volunteers, if you will). Then they must do a paper and oral report that synthesize their reading (about domestic violence, for example, if their site is a battered women's shelter), the insights they have gained on the site, and analyses of the concepts and theories they have learned from class and assigned readings about race/class/culture/gender.

I am convinced by our students and our observations that teaching in these new ways, being very conscious of what we teach and why we teach what we teach, which bell hooks has described as adopting a revolutionary feminist pedagogy, has the potential for real change in our students. The class I co-taught last year with Johnnetta Betsch Cole was an unusual one for Spelman. The lone white student, who was from Agnes Scott College (a white women's college in Atlanta), admitted on the first day that she was very nervous and had never experienced being a minority in a classroom. Two students from Morehouse College (a historically Black, all-male college in Atlanta) also were nervous and huddled close to Johnnetta and me on the first day.

Within three weeks, one of the men (who died tragically in a fraternity hazing incident during the semester of the class) was talking openly about his new ideas about being a good father, especially in terms of raising a daughter, which he admitted he preferred to a son. His friend talked honestly about violent behavior in his relations with his sister and why it was necessary to reconceptualize notions of masculinity. He chose as his site Men Against Violence, a self-help group for men attempting to understand domestic violence. The Agnes Scott student spent a semester interning in Washington, D.C., at a nonprofit minority organization and wrote to us after the recent governor's election in Georgia that her grandfather had voted for Andy Young. This astounded her, she explained, because he had been the person who, in his role as jailer, locked up Martin Luther King, Jr., during his early jail experience in Georgia.

I am convinced that what happened in that class is suitable—even critical—for students everywhere. Students left this Afrocentric, women-centered class knowing more about themselves and the world in which they live but also feeling connected to the people about whom they studied and among whom they worked.

We have tremendous power as teachers to influence the direction in which this country will move as we approach the twenty-first first century. White students need an inclusive curriculum and "oppositional" pedagogy as much as "ethnic" students do. We must not lose sight of the ultimate purpose of "revolutionary" pedagogies: educating students who will work to make this planet a better place for all humans to live. We must prepare students for a world in which non-Western women of color are the world's majority. We must not teach only "the canon," which consistently has excluded or devalued the experiences of people of color and women. We must discontinue the harmful practice of educating many students away from themselves. We must disrupt the practice of "miseducating" the majority of our students. Sensitivity to issues of race, class, ethnicity, and gender would begin the process of cultural literacy and rid us of the ignorance in which we have basked so blissfully and arrogantly for decades. Our collective human survival—and the freedom and dignity in which some of us can live—will depend, in large part, on our commitment as educators to helping eradicate racism, sexism, and other forms of domination.

Notes

[1] bell hooks, *Talking Back: Thinking Feminist, Thinking Black* (Boston: South End Press, 1989), 49.

[2] Ibid., 50.

[3] I am indebted to Professor Elsa Barkley Brown for her important scholarly work and insights about curriculum transformation as it relates to women and people of color, and to her innovative pedagogical strategies. Professors Johnnella Butler, Margaret Anderson, and Peggy McIntosh's work on the inclusive curriculum also have been helpful.

4. Breaking the Silence: A Black Feminist Response to the Thomas/Hill Hearings (1992)

(for Audre Lorde)

There are a number of disturbing issues raised by the recent appointment of Clarence Thomas to the Supreme Court even if Anita Hill's allegations of sexual harassment had not surfaced: his unfitness to serve on the High Court due to inadequate judicial experience and overall mediocrity; his views on affirmative action and abortion; his record at EEOC; his disavowal of deeply held, frequently stated right-wing views; his portrayal of his hard-working, supportive sister as a disgusting welfare mother; and his obvious lying—he claims not to have read a report, which he signed, opposing abortion. He claims to have never discussed *Roe v. Wade.* In a historic statement in support of Anita Hill, which appeared in the November 18, 1991, issue of the *New York Times,* titled "African American Women in Defense of Ourselves," 1,642 black women[1] reminded the nation of Thomas's persistent failure, despite his own racial history and professional opportunities, to respond to the urgency of civil rights for disadvantaged groups in this country: "...this consolidation of the conservative majority on the Supreme Court seriously endangers the rights of all women, poor and working class people, and the elderly . . . we know that the seating of Clarence Thomas is an affront to African American women and men and all those concerned with social justice."

The overwhelming reaction among Blacks to Anita Hill's sexual harassment charges against Judge Thomas during the nomination proceedings, despite what the polls may have revealed, seems to have been that even if the allegations were true, she should have remained silent. I have encountered very few Blacks, men or women, who believe that Thomas was telling the truth when he categorically and unequivocally denied having engaged in sexually inappropriate conduct, including pressuring Hill for dates and making offensive sexual comments, while he was her boss. I became even more convinced of the "reality" of my observations when I asked my eighty-year-old father, who has lived in Memphis, Tennessee, all his life and understands the painful reality of racism and the particular plight of Southern Black men, about his reactions to what he saw on television. He responded very quickly and calmly and without any racial references this way: "Well, of course Thomas is lying, and Hill is a very good girl. Anyone should be able to see that. Men have been taking advantage of nice girls for as far back as I can remember."

When I asked him whether he thought Hill should have come forth after being pressured to do so by the Judiciary Committee, he stated very forcefully, "Of course." Even conservative Orlando Patterson, a Black Harvard professor and one of Thomas's most ardent supporters, argues, much to my dismay, that "Judge Thomas was justified in denying making the remarks, even if he had in fact made them."[2] Perhaps the best explanation of this tendency on the part of large numbers of African Americans, men and women, to vehemently oppose Anita Hill's public exposure of Thomas's sexual harassment of her (I wonder if the response would have been different if the hearings hadn't been televised) is that she violated a deeply held Black cultural taboo, which is that we shouldn't air our racial dirty linen in front of white folks. This prohibition has engendered the most anger when it is Black women "breaking the silence" about our experiences, especially sexual, with Black men. I am reminded at this point of the need to contextualize the Thomas/Hill hearings and to analyze them within a framework that enables us to see this drama as part and parcel of a larger scenario that has been brewing for more than a decade.[3]

Twelve years ago (August 27, 1979, issue of *Newsweek*), "a new black struggle" was chronicled. This came on the heels of Ntozake Shange's award-winning Broadway play *For Colored Girls Who Have Considered Suicide/When the Rainbow is Enuff* (1976) and Michele Wallace's controversial book *Black Macho and the Myth of the Superwoman* (1979). Both writers were demonized among large segments of the Black community:

> It's the newest wrinkle in the Black experience in America—a growing distrust, if not antagonism, between black men and women that is tearing marriages apart and fracturing personal relationships. But while the strains between Blacks are much the same as those between the sexes in general, their impact on (Blacks) seems unusually severe.

The issue of sexual politics within the African American community soon became a hotly debated topic in such publications as *The Black Scholar* (March/April 1979), *Freedomways*, and *Black Books Bulletin*, and provided the catalyst for the founding of a short-lived bimonthly magazine, *Black Male/Female Relationships*, by Nathan and Julia Hare. A decade later, the controversy continued and grew more virulent, the most obvious manifestations of which were loud and angry litanies, especially among Black professional men, about the portrayal of Black male characters by contemporary Black women writers. Alice Walker's novel *The Color Purple* (1982) and Steven Spielberg's film adaptation sparked the most vitriolic responses. Shaharazad Ali's self-published *The Blackman's Guide to Understanding the Blackwoman* (1990) is the latest and most disturbing publication in this decade-old family battle and reminds us, once again, of a perceptible but unspeakable misogynist strain in African American thinking.

Black women too often become suspect and discredited in our communities when we raise issues of sexism, such as sexual harassment, rape, incest, battering, date rape, or when we speak openly and honestly about what we have experienced as women under patriarchy, a structure of domination that exists in the larger society and also within the Black community. We become associated with the "F" word—feminism—and are assumed to be man-hating or, worse, lesbian. Historically, we have been accused of being traitors to the race when we align ourselves with women's liberation struggles, as we've consistently done since the nineteenth century despite the racism of white women and the scorn of many Black men and some Black women. And so, as one Black feminist activist reminds us in her analysis of the ironies embedded in the Thomas/Hill hearings:

> Black women must always put duty to the race first. No mention was made of how Clarence Thomas had failed in his duty to the race, especially to Black women. This deeply held ethic that Black women have a duty to the race while Black men are allowed to have a duty only to themselves, can only be challenged by a Black feminist analysis that emphasizes the importance of Black women's lives. (Hammonds, p. 6)

As we prepare ourselves for the most difficult time of our sojourn in America since slavery, it is imperative that Black men and women rid ourselves of all ideas and behaviors that will result in our individual and collective underdevelopment and debasement. There are deadly dragons to slay, and men and women must be prepared equally for struggle, especially in this menacing Republican era made worse by a Supreme Court seemingly dedicated to undoing the work of justices like Thurgood Marshall with respect to the rights of minorities and women. Black men do not need subservient women who remain silent about the abuse and suffering they experience, no matter who is the victimizer. We must reject antiquated and counterproductive notions of manhood which dictate that men maintain power over women and prevent them from speaking, even in their own behalf. The Black community will continue to survive, despite the recent hearings, though we will fare better when we commit ourselves to dealing honestly with our problems—whether it is the racism and sexism in the dominant culture or the internalized racism and sexism within our own communities. We must heed the admonishment of Audre Lorde to her sisters: "So it is better to speak/ remembering/ we were never meant to survive."[4]

NOTES

[1] Though Black female voices were conspicuously absent as commentators during the Thomas/Hill hearings, a number of important statements by enlightened Black women are beginning to emerge in print. See Jill Nelson, "Back Talk: Hill Versus Thomas," *Essence,* December 1991, p. 134; Evelynn M. Hammonds, "Viewpoint: Who Speaks for Black Women?" *Sojourner: The Women's Forum,* November 1991, pp. 7-8. Upcoming publications include a Forum on the Thomas/Hill hearings in a special issue of *SAGE: A Scholarly Journal on Black Women on relationships,* which will include essays by Gloria Wade-Gayles, Nellie McKay, and others; and a collection of essays edited by Toni Morrison, which will include Paula Giddings, Cornel West, and others.

[2] See the *New York Times* Op-Ed, "Race, Gender and Liberal Fallacies," October 20, 1991.

[3] This part of my analysis was sparked initially by my revulsion at the publication of Shaharazad Ali's *The Blackman's Guide to Understanding the Blackwoman* (1990), one of the most blatantly misogynist and racist texts that has appeared in print during this period. See my essay, "Exacerbating the Problem," in *Confusion by Any Other Name: Essays Exploring the Negative Impact . . .,* edited by Haki R. Madhubuti, Chicago: Third World Press, 1990.

[4] See her "A Litany for Survival," *The Black Unicorn.* New York: W. W. Norton, 1978, pp. 31-32.

Part II

Black Feminism

5. The Evolution of Feminist Consciousness Among African American Women: WORDS OF FIRE (1995)

Black women both shape the world and are shaped by it ... [they] create their own black feminist theory. They come to feminist theory and practice out of the oppression they experience as people who are poor and black and women .... black feminism has evolved historically over centuries, outside traditional white feminine roles.

Kesho Yvonne Scott, *The Habit of Surviving*

The struggle for black women's liberation that began to emerge in the mid-1960s is a continuation of both intellectual and activist traditions whose seeds were sown during slavery and flowered during the antislavery fervor of the 1830s. When a small group of free black "feminist-abolitionists" in the North surfaced during the early nineteenth century, among whom were Maria Stewart, Sojourner Truth, and Frances E. W. Harper, the history of African American feminism began.[1] Their involvement in abolitionist and other reform movements as lecturers, writers, and journalists—traditionally male domains—met with resistance and violated the Victorian ethic of "true womanhood," which stressed piety, chastity, submissiveness, and domesticity (Welter, 151).*

The argument that African American women confront both a "woman question and a race problem" (Cooper, 134) captured the essence of black feminist thought in the nineteenth century and would reverberate among intellectuals, journalists, activists, writers, educators, artists, and community leaders, both male and female, for generations. While feminist perspectives have been a persistent and important component of the African American literary and intellectual traditions for generations, scholars have focused primarily on racial overtones.[2] This tendency to ignore long years of political struggle aimed at eradicating the multiple oppressions that black women experience resulted in erroneous notions about the relevance of feminism to the black community during the second wave of the women's movement. Rewriting black history using gender as one category of analysis should render obsolete the notion that feminist thinking is alien to African American women or that they have been misguided imitators of white women. An analysis of the feminist activism of black women also suggests the necessity of reconceptualizing women's issues to include poverty, racism, imperialism, lynching, welfare, economic exploitation, sterilization abuse, decent housing, and a host of other concerns that generations of black women foregrounded.

While black feminism is not a monolithic, static ideology, and there is considerable diversity among African American feminists, certain premises are constant: 1) black women experience a special kind of oppression and suffering in this country which is racist, sexist, and classist because of their dual racial and gender identity and their limited access to economic resources; 2) this "triple jeopardy" has meant that the problems, concerns, and needs of black women are different in many ways from those of both white women and black men; 3) black women must struggle for black liberation and gender equality simultaneously; 4) there is no inherent contradiction in the struggle to eradicate sexism and racism as well as the other "isms" which plague the human community, such as classism and heterosexism; 5) black women's commitment to the liberation of blacks and women is profoundly rooted in their lived experience.

Discussions about the evolution of feminist consciousness[3] among African American women usually begin with abolitionist Sojourner Truth (less often with abolitionist Maria Stewart), since the catalyst for the emergence of women's rights in the mid-nineteenth century was the movement to eradicate slavery. There is certainly little disagreement among historians about the link between women's rights and abolition: "It was in the abolition movement that women first learned to organize, to hold public meetings, to conduct petition campaigns. For a quarter of a century the two movements, to free the slave and liberate the woman, nourished and strengthened one another" (Flexner, 41). But it was the horrendous circumstances that enslaved African women endured since 1619, not the abolition movement, that inspired their first yearnings for freedom and rebellious spirit. They resisted beatings, involuntary breeding, sexual exploitation by white masters, family separation, debilitating work schedules, bad living conditions, and even bringing into the world children who would be slaves. A few of their life stories called attention to the peculiar plight of black women and their strategies for resistance.[4] In her antebellum autobiography, *Incidents in the Life of a Slave Girl: Written by Herself* (1861), Harriet Jacobs publicized her sexual vulnerability and stated unequivocally that "slavery is terrible for men; but it is far more terrible for women. Superadded to the burden common to all, they have wrongs, and sufferings, and mortifications peculiarly their own" (Yellin, 77). Covert use of contraceptives, the practice of abortion, and desperate attempts to control the fate of their children, including occasionally infanticide, provided some slave women a measure of control over their bodies and their reproductive capacity. The most well-documented case of infanticide concerns Margaret Garner, who escaped slavery in Kentucky in 1856, and during her capture in Cincinnati killed her baby daughter rather than have her returned to her master. This saga inspired Toni Morrison's award-winning novel, *Beloved,* which was published in 1987.

Manifestations of black women's race and gender consciousness are also found in the single-sex, self-help organizations which free Northern black women formed in the early 1800s because it was difficult for them to become leaders in organizations with black men, or because they were denied membership in white women's groups. It was also easier for black women to attend to their own political, cultural, and intellectual agendas with the establishment of separate literary, debating, abolitionist, or other reform organizations. Located primarily in the northeast, one of the earliest of these organizations was the Afric-American Female Intelligence Society of Boston, founded in 1831. In 1832, free women of color were also responsible for organizing the first female abolitionist group, the Salem Massachusetts Female Antislavery Society, a year before the founding in Philadelphia of the all-male American Anti-Slavery Society (AAS), the most prominent abolitionist organization. The racially mixed Philadelphia Female AntiSlavery Society, also founded in 1833, emerged because the AAS prohibited female membership. Though ignored by historians attempting to document the development of feminism in the mid-nineteenth century, black women's self-help, abolitionist, and other reform activities also contributed to a climate of discontent which foreshadowed the historic women's rights gathering at Seneca Falls in 1848.

In 1832, Maria W. Stewart (1803-1879), a free black from Connecticut with abolitionist and feminist impulses, delivered four public lectures in Boston, the first one before the Afric-American Female Intelligence Society. She was probably the first black woman to speak publicly in defense of women's rights, though she is remembered primarily as the first American born woman of any race to lecture publicly about political matters to racially mixed audiences of women and men. Though she spoke on a variety of issues relevant to the black community—literacy, abolition, economic empowerment, and racial unity—she admonished black women to break free from stifling gender definitions and reach their fullest potential by pursuing formal education and careers, especially teaching, outside the home. She was also adamant that black women assume leadership roles. These were all familiar themes in what we now label a black feminist agenda. Passionate in her defense of black womanhood, she queried: "How long shall the fair daughters of Africa be compelled to bury their minds and talents beneath a load of iron pots and kettles? ... Possess the spirit of independence .... Sue for your rights and privileges" (Richardson, 38).

Discouraged by criticism from black men about her inappropriate female behavior (political activism and lecturing in public), Stewart left the lecture circuit a year later, in 1833, but not without defending womanhood in the most glowing terms by alluding to historical and biblical precedents of women leaders and scholars. She also warned against a paradoxical problem which would plague the black community for generations—preaching against prejudice in the white community but being discriminatory in its own backyard.

During the 1830s and 1840s, other American women, like Stewart, began lecturing against slavery and discovered that they had to defend their right to speak in public, which motivated them to demand their own emancipation. In 1840, the mostly white male American delegates to the World's Anti-Slavery Convention arrived in London to find the women delegates among them excluded from participation. While seated in the gallery behind a curtain with the rest of the women, Elizabeth Cady Stanton and Lucretia Mott felt the striking similarity between themselves, as white women, and black slaves, a common theme in early white feminist discourse. During ten frustrating days, they became friends and agreed to hold a women's rights convention on their return to America. Eight years later, the Seneca Falls convention, most of whose participants were white female abolitionists, was held in New York; this convention signaled the beginning of the United States women's movement. Frederick Douglass, prominent abolitionist and women's rights advocate, was the lone black in attendance.

While Frederick Douglass believed the antislavery movement was helping to empower women, he understood the need for an independent, organized movement to achieve equal rights for women. On July 14, 1848, his *North Star* carried the announcement of the Seneca Falls Convention. A constant reminder to readers of his commitment to the rights of women was the newspaper's slogan — "Right Is of No Sex." At Seneca Falls, when it appeared that Elizabeth Cady Stanton's resolution for woman suffrage was headed for defeat, Douglass at a critical juncture asked for the floor and delivered an eloquent plea on behalf of women's suffrage. The resolution was then put to vote and carried by a small margin.

Serious involvement on the part of black women in the "first-wave" women's rights movement is manifest in the life of Sojourner Truth, the most revered black feminist-abolitionist. Though she could neither read nor write, we know of the details of her life because she dictated her autobiography to a friend. Truth, whose slave name was Isabella, was born around 1797 to parents in Africa and sold as a slave in the state of New York. At age nine, she was sold away from her parents to John Nealy for $100 and sold twice more before she was twelve years old. Her last master, John Dumont, raped her, and later married her to an older slave, Thomas, by whom she had several children. Although slavery was ended by law in New York in 1817, her master delayed her emancipation. She was finally freed by another master in 1827. For a number of years, she worked in New York City as a domestic, the major source of work for black women in the North during this period. Feeling called by God, she left New York in 1843, abandoned her slave name, Isabella, became an itinerant preacher, and attended many antislavery gatherings. In 1850, she attended the second women's rights convention in Salem, Ohio (as did Douglass), and spoke at the third women's rights convention, in Worcester, Massachusetts. Her legendary, but now controversial, "Ain't I a Woman" speech, delivered at the Akron, Ohio, women's rights convention in 1851, is an eloquent statement of black feminist thought because of the implicit links it makes between race and gender in the lives of black women. Truth also reminds her audience that poor black women, whose experiences are radically different from those of white women, must be considered in notions about womanhood.[5]

In 1866, following the Civil War, Douglass and Charles Remond were among the vice presidents chosen for the newly formed Equal Rights Association (ERA) after the American Anti-Slavery Society disbanded. At the first annual meeting of the ERA in 1867, Sojourner Truth addressed women's rights again, but worried that the freedom of black men was getting more attention than black women's liberation. Two years later, a major split occurred in the women's movement over women's suffrage. At the proceedings of the ERA meeting in New York in 1869, the famous debate between Frederick Douglas and white feminists occurred during which he argued for the greater urgency of race over gender. He believed it was the Negro's hour, and women's rights could wait since linking women's suffrage to Negro suffrage at this point would seriously reduce the chances of securing the ballot for Black men, and for Black (males), Douglass reiterated, the ballot was urgent. When asked whether this was true for Black women as well, he quickly responded, "Yes, yes, yes ... but not because she is a woman, but because she is black" (Foner, 87). Frances E. W. Harper, a prominent black feminist-abolitionist, supported Douglass, while Sojourner Truth supported white suffragists, believing that if black men got the vote they would dominate black women.

Following this meeting, Stanton and Anthony organized the women only National Woman Suffrage Association (NWSA) because they believed male leaders had betrayed their interests. In 1869, in Cleveland, the American Woman Suffrage Association (AWSA) was organized with Lucy Stone as chair. By the fall of 1873, even though the Fifteenth Amendment granted black male suffrage and excluded women from voting, white women were anxious to reconcile their differences with Douglass. Peace was finally restored with black abolitionists at the 1876 convention of NWSA, during which Douglass was told that he was needed in the continuing struggle for women's rights. Though he was still somewhat bitter about the racism that surfaced during the battle over the Fifteenth Amendment, he announced that he was willing to work for women's emancipation and became a familiar figure at women's rights conventions again.

An examination of the extraordinary saga of black women journalists during this period provides another perspective on their feminist vision. Mary Shadd Cary (1823-1893), born in Delaware to abolitionist parents, was the first black female newspaper editor in North America. Her pioneering publishing efforts in the 1850s mark the beginning of black women's leadership roles in the male-dominated field of journalism. She migrated to Canada with her brother after the passage of the Fugitive Slave Act in 1850 and a year later solicited the help of Samuel Ringgold Ward, abolitionist and fugitive slave, in the founding of their own abolitionist newspaper, the *Provincial Freeman*, which would also be a publishing outlet for other black women whom she encouraged to write. Its motto was "Self-Reliance Is the True Road to Independence," which was consistent with her ideas about black female empowerment. After the death of her husband, she returned to the United States in 1863, started a school for black children in Washington, D.C., and joined the antislavery lecture circuit. She also became the first black woman lawyer in the United States, graduating from Howard Law School in 1870. In 1880, she founded the Colored Women's Progressive Franchise Association in Washington, D.C., one of the earliest women's rights organizations for African American women. Though gaining suffrage for black women was the major objective, the Association's twenty-point agenda included broadening occupations for black women and establishing newspapers that black women would control.

The black women's club movement, which emerged on the national level in the 1890s as did white women's clubs, must be reconceptualized as a manifestation of middle-class black women's race *and* gender obligations, though scholars locate it primarily within the context of self-help and racial uplift. During the 1870s, middle-class white women, freed from the drudgery of housework because of advances in technology, the availability of immigrant domestics, and access to education and leisure, organized clubs for themselves for the purpose of self and community improvement. Sorosis and the New England Women's Club were among the first of these local organizations, but they quickly proliferated throughout the country, and by 1890 the largely white General Federation of Women's Clubs was founded as an umbrella entity. Black women's clubs emerged not only because white women's clubs prohibited their membership, except in New England, but because they had a unique set of issues—defending black womanhood, uplifting the masses, and improving family life, to name a few.

Five years after the General Federation of Women's Clubs was organized, the first national convention of black women's clubs took place in Boston in 1895. The specific catalyst was a letter that Florence Belgarnie, an officer of the Anti-Lynching Committee in London, received from John Jacks, an American newspaper editor. Angry over Belgarnie's antilynching activities, which had been encouraged by Ida Wells Barnett's anti-lynching crusade in England, Jacks wrote her a letter defending the white South and maligning black women for their immorality. In turn, Belgarnie sent a copy of the letter to Josephine St. Pierre Ruffin, a black member of the largely white New England Women's Club and founder, of the New Era Club (1892-1894) for black women. Later she distributed the letter to numerous black women's clubs and called for a national conference in Boston in 1895, which resulted in the formation of the National Federation of Afro-American Women. When this historic gathering of black clubwomen occurred, a number of items were on the agenda—temperance, higher education, home life, morality, and education for girls and boys. However, it was also clear that black female empowerment for individual and race advancement was the overriding objective:

> ... we need to talk over not only those things which are of vital importance to us as women, but also the things that are of especial interest to us as colored women ... what we especially can do in the moral education of the race ... our mental elevation and physical development ... how to make the most of our own ... limited opportunities ... (*The Woman's Era,* September 1895, 2).

An important goal of the meeting was vindicating the honor of black women and denouncing Jacks. In 1896, the National Association of Colored Women (NACW) was formed as a result of a merger between the Federation and Mary Church Terrell's National League of Colored Women of Washington, D.C.

A pivotal moment in black women's publishing history and the coming of age politically for clubwomen occurred with the founding of *Woman's Era.* In the 1890s, Josephine St. Pierre Ruffin organized the Woman's Era Club in Boston and initiated its newspaper, which eventually became the official organ of the NACW. The first issue came out March 24, 1894, and twenty-four issues were published through 1897. Since it was founded, edited, and published by suffragist Ruffin, it is not surprising to find in the publication a strong advocacy of women's suffrage, especially for black women.

The front page of the first issue carried a portrait and feature article on the women's rights leader Lucy Stone. The first issue also contained an article on the closing meetings of the New England Woman Suffrage Association, of which Ruffin was a member. There was also strong advocacy for black women entering the public arena to solve their unique problems. An awareness of the dilemma that black women faced because of the "double jeopardy" of race and gender is apparent throughout *Woman's Era,* the most significant outlet for the expression of their political views and aspirations during the Progressive Era.

In 1892, clubwoman and educator Anna Julia Cooper published *A Voice from the South: By a Black Woman of the South,* the first book-length feminist analysis of the condition of African Americans. Cooper was born a slave during the Civil War, in Raleigh, North Carolina. At the age of nine, she attended St. Augustine's Normal School and eventually became a teacher there. An early manifestation of her sensitivity to sexism was her protesting female students' exclusion from Greek classes, which were only open to male theology students. She boldly appealed to the principal and was finally granted permission to enroll as the lone female. Her experiences with respect to male privilege at St. Augustine awakened in her a sensitivity to the urgent need for gender equality in the educational arena. Cooper's collection of essays, many of which were speeches delivered to black organizations, is also a progressive discussion of the oppressed status of black women. Not content with simply describing their plight, she argued that black women needed to speak out for themselves and stop allowing others, including black men, to speak for them. Commenting on black women's unique status, she advanced the argument of "double jeopardy," since black women experienced both gender and race problems. A strong advocate for black women's liberation, Cooper was especially concerned about the accessibility of higher education for black women. She also felt that elevating the status of black women would uplift the entire black race, a persistent theme in the writings of Josephine St. Pierre Ruffin and Mary Church Terrell (the first president of NACW), both of whom consistently espoused feminist ideas in their speeches and articles. Cooper was critical of black men who were unsupportive of black female equality, and she frequently spoke at black male gatherings about the importance of women in the struggle for racial uplift. In fact, she believed that women, because of their special qualities and moral values, should be in the forefront of the fight for racial equality. Though she was aware of the double burden of race and gender which was particular to black women, she also felt that black women shared many problems with black males, because of racial oppression, that white women did not share with their men. Cooper also analyzed relationships between black men and women and the problematic nature of those relationships—an analysis that links her to contemporary black feminists.

The next generation of clubwomen would continue and expand the work that Ruffin and Cooper initiated. NACW member Nannie Burroughs (1879-1961), who had Mary Church Terrell and Anna Julia Cooper for teachers and role models at M Street High School in Washington, D.C., worked for the race and for women within a religious context. One of the founders of the Women's Convention, an auxiliary group of the National Baptist Convention and the largest membership organization of black women in the United States, she attended the founding meeting in 1900 in Richmond, Virginia, and spoke, when she was only twenty-one, on "How the Sisters Are Hindered from Helping." This feminist critique of sexism within the church catapulted her into national prominence.[6] A strong advocate for woman suffrage, she also criticized the church for failing to assist in the political development of women, and argued in the *Crisis* (August 1915), the official organ for the National Association for the Advancement of Colored People (NAACP), that the vote would enable women to fight male dominance. In 1909, she founded the National Training School for Women and Girls in Washington, D.C., which stressed industrial education, because she wanted to prepare black women for employment in areas that were open to them.

A few years later, in 1914, the outbreak of World War I precipitated a number of advocacy efforts for the many working women who were leaving domestic service in the South for jobs in northern industry. These included the founding of the Women Wage Earners Association in Washington, D.C., by clubwomen such as Mary Church Terrell and Julia F. Coleman, and efforts to unionize black women workers. After the War ended in 1918, black women found themselves in desperate straits economically given their loss of jobs after the men returned home from Europe. Nannie Burroughs's concern for the plight of black working-class women, particularly domestic servants, resulted in her organizing the National Association of Wage Earners, in 1920. Her intense feelings of racial pride were also manifested in her rejection of white standards of beauty, and she accused her sisters of "color phobia" if they used hair straighteners and skin bleachers. After the Nineteenth Amendment was passed in 1919, she worked with the NACW to mobilize black women voters and in 1924 became president of the National League of Republican Colored Women.

During this same period, the International Council of Women of the Darker Races (which sometimes met in Washington, D.C., at Nannie Burroughs's school) was spawned by the racial uplift impulses and the international educational projects of the black women's club movement. Organized by several club women in 1924, most notably Margaret Murray Washington, founder of the Tuskegee Women's Club and President of NACW from 1914-1918, its purpose was to study the history of peoples of color throughout the world and disseminate knowledge about them for the purpose of engendering racial pride. Study groups, which were called Committees of Seven, were also formed to infuse public school curricula with material on blacks (a precursor of Black Studies) and other people of color, and field trips were organized to gain firsthand experience of other cultures. The Council also studied the situation of women and children of color internationally. Like Cooper, who mentioned Muslim harems and the Chinese practice of foot binding on the first page of *A Voice from the South,* council members were aware of the differential experiences of women because of their travel to international conferences. Washington taught a course at Tuskegee Institute on the condition and status of women throughout the world.

The Pan-African Congress, which stressed the unity of all African peoples, was organized in 1919 in Paris by William E. B. Du Bois, a strong supporter of black women's liberation. Cooper, who spoke on "The Negro Problem in America," was one of only two black women to address this international gathering of people of African descent. The Council also cosponsored, with the Chicago Women's Club, a fund-raising activity to support Pan-Africanist feminist Adelaide Casely-Hayford's efforts to build a school in Sierra Leone.

She was married to a prominent Ghanaian lawyer who edited *Gold Coast Leader,* a leading Pan-Africanist publication. This work of the council is reminiscent of more recent attempts by black feminist activists to learn about and establish linkages with women of color internationally and to struggle for the elimination of sexism and racism globally. In July 1960, for example, African American women attended the First Conference of African Women and Women of African Descent held in Accra, Ghana.

A frequently overlooked aspect of black women's activism during this period, especially within the context of Pan-Africanism or nationalism was their battle against gender oppression, though black liberation would be their major priority. In 1925, Elise McDougald, Harlem teacher and journalist, discussed the economic plight of a particular class of African American women. She also acknowledged that black women's "feminist efforts are directed chiefly toward the realization of the equality of the races, the sex struggle assuming a subordinate place" (McDougald, "The Double Task: The Struggle of Negro Women for Sex and Race Emancipation" *Survey Graphic* [October 1924-March 1925).) This granting of greater urgency to racial concerns was predictable given the pervasiveness of white supremacy.

The feminist-pan-Africanist views of Amy Jacques Garvey (1896-1973), Marcus Garvey's second wife, are especially important to consider during this period because of their potential impact on thousands of working class urban blacks involved with the most powerful nationalist organization in the United States—the Universal Negro Improvement Association (UNIA), which her husband founded in Jamaica in 1914 with his first wife, Amy Ashwood.[7] As a young man, Garvey was outraged by the exploitation of blacks in the Caribbean. A trip to London in 1912 brought him in contact with Africans who inspired him to struggle against colonialism. When he returned to Jamaica, he organized the UNIA for the promotion of racial solidarity and self-determination among African peoples throughout the world. From the beginning, women were crucial in the hierarchy of the organization, and women's issues were discussed, among them the question of whether a woman's intellect was as highly developed as a man's. Scholars of the Garvey movement also agree that a distinguishing characteristic of the UNIA was the opportunity it provided for black women's political development.

As editor from 1924-1927 of the Women's Page of the *Negro World,* the UNIA's weekly newspaper, Amy Jacques Garvey wrote passionately in "Our Women and What They Think" about the evils of imperialism, racism, capitalism, and the interlocking race, class, and gender oppression that black and other women experienced globally, particularly in colonial contexts. She believed the women's movement was one of the most significant struggles in human history, and that the emancipation of women was imperative. She called for women to participate in all spheres of public life despite their important duties as wives and mothers. She also felt that women were central to the success of black liberation struggles both in the United States and abroad, and she urged them to struggle against imperialist domination as well as their own oppression within their communities. Echoing Sojourner Truth and Anna Julia Cooper, she espoused a feminist vision of the world in which women would set things right: "You [men] had your day at the helm of the world, and a pretty mess you have made of it ... and perhaps women's rule will usher in the era of real brotherhood, when national and racial lines will disappear, leaving mankind in peace and harmony one with another" (Garvey, *Negro World*, 1926, 5). She also had a special warning for black men: " ... watch your step! Ethiopia's queens will reign again and her Amazons protect her shores and people. Strengthen your shaking knees and move forward, or we will displace you and lead on to victory and glory" (Lerner, 579). Concerned about the status of women globally, particularly in Asia and Africa, she applauded Egyptian women's removal of the veil and women's political gains in India, Russia, and China. A "training ground for black feminists of the 1930s," both in the United States and Jamaica (Lewis and Bryan, 82), the UNIA deserves a place in the history of black feminism in the diaspora.

Despite the decline in black fertility rates since the turn of the century, advocating for birth control was another black feminist agenda item during the 1920s and 1930s.[8] It is important to point out that the covert use among slave women of contraceptives and abortifacients was perhaps the earliest manifestation of black women's exercising reproductive freedom, a major demand of contemporary feminists. Having fewer children was a deliberate choice of some women to enhance their family's standard of living as well as a strategy espoused in the black press for ensuring the community's economic well-being, particularly during the Depression. Black women also had a feminist perspective on excessive childbearing, linking it to burdensome physical and mental problems, and were also concerned about sterilization abuse. On a national level, Margaret Sanger, prominent white birth control crusader, launched a major campaign in 1915 to legalize the dissemination of information about birth control methods and founded the American

Birth Control League in 1921.[9] The Women's Political Association of Harlem, founded in 1918 and concerned about all aspects of black women's leadership, was the first black organization to advocate birth control, though numerous birth control clinics appeared nationwide in the black community from 1925-1945. The Association also supported Sanger's desire to establish a birth control clinic in Harlem. In September 1919, Sanger's *Birth Control Review* published a special issue on "The New Emancipation: The Negroes' Need for Birth Control, as Seen by Themselves." This issue included the work of black women writers—a feminist play by Mary Burrill, *They That Sit in Darkness*, which dramatizes the tragedy of too many children, and a short story, "The Closing Door," by Angelina Weld Grimke, the niece of the white Grimke sisters who were famous feminist abolitionists.

The two most important civil rights organizations in the black community—the National Urban League and the NAACP—supported the use of birth control because they believed that smaller families were more viable economically. This issue sparked controversy, however, within certain circles as nationalist concerns about racial extinction and traditional male views about women's primary role as mothers clashed with feminist demands for sexual autonomy among black women. There was a range of attitudes among black leaders on this issue. Marcus Garvey felt that contraceptives were retarding the growth of the race. Sociologist and PanAfricanist William E. B. Du Bois, one of the founders of the NAACP, argued in "The Damnation of Women" (1925) that women must be free to choose motherhood, and he repeated this progressive stance in "Black Folks and Birth Control" in the June 1932 issue of *Birth Control Review.*

Concern for black working women also fueled black women's activism during the 1940s and the aftermath of World War II. Because of the labor shortage with men at war, thousands of black women left the rural South again and migrated to the North for better jobs in industry. The promise of a better life had remained elusive, however, since they were relegated to the most menial, hazardous, low-paying factory jobs. Poor living conditions in crowded urban settings, job discrimination, the absence of childcare facilities, and segregated, substandard housing produced a climate ripe for agitation.

One of the most radical voices during this era was Claudia Jones, whose family had migrated to Harlem from Trinidad in 1924. Economic hardship during the Depression caused her to drop out of school and get a factory job. At age eighteen, she joined the Young Communist League along with many other working-class Harlemites during the 1930s. During the 1940s, she became one of the most outspoken black communists on the issue of women's rights; in a 1947 issue of *Political Affairs*, a Communist Party journal, she argued that black women, "as workers, as Negroes, and as women" were "the most oppressed stratum of the whole population" (Jones, 4). In her passionate analysis of the situation of black women historically, the plight of the contemporary worker, and the struggles of militant "Negro women" for peace, civil rights, and economic justice, she anticipated a sophisticated black feminist discourse that was a generation away. Though she applauded women in organizations such as the National Association of Negro Women and trade unionists, she chastised the latter for being insensitive to the misery and urgent needs of domestic workers, who were unprotected by labor legislation. She also made insightful connection between the sexist treatment of black domestics and the dehumanizing treatment of black women in general. Reminiscent of Cooper and other nineteenth-century black women feminist-abolitionists, she exposed the racism of white women and reminded them that it was in their own self-interest to work for black women's liberation "inasmuch as the super exploitation and oppression of Negro women tends to depress the standards of all women" (Jones, 12). Her prophetic call for the women's movement to embrace an antiracist agenda anticipated similar pleas by black feminists two generations later. "A developing consciousness on the woman question today ... must not fail to recognize that the Negro question ... is *prior* to, and not equal to, the woman question; that only to the extent that we fight all chauvinist expressions and actions as regards the Negro people, and [the] right for the full equality of the Negro people, can women as a whole advance their struggle for equal rights" (Jones, 15).

In the 1960s, black feminist struggle came to the forefront in a more sustained manner and among a larger group, mainly because of the failure of the Civil Rights and women's rights movements to address the concerns of black women. Heightened consciousness about the confluence of racism and sexism in their lives was one result of their experiences with male chauvinism within the Civil Rights Movement. In her autobiography, *The Trumpet Sounds* (1964), Anna Arnold Hedgeman describes her feelings about the male-dominant civil rights leadership and her experiences as the only woman on the planning committee for the 1963 March on Washington. When she discovered the omission of women as speakers on the program, she was appalled and wrote a letter to director A. Philip Randolph in which she alluded to black women's important roles in the Civil Rights Movement. She also argued that "since the 'Big Six' [civil rights leaders] [had] not given women the quality of participation which they [had] earned through the years," (Hedgeman, 179), it was even more imperative that black women be allowed to speak. The outcome, according to Hedgeman, was that on the day of the March the wives of the civil rights leaders and a few other black women were asked to sit on the dais, Daisy Bates was asked to say a few words, and Rosa Parks was presented, but didn't speak. Hedgeman's response that historic day was one of disappointment: "We grinned, some of us, as we recognized anew that Negro women are second-class citizens in the same way that white women are in our culture" (Hedgeman, 180).

In 1964, Mary King and Casey Hayden, white Student Nonviolent Coordinating Committee (SNCC) staffers, discussed the sexist treatment of women in SNCC in a position paper entitled "Women of the Movement," which they delivered at SNCC's Waveland Conference.[10] Ruby Doris Smith Robinson, SNCC executive secretary (1966), died of cancer a year later at age twenty-five, and Kathleen Cleaver, a former SNCC worker and Black Panther, believed Robinson's death was caused in part by overwork and "the constant struggles that she was subjected to because she was a woman" (Cleaver, 55). Similarly, Septima Clark, the Southern Christian Leadership Conference's (SCLC) director of education in 1961, criticized the sexism of SCLC in her autobiography *Ready from Within*: "... those men didn't have any faith in women, none whatsoever. They just thought that women were sex symbols and had no contributions to make ... I had a great feeling that Dr. King didn't think much of women either ... " (Crawford, 195-96). She also confronted King about his nondemocratic style of leadership and eventually joined the National Organization for Women (NOW) in 1968 because of its women's rights agenda.

The publication in 1970 of Toni Cade's *The Black Woman: An Anthology,* Shirley Chisholm's autobiography *Unbought and Unbossed,* Toni Morrison's *The Bluest Eye,* and Audre Lorde's *Cables to Rage* signaled awakening among black women and the beginning of a clearly defined black women's liberation movement that would have priorities different from those of white feminists, and generate considerable debate, even hostility, within the black community. Cade's antiracist, antisexist, anti-imperialist agenda captures the essence of contemporary black feminism: conduct a comparative study of women's roles in the Third World; debunk myths of the black matriarch and "the evil black bitch"; study black women's history and honor woman warriors such as Harriet Tubman and Fannie Lou Hamer; do oral histories of ordinary black women (migrant workers, quilters, UNIA grandmothers); study sexuality; establish linkages with other women of color globally (Cade, 11). The anthology includes SNCC activist Frances Beale's pioneering essay on the "double jeopardy" of black women, which highlights their sexual and economic exploitation, the inappropriateness of white models of womanhood, black male sexism, sterilization abuse of women of color globally, abortion rights, and Sojourner Truth's 1851 women's rights speech. Beale also voices her disapproval of black nationalist demands that women be subordinate to men and the assumption that women's most important contribution to the revolution is having babies: "To assign women the role of housekeeper and mother while men go forth into battle is a highly questionable doctrine to maintain" (Cade, 100).

In 1973, the National Black Feminist Organization (NBFO) would emerge in part as a reminder to the black liberation movement that "there can't be liberation for half the race."[11] Activist lawyer Flo Kennedy and Margaret Sloan decided to convene a small gathering of black feminists in May so that they could discuss their experiences within the racist women's movement and what it meant to be black, female, and feminist. In their statement of purpose, they objected to the women's movement's being seen as white, and their involvement in it as disloyal to the race. Emphasizing black women's need for self-definition, they identified racism from without and sexism from within as destructive to the black community.

The National Black Feminist Organization officially began in November 1973, at an Eastern Regional Conference in New York City at the Cathedral of St. John the Divine. This was a historic gathering of the first explicitly black feminist organization committed to the eradication of sexism, racism, and heterosexism. Workshops focused on a variety of issues — childcare, the church, welfare, women's liberation, lesbianism, prisons, education, addiction, work, female sexuality, and domestic violence. Among those present were Shirley Chisholm, Alice Walker, Eleanor Holmes Norton, Flo Kennedy, and Margaret Sloan, NBFO's first and only president. [12]

A year after the founding meeting, the Boston chapter of NBFO decided to form a more radical organization, according to lesbian feminist writer Barbara Smith, and named itself in 1975 the Combahee River Collective after Harriet Tubman's "military campaign" in South Carolina (1863), which freed nearly 800 slaves. In 1977, after meeting informally for three years and doing intense consciousness-raising (the major strategy for feminist organizing in the 1970s), a black feminist lesbian manifesto was issued that foregrounded sexuality and asserted that "sexual politics under patriarchy is as pervasive in black women's lives as the politics of class and race" (Hull, Bell Scott, and Smith, 16). Emphasizing the "simultaneity" of racial, gender, heterosexist, and class oppression in the lives of black and other women of color, they affirmed their connection to an activist tradition among black women going back to the nineteenth century as well as to black liberation struggles of the 1960s. Despite the difficulty of sustaining a socialist black feminist organization with lesbian leadership for six years, they worked untiringly on a variety of "revolutionary" issues—reproductive rights, rape, prison reform, sterilization abuse, violence against women, health care, and racism within the white women's movement. They also understood the importance of coalition building and worked with other women of color, white feminists, and progressive men. Equally important was their breaking the silence about homophobia within the black community and providing lesbians and heterosexual women with opportunities to work together.

In 1975, Michele Wallace wrote an article for the *Village Voice* entitled "A Black Feminist's Search for Sisterhood," and precipitated an intense controversy within the black community when *Black Macho and the Myth of the Superwoman* appeared three years later. Wallace, a founding member of NBFO, critiqued black male sexism and the misogyny of black liberation struggles. Echoing Wallace, the August 17, 1979, issue of *Newsweek* included a significant article, "A New Black Struggle," that underscored intraracial tensions based on gender: "It's the newest wrinkle in the black experience in America—a growing distrust, if not antagonism, between black men and women that is tearing marriages apart and fracturing personal relationships." This "wake-up call" came on the heels of Ntozake Shange's award-winning Broadway play *For Colored Girls Who Have Considered Suicide/When the Rainbow is Enuf* (1976) and Wallace's polemic *Black Macho,* which were demonized because of their negative assessments of black men. The issue of sexual politics within the African American community became a hotly debated topic in journals such as *The Black Scholar, Freedomways,* and *Black Books Bulletin,* and provided the catalyst for the founding of a short-lived bimonthly magazine, *Black Male/Female Relationships,* by sociologists Nathan and Julia Hare. *Black Scholar,* however, would provide the most extensive and sober treatment of the debate generated by Wallace's and Shange's controversial feminist writings. The April 1973 issue on "Black Women's Liberation" led the way, followed by the March 1975 issue, "The Black Woman," the 1979 "Black Sexism Debate" issue, and the 1986 "Black Women and Feminism" issue. Robert Staples's essay "The Myth of

Black Macho: A Response to Angry Black Feminists," which appeared in the March/April 1979 issue, was a feminist-bashing response to Wallace and Shange, whom he accused of black male bashing; it stimulated a Readers' Forum in the subsequent May/June 1979 issue, in which the battle lines were drawn. Robert Chrisman's editorial for this special issue acknowledged in very strong terms the validity of the accusations and called for a reconciliation between black men and women: "Black feminists have raised criticisms of black male sexism .... We believe that the effort to clarify the nature of black male/ female relationships is an important step in the process of reuniting our people and revitalizing the struggle against oppression ... the problems of black male/female relationships are neither new nor solely the creation of the white media."

A decade later, the controversy continued and grew more virulent; its most obvious manifestations were loud and angry litanies, especially among black professional men, about the portrayal of black male characters in the fiction of contemporary black women writers. Alice Walker's novel *The Color Purple* (1982) and Steven Spielberg's film adaptation sparked the most vitriolic responses. Shahrazad Ali's self-published *The Blackman's Guide to Understanding the Blackwoman* (1990) was one of the most disturbing publications during this decade-and-a-half-old family battle and is one of the most blatantly misogynist and racist texts to appear in print. Black feminist writing proliferated during this period amid rancorous debate within the black community about the relevance of the contemporary white women's movement to black women. One of the most passionate defenders of feminist ideology to emerge, though she also delivered scathing critiques of white feminism, was bell hooks, whose pioneering monograph, *Ain't I a Woman: Black Women and Feminism* (1981) delineated the impact of sexism on the lives of black women; analyzed the devaluation of black womanhood, both historically and contemporaneously; and discussed the persistence of racism in the women's movement and the involvement of black women in struggles to achieve gender equality. The chapter on "Sexism and the Black Female Experience" advanced the new thesis that slavery, a reflection of a patriarchal and racist social order, not only oppressed black men but also defeminized slave women. Over the next decade and a half, a substantial group of black feminist writers, among whom were Audre Lorde, Barbara Smith, Angela Davis, Alice Walker, Gloria Joseph, June Jordan, Ntozake Shange, Gloria Hull, Paula Giddings, and Barbara Christian, would redefine feminism as a broad political movement to end all forms of domination. In the words of hooks, " ... feminism is not simply a struggle to end male chauvinism or a movement to ensure that women have equal rights with men; it is a commitment to eradicating the ideology of domination that permeates Western culture on various levels—sex, race, and class, to name a few—and a commitment to reorganizing U.S. society so that the self-development of people can take precedence over imperialism, economic expansion, and material desires" (hooks, 1981, 194).

Reminiscent of the 1890s, writing, publishing, and organizing became a major preoccupation of black feminists during the 1980s, and heeding Cooper's words, black women were clearly speaking for themselves. Other groundbreaking texts were Barbara Christian's *Black Women Novelists* (1980); Angela Davis's *Women, Race, and Class* (1981); Filomina Chioma Steady's *The Black Woman Cross-Culturally* (1981); Hull, Bell Scott, and Smith's *All the Women Are White, All the Blacks are Men, But Some of Us Are Brave: Black Women's Studies* (1982); Paula Gidding's *When and Where I Enter: The Impact of Black Women on Sex and Race in America* (1984); Alice Walker's I*n Search of Our Mother's Gardens: Womanist Prose* (1983); Barbara Smith's *Home Girls: A Black Feminist Anthology* (1983); Audre Lorde's *Sister Outsider: Essays and Speeches* (1984); Deborah Gray White's *Ain't I a Woman?: Female Slaves in the Plantation South* (1985); and Hazel Carby's *Recontructing Womanhood: The Emergence of the Afro-American Woman Novelist* (1987). Kitchen Table: Women of Color Press was founded in 1980 by Audre Lorde and Barbara Smith for the purpose of publishing mainly feminist women of color; its mission was also to provide a "political support network for feminists and lesbians of color as well."

The first explicitly black feminist periodical devoted exclusively to the experiences of women of African descent in the United States and throughout the world was founded in 1984 in Atlanta, Georgia, and hosted by Spelman College's Women's Research and Resource Center, the first feminist institute on a historically black college campus. *SAGE: A Scholarly Journal on Black Women* would provide a major outlet for feminist perspectives on a variety of issues including mother-daughter relationships in the black community, health, science and technology, and the situation of women in rural Africa. During its founding conference in 1983, the National Black Women's Health Project, whose newsletter *Vital Signs* provides black feminist perspectives on health, attracted the largest group of black women ever to assemble on Spelman's campus.

Black feminist theory would come of age during the 1990s and move from the margins to the center of mainstream feminist discourse. Patricia Hill Collin's landmark *Black Feminist Thought* identified the fusion of activism and theory as its distinguishing characteristic and analyzed its three core themes: the interlocking nature of race, class, and gender oppression in black women's personal, domestic, and work lives; the necessity of internalizing positive self-definitions and rejecting the denigrating, stereotypical, and controlling images (mammy, matriarch, welfare mother, whore) of others both within and without the black community; and the need for active struggle to resist oppression and realize individual and group empowerment (Collins, 23, 32, 83-84). The Collins text would further establish, along with Toni Cade's *The Black Woman* and bell hooks's *Ain't I a Woman,* a continuous black feminist intellectual tradition going back to the publication of Cooper's *A Voice from the South* a hundred years earlier.

Despite their commitment to ending sexism, however, some black women continue to be alienated by the term "feminist." Alice Walker's *In Search of Mother's Gardens* (1983) provided the alternative term "womanist" as a more culturally appropriate label for black feminists or feminists of color. "Womanist" recalled a black folk expression of mothers admonishing their daughters to refrain from "womanish" behavior. According to Walker, a "womanist" prefers women's culture, is committed to the survival of the entire group, is serious, "loves struggle, *loves* the folk, and loves herself" (Walker, *In Search of Our Mothers' Gardens,* xi-xii). Inspired by Walker, scholars such as Cheryl Gilkes, Katie Cannon, Jacquelyn Grant, Delores Williams, Renita Weems, and Emily Townes, for example, self-identity as "womanist" theologians as a way of differentiating themselves from white feminist theologians.

President George Bush's 1991 nomination of Judge Clarence Thomas to the Supreme Court and Professor Anita Hill's subsequent allegations of sexual harassment, which resulted in televised hearings for three days in October, sparked perhaps the most profound intraracial tensions around sexual politics that the modern African American community ever experienced. Despite Hill's allegations that Thomas had sexually harassed her while she worked under him at the Department of Education and the Equal Employment Opportunity Commission (EEOC), on October 16 the Senate confirmed, 52-48, Clarence Thomas as Associate Justice of the Supreme Court, replacing outgoing Thurgood Marshall. A month later, a cogent statement opposing the racist and sexist treatment of Anita Hill appeared in the November 17, 1991, issue of the *New York Times* (A-53, "African American Women in Defense of Ourselves." Over 1,600 black women reminded the nation of Thomas's persistent failure, despite his own racial history and professional opportunities, to respond to the urgency of civil rights for disadvantaged groups. Furthermore, the statement called attention to a long history of sexual abuse and stereotyping of black women as "immoral, insatiable, perverse." The failure of Congress to take seriously Hill's sexual harassment charges was perceived as an attack on the collective character of black women (Chrisman and Allen, 292).

More than any other episode in recent memory, including the angry responses to *Black Macho, For Colored Girls,* and *The Color Purple,* the Thomas/Hill saga unmasked problematic gender attitudes within the black community and in some cases outright misogyny. Because Hill had violated a deeply held cultural taboo—that racial dirty linen shouldn't be aired in public—she epitomized black female treachery in breaking the silence about objectionable black male behavior. For over a decade, black women had been labeled traitors among some segments of the community because of their advocacy of feminism, which was associated with white women. Despite the criticism, however, contemporary black feminists, like their nineteenth-century counterparts, mobilized for struggle with the hope that eradicating the twin evils of racism and sexism would become a battle cry within the entire community. In the aftermath of the Thomas/Hill hearings, black women witnessed rancorous public dialogue about their character, which sparked the formation of a new feminist organization, African American Women in Defense of Ourselves.

In January 1994, the largest gathering of black feminist scholars and activists took place at the Massachusetts Institute of Technology (MIT) during a national conference entitled "Black Women in the Academy: Defending Our Name, 1894-1994." Ironically, nearly one hundred years after the historic gathering of clubwomen in Boston in 1895, over 2,000 mostly academic black women gathered again. Like black women in the 1890s, they found themselves under attack, much of which was generated by the Thomas/Hill hearings and the propaganda associated with welfare reform and "family values." In addition, two prominent black academic women with liberal politics, Johnnetta Betsch Cole and Lani Guinier (both of whom were keynoters at MIT), had been viciously attacked by the Right; as a result, both of them were abandoned as appointees of the Clinton administration. Twenty-five years earlier, Angela Davis (the third keynoter) had been fired from her faculty job at the University of California, Los Angeles, by Governor Ronald Reagan because of her political views and Communist Party membership.

Among other things, the MIT conference demonstrated the persistence of black women intellectuals' commitment to feminist discourse and action, despite the absence of common ground on several issues. A resolution was drafted and sent to President Clinton which, first of all, acknowledged the "complexity of social categories such as race, class, gender, and sexual orientation."[13] It called for a blue ribbon panel on race relations in the United States; underscored the importance of research on black women that would promote the interests of the entire African American community; called for an examination of career advancement issues for women of color in higher education; and requested increased funding for community-based organizations serving poor black families and others in need. This document articulates the contours of contemporary black feminism and suggests a blueprint for the future.

As we approach the beginning of the twenty-first century, it is apparent that the lives of many women around the world have been unaffected by centuries-old struggles for gender equality. In most places, women are poorer than men, in some places, daughters are still valued less than sons, and a global epidemic of violence against women remains unchecked. It is also the case that the promise of feminism—that females can live better lives with a wider range of choices and resources—is a reality for some women three decades after the beginning of the "second wave" of the United States women's movement even though poverty, racism, and heterosexual privilege remain deeply entrenched. More of us, women and men, must heed the challenge set before us by bell hooks in her first book on black feminism: "Only a few black women have rekindled the spirit of feminist struggle that stirred the hearts and minds of our nineteenth century sisters. We, black women who advocate feminist ideology, are pioneers. We are clearing a path for ourselves and our sisters. We hope that as long as they see us reach our goal—no longer victimized, no longer unrecognized, no longer afraid—they will take courage and follow" (*Ain't I a Woman,* 196). The struggle continues.[14]

NOTES

* Barbara Welter, "The Cult of True Womanhood," *American Quarterly* 18 (Summer 1966), 151.
Claudia Jones, "An End to the Neglect of the Problems of the Negro Woman," *PUBLIC AFFAIRS*, June 1949, p. 4

• • •

[1] Blanche Glassman Hersh's *Slavery of Sex: Feminist-Abolitionists in America* (Urbana: University of Illinois Press, 1978) excludes black women abolitionists from her discussion of feminist-abolitionists (her terminology) because of her erroneous assessment of their minimal involvement in the first wave of the women's movement, which she describes as largely white. Jean Yellin and John Van Horne's collection of essays, *The Abolitionist Sisterhood* (Ithaca: Cornell University Press 1994), corrects Hersh's assumptions by including extensive discussions of women of African descent in their category of antislavery feminist, "that small circle of black and white American women who, in the 1830s and 1840s, initially banded together to remedy the public evils of slavery and racism and who ultimately struggled for equal rights for women as well as slaves" (3). Yellin and Van Horne also complicate the analysis by indicating that this group was diverse and included more traditional women who were not feminist.
[2] See Shirley J. Yee's *Black Women Abolitionists: A Study in Activism, 1828-1860* (Knoxville: University of Tennessee Press, 1992) for an excellent analysis of the emergence of black feminism in the early nineteenth century.
[3] Gerda Lerner's *The Creation of Feminist Consciousness: From the Middle Ages to Eighteen-Seventy* (New York: Oxford University Press 1993) documents the twelve-hundred-year struggle of women in the West to free their minds of patriarchal thinking, the roots of which can be found in institutional barriers to their intellectual development. Her brief discussion of African American women focuses on evangelists such as Sojourner Truth, whom she singles out as being "virtually alone among black women in the nineteenth century in staunchly combining the defense of her race with a defense of her sex" (106). Lerner also defines feminist consciousness as women's awareness that they belong to a subordinate group which has suffered because of societal constructs. As a result, they need to develop sisterly bonds with other women and work to change their subordinate status (274).
[4] See Angela Davis's pioneering essay, "Reflections on the Black Woman's Role in the Community of Slaves," *Black Scholar* 3 (December 1971): 4-15, which rewrites the history of slave resistance. Deborah Gray White's *Ain't I a Woman? Female Slaves in the Plantation South* (New York; W.W. Norton, 1985) also focuses on the black female slave experience.
[5] Frances Dana Gage, a white abolitionist who chaired the historic meeting in Akron, is responsible for the details of this gathering, which focus on Truth's presence and what she did and said. The speech, which Gage is reputed to have recorded, appears appears in Elizabeth Cady Stanton, Susan B. Anthony and Matilda Joslyn Gage's

History of Woman Suffrage, 6 vols. (1889-1992), 2: 193. See Nell Irvin Painter'"Difference, Slavery, and Memory: Sojourner Truth in Feminist Abolitionism," in *The Abolitionist Sisterhood,* eds. Yellin and Van Horne, and her "Sojourner Truth in Life and Memory," in *Gender and History* 2 (Spring 1990): 3-16, which raise doubts about Gage's version of the Sojourner Truth saga in Akron, Ohio.

[6] See Evelyn Brooks Higginbotham's award-winning book *Righteous Discontent: The Women's Movement in the Black Baptist Church, 1880-1920* (Cambridge: Harvard University Press, 1993) for a discussion of the feminist theology of black Baptist women, Nannie Burroughs's struggles against racism and sexism, and the role of black women's organizations, such as the Women's Convention of the National Baptist Convention, in self-determination.

[7] As is frequently the case with women married to prominent men, Amy Jacques Garvey has been largely overlooked in the scholarship on the Garvey movement. Exceptions are Mark D. Matthews," 'Our Women and What They Think': Amy Jacques Garvey and *The Negro World,*" *Black Scholar* (May-June 1979): 2-13; "'Always Leading Our Men in Service and Sacrifice': Amy Jacques Garvey, Feminist Black and Nationalist," *Gender and Society* 6 (September 1992): 346-375; and the work of Professor Ula Taylor. For discussions of women in the Garvey movement, see *Garvey: His Work and Impact,* eds. Rupert Lewis and Patrick Bryan (Trenton, N.J.: Africa World Press, 1991), which contains an essay by Tony Martin and Honor Ford Smith.

[8] See Jessie M. Rodrique's "The Black Community and the Birth Control Movement," *Passion and Power: Sexuality in History,* eds. Kathy Peiss and Christina Simmons (Philadelphia: Temple University Press, 1989) for a discussion of the decline in fertility among blacks from the late nineteenth century to World War II (1880-1945), and a comprehensive analysis of the black community's considerable involvement with the issue of birth control from 1915 to 1945, though this has been overlooked in chronicles of the birth control movement in the United States.

[9] See Angela Davis, *Women, Race, and Class* (New York: Random House, 1981) for a thoughtful analysis and critique of Margaret Sanger's racism.

[10] Mary King, *Freedom Song: A Personal Story of the 1960s Civil Rights Movement* (New York: William Morrow, 1987), 567-569.

[11] "Statement of Purpose," in *Feminism in Our Time,* ed. Miriam Schneir (New York: Vintage Books, 1994), 171-174.

[12] See Beverly Davis, "To Seize the Moment: A Retrospective on the National Black Feminist Organization," *SAGE: A Scholarly Journal on Black Women (Fall 1988)*: 43-46, for a detailed history of NBFO.

[13] See *Black Scholar* 24 (Winter 1994): 6.

[14] Portions of this introduction appear in my dissertation *Daughters of Sorrow: Attitudes Toward Black Women, 1880-1920* (Carlson, 1990) and in "Remembering Sojourner Truth: On Black Feminism," *Catalyst* 1 (Fall 1986): 54-57.

6. Gender Talk, (Introduction with Johnnetta Betsch Cole) (2000)

As members of this panel on gender identity, we would like to share with you our vision of perhaps our most challenging publishing project. We are writing a book, tentatively titled *Gender Talk,* in which we will probe a range of complex gender issues within African-American communities as a way of illuminating some aspects of the state of Black America at the beginning of this new century. In this book project, we are asking, very simply, what would it mean to take gender seriously in our analysis of what ails Black America? We would like to begin our response by remembering Audre Lorde, who perhaps more than anyone we know taught us about the tyranny of silence and the fears we need to overcome in our collective struggles against racism, sexism, classism, and heterosexism. Audre Lorde also reminded us of the problem of difference within African-American communities and the courage we need to address a range of intracommunity issues despite our history of racial oppression:

> Within Black communities where racism is a living reality, differences among us often seem dangerous and suspect. The need for unity is often misnamed as a need for homogeneity, and a Black feminist vision mistaken for betrayal of our common interests as a people. Because of the continuous battle against racial erasure that Black women and Black men share, some Black women still refuse to recognize that we are also oppressed as women, and that sexual hostility against Black women is practiced not only by the white racist society, but implemented within our Black communities as well. It is a disease striking the heart of Black nationhood, and silence will not make it disappear.[1]

Despite Audre Lorde's call for Black women to speak, there has been an even louder call from various segments of our community to remain silent, and if we persist in naming our problems, we are often labeled race traitors. We see *Gender Talk* as yet another attempt on the part of those of us who self-identify as Black feminists to participate in race regeneration.

At the turn of the twentieth century, Anna Julia Cooper wrote an important text, *A Voice from the South: By a Black Woman of the South* (1892), in which she provided a feminist analysis of the state of Black America and in different terms and a very different cultural context probed some of the questions that preoccupy us in *Gender Talk:* What would a vision of

Black community transformation look like if gender were more central to our analytic frameworks? What would it mean to make more visible, to engage in more systematic analyses of the convergence of race and gender within the African-American context? How might we begin to conceptualize race loyalty differently? Twenty-seven years removed from slavery and preoccupied by the challenges of "race regeneration" after the long nightmare of slavery, Cooper was unapologetic about the urgency of analyzing our past failures and achievements, our present "difficulties and embarrassments," and our "mingled hopes and fears for the future." She boldly asserted that it was now time "to pause a moment for retrospection, introspection, and prospection."[2] In addition to analyzing the legacy of slavery and the racism of the white women's movement, Cooper also provided what we would now call an internal critique, an analysis of sexism within the Black community. She was particularly perturbed that "while our men seem thoroughly abreast of the times on almost every other subject, when they strike the woman question they drop back into sixteenth century logic."[3]

We feel it is time again to pause for retrospection and introspection, borrowing Cooper's terminology, during these difficult times, despite all the rhetoric to the contrary about how well we're faring as a community. We are mindful as well of a body of work by Black women, in the tradition of Cooper, that analyzes and debates issues and arrives at diagnoses and solutions that are frequently at odds with the more visible, hegemonic Black male discourse about the state of Black America and what ails us. Certainly, what we are attempting to do in *Gender Talk* is not entirely new. There is the insightful though often maligned work of a group of Black feminist writers, activists, and intellectuals that began with Toni Cade's 1970 anthology, *The Black Woman,* with which our book shares a similar mission and political perspective. There is also a broad range of writing by Black women and men with differing ideological perspectives that examines gender issues within AfricanAmerican communities, though these analyses and narratives are always situated within the broader context of white racism, which will be true of *Gender Talk* as well. We are referring to Paula Giddings's *When and Where I Enter: The Impact of Black Women on Race and Sex in America* (1984); numerous books by bell hooks on Black feminism; Barbara Omolade's *The Rising Song of African American Women* (1994); Jill Nelson's *Straight, No Chaser* (1997); Michael Dyson's *Race Rules: Navigating the Color Line* (1996); Orlando Patterson's *Rituals of Blood: Consequences of Slavery in Two American Centuries* (1998); Deborah Gray

White's *Too Heavy a Load: Black Women in Defense of Themselves, 1894-1994* (1999); and Charles Michael Smith's *Fighting Words: Personal Essays by Black Gay Men* (1999).

As important are works that provide a gendered analysis of the civil rights movement and a more nuanced history of Black political activism in the contemporary period. Belinda Robnett's *How Long? How Long?: African-American Women in the Struggle for Civil Rights* (1997) is in this category and analyzes, among other things, the impact of Black Power ideology and the move to more hierarchical structures within organizations such as the Student Nonviolent Coordinating Committee (SNCC), which adversely affected women's leadership roles after 1965. Kimberly Springer's *Still Lifting, Still Climbing* (1999) is the first collection of critical essays to examine the broad range of political activism on the part of African-American women over the past four decades, including male-dominated Pan-African organizations. Black nationalist imperatives in the late 1960s and assertions about the need to reclaim Black manhood were accompanied by calls for Black women to "step back." Angela Davis alludes to her experiences with nationalist organizations in Paula Giddings's *When and Where I Enter*:

> Some of the brothers came around only for staff meetings, ... and whenever we women were involved in something important, they began to talk about "women taking over the organization"—calling it a matriarchal coup d'etat. All the myths about black women surfaced. [We] were too domineering; we were trying to control everything, including the men, which meant by extension that we wanted to rob them of their manhood. By playing such a leading role in the organization, some of them insisted, we were aiding and abetting the enemy, who wanted to see Black men weak and unable to hold their own.[4]

Similarly, Elaine Brown's autobiographical *A Taste of Power* is a powerful behind-the-scenes analysis of the gender politics within the Black Panther Party.

At this juncture, we want to provide a broader historical context for *Gender Talk* by calling attention to several important moments in the history of the United States in which the collision of race and gender issues had a palpable and divisive impact on the African-American community. It is also the case that during these episodes the issue of race loyalty became a prominent feature of public discourse within Black communities. There were also profound differences between Black women and men, and among Black women, about how to deal with these incidents, particularly in the recent past when a series of highly public and controversial events—the Clarence Thomas/Anita Hill Supreme Court hearings, the Mike Tyson, O. J. Simpson, and Reverend Henry

Lyons trials—forced the Black community to respond to what it perceived to be harmful airing of dirty racial linen in public. We have our memories of these debates, since we lived through them, but also articles and books that help us make sense of the range of responses within Black communities, especially about Clarence Thomas and O. J. Simpson.

Before turning to the more contentious contemporary scene, we should recall 1869 and the debate over the Fifteenth Amendment to the Constitution, which would grant Black male suffrage. This issue precipitated a major split within the women's movement and debate within the Black community as well. At the first annual meeting of the Equal Rights Association in New York in 1869, the famous debate between Frederick Douglass and white suffragists occurred over the Fifteenth Amendment, during which he argued for the greater urgency of race over gender. He believed it was the "Negro's hour," and that women's rights could wait, since linking woman suffrage to Negro suffrage at that historical juncture would seriously reduce the chances of securing the ballot for Black men, and for African Americans, Douglass reiterated, the ballot was urgent. When asked at the American Equal Rights Association Convention in New York City, May 12, 1869, whether suffrage was as urgent for Black women, he quickly responded, "Yes, yes, yes, . . . but not because she is a woman; but because she is black."[5] Frances E. W. Harper, a prominent Black feminist and abolitionist, supported Douglass, whereas Sojourner Truth supported white suffragists, believing that if Black men got the vote, they would dominate Black women.

From our perspective at the turn of the twenty-first century, what is important is not who was right but how we might reinterpret this historic moment. The historian Darlene Clark Hine provides a cogent analysis, a useful way of assessing the meaning of this nineteenth-century race/gender debate. She argues that given the reality of U.S. patriarchy in 1869, most Black women and men applauded the adoption of the Fifteenth Amendment, but that "inauspiciously, this amendment in some ways cemented a gender breach in black culture" because it created fundamental inequalities between Black men and women with respect to their access to power. "Once black men gained the right to vote, black women had no alternative but to negotiate with and convince their male relatives to use the ballot to advance group as opposed to individual interests.... They worked to persuade men that their individual ballots were in reality their collective propeny."[6] Hine goes on to argue that what was perhaps even more problematic as far as Black women were concerned was that this differential power base enabled Black men to determine the public agenda for the race. One consequence of this imbalance of power was that the perspectives of Black women were relegated to the back burner.

A contemporary manifestation of the political marginalization of Black women was the decision on the part of male civil rights leaders not to allow Black women to speak at the March on Washington in 1963. In her 1964 autobiography, *The Trumpet Sounds*, Anna Arnold Hedgeman describes her feelings about the male-dominant civil rights leadership and her experiences as the only woman on the planning committee for the March on Washington. When she discovered that women were not speaking on the program, she wrote a letter to the director A. Philip Randolph in which she alluded to Black women's important roles in the civil rights movement. She also argued that since the "Big Six" civil rights leaders (Randolph, Martin Luther King Jr., Roy Wilkins, John Lewis, James Farmer, and Whitney Young) had consistently ignored the important contributions of women, it was even more imperative that they be allowed to speak. Despite her admonitions, however, their masculinist solution was to allow the wives of the civil rights leaders and a few other Black women to sit on the dais. Rosa Parks was presented but didn't speak.

In Jervis Anderson's biography of Bayard Rustin, a prominent gay civil rights leader, an adviser to King, a Southern Christian Leadership Conference (SCLC) staffer, and the chief strategist for the march, there is a behind-the-scenes narrative about the march, which, according to Rustin, required careful negotiations and compromise among the various organizational leaders who had not previously collaborated on a national project. There is also a discussion of the "brooding feminist rebellion behind the scenes," in the words of Anderson. He also reports that Black women activists resented that no woman had been invited to deliver a major address. Daisy Bates, who was a leader in the desegregation of Little Rock's Central High School in 1957, was allowed a brief moment at the platform to introduce five "Negro women fighters for freedom," among whom was Rosa Parks. A week before the march, Pauli Murray, a civil rights attorney and feminist activist, sent a letter to Randolph in which she expressed her disgust with the blatant sexism of the male leaders and their failure to see the connection between racial bias and gender bias:

> I have been increasingly perturbed over the blatant disparity between the major role which Negro women have played and are playing at the crucial grass-roots levels of our struggle and the minor role of leadership they have been assigned in the national policy-making decisions ... It is indefensible to call a national March on Washington

> and send out a Call which contains the name of not a single woman leader. Nor can this glaring omission be glossed over by inviting several Negro women to appear on the August 28 program. The time has come to say to you quite candidly, Mr. Randolph, that "tokenism" is as offensive when applied to women as when applied to Negroes, and that I have not devoted the greater part of my adult life to the implementation of human rights to [now] condone any policy which is not inclusive.[7]

A decade later, Black women activists helped to catalyze a women's movement that would generate a sustained discourse within the African-American community about the relevance of women's liberation to Black people. Indeed, rancorous debates within the African-American community surrounding sexual politics began with the publication of Michele Wallace's *Black Macho and the Myth of the Superwoman* (1978), in which she criticized Black male sexism and the misogyny of Black liberation struggles of the sixties. Echoing Wallace, the August 27, 1979, issue of *Newsweek* chronicled a new Black struggle that underscored intraracial tensions based on gender: "It's the newest wrinkle in the black experience in America-a growing distrust, if not antagonism, between black men and women that is tearing apart marriages and fracturing personal relationships."[8] This "wake-up call" came on the heels of Ntozake Shange's award-winning Broadway play, *For Colored Girls Who Have Considered Suicide/When the Rainbow Is Enuf* (1976) and Wallace's polemic, *Black Macho*. The demonization of Shange and Wallace by many within the Black community (men and women) for their so-called bashing of Black men was the beginning of an all-too-familiar (by now) assault on Black feminists for their airing of dirty linen in public.

Surely, Black sexual politics left the closet, so to speak, in the 1970s and became a highly contentious topic within African-American communities and subsequently in the national media. The issue of sexual politics was a hotly debated topic in journals such as *The Black Scholar. Freedomways*, and *Black Books Bulletin* and provided the catalyst for the founding of a short-lived bi-monthly magazine by the sociologists Nathan and Julia Hare, *Black Male/Female Relationships*. In a talk show on Black Entertainment Television on October 17, 1991 (a few days after the Thomas/Hill hearings began), Nathan and Julia Hare instructed the largely Black audience about what they called a long, destructive history of Black women's betrayal of the race that they argued began when slave women collaborated with their white masters. Disloyalty to the race would continue, they boldly asserted, as contemporary Black women collaborated with white feminists.

The Black Scholar would provide the most extensive and sober treatment of the debate generated by Wallace's and Shange's controversial feminist writings in five very important issues that began with its April 1973 issue on Black Women's Liberation. The March/April 1979, Black Sexism Debate issue, in which the sociologist Robert Staples's controversial essay, "The Myth of Black Macho: A Response to Angry Black Feminists" appeared, spawned an even angrier response a month later in the May/June, issue which included Audre Lorde's angry essay, "Sexism: An American Disease in Blackface." Calling for dialogue between Black men and women, Lorde delivered a passionate plea for a serious consideration of the damaging effects of sexism in our communities:

> In our work, we posit the equal importance of changing the condition of Black women and children and assert that without attention to gender matters, there can be no long-lasting solutions to many of our race problems. Freedom and future for Blacks does not mean absorbing the dominant white male disease of sexism. . .. the Black male consciousness must be raised to the realization that sexism and woman-hating are critically dysfunctional to his liberation as a Black man because they arise out of the same constellation that engenders racism and homophobia. Until that consciousness is developed, Black men will view sexism and the destruction of Black women as tangential to Black liberation rather than as central to that struggle.[9]

A decade later, the controversy continued and grew more virulent; its most obvious manifestations were loud and angry litanies, especially among Black professional men, about the portrayals of Black male characters in the novels of contemporary Black women writers. Alice Walker's 1982 novel *The Color Purple* and Steven Spielberg's film adaptation sparked the most lasting and vitriolic responses. "The Same River Twice" (1996), Alice Walker's meditation on the making of the film, includes a variety of responses from the Black community, including the Coalition Against Black Exploitation and other persons who castigated the film and Walker for celebrating lesbianism, which was perceived to be akin to drug addiction and violence as new evils destroying the Black community. Distorting the message of a film he refused to see in his commentary on *The Color Purple*, the journalist Tony Brown, the quintessential apologist for Black men, celebrated Nelson Mandela, Martin Luther King, and Malcolm X, who, he argues, "overcame the system's psychological warfare and produced healthy, non-incestuous, non-brutalizing relationships with women." Ridiculing the text's woman bonding, he sarcastically asserts, "their women never needed a 'Shug.' "[10]

What this brief historical context underscores is the need for us to pause again for retrospection and introspection. In the words of bell hooks,

> one of the major barriers impeding our capacity as black people to collectively challenge sexism and sexist oppression is the continued equation of black liberation with the development of black patriarchy ... our efforts to create renewed black liberation struggle are seriously impeded by the fact that in diverse black settings the assumption prevails that we need only listen to patriarchal men, that our very capacity to move forward as a people depends on strong black male leadership.[11]

Continuing a tradition of Black feminist writing that began in the 1830s with Maria Stewart's speeches, there is a significant body of contemporary work by African-American women and men that falls under the rubric of Black feminism or womanism. This body of work is predictably smaller and less well known than the proliferation of writing in the popular Black press and in what is a growing profusion of books and articles that oversimplify the status of Black women versus Black men. There is also the very popular notion that Black men are an endangered species, which has given the impression that all is well with Black women. The metaphor of the "endangered Black male" calls attention to a several demographic realities; for example, one in four Black males is in some way involved with the criminal justice system; Black male-on-male homicide is the leading cause of death among young Blacks between the ages of seventeen and twenty-six. The endangered Black male metaphor, however, reinforces the myth that changing the status of Black men will single-handedly solve all the complex problems facing African-American communities. In our work, we posit the equal importance of changing the condition of Black women and children and assert that without attention to gender matters, there can be no long-lasting solutions to many of our race problems.

This is a particularly critical time for *Gender Talk*, for today there is in full swing a backlash against Black feminism and Black feminists. This backlash is alive and well in the popular press, including Black media, and is increasingly a theme in sit-coms, talk shows, and everyday conversations. A concrete example involved the demonizing of the feminist activist Angela Davis in the *Amsterdam News* because of her public criticism of the 1995 Million Man March. As we travel to college and university campuses, we hear among some Black students, female and male, strong attacks against anything that they perceive to be feminist. This includes discussions about taking a women's studies class, challenges to homophobia, or simply the need for all-female gatherings. There is a similar backlash, as well, against feminism among white students.

Today, in African-American communities, there is a great deal of anger about the so-called trashing of successful Black men. Earl Ofari Hutchinson's *The Assassination of the Black Male Image* (1994) is a good example of this kind of thinking. These accusations of "Black male bashing" have escalated as a result of the high visibility of the Thomas/Hill hearings; the Mike Tyson and O. J. Simpson trials; the court-martial of Army Sergeant Major Gene McKinney; and, most recently, the trial of Rev. Henry Lyons. It is frequently Black women who are singled out for scorn because of our public pronouncements and writings about the problems of sexism within Black communities and the behavior of particular Black men. In fact, feminism itself is frequently blamed as a major source of the problems that confront Black America.

Within this woman-blaming climate, there is a proliferation of books that purport to cure what ails Black communities, much of which focuses on strengthening Black families and male/female relationships. These heterosexist texts include rigidly prescriptive advice for "good" Black women (meaning "not feminist") who are engaged in what is considered a righteous search for a Black man. Examples of this genre are Ronn Elmore's *How to Love a Black Man* and Dene Miller's *The Sistah 's Rules: Secrets for Meeting, Getting and Keeping a Good Man* (1997). Popular magazines like *Ebony* frequently include articles such as "Ten Biggest Mistakes Women Make in Relationships" (May 1998) that repeat old stereotypes about evil Black women and remind readers that "hell hath no fury like a black woman scorned." There is also the myth, yet again, of the emasculating Black woman. In one such article in the same issue of *Ebony*, Black women are chastised directly: "Whatever you care to call it—dissin', putting in check, low rating, fronting off, downing—all the names stand for the same thing, disrespect [of the Black man]."

There is no shortage in Black popular culture of blatant calls for Black women to be subservient to the wishes and demands of Black men. Shahrazad Ali's enormously popular *The Blackman's Guide to Understanding the Blackwoman* (1990) is a stark example of this misogynist genre. Simply put, the major thesis of her propaganda is that Black women are to be blamed for all the problems that Black men (and by extension the Black family and the Black community) are experiencing. Since Black women are out of control, the Black man must "take [his] rightful place as ruler of the universe and everything in it, including the black woman."[12]

There has also been an upsurge in conservative Black nationalist antidotes for what ails us as a community, which bell hooks and other Black feminists have also observed:

> Nationalist black leaders male and female, whether they be in conservative religious organizations or represent themselves as spokespersons of more radical movements for liberation, continue to suffer failures of insight that lead them to invest in the notion that patriarchy is the only possible system of social organization that can bring stability to black family life and to the race.[13]

This socially conservative strand in Black nationalist thought is characterized by a call for traditional gender roles, an emphasis on so-called family values, an embrace of patriarchy or hypermasculine constructions, and an abhorrence of gay and lesbian sexuality. The analysis in *Gender Talk* focuses on the intersection of race and gender, not only because of their centrality in the lives of African Americans, but also because analyses of "the race problem" have been so male-centered. For example, discussions of violence tend to focus on Black male-on-male homicide or police brutality far more than on rape or spousal abuse. This is the case despite the fact that homicide is one of the ten leading causes of death for African American women, the reported rape rate for Black women is almost three times that of white women, and Black rape victims have a harder time getting police and medical professionals to believe them. In a male-dominant society, however, Black men experience gender privilege that enables them to oppress Black women at the same time that they experience the ravages of white racism and poverty.

As we look toward the future, we suggest how we might begin to conceptualize race loyalty differently. We articulate the consequences of our discomfort as a community about seriously considering gender issues in our strategies for improving the race, and we make suggestions about how we might begin to build new Black communities. Finally, we assert that although our work focuses on African-American communities, perhaps its most useful analysis will underscore what ails us as a nation still deeply committed to the maintenance of racism, sexism, classism, and heterosexism. We believe that this "truth telling" about issues within Black America will also unmask the ugliness and complexity of race, gender, and class matters in the broader body politic.

NOTES

[1] Audre Lorde, *Sister Outsider* (Trumansburg, N.Y.: Crossing Press, 1984), pp. 119-120.
[2] Anna Julia Cooper, *A Voice from the South: By a Black Woman of the South* (Xenia, O hio: Aldine Printing House, 1892), pp. 26-27.
[3] Ibid., p. 75.
[4] Paula Giddings, ed., *When and Where 1 Enter: The Impact of Black Women on Sex and Race in America* (New York: William Morrow, 1984), p. 316.
[5] Philip S. Foner, ed., *Frederick Douglass on Women's Rights* (New York: Da Capo Press, 1992), p. 87.
[6] Darlene Clark Hine, '"In the Kingdom of Culture': Black Women and the Intersection of Race, Gender, and Class," in Gerald Early, ed., *Lure and Loathing: Essays on Race, Identity, and the Ambivalence of Assimilation* (New York: Penguin Books, 1993), p. 344.
[7] Quoted in Jervis Anderson, *Bayard Rustin: Troubles I've Seen* (New York: HarperCollins, 1997), p. 259.
[8] "A New Black Struggle," *Newsweek*, August 27, 1979, p. 58.
[9] Lorde, *Sister Outsider*, pp. 63-64.
[10] Tony Brown, "Blacks Need to Love One Another," in Alice Walker, *The Same River Twice: Honoring the Difficult* (New York: Scribner, 1996), pp. 224-225.
[11] bell hooks, *Killing Rage: Ending Racism* (New York: Henry Holt & Company, 1995), pp. 63-64.
[12] Shahrazad Ali, *The Blackman's Guide to Understanding the Blackwoman* (Philadelphia: Civilized Publications, 1990).
[13] hooks, *Killing Rage: Ending Racism*, p. 94. See also Patricia Hill Collins's cogent analysis of Black nationalist ideologies, particularly Afrocentricism, in *Fighting Words: Black Women and the Search for Justice* (Minneapolis: University of Minnesota Press, 1998).

7. African Feminist Discourse: A Review Essay (2003)

Despite the pervasiveness of Western feminist theory in academic discourse, there is a growing body of creative (fiction, visual art, film)[1], scholarly, and political work by African women[2] which can be placed under the rubric of "African feminism." These discursive, imaginative, and activist projects are important sites of resistance among African women in various cultural contexts and they compel us to re-imagine what is meant by 'feminism' in a global context. While a comprehensive examination of African feminisms would take into consideration this broad range of work throughout the continent, this briefing focuses on the analytical prose of African women from sub-Saharan Africa.

At a conference on 'Women in the African Diaspora' held at Howard University in 1983, Sierra Leonian anthropologist Filomina Chioma Steady's keynote address, "African Feminism: A Worldwide Perspective," was an expansion of the introductory essay in her pioneering anthology, *The Black Woman Cross-Culturally* (1981). It provided a conceptual framework for the comparative study of black women in Africa, the Caribbean, Latin America, and the United States. Steady described the relationship between women of African descent and the mainstream women's movement in the West as problematic and argued that the former have evolved their own brand of feminism and for them the struggle against gender oppression has always been (1981:34) *fused with liberation from other forms of oppression, namely slavery, colonialism, neocolonialism, racism, poverty, illiteracy, and disease.*[3]

Steady amplified this concept of the simultaneity of oppressions in the lives of black women during her keynote address in which she called for a theory of African feminism in the study of women throughout the African diaspora.

Nearly a decade later, prominent Ghanaian writer, Ama Ata Aidoo, similarly engaged the debate about African women and feminism. She was unequivocal in her assertion about the value of this liberatory politic for a new Africa in her keynote address, "The African Woman Today," at another historic conference[4] (Nnaemeka, 1998:47):

> When people ask me rather bluntly every now and then whether I am a feminist, I not only answer yes, but I go on to insist that every woman and every man should be a feminist - especially if they believe that Africans should take charge of African

> land, African wealth, African lives, and the burden of African development. It is not possible to advocate independence for the African continent without also believing that African women must have the best that the environment can offer. For some of us this is the crucial element in our feminism.

Adding to this, Trinidadian literary critic and scholar, Carole Boyce Davies, articulated one of the most cogent definitions of African feminism in her pioneering introduction to *Ngambika* (1986), the first anthology of critical essays on women in African literature (Boyce Davies and Adam Graves, 1986:8-10):

> African feminism...recognizes a common struggle with African men for the removal of the yokes of foreign domination and European/American exploitation. It is not antagonistic to African men but challenges them to be aware of certain salient aspects of women's subjugation which differ from the generalized oppression of all African peoples...[it] recognizes that certain inequities and limitations existed/exist in traditional societies and that colonialism reinforced them and introduced others...
>
> It acknowledges its affinities with international feminisms, but delineates a specific African feminism with certain specific needs and goals arising out of the concrete realities of women's lives in African societies for institutions which are of value to women and rejects those which work to their detriment and does not simply import Western women's agendas. Thus, it respects African woman's status as mother but questions obligatory motherhood and the traditional favoring of sons... it respects African woman's self-reliance and the penchant to cooperative work and social organization...[it]understands the interconnectedness of race, class, and sex oppression.

One of the earliest non-fictional texts written from an African feminist perspective is Awa Thiam's, *Black Sisters Speak Out: Feminism and Oppression in Black Africa* (1978). In this scathing critique of oppressive and patriarchal African traditions, such as polygamy, forced marriages, and female circumcision, she asserts in the opening paragraph that: black women have been silent for too long... . Women must assume their own voices— speak out for themselves (1978:11).

What distinguishes this text from subsequent examples of African feminist thought is its inclusion of the voices of various African women who speak about their personal experiences in patriarchal West African societies, particularly in Senegal. She also discusses the negative impact of colonialism on African women and articulates the concept of multiple jeopardy, a familiar theme in African American feminist thought (1978:118):

> ...the Black woman of Africa suffers a threefold oppression: by virtue of her sex, she is dominated by man in a patriarchal society; by virtue of her class she is at the mercy of capitalist exploitation; by virtue of her race lives in African societies... she suffers

> from the appropriation of her country by colonial or neo-colonial powers. Sexism, racism, class division; three plagues...

Any discussion of the multiple jeopardy confronted by African feminism is likely to make reference to the foundational work of scholars such as Molara Ogundipe-Leslie, a Yoruba writer, critic, intellectual, and scholar who has been writing about the issue of gender politics and social transformation within the African context for over three decades.[6] Her essay, "African Women, Culture, and Another Development," is explicit about the nature of African women's oppression. She discusses the six mountains on their backs which include oppression from the outside, especially the ravages of colonialism, some African cultural traditions, the backwardness of the African woman, men, race, and herself (1994). One of the most compelling treatises in her collection of essays, *Re-Creating Ourselves: African Women & Critical Transformations* (1994), is "Stiwanism: Feminism in an African context," which I would compare with the Combahee River Collective manifesto which captures the essence of African-American feminism[6], namely the idea that black women experience multiple jeopardies, including racial, class, and gender oppression. She was a founding member of Women in Nigeria (WIN), a feminist women's research and activist group, as well as of another African feminist organization, the Association of African Women for Research and Development (AAWORD) located in Dakar, Senegal. One of the leading African woman intellectuals (whose work in my opinion has not received the attention it deserves), Ogundipe-Leslie, argues that gender asymmetry was an integral part of many pre-colonial societies, even though African women's position relative to men certainly deteriorated under colonialism. She also argues, as do African-American feminists, that there are also traditions of resistance and activism among African women going back to pre-colonial times. In other words, there were indigenous 'feminisms' prior to contact with Europeans, just as there were indigenous modes of rebellion and resistance throughout the period of colonial domination. What this means is that the struggle for women's rights is not the result of contamination by the West or of simple imitation by African women of Euro-American values. In addition, she reminds us that in most cultures there have always been indigenous manifestations of 'feminism' that take various forms, albeit very different forms, in particular cultural contexts. An important task for African scholars has therefore been to identify, excavate and analyse these indigenous forms of feminist resistance.

Other sites for the production of African feminist scholarship include various research organizations, for example, the Council for the Development of Social Science Research in Africa (CODESRIA), which has its headquarters in Senegal. It publishes a quarterly journal, *Africa Development*, the longest standing Africa-based journal, and it organizes workshops and other forums which facilitate the exchange of ideas and information among African researchers. In this regard, it sponsored a workshop aimed at advancing knowledge about gender, particularly in and for Africa. The conference proceedings, *Engendering African Sciences* (Imam *et al*, 1997), was important for its gender-sensitive scholarship and it employed an African feminist framework. The conference proceedings included some of the most productive African women scholars such as Aretha M Imam (Nigeria), Fatou Sow (Senegal), Amina Mama (Nigeria), N'Dri Thérese Assié-Lumumba (Cote d'Ivoire) and Rudo B Gaidzanwa (Zimbabwe).

Southern Africa is another critically important site for the production of African feminist thought. One of the most prolific and compelling African woman intellectuals and activists is anthropologist Patricia McFadden, who was born in Swaziland and spent much of her professional life in Zimbabwe. She is presently in the United States completing a book on feminism and nationalism. She has been associated with the Southern Africa Political Economy Series (SAPES) Trust and its Gender Project[7], as well as with the South African Research Institute for Policy Studies (SARIPS), and edited its *South African Political Economy Monthly*. She has also produced an important body of hard-hitting feminist work that has been shaped by the particularities of the southern African context. Her pioneering scholarship can be characterized as radical African feminist theory (to use her own self-description of being a radical African feminist), and includes analyses of sexuality in the African context, a taboo topic, especially before the ravages of HIV/AIDS. I also characterize her work as 'radical' because of its unrelenting critiques of African patriarchy, Western capitalism, and neo-colonialist interventions. It also rejects heterosexist analytical paradigms and it uncompromisingly calls for progressive African gender ideologies and the empowerment of African women on their own terms. Her criticism of African cultural practices includes:

> those legal systems that are partial and often blatantly patriarchal: for example, the persistence of notions of male conjugal rights; refusals to recognize marital rape as a crime; allowance of polygamy and rampant sexual mobility; notions of paternity which define children as the property of the man rather than emphasizing the responsibilities and obligations of parenting in democratic family relationships;

> inheritance practices that allow men to inherit women as a form of property/as slaves of male controlled families (2001:4).

In a lecture delivered at the Feminist Institute of the African Women's Leadership, she offered a challenge to African women at the dawn of the 21st century. After discussing African women's legacy of struggle, HIV/AIDS, gender violence, bodily integrity, indigenous women's movements in Africa, reproductive rights, female circumcision, sexuality, the rise of religious fundamentalisms, civil strife, as well as the insensitivity of the Organization of African Unity (OAU) to the plight of women, she asserted:

We bring the African feminist tradition of thinking and problem solving to the global women's movement and participate in the formulation of new theories and methodologies... . We must write about ourselves and speak for ourselves. We have nothing to lose by envisioning and crafting a new future, and we have every reason to want something different for Africa in the 21st century (McFadden, 1997).

South Africa is also home to several feminist publications including *Agenda: Empowering Women for Gender Equity,* based in Durban, South Africa. This journal included two earlier special issues on 'African Feminisms' (No 50, 2001, and No 54, 2002). There is also the *Southern African Feminist Review,* published by the Southern African Institute for Policy Studies, Harare, Zimbabwe; and *Feminist Africa* based at the African Gender Institute, University of Cape Town, South Africa, founded in 2002.[8]

This briefing makes no claims to having surveyed the considerable body of work that can be characterized as "African feminism." An outpouring of black feminist intellectual production over the past decade in Africa, the United States, Canada, the Caribbean, Brazil and Black Britain, in particular, underscores the importance of taking seriously the voices of women of African descent with respect to a range of social justice issues. A comprehensive examination of African feminisms, both the scholarship and activism, is certainly long overdue. Such a sustained project would help to contest the hegemony of Western, white feminist analytical frameworks and broaden our knowledge about a region of the world that continues to be misunderstood, devalued and, in some cases, romanticized, especially with respect to gender constructs. This briefing has gestured to the richness and complexity of African feminist politics and its potential for profound social change on the continent and throughout the diaspora.

Notes

[1] The earliest scholarship related to African feminism dealt with the fiction of African women writers such as Bunch Emecheta (1979; 1974); Flora Nwapa (1966); Mariama Ba (1980) and Bessie Head (1992). Useful feminist literary criticism by African women scholars includes D'Almeida (1994); Chukwuma (1994); Nnaemeka (1997); Makuchi Nfah-Abben yi (1997); Kolawole (1997); and Ogunyemi (1996). Literary critic Ogunyemi also articulated the concept of African womanism and indicates that she arrived at the term 'womanism' independently of Alice Walker who conceptualized 'womanism' in the African American context and popularized this alternative conception of feminism (Ogunyemi, 1985).

[2] I am including women whose family of origin would be sub-Saharan Africa though they may reside in various parts of the African diaspora, especially the US and Britain.

[3] For the entire conference proceedings see Terborg-Penn, Harley and Benton (1987).

[4] This international women's conference took place in Nsukka, Nigeria in 1992.

[5] See also the work of other Nigerian feminist scholars, including Obioma Nnaemaka, such as Amadiume (1987) and Akachi Ezeigbo (1996) or African women scholars writing about gender issues such as Acholonu (1991); Oyewumi, (1997) and Oyewumi (1993). A useful analysis of African feminism by a German scholar of African literatures is Arndt (2002).

[6] The Combahee River Collective document is included in Beverly Guy-Sheftall (ed) (1995), *Words of Fire: African American Feminist Thought*, New York: New Press.

[7] See Ruth Meena (ed) (1992) *Gender in Southern Africa: Conceptual and Theoretical Issues* (Harare: SAPES Trust), which is the result of a gender planning workshop organized by the SAPES Gender Project in July 1991.

[8] See also *Sauti Ya Siti*, the official publication of the Tanzania Media Women's Association (TAMWA), based in Dar es Salaam; *the African Journal of Reproductive Health*, based in Benin City, Nigeria, at the Women's Health and Action Research Centre; *Echo: Bilirtgual Quarterly Newsletter of the Association of African Women for Research and Development*, based in Dakar, Senegal; and *Jen da: A Journal of Culture and African Women Studies* (www.jendajoumal.com); *Fippu*, founded in 1987, based in Dakar, Senegal, and the magazine of the feminist organization which bears its name.

References

Arndt S (2002). *The Dynamics of African Feminism: Defining and Classifying African Feminist Literature,* Trenton: Africa World Press.

Acholonu CO (1991). *Motherism: The Afrocentric Alternative to Feminism,* Lagos: NIIA.

Akachi Ezeigbo T (1996). *Gender Issues in Nigeria: A Feminine Perspective,* Lagos: Vista Books.

Amadiume I (1987). *Male Daughters, Female Husbands: Gender and Sex in an African Society,* London: Zed Books.

Ba M (1980). *So Long a Letter,* London: Heinemann. Boyce Davies C & Adams Greeves A (eds) (1986). *Ngambika Studies of Women in African Literature,* Trenton NJ: Africa World Press.

Chukwuma H (ed) (1994). *Feminism in African Literature: Essays on Criticism,* New Enuga Nigeria: Generation Books.

D'Almeida IA (1994). *Francophone African Women Writers: Destroying the Emptiness of Silence,* Gainesville: University Press of Florida. Emecheta B (1979). *Joys of Motherhood,* New York: George Braziller.

Emecheta B (1987). *Second Class Citizen,* London: Flamingo.

Head B (1977). *The Collector of Treasures and Other Botswana Village Tales,* London: Heinemann.

Imam A, Mama M & Sow F (eds) (1997). *Engendering African Social Sciences,* Dakar: CODESRIA.

Kolawole ME (1997). *Womanism and African Consciousness,* Trenton: Africa World Press.

McFadden, Patricia (2001). 'Political power: the challenges of sexuality, patriarchy and globalization in Africa' paper delivered in Port Louis, Mauritius, February 12-17, published in *Women's World,* 3, available at: www.wworld.org/programs/regions/africa/patrici a_mcfadden2_p.htm

Nnaemeka O (ed) (1997). *The Politics of (M)othering: Womanhood, Identity, and Resistance in African Literature,* London: Routledge.

Nnaemeka O (ed) (1998). *Sisterhood, Feminisms, and Power: From Africa to the Diaspora,* Trenton, NJ: Africa World Press.

Makuchi Nfah-Abbenyi J (1997). *Gender in African Women's Writing: Identity, Sexuality and Difference,* Bloomington: Indiana University Press.

Nwapa F (1966). *Efuru,* London Heinemann.

McFadden P (1997). 'The Challenges and Prospect for the African Women's Movement in the 21st Century' in *Women in Action,* I.

Ogundipe-Leslie (1994). *Re-creating Ourselves: African Women and Critical Transformations,* Trenton: Africa World Press.

Ogunyemi CO (1996). *Africa Wo/Man Palava: The Nigerian Novel* by Women,·Chicago: University of Chicago Press.

Ogunyemi CO (1985). 'Womanism: the dynamics of the contemporary Black female novel in English' in *Signs*, 11.

Oyewumi O (1997). *The Invention of Women: Making an African Sense of Western Gender Discourses*, Minneapolis: University of Minnesota Press.

Oyewumi O (ed) (1993). *African Women and Feminism: Reflecting on the Politics of Sisterhood*, Trenton: African World Press.

Steady FC (ed) (1981). *The Black Woman Cross Culturally*, Cambridge, Mass: Schenkman Publishing Company, Inc.

Terborg-Penn R, Harley S & Benton Rushing A (eds) (1987). *Women in Africa and the African Diaspora*, Washington, DC: Howard University Press.

Thiam A (1978.) *La Parole aux Negresses (trans) Black Sisters Speak Out: Feminism and Oppression in Black Africa*, Paris: Editions Denoel. (Second edition published oy Pluto Press, 1986).

8.1 Remembering Our Feminist Forefathers (2006)

I wonder what it would take to fully integrate gender and sexuality into Black political consciousness. What would it take for our public intellectuals, the self-appointed spokespersons, the opinion leaders and the like, to go beyond lip service given to "unity" and "common interest" to articulate a political sensibility that embraces substantive equality as a value within our community?

Kimberle Williams Crenshaw, in
Black Men on Race, Gender, and Sexuality,
Devon Carbado, 1999

Not only have Black women made contributions to feminist history, Black men have made contributions as well.

Aaronette M. White, *Womanist,* 2001-2002

African American men's contributions to progressive gender or profeminist activism have been largely ignored in black political history. This is so even though there is a growing body of scholarly work about black men and black masculinities.[1] These silences surrounding a significant aspect of black men's commitments to social justice compelled the publication of *Traps: African American Men on Gender and Sexuality.*[2] This anthology, which I coedited with Rudolph P. Byrd, is the first of its kind that historicizes writings by black men who have examined the meanings of the overlapping categories of race, gender, and sexuality and who have theorized these categories in the most expansive and progressive terms. The first imperative of *Traps* was to contest and to dispel the widely accepted notion that black men have been hostile to feminism and played no part in its development. This erasure has occurred within the scholarship concerning the evolution of feminism in the United States and discussions of black politics as well. It is important to recall that Frederick Douglass was among the first men in the United States to publicly endorse and support the elective franchise for women. He was the only black person and one of only thirty-two men to attend the historic Women's Rights Convention in Seneca Falls, New York, in 1848. In one sense, *Traps* calls all American men, but particularly African American men, to reclaim a radical tradition of commitment to feminist struggle and to remember our gender-progressive forefathers.

Despite the commitment of some African American men to eradicate sexism and heterosexism, black liberation has been conceptualized, generally speaking, in narrow terms that focus heavily on recuperating black manhood, on constructing patriarchal families, and on ending racism. Hegemonic black nationalist discourse, characterized by both masculinist and heterosexist frameworks, has been particularly influential within activist and intellectual communities and has stifled the development of more egalitarian models of black empowerment free from the ideological traps of sexism and homophobia. Put another way, the tendency to conflate black freedom with black manhood, our uncritical acceptance of traditional conceptions of gender, the celebration of normative and rigid constructions of black masculinity, and persistent denials about homosexuality have prevented African Americans from establishing the truly revolutionary communities that Toni Cade Bambara challenged us to imagine over thirty years ago in her groundbreaking anthology, *The Black Woman*.[3] Her compelling essay, "On the Issue of Roles," was the first to interrogate the pitfalls of the African American community's uncritical embrace of dominant cultural definitions of masculinity and femininity: "Generally speaking, in a capitalist society, a man is expected to be an aggressive, uncompromising, factual, lusty, intelligent provider of goods, and the woman, a retiring, gracious, emotional, intuitive, attractive consumer of goods .... [W]e have not been immune to the conditioning; we are just as jammed in the rigid confines of those basically oppressive socially contrived roles."[4] Anticipating a fundamental premise of the emerging field of women's studies, she understands from her study of postcolonial Africa, Asia, the South Seas, and the Americas that gender—conceptions of what it means to be male and female—is a cultural construction. She noted, "Cultures have conceived of man/woman in a variety of ways [and] 'human nature' is a pretty malleable quality."[5] Recalling the more egalitarian nature of some societies before contact with Europeans and Christianity, she explained, "There is nothing to indicate that the Sioux, Seminole, Iroquois, or other 'Indian' nations felt oppressed or threatened by their women, who had mobility, privileges and a voice in the governing of the commune."[6] With respect to our African ancestors, she asserted, "the woman was neither subordinate nor dominant, but a sharer in policymaking and privileges."[7] Painfully aware of the "antagonism between the sexes,"[8] Cade (original surname) insists that we fashion "revolutionary selves, revolutionary lives, revolutionary relationships"[9] by abandoning dysfunctional definitions of manhood and womanhood, which stifle the development of healthy black communities. It is fair to assert that Cade is in some ways a spiritual daughter of Du Bois and like-minded black foremothers who envisioned a gender-progressive world very different from the one in which they were socialized.

Although it is clear that Cade's admonitions were largely ignored during the male-dominant revolutionary Sixties, and later, many of us would like to believe that a gender revolution within our communities is still possible. Literary critic Michael Awkward, echoing Cade in his admonitions concerning the necessity of an active disloyalty to patriarchy, wrote a pioneering essay, in which he reminded us that "androcentric practices are learned, are transmitted by means of specific sociocultural practices in such effective ways that they come to appear natural." However, "through an informed investigation of androcentric and feminist ideologies, individual men can work to resist the lure of the normatively masculine."[10] In his call for theorizing a black male feminism, Awkward went on to assert that "while gendered difference might be said to complicate the prospect of a non-phallocentric black male feminism, it does not render such a project impossible."[11] What is needed, he argued, is an acknowledgment that "feminism represents . . . an incomparably productive, influential, and resilient ideology and institution" and that *"certain instances of afrocentric feminism provide Afro-American men with an invaluable means of rewriting—of re-vis(ion)ing—our selves, our history and literary tradition, and our future."*[12] After a description of his childhood, in which he articulated his difficulty achieving a "gendered self-definition" because he was only able to define himself with regard to his gender in oppositional ways—that is, what he did not want to become—he asserted the value of black feminism, and Afro-American women's literature, which he embraced as a sophomore student at Brandeis University in 1977. "[It] helped me move toward a comprehension of the world, of aspects of my mother's life, and what a man against patriarchy could be and do."[13]

The radicalizing and transformative potential of an embrace of black feminist discourse among young black men would become even more apparent over the next two decades. Listen to the transgressive discourse of a small group of Morehouse College students who founded an organization called "Black Men for the Eradication of Sexism" in 1994. Their mission statement asserts the following:

> We believe that although we are oppressed because of our color, we are privileged because of our sex and must therefore take responsibility for ending that privilege;
> We believe that our relationships with women must be based on the principle of equality;

> We recognize that present Eurocentric notions of manhood and masculinity are damaging to the psyche of Black men and must be replaced with a holistic interpretation of manhood that acknowledges the oneness of women and men;
>
> We believe that sexism is a global form of oppression of no less importance than any other form of oppression;
>
> We believe that sexist oppression against women pervades every aspect of our communities and must be eradicated.[14]

Their final statement is a testament to their solidarity with black women and offers the possibility of reconciliation: "As we fight alongside our sisters we struggle to become whole, to deprogram ourselves. We have organized into one body because we know in our hearts and minds that as we hold our sisters back so will we hold ourselves back."[15]

FEMINIST FOREFATHERS: MAYS, DOUGLASS, AND DU BOIS

Benjamin Elijah Mays

Though the young Morehouse men may have been unaware of their connections to a small group of feminist forefathers, their departed elders, it is instructive to remember the legacy of black men whose progressive writings about gender and the oppression of black women are a significant, if invisible, aspect of black political discourse. I daresay that these Morehouse students may have also been surprised to learn that they were connected as well to one of the most revered figures in the history of the college. In his autobiography, *Born to Rebel* (New York: Scribner, 1971), former president of Morehouse College Benjamin Elijah Mays reveals the origins of his feminist sensibility with respect to the treatment of black women as he recalls his own patriarchal, abusive household and the impact it had on his own adult behavior.

> I cannot say that my home life was pleasant. Quarreling, wrangling, and sometimes fighting went on in our house. I got the impression early on that Father was mean to our mother. He fussed at her; and when he drank too much he wanted to fight and sometimes did. All too many times we children had to hold him to keep him from hurting Mother. He would take out his knife and threaten to cut her. Often at night, we were kept awake by Father's loud and abusive raging. I think if Mother had said nothing, there would have been fewer arguments. But Mother had to talk back. Our sympathy was with her .... Largely under the influence of my mother, I made a vow at twelve years of age that I would never drink liquor .... My decision was not based on religious or moral grounds but on what I saw drinking do to my father and our family. (p. 9-10)

Though Mays, perceived primarily as a race man, was not privy as an undergraduate at Bates College to the kinds of classes Awkward and Morehouse students would take long after he left the presidency, his autobiography does reveal an understanding of the evils of male dominance, at least in the domestic arena.

Frederick Douglass

An examination of the still-neglected topic of African American men and feminism usually begins with the writings and activism of Frederick Douglass and William E. B. Du Bois.[16] Without question, Douglass was one of the most outspoken advocates during the nineteenth century for the full emancipation of women in all areas of their public lives. A fellow suffragist, Fannie Barrier Williams, acknowledged shortly after Douglass's death in 1895 the debt owed to him by lovers of liberty everywhere, especially women:

> He so lived not only that men might be free and equal and exalted, but that women, too, by the same emancipating forces, might come equally into the estate of freedom .... His eloquence on behalf of women's rights to the equalities of citizenship is a lasting justification of woman's claims and contentions for perfect liberty. By right of his manly confidence in woman ... Mr. Douglass was easily the strongest and best friend American women ever had among the great men of the republic. The history of progressive women in this country cannot be written without grateful acknowledgment to the helpful and inspiring influence of the incomparable friend of all humanity, Frederick Douglass.[17]

Though Douglass is known primarily as an anti-slavery crusader, he was deeply committed to an independent, organized movement to achieve equal rights for women. On July 14, 1848, his newspaper, the *North Star*, carried the historic announcement of the Seneca Falls Convention, the first women's rights gathering in the United States. In addition, a constant reminder to his readers of his commitment to the rights of women was the slogan, which appeared on every issue of the *North Star*—"Right Is of No Sex." At the 1848 convention, when Elizabeth Cady Stanton's resolution that "it was the duty of the women of this country to secure for themselves their sacred right to the elective franchise" seemed headed for defeat, Douglass, at a critical juncture, asked for the floor and delivered an eloquent plea on behalf of woman's right to the vote.[18] The resolution was then put to a vote and was carried by a small margin. In 1888, a few years before his death, Douglass recalled his role at the Seneca Falls Convention and told the International Council of Women:

> There are few facts in my humble history to which I look back with more satisfaction than to the fact ... that I was sufficiently enlightened at that early day, when only a few years from slavery, to support your resolution for woman suffrage. I have done very little in this world in which to glory except this one act—and I certainly

> glory in that. When I ran away from slavery, it was for myself; when I advocated emancipation, it was for my people; but when I stood up for the rights of woman, self was out of the question, and I found a little nobility in the act.[19]

Similarly, in his autobiography he explained why he became a woman's rights man: He believed that all persons are created equal and should therefore have the right to participate fully in the affairs of government.

> Recognizing not sex nor physical strength, but moral intelligence and the ability to discern right from wrong, good from evil, and the power to choose between them, as the true basis of republican government ...I was not long in reaching the conclusion that there was no foundation in reason or justice for woman's exclusion from the right of choice m the selection of the persons who should frame the laws, and thus shape the destiny of all the people, irrespective of sex. [20]

W. E. B. Du Bois

In her compelling essay, "The Souls of Black Women Folk in the Writings of W. E. B. Du Bois," literary critic Nellie Y. McKay called our attention to what makes Du Bois a unique figure in African American life: "The extent to which he includes the influences of women's experiences, and especially those of black women, on his thinking; his recognition of gender oppression; and his acceptance of the worth of his emotional and spiritual feelings makes his works distinctive."[21] Here McKay is referring to his emphasis on the soul – the sensitive, feeling component to the self—as opposed to the intellectual, rational component stereotypically considered to represent masculinity. She also asserted that Du Bois' three autobiographies "demonstrate that Black women have been central to the development of his intellectual thought."[22] McKay reminded us of his indication in The *Autobiography of W. E. B. Du Bois: A Soliloquy on Viewing My Life from the Last Decade of Its First Century* that "he always had more friends among Black women than among Black men; that he was less attracted to relationships with the men of the race because many of them "imitated an American culture which [he] did not share."[23] McKay also went on to assert, "We also know that he was aware that the folk were not all men. If anything can be said about his views on the souls of Black women folk, it is that he felt that they had struggled through to an even higher plane than Black Men had."[24] Furthermore, his perceptions of the 'souls of Black folk'—that spiritual essence that made survival and transcendence possible for an entire race in spite of indescribable oppression, was most obvious in his discourse on Black women."[25]

Though largely ignored, Du Bois's essay "Of the Meaning of Progress," which appears in *The Souls of Black Folk*, reveals his progressive gender politics, which he seemed to have developed at a fairly early age."[26] While he was an undergraduate student at Fisk University in 1886, he went for two consecutive summers to teach at a school for poor rural blacks in Tennessee. The essay includes the heroic, long suffering black figure Josie—the young schoolgirl who had impacted him most—and one of the most poignant portraits of a black community struggling to survive and trying to maintain a sense of dignity in the most desperate circumstances. The plight of females in this tiny community is perhaps the most memorable aspect of his recollections. Ten years after graduating from Fisk, Du Bois returned to the hills of Tennessee and learned of Josie's death and the troubles her family and others had endured; her life, like the lives of many poor black women, had been tough and consumed with unrelenting labor and very little happiness. Following the tragedy of her brother Jim having to leave town because of a racial incident, "Josie grew thin and silent, yet worked the more."[27] Unfulfilled as an adult, "Josie shivered and worked on, with the vision of schooldays all fled, with a face wan and tired,—worked until, on a summer's day, someone married another; then Josie crept to her mother like a hurt child, and slept—and sleeps."[28] Here Du Bois reminded us of her unfulfilled dreams and her loneliness. Listening to the life struggles of another family, Du Bois learned from Uncle Bird that a neighbor, "Thenie came wandering back to her home over yonder, to escape the blows of her husband. And next morning she died in the home that the little bow-legged brother, working and saving, had bought for their widowed mother."[29] This brief allusion to domestic violence illustrates Du Bois's sensitivity to the particular plight of women; in this case, black families suffer the indignities of racial oppression, including lynching and poverty. Black women also suffer at the hands of their menfolk.

In his riveting essay, "The Damnation of Women," which McKay referred to as "one of his most moving discourses on the plight of Black women,"[30] Du Bois, as committed to women's rights as was Douglass, spoke autobiographically and politically about the women of his youth: "my mother, cousin Inez, Emma, and Ide Fuller. They represented the problem of the widow, the wife, the maiden, and the outcast .... They existed not for themselves, but for men; they were named after the men to whom they were related and not after the fashion of their own souls."[31] In his feminist critique of patriarchy, which renders women unable to forge their own identities, Du Bois anticipated the contemporary women's movement, which would articulate the plight of disempowered women in male-dominant societies. He was also critical of the institution of marriage, which in the case of his cousin, Inez, resulted in a life of misery. "What was marriage? We did not know, neither did she, poor thing! It came to mean for her a litter of children, poverty, a drunken, cruel companion, sickness, and death."[32] Du Bois' use of the term "litter" to describe Inez's family situation suggests an oppositional viewpoint with respect to the joys of motherhood. His refusal to idealize matrimony and mothering is underscored in his subsequent analysis of the urgency of forging a new world for women. He imagined a world of free women, set loose from the traps of patriarchy, ignorance, economic dependence, obligatory motherhood, and domestic confinement. "The future woman must have a life work and economic independence. She must have knowledge. She must have the right of motherhood at her own discretion. The present mincing horror at free womanhood must pass if we are ever to be rid of the bestiality of free manhood; not by guarding the weak in weakness do we gain strength, but by making weakness free and strong."[33]

Throughout the essay, he spoke eloquently about both the plight and contributions of black women. In the 1920s, this was his assessment of the race with respect to gender matters: "As I look about me today in this veiled world of mine, despite the noisier and more spectacular advance of my brothers, I instinctively feel and know that it is the five million women of my race who really count."[34] Furthermore, the accumulated assets of the black community were "wrung [largely] from the hearts of servant girls and washer women" who "toil hard" and have their value "trod under the feet of men."[35] He also defended the beauty of black women against the "defective eyesight" of the white world and sang the praises of such heroic figures as Sojourner Truth and Harriet Tubman. And then there is his most moving tribute to black women, which captures his sensitivity to the peculiar history of African American women:

> For their hard past, I honor the women of my race. Their beauty-their dark and mysterious beauty of midnight eyes, crumpled hair, and soft, full-featured faces ... No other women on earth could have emerged from the hell of force and temptation which once engulfed and still surrounds Black women in America with half the modesty and womanliness they retain. I have always felt like bowing myself before them in all abasement, searching to bring some tribute to these long-suffering victims, these burdened sisters of mine, whom the world, the wise, white world, loves to affront and ridicule and wantonly to insult.[36]

And finally, he offered this particularly scathing attack on white America: "I shall forgive the white South much in its final judgment day; I shall forgive its slavery, for slavery is a world-old habit; I shall forgive its fighting for a well-lost cause ... but one thing I shall never forgive, neither in this world nor the world to come: its wanton and continued and persistent insulting of the Black womanhood which it sought and seeks to prostitute to its lust.[37]

Conclusion

Mays, Douglass, and Du Bois are our feminist forefathers. Given, in particular, Douglass's and Du Bois' passionate commitment to the eradication of gender oppression and Du Bois' unusual sensitivity to the plight of black women historically, I articulate here how we might make use of this legacy's embrace of feminist ideologies in a contemporary context.[38] Du Bois is certainly an important male figure with respect to his contributions to our understanding of the need for struggle around the emancipation of women, especially African American women, but I believe his writings represent new visions of manhood that are liberating and healing. At the beginning of this new century, black women and men—indeed, all men and women—must struggle for "revolutionary selves, revolutionary lives, revolutionary relationships,"[39] which Toni Cade Bambara asserted three decades ago. Rejecting the traps of patriarchy and sexism, which Du Bois compelled us to do sixty years ago, black folk, in particular, might continue our journey toward freedom in racist America in even more compelling ways and will offer new visions and possibilities for this nation, the world, and generations yet unborn. Du Bois boldly asserted in 1920 that "the uplift of women is, next to the problem of the color line and the peace movement, our greatest modern cause," though what is mainly remembered is what he said about the color line.[40] These three urgent issues remain: the eradication of the oppression of women and people of color and building and sustaining a world of peace with justice. Embracing Du Bois' prophetic vision would have pointed the way toward the creation of a world in which racism, sexism, and violence might be relics of the past. Du Bois' rejection of a patriarchal political culture, which stifles women and robs the world of their potential contributions, is one example of gender-progressive thinking on the part of an African American male who remains one of our most revered intellectuals. It is important to remember and honor the legacy of the feminist forefathers who understood that eradicating the twin evils of racism and sexism was urgent. We can now imagine the viability of the idea of progressive black masculinity in all its complexity because of them.

NOTES

[1] Useful texts in this regard include Richard G. Majors and Jacob U. Gordon, eds., *The American Black Male: His Present Status and His Future* (Chicago: Nelson-Hall Publishers, 1994); Majors and Janet Mancini Bilson, *Cool Pose: The Dilemmas of Black Manhood in America* (New York: Lexington Books, 1992); Darlene Clark Hine and Earnestine Jenkins, eds., *A Question of Manhood: A Reader in U.S. Black Men's History and Masculinity, vols. 1 and 2* (Bloomington: Indiana University Press, 1999); Devon W. Carbado, *Black Men on Race, Gender, and Sexuality* (New York: New York University Press, 1999); Donald Belton, ed., *Speak My Name: Black Men on Masculinity and the American Dream* (Boston: Beacon Press, 1975); Christopher B. Booker, "I Will Wear No Chain!": A Social History of African American Males (Westport, CT: Praeger, 2000); Daniel Black, Dismantling Washington Square Press, 2002); and W. Lawrence Hogue, The African American Male, Writing, and Difference: A PolycentricApproach to African American Literature, Criticism, and History (Albany: State University of New York Press, 2003).

[2] See Rudolph P. Byrd and Beverly Guy-Sheftall, eds., T*raps: African American Men on Gender and Sexuality* (Bloomington: Indiana University Press, 2001).

[3] Toni Cade, ed., *The Black Woman: An Anthology* (New York: Mentor, 1970), 102. See Farah Jasmine Griffin, "Conflict and Chorus: Reconsidering Toni Cade's The Black Woman: An Anthology," in *Is It Nation Time?: Contemporary Essays on Black Power and Black Nationalism,* ed. Eddie S. Glaude, Jr. (Chicago: University of Chicago Press, 2002), for a discussion of gender issues.

[4] Cade, *Black Woman,* 102.

[5] Ibid., 103.

[6] Ibid., 104.

[7] Ibid., 103.

[8] Ibid., 101.

[9] Ibid., 110.

[10] Michael Awkward, "A Black Man's Place in Black Feminist Criticism," in Byrd and Guy-Sheftall, *Traps,* 178.

[11] Ibid., 179.

[12] Ibid., 181-82.

[13] Ibid., 187.

[14] Reprinted in Byrd and Guy-Sheftall, *Traps,* 201.

[15] Ibid.

[16] See the pioneering work of Gary L. Lemons, who has written extensively about black men's feminist forefathers. Lemons, "To Be Black, Male, and Feminist: Making Womanist Space for Black Men on the Eve of a New Millennium," in *Feminism and Men: Reconstructing Gender Relations,* ed., Steven P. Schacht and Doris W. Ewing (New York: New York University Press, 1998), 43; and *Lemons,* "'When and Where

[We] Enter': In Search of a Feminist Forefather-Reclaiming the Womanist Legacy of W. E. B. Du Bois," in Byrd and Guy-Sheftall, *Traps,* 71. His unpublished manuscript, *Memoir of a Black Boy Outsider: From the Margin of Masculinity to Pro Feminist Professor,* is also useful in this regard. Also see Philip Foner, ed., Frederick Douglass on Women's Rights (Westport, CT: Greenwood Press, 1976); Kalamu ya Salaam, *Our Women Keep Our Skies from Falling* (New Orleans: Nkombo, 1994); Nellie Y. McKay, "The Souls of Black Women Folk in the Writing of W. E. B. Du Bois," in *Reading Black, Reading Feminist: A Critical Anthology,* ed., Henry Louis Gates, Jr. (New York: Meridian, 1990); Aaronette M. White, "Ain't I a Feminist?: Black Men as Advocates of Feminism," Womanist Theory and Research 3, no. 2 (2001- 2002); Luke Charles Harris, "The Challenge and Possibility for Black Males to Embrace Feminism," in *Black Men on Race, Gender, and Sexuality: A Critical Reader,* ed., Devon Carbado (New York: New York University Press, 1999); and Joy James, *Shadowboxing: Representations of Black Feminist Politics,* particularly the essay "Fostering Alliances: Black Female Profeminisms" (New York: St. Martin's, 1999).

[17] Fannie Barrier Williams, Woman's Era 2 (April 1895).

[18] Foner, Frederick Douglass, 13-14.

[19] Ibid., 113.

[20] *Frederick Douglass, Life and Times of Frederick Douglass* (New York: Macmillan, 1962), 472-73.

[21] Nellie Y. McKay, "The Souls of Black Women Folk in the Writing of W. E. B. Du Bois," in Henry Louis Gates, Jr., ed., Reading Black, Reading Feminist: A Critical Anthology (New York: Meridian, 1990), 229.

[22] Ibid.

[23] Ibid. See W. E. B. Du Bois, *Autobiography of W.E.B. Dubois: A Soliloquy on Viewing My Life from the Last Decade of Its First Century,* ed., Herbert Aptheker (New York: International Publishers, 1968).

[24] Ibid.

[25] Ibid., 230.

[26] *Du Bois, The Souls of Black Folk* (New York: Penguin, 1996), originally published in 1903.

[27] Ibid., 58.

[28] Ibid., 58-59.

[29] Ibid., 61-62.

[30] McKay, "Souls," 236-37.

[31] *Du Bois, Darkwater: Voices from within the Veil* (New York: Harcourt, Brace, 1921), 163.

[32] Ibid.

[33] Ibid, 164-65.

[34] Ibid., 179.

[35] Ibid., 179, 182.

[36] Ibid., 185-86.
[37] Ibid., 172.
[38] In this chapter, I am concerned with Du Bois' critiques of patriarchal gender conventions, that is, his progressive writings about gender matters. Here I am not examining his own behavior or what we know about his personal life and his treatment of women, as these have been revealed in several biographies, including Gerald Horne, *Race Woman: The Lives of Shirley Graham Du Bois* (New York: New York University Press, 2000), a biography of Du Bois' second wife, or David Levering Lewis, *W.E.B. Du Bois: Biography of a Race, 1868-1919* (New York: Henry Holt, 1993) 2 vols., a comprehensive biography of Du Bois. The discrepancy between Du Bois' gender ideologies and his actual practice is the subject of another work. The work of Lemons is important in this regard, however. See also Round Table Discussion of W.E.B. Du Bois' "The Damnation of Women," coordinated by Shirley L. Poole, Crisis XX (November-December 2000):1-16, which includes a multilogue among a group of women, myself included, that discusses the essay from their contemporary vantage points.
[39] Cade, *Black Woman,* 110.
[40] Du Bois, *Darkwater,* 181.

9. Black Feminist Studies: The Case of Anna Julia Cooper (2009)

Anna Julia Cooper—feminist, human rights advocate, educational reformer . . . teacher, lecturer, scholar, the author of essays, vignettes, and poems.

Louise Daniel Hutchinson
Anna J. Cooper: A Voice from the South,
Smithsonian Institution Press, 1982

Black feminist studies, which emerged in the 1970s as a corrective to both black studies and women's studies, probes the silences, erasures, distortions, and complexities surrounding the experiences of peoples of African descent wherever they live. The early scholarship was comparable to the painstaking excavation projects of an archaeologist digging for hidden treasures. A small group of mainly black feminist scholars have been responsible for reconstructing the androcentric African American literary tradition by establishing the importance of black women's literature going back to the nineteenth century. In this regard, the early work of Mary Helen Washington and Barbara Christian comes to mind—as well as that of Alice Walker, who is responsible for rescuing Zora Neale Hurston from the shadows and possibly from oblivion.[1] When Roseann P. Bell, Bettye J. Parker, and I published *Sturdy Black Bridges: Visions of Black Women in Literature,* it was the first anthology of black women's literature and would signal the importance of reclamation projects in the development of a case for a robust black women's intellectual tradition. When *Words of Fire: An Anthology of African-American Feminist Thought* was published, the maturity of black feminist studies, as well as recognition of the significance of founding texts in the evolving field, could be claimed.

In this historic symposium on Anna Julia Cooper (1858-1964), it is appropriate to begin with an assessment of the scholarly criticism about her life and legacy. Beginning with the reception she received from her peers, to the rediscovery of her seminal 1892 text *A Voice from the South: By a Black Woman of the South* by contemporary black feminist scholars, this essay chronicles significant junctures in Cooper criticism.[2] It also calls attention to the silences and gaps in the scholarship on Cooper while simultaneously bearing witness to her significance in the development of black feminist discourse and its theory-building around intersectionality.

The publication of Gerda Lerner's documentary history *Black Women in White America* (1972), a foundational text in the development of black women's history, situates Cooper, for the first time, among a small group of nineteenth-century black feminist leaders that included Maria Stewart, Sojourner Truth, Fannie Barrier Williams, and Mary Church Terrell. In her final section, "Black Women Speak of Womanhood," Lerner includes a very brief excerpt from Anna Julia Cooper's *A Voice from the South* in which there is the now-famous quote about the peculiar and special burdens of black women: "The Colored Woman of to-day occupies, one may say, a unique position in this country. In a period of itself transitional and unsettled, her status seems one of the least ascertainable and definitive of all the forces which make for our civilization. She is confronted by both a woman question and a race problem, and is as yet an unknown or an unacknowledged factor in both" (Cooper qtd. in Lerner 572-73).

Six years later, the first collection of scholarly essays on the neglected history of African American women would make an important contribution to our understanding of the importance of black women's history as a corrective to American, African American, and women's movement historiography. *The Afro-American Woman: Struggles and Images* (1978), edited by two pioneering black women historians, Sharon Harley and Rosalyn Terborg-Penn, includes the first assessment of Cooper's importance in an essay entitled "Anna J. Cooper: A Voice for Black Women." Here Harley chronicles the important details of her life as a women's rights and human rights crusader and educator, her role in the black women's club movement, her struggles with both racism and sexism, as well as her personal crises within Washington, D.C. black communities.

In 1981, staff historian Louise Daniel Hutchinson wrote the catalogue for the first exhibition on Cooper's life and legacy, *Anna Julia Cooper: A Voice from the South,* which was held at the Anacostia Neighborhood Museum of the Smithsonian Institution in Washington, D.C. Still the most comprehensive chronicling of her extraordinary life, the exhibit and accompanying monograph, a year in the making, were influenced in part by the unpublished manuscript of the late Leona C. Gabel's *From Slavery to the Sorbonne and Beyond: The Life & Writings of Anna Julia Cooper* (Smith College, 1982), the second Cooper biography. Paula Giddings's 1984 work *When and Where I Enter: The Impact of Black Women on Sex and Race in America,* the first contemporary feminist history of African American women, immortalizes Cooper in many ways by using a quote from *A Voice from the South* in her title. She also establishes both

Cooper's significance in the black women's club movement and her status as an influential political thinker during the Progressive Era.

Three years later, literary critic Hazel Carby's landmark text, *Reconstructing Womanhood: The Emergence of the Afro-American Woman Novelist* (1987), challenged the commonly held belief that the late-nineteenth and early-twentieth centuries were the Age of Washington and Du Bois with respect to African American political and intellectual history. In her compelling examination of a nineteenth-century "black women's renaissance" (7), Carby makes visible for the first time the development of black feminist theory—its history and tendencies—in the work of Frances E. W. Harper, Fannie Barrier Williams, Fannie Jackson Coppin, Sarah J. Early, Hallie Quinn Brown, Ida B. Wells, and, of course, Anna Julia Cooper. Her chapter, "'In the Quiet, Undisputed Dignity of My Womanhood': Black Feminist Thought after Emancipation," foregrounds the existence of an evolving black female intellectual tradition and black women's movement, and includes the first scholarly analysis of Cooper's *A Voice from the South* (95-120).[3] Not surprising is Carby's allusion to one of the most memorable sections of *Voice* in the chapter title: "Only the Black Woman can say when and where I enter, in the quiet, undisputed dignity of my womanhood, without violence and without suing or special patronage, then and there the whole Negro race enters with me'" (Cooper qtd. in Carby 99). Carby can be credited with identifying Cooper's (and Wells's) pioneering role in the evolution of black feminist theory, which marks the importance of intersectionality in the lives of women: "Both Cooper and Wells theorized the relationships among race, gender, and patriarchy in their writing" (96). Carby also analyzes Cooper's insightful discourse on "the nature of imperialism and racism as hegemonic ideologies" (97) and her claim, extraordinary for the time, that imperialist or expansionist impulses, "with [their] ideology of racial hierarchies" are "a supreme instance of patriarchal power" (101).

A year after Carby's book was published, literary critic Mary Helen Washington wrote the first scholarly assessment of the significance of Cooper's life and body of work in her introduction to Henry Louis Gates, Jr.'s 1988 multi-volume *Schomburg Library of Nineteenth-Century Black Women Writers*. Cooper's *A Voice from the South* was now available in a new edition for the first time since it had been released in 1892 by the Aldine Publishing Company. In his foreword to the thirty-volume set, Gates announced her significance: ". . . Anna Julia Cooper, a prototypical black feminist whose 1892 *A Voice from the South* can be considered to be one of the original texts of the black feminist movement. It was Cooper who first analyzed the fallacy of referring to 'the Black man' when speaking of black people. . . . Gender and race, she argues, cannot be conflated except in the instance of a black woman's voice and it is this voice which must be uttered and to which we must listen" (xiii-xiv).

Despite Cooper's "unparalleled articulation of black feminist thought" (Washington xvii) and her unprecedented leadership in the African American community for over a half a century, Washington raises the question, "why is Anna Cooper a neglected figure" (xxvii), especially when one considers her more well-known contemporaries Ida B. Wells and Mary Church Terrell? Much of her introduction captures Cooper's importance and provides an explanation for Cooper's erasure from black intellectual history. Her compelling argument is that "the intellectual discourse of black women of the 1890s, and particularly Cooper's embryonic black feminist analysis" was ignored because of sexism—"because it was by and about women and therefore thought not to be as significantly about the race as writings by and about men" (Washington xxviii). Washington also painstakingly chronicles the ways in which prominent black male contemporaries ignored Cooper (and other black women intellectuals), and remarks that when the American Negro Academy was founded in 1897, women were excluded from membership. Washington is especially critical of Du Bois and his repeated failures to respond to Cooper's inquiries and requests. In the first book-length analysis of Cooper, *A Singing Something: Womanist Reflections on Anna Julia Cooper,* womanist theologian Karen Baker-Fletcher asserts, that "in the midst of an intellectual world dominated by men, Anna Cooper never received the full respect or credit she deserved for her work" (49).

While Washington captures the significance of Cooper as an important though neglected black female intellectual, she also critiques what she perceives to be her elitism with respect to ordinary black women and her uncritical attachment to the conservative ideology of true womanhood because of her own middle-class status. Washington asks a provocative question which she then attempts to answer: "How did Cooper, a woman who in some ways is so clear-eyed about the need to resist the subordination of women in all its forms, get trapped in the ideological underbrush of true womanhood?" (xlvi). Not surprisingly, she links Cooper with her middle-class sisters whose notions about racial uplift distanced them from the masses of working, less respectable black women. "As a middle-class black woman," Washington writes, "Cooper, like all of her contemporaries . . . had a great stake in the prestige, the respectability, and the gentility guaranteed by the politics of true womanhood. . . . Burdened by the race's morality, black women could not be as free as white women or black men to think outside of these boundaries of 'uplift'" (xlvii).

The emergence of what can now be called Cooper studies would be enhanced by the publication in 1988 of Frances Richardson Keller's translation into English of Cooper's 1925 dissertation, *L'Attitude de la France a l'egard de l'esclavage pendant la Revolution* (Slavery and the French Revolutionists, 1788-1805), published by the Edwin Mellen Press; Charles Lemert and Esme Bhan's edited collection of the bulk of Cooper's writings, *The Voice of Anna Julia Cooper* (Rowman & Littlefield, 1998); the aforementioned first book-length study, Karen Baker-Fletcher's *A Singing Something,* in which the argument is made that *A Voice from the South* is a theological text; Karen Johnson's *Uplifting the Women and the Race: The Educational Philosophies and Social Activism of Anna Julia Cooper and Nannie Helen Burroughs* (Garland, 2000); and several substantive journal articles and book chapters.[4]

Over a decade later, Vivian May's *Anna Julia Cooper, Visionary Black Feminist: A Critical Introduction* has the distinction of now being the most comprehensive and theoretically sophisticated book-length study of Cooper's substantial body of work. Not only does she establish that *A Voice from the South* is "a significant theoretical and political work" (2), but she also analyzes the broad range of her work, including her doctoral dissertation, which was completed in 1925 at the Sorbonne when she was sixty-six years old. She also makes a compelling case for Cooper as a visionary social theorist and activist whose "insurgent" and "prophetic" ideas have still not received the attention they deserve despite an increase in Cooper scholarship, most of which still focuses on her 1892 text. Even in the fields of social philosophy and feminist theory, May reminds us, Cooper's radical work as a public intellectual is invisible or marginalized. Even in Africana studies, May argues, "figures such as W. E. B. Du Bois, Carter G. Woodson, and Alain Locke are readily cited for their forethought and innovation, while Cooper's work, for example, is rarely pointed to, much less acknowledged in a substantial way" (173-74). In her final chapter, "Tracing Resistant Legacies, Rethinking Intellectual Genealogies: Reflections on Cooper's Black Feminist Theorizing," May captures the uniqueness of her scholar/activism and her fluency in multiple discourses in this way: "Whether in linguistics, history, social work, educational leadership, philosophy, literature, theology, labor analysis, or political organizing, Cooper speaks from the margins to develop and deploy an interstitial political and analytic method" (172-73). May's text is also important because in her reassessment of Cooper's personal life, she challenges some of the erroneous claims of her biographers (especially that she was isolated and solitary), as well as identifies some of the pitfalls of a preoccupation with the lives of women thinkers rather than their ideas. Extremely illuminating is her cogent summary analysis of the distinguishing characteristics of Cooper's feminist theories (182–87).

The disciplines of philosophy, education, theology, and rhetoric, as well as the interdisciplinary fields of women's studies and African American studies (especially black feminist theory), have contributed the most important Cooper scholarship over the past two decades.[5] Analyses of African American intellectuals are finally paying attention to Cooper, though they tend to be limited by their narrow focus on *A Voice from the South*.[6] When I was completing *Words of Fire*, I attempted to capture the significance of our first book-length black feminist text: "This collection of essays provides a global perspective on racism, imperialism, and colonialism; praises black achievements; advocates black women's education; and critiques black male sexism and the racism of white women" (43). With the publication of now two monographs on Cooper's writings and a new generation of women's studies and African American studies students now being exposed to her writing in their courses, it is now possible to imagine an outpouring of scholarship on Cooper over the next decade. As Vivian May demonstrates in her definitive work on Cooper, there is considerably more work to be done before Cooper is fully appreciated as a major American thinker and theorist.

Notes

[1] Pioneering and foundational critical essays and monographs in black feminist literary studies include Mary Helen Washington, "Black Women Image Makers: Their Fiction Becomes Our Reality," *Black World* 23.10 (August 1974), 10-18; June Jordan, "On Richard Wright and Zora Neale Hurston: Notes Toward a Balancing of Love and Hatred," *Black World* 23.10 (August 1974), 4-8; Barbara Smith, "Toward a Black Feminist Criticism," Conditions: Two 1.2 (October 1977), 24-44; Deborah McDowell, "New Directions for Black Feminist Criticism," *Black American Literature Forum* 14.4 (Winter 1980), 153-59; Barbara Christian, *Black Women Novelists: The Development of a Tradition,* 1892-1976 (Westport, CT: Greenwood, 1980) and *Black Feminist Criticism: Perspectives on Black Women Writers* (Oxford, UK: Pergamon, 1985); and Hazel Carby, *Reconstructing Womanhood.*

[2] See Lawson A. Scruggs, *Women of Distinction: Remarkable in Works and Invincible in Character* (Raleigh, NC: E. M. Uzzeli, 1892); May Wright Sewall, ed., *World's Congress of Representative Women* (Chicago: Rand McNally, 1894); Monroe Majors, *Noted Negro Women: Their Triumphs and Activities* (Chicago: Donohue & Henneberry, 1893); John E. MacBrady, ed., *A New Negro for a New Century* (Chicago: American Publishing House, 1900); and Henry F. Kletzing and William Henry Crogman, *Progress of a Race,* or, *The Remarkable Advancement of the Afro-American Negro: From the Bondage of Slavery, Ignorance, and Poverty to the Freedom of Citizenship, Intelligence, Affluence, Honor, and Trust* (Atlanta: J. L. Nichols, 1897).

[3] See an earlier version of this chapter, "'On the Threshold of Woman's Era': Lynching, Empire and Sexuality in Black Feminist Theory," in *Critical Inquiry* 12.1 (Autumn 1985), 262-77.

[4] These include Elizabeth Alexander, "'We Must Be About Our Father's Business': Anna Julia Cooper and the Incorporation of the Nineteenth-Century African American Woman Intellectual," *Signs* 20.2 (Winter 1995), 336-56; Kathy L. Glass, "Tending to the Roots: Anna Julia Cooper's Sociopolitical Thought and Activism," *Meridians* 6.1 (October 2005), 23-55; David W. H. Pellow, "Anna J. Cooper: The International Dimensions," in *Recovered Writers/Recovered Texts: Race, Class, and Gender in Black Women's Literature,* Dolan Hubbard, ed. (Knoxville: U of Tennessee P, 1997), 60-74; Cathryn Bailey, "Anna Julia Cooper: 'Dedicated in the Name of My Slave Mother to the Education of Colored Working People,'" *Hypatia* 19.2 (Spring 2004), 56-73; Frances Richardson Keller, "An Educational Controversy: Anna Julia Cooper's Vision of Resolution," *NWSA Journal* 11.3 (Fall 1999), 49-67; Vivian M. May, "Thinking from the Margins, Acting at the Intersections: Anna Julia Cooper's A Voice from the South," *Hypatia* 19.2 (Spring 2004), 74-91; Barbara McCaskill, "Anna Julia Cooper, Pauline Elizabeth Hopkins, and the African American Feminization of Du Bois's Discourse," in *The Souls of Black Folk: One Hundred Years Later,* Dolan Hubbard, ed. (Columbia:

U of Missouri P, 2003), 70-84; Margaret Nash, "'Patient Persistence': The Political and Educational Values of Anna Julia Cooper and Mary Church Terrell," Educational Studies 35.2 (2004), 122-36; Elizabeth West, "Cooper and Crummell: Dialogics of Race and Womanhood," in Rhetorical Women: Roles and Representations, Hildy Miller and Lillian Bridwell-Bowles, eds. (Tuscaloosa: U of Alabama P, 2005), 81-102. For the most extensive and up-to-date bibliography on Cooper, see May.

5 Only recently have African American philosophers taken seriously the work of Cooper; see especially Tommy L. Lott and John P. Pittman, eds., *A Companion to African-American Philosophy* (Oxford, UK: Blackwell, 2003); and Anthony Bogues, *Black Heretics, Black Prophets: Radical Political Intellectuals* (New York: Routledge, 2003). See also Jacqueline Jones Royster, *Traces of a Stream: Literacy and Social Change Among African American Women* (Pittsburgh: U of Pittsburgh P, 2000).

6 These would include Robin D. G. Kelley, *Freedom Dreams: The Black Radical Imagination* (Boston: Beacon, 2002); Joy James, *Transcending the Talented Tenth: Black Leaders and American Intellectuals* (New York: Routledge, 1997); and Kevin K. Gaines, *Uplifting the Race: Black Leadership, Politics, and Culture in the Twentieth Century* (Chapel Hill: U of North Carolina P, 1996).

Works Cited

Baker-Fletcher, Karen. *A Singing Something: Womanist Reflections on Anna Julia Cooper*. New York: Crossroad, 1994.

Bell, Roseanne P., Bettye J. Parker, and Beverly Guy-Sheftall, eds. *Sturdy Black Bridges: Visions of Black Women in Literature*. Garden City, NY: Anchor P, 1979.

Carby, Hazel V. *Reconstructing Womanhood: The Emergence of the Afro-American Woman Novelist*. New York: Oxford UP, 1987.

Cooper, Anna Julia. *A Voice from the South: By A Black Woman of the South*. 1892. *The Schomburg Library of Nineteenth-Century Black Woman Writers*. Ed. Henry Louis Gates, Jr. New York: Oxford UP, 1990.

—. *Slavery and the French Revolutionists, 1788-1805*. Trans. Frances Richardson Keller. Lewiston, NY: Edwin Mellen P, 1988.

Gabel, Leona C. *From Slavery to the Sorbonne and Beyond: The Life & Writings of Anna Julia Cooper*. Unpublished ms., Smith College, 1982.

Gates, Henry Louis Jr. "Foreword: In Her Own Write." *A Voice from the South* vii-xxvi.

Giddings, Paula. *When and Where I Enter: The Impact of Black Women on Sex and Race in America*. New York: William Morrow, 1996.

Guy-Sheftall, Beverly, ed. *Words of Fire: An Anthology of African American Feminist Thought*. New York: New P, 1995.

Harley, Sharon, and Rosalyn Terborg-Penn, eds. *The Afro-American Woman: Struggles and Images*. Port Washington, NY: Kennikat, 1978.

Johnson, Karen. *Uplifting the Women and the Race: The Educational Philosophies and Social Activism of Anna Julia Cooper and Nannie Helen Burroughs*. New York: Garland P, 2000.

Lemert, Charles, and Esme Bhan, eds. *The Voice of Anna Julia Cooper,* Including *A Voice from the South* and *Other Important Essays, Papers, and Letters*. Lanham, MD: Rowman and Littlefield, 1998.

Lerner, Gerda, ed. *Black Women in White America: A Documentary History*. New York: Random House, 1972.

May, Vivian. Anna Julia Cooper, *Visionary Black Feminist: A Critical Introduction*. New York:

Routledge, 2007. Washington, Mary Helen. Introduction. *A Voice from the South* xxvii-liv.

PART III

Black Studies — Women's Studies

10. The Promise and Challenge of Black Women's Studies:

A Report from the Spelman Conference, May 25-26, 1990, with Patricia Bell-Scott and Jacqueline Jones Royster **(1991)**

A rich legacy of excellence in the education of women makes Spelman College, founded in 1881, the nation's oldest liberal arts institution devoted exclusively to the education of women of African descent. Spelman is thus an ideal home for the first women's research center to be established at a historically Black college and a logical setting for the recent conference on Black Women's Studies.[1] Established in 1981 with a grant from the Charles Stewart Mott Foundation, the Spelman College Women's Research and Resource Center was strengthened in 1983 with a two-year grant from the Ford Foundation for the implementation of a pioneering curriculum development project in Black women's studies at selected southern colleges. As a result of this project, Spelman now has the distinction of being the only historically Black college with a Women's Studies program *and* a "mainstreaming" project in Women's Studies. Spelman's project is also unique because of its special attention to women of color and its cross-cultural perspective.[2]

Though Spelman's formal involvement in women's studies is relatively recent, its involvement as a sponsor of seminars and conferences on issues related to Black women is considerably older. In 1944, for example, Spelman was the site of the Conference on Current Problems and Programs in the Higher Education of Negro Women, during which representatives of several historically Black colleges focused on directions for postwar education. More recently the Spelman Center has played a significant role in national discussions relating to the intersection of race, gender, and class within women's studies. The center has also emerged as a site for national conferences that address critical issues facing women in general and Black women in particular. Among these have been the Conference on Black Women and Public Policy in 1982; the First National Conference on Black Women's Health organized by the National Black Women's Health Network in 1983; the Tenth Anniversary Conference of the National Women's Studies Association in 1987; and the Spelman College Presidential Inaugural Symposium on the Education and Empowerment of Black Women in 1988. Perhaps the most visible and explicit manifestation of the college's commitment to the development of Black women's studies is its provision of an editorial office for *SAGE: A Scholarly Journal on Black Women.* The journal premiered in 1984 with an issue on Black women's education. A student internship program with the journal is cosponsored by the college's Comprehensive Writing Program and the Women's Center.[3]

Because Spelman has played a central role in the education of Black women and the development of the contemporary Black women's studies movement, the college provided an ideal setting in which to host a dialogue about the promise and challenge of Black women's studies. Thus, on May 25-26, 1990, with funding from the Ford Foundation, Spelman College sponsored a conference on Black women's studies. This conference was the final activity of a curriculum development project in Black women's studies at selected southern colleges. It was designed to bring together a small group of teacher/scholars, writers, and activists from a variety of settings to explore curriculum integration strategies that have been successful in incorporating material on women of color into women's studies and other courses across the disciplines and to examine Black feminist perspectives in American scholarship over time. The conference also focused on assessing the state of Black women's studies in terms of research and pedagogy and developing a global liberal arts curriculum by including cross-cultural perspectives on women into college and university courses.

The goal was to hold an intensely interactive dialogue that would be inclusive of a range of voices, experiences, and areas of expertise. Participants were drawn from colleges, universities, and community-based organizations. In addition to Black and women's studies perspectives, participants also contributed perspectives from their disciplines, which included anthropology, history, literature, psychology, Romance languages, sociology, theology, and the biological sciences. Session topics included "The Impact of Black Women's Studies on the Disciplines," "Caribbean and African Women Writers: Teaching and Research Strategies," "Teaching About Black Women and Religion," "Doing Research in Black Women's Studies: Conceptual and Methodological Issues," "Global/Cross-Cultural Perspectives on Black Women: Teaching and Research Strategies," "Innovative Projects on Black Women," and "Teaching About Black Women: Male Perspectives." Each session was set up as an open discussion evolving from short panel presentations. This structure gave participants the opportunity to switch comfortably from presenter to audience to resource person in the interest of a fruitful, multidisciplinary dialectic. The resulting conversations throughout the conference enabled participants to see dimensions of issues more fully and to think reflectively and proactively about teaching and learning.

In addition, *SAGE*, a conference co-sponsor, presented two awards. The Hilda A. Davis Award was given to Leah Creque-Harris in recognition of distinguished service to the journal, and the first Anna Julia Cooper Award was given to Paula Giddings in recognition of outstanding scholarship in Black women's studies. As a closing event, writers Mari Evans and Pearl Cleage read from their recent work.

Conference participants generally concurred that efforts in Black women's studies have been painfully slow and frequently met with hostility and opposition—even on campuses with established Black and/or women's studies programs. At the opening plenary session, historian Elsa Barkley Brown described the current state of affairs succinctly: "Much has changed and little has changed." And it is precisely this situation—one of promise and challenge—on which the conferees concentrated for two days.

Of particular promise has been the redefinition of politics, community, and family within several disciplines. This redefining process also has been accompanied by a movement away from hierarchical thinking among a few feminist and Black theorists. The enormous volume of literary criticism and works by creative women writers throughout the African diaspora; the emergence of models and constructs in sociology, psychology, and theology that capture Black women as agents of change with complex and multifaceted lives; and the consideration of the scholar/subject dialectic in the conduct of science, biography, and history are equally encouraging.

Despite these progressive developments, conference participants identified several major challenges. Conferees stressed the need to place Black and other women of color at the center rather than the margin of Black and women's studies. Though the invisibility and distortion of Black and women's experiences in the traditional disciplines provided impetus for the establishment of Black and women's studies programs, these programs—now commonplace on many campuses—are predominantly male and white in their administration, faculty, and curriculum. Myra Burnett, psychologist, and Jacquelyn Grant, theologian, reported that some leading proponents of the Black psychology and Black liberation theology movements continue to be blatantly chauvinistic. Paula Giddings, historian, and Beverly Guy-Sheftall, conference co-organizer, spoke of the tendency among women's studies scholars to see scholarship on Black and other women of color as narrow and peripheral to understanding women's experiences generally. All asserted that the study of persons in whom the forces of race, sex, and class oppression converge is obviously among the broadest and most complex inquiries of the human experience. Hence, rather than being marginal, Black women's studies is central to understanding women's and Black experiences.[4]

Focusing on the need for theory, frameworks, and language through which the complexity and diversity of Black women's lives can be considered and named from Black women's viewpoints, Mona Phillips, Myra Burnett, and Sheila Walker described the biases of sociological, psychological, and anthropological discourse respectively. These disciplines historically have characterized Black women as low status, dysfunctional primitives. Moreover, neither Black nor women's studies has offered a language totally usable or meaningful for describing Black women's experiences. In response to this situation, some scholars have tried to reform existing theory and frameworks by arguing for Black women's inclusion. Not surprisingly, efforts that simply add the experiences of a few famous Black women to the curriculum have presented no threat to the Eurocentric worldview upon which the disciplines rest. Others have given new meaning to pejorative language. Walker and her African American anthropologist colleagues, for example, named their newsletter "Notes from the Natives." Still others have developed new language—as is the case with Jacquelyn Grant who has adopted the term "womanist" coined by Alice Walker. This term, Grant asserted, is free of the distortions and limitations associated with much of feminist and Black theology. And finally, some scholars have argued for a deliberative and radical transformation of the knowledge-building process, utilizing the experiences of people of color as the foundation for theory.[5]

Carol Boyce Davies and Miriam DeCosta-Willis addressed the limitations of Western notions about race and feminism in studying non-U.S. women and emphasized the need to employ international and comparative perspectives. Davies, a literary scholar, detailed the pitfalls of exporting the Eurocentric canon to Africa and the Caribbean, the inability of most critics to place works by non-U.S. writers in an international context, and the devaluing of the vast and multicultural nature of the African continent. DeCosta-Willis, a Romance languages and literary scholar, stressed the importance of learning the writer's language so as better to understand the nuances. She also discussed how Afro-Hispanic writers, many of whom write in English, are excluded from the curricula in Spanish, English, Black and women's studies.[6]

Brown and Patricia Bell-Scott, conference co-organizer, explained the importance of multiple voices in analyzing African American women's lives. To illustrate this point, Brown recalled how she shared, in a letter to her mother, the ambitions and frustrations she felt while working to support a husband who was in graduate school and longing to pursue an advanced degree herself. Brown's mother wrote back advising that family and not graduate school should be her daughter's priority. And yet, in this same letter, was a check for Brown's graduate school tuition—"contradicting" the written message and indicating a mother's understanding of a daughter's dreams. Bell-Scott also described how one's willingness to hear contrasting voices is critical to writing about/constructing a life story, as these voices often reflect a woman's most deeply held dreams and values, as well as the conflict of these with her daily realities. Both Brown and Bell-Scott called for the use of multimethod strategies that draw from what women write, what they say about themselves, what they do, as well as how they are perceived by contemporaries and scholars.[7]

Outlining the important role that academic politics play in the interpretation of Black women's lives, Davies suggested the need to address power issues in the interpretation of Black women's lives. She discussed how scholars anointed by the "politics of citation or mention" assume power as official interpreters of Black women's experiences. Bell-Scott and Walker described their efforts to empower the knowledge source, that is, Black women, as interpreter(s) and to minimize or at least delineate very carefully the scholar's interpretative role. Bell-Scott discussed the use of negotiated interpretation—a strategy whereby scholars share their understanding of women's lives with the women themselves and incorporate women's viewpoints into the life story—a useful tool for biographers. Walker, on the other hand, explained her preference for the use of film and photographs in studying communities, suggesting that visuals directed or produced by Black women allow the scholar to get out of the way.[8]

Johnnetta B. Cole, anthropologist and Spelman College president, reminded those present of the need for ongoing consideration of the relationships among research, community, and social action. She urged conferees to examine the role of research in Black women's empowerment and posed several questions: "Do rich Black women have more in common with rich white men or poor women?" "How can middle-class Black women express genuine solidarity with Black women in South Africa, the favelas of Brazil, and the underclass in the U.S.?" "How does the Black woman/man drama get played out in non-

U.S. contexts?" "Will Black women find more ways to connect via the new technology or will they be isolated by that technology?" "What is/should be the particular role of the Black woman professoriate?" Janet Sims-Wood, librarian/ bibliographer, and Naima Major, health activist, reported on Black Women's Voices and the National Black Women's Health Project—two community-based efforts that bring together the education and research processes.[9]

In addition to these challenges, many spoke of the struggle to find space, time, and a supportive, or at least a neutral, environment in which to do one's work. Several reported attempts by colleagues and superiors to discourage work on Black women. Dialogue also focused on the critical role that homophobia, class bias, and colorism play in the distortion of Black women's experiences. Maceo Dailey, Jr. and Selwyn Cudjoe, two Black males who teach courses in Black women's history and literature, respectively, shared new insights and alternative interpretations gained/learned from women students. Dailey spoke personally about the "narcotic effect" of male thinking on the knowledge-building process. Stories of academic politics resonated throughout the conference. Examples of scholars with no previous background in Black women's studies, who declare themselves to be experts and are given credibility by the academic establishment were plentiful—as were examples of Black women scholars with decades of work to their name and little or no job security, grant support, or recognition from colleagues.

Despite the scope of the challenges and issues identified, participants revealed that the conference left them intellectually and spiritually renewed. As the organizers, we concluded that Black women's studies is maturing as a field. We are, however, concerned that this maturation will be accompanied by an ahistorical, depolitical attempt to reform the traditional disciplines rather than to transform the knowledge-building process. It is also clear that a distinguished cadre of teacher/scholar/activists remains committed to the growth and vitality of this field; yet they are sorely in need of nourishment and recognition for the work they do in the academy and the community. Furthermore, the rejuvenation experienced by all at Spelman requires that dialogues such as this one be ongoing in educational institutions, especially in settings where Black women work and live. Education that does not center the learner in theory and praxis promotes denial of self and the eventual destruction of community. In short, Black women's studies must consider as primary the knowledge that will save Black women's lives.[10] Our hope is that this conference has moved us a little closer toward this end.

NOTES

[1] The authors wish to thank the conference participants and the Ford Foundation for making this dialogue possible. Conference presenters included Patricia Bell-Scott, University of Connecticut; Elsa Barkley Brown, State University of New York at Binghamton; Myra Burnett, Spelman College; Pearl Cleage, Spelman College; Johnnetta B. Cole, Spelman College; Selwyn Cudjoe, Wellesley College; Maceo Dailey, Jr., Spelman College; Carol Boyce Davies, State University of New York at Binghamton; Miriam DeCosta-Willis, George Mason University; Noel Erskine, Emory University; Mari Evans, Spelman College; Vanessa Northington Gamble, University of Wisconsin, Madison; Paula Giddings, Douglass College/ Rutgers University; Jacquelyn Grant, Interdenominational Theological Center; Beverly Guy-Sheftall, Spelman College; Jacqueline Jones Royster, Spelman College; Ruth Simmons, Spelman College; Janet Sims-Wood, Howard University; Mona Phillips, Spelman College; and Sheila Walker, William and Mary College.

[2] Curriculum development projects at Spelman and other institutions are detailed in Beverly Guy-Sheftall, "Black Women and Higher Education: Spelman and Bennett Colleges Revisited," *Journal of Negro Education* 51 (Summer 1982): 275-87 and "Women's Studies at Spelman: Reminiscences from the Director," *Women's Studies International Forum* 9, no. 2 (1986): 151-55; Guy-Sheftall and Patricia Bell-Scott, "Black Women's Studies: A View from the Margin," in *Educating the Majority: Woman Challege Tradition in Higher Education,* ed. Carol S. Peanon, Donna L. Shavlik, and Judy G. Touchton (New York: Macmillan, 1989), 205-17. See SAGE 6, no. I (1989) for a general discussion of pedagogical and research issues in Black women's studies.

[3] For a detailed discussion of the *SAGE* journal/student internship program see, Jacqueline Jones Royster, *Looking from the Margins: A Tale, of Curriculum Reform* (Minneapolis: University of Minnesota, Center for Interdisciplinary Studies of Writing, 1990); "A Something from Within: Black Women's Pathways to Intellectual Empowerment," in *Composition, Gender and Culture,* ed. Deborah H. Holdstein (New York: Modern Language Association, forthcoming); and Royster and Guy-Sheftall, "Reflections on the SAGE Women as Writers/ Scholars Internship Program," Student supplement SAGE (1988): 4-6. The 1988 supplement was produced by student interns and partially supported by the Fund for the Improvement of Postsecondary Education. Copies are available from the Spelman College Women's Research and Resource Center.

[4] The marginalization of Black and other women of color in women's studies is confirmed by data gathered in a national survey on minority content and presence in women's studies coordinated by Bell-Scott and Guy-Sheftall. A report from this project is forthcoming. For a discussion of the philosophical/disciplinary underpinnings of the marginalization of Black and other women of color in women's studies and/or feminist theory see, Patricia Hill Collins, *Black Feminist Thought: Knowledge, Consciousness,*

and the Politics of Empowerment (Cambridge, Mass.: Unwin Hyman, 1990); bell hooks, *Feminist Theory: Margin to Center* (Boston: South End Press, 1984); and Elizabeth V. Spelman, *Inessential Woman: Problems of Exclusion in Feminist Thought* (Boston: Beacon Press, 1988).

[5] See Jacquelyn Grant, *White Women's Christ and Black Women's Jesus: Feminist Christology and Womanist Response,* (Atlanta, Ga.: Scholars Press, 1989) for a discussion of black womanist theology; Collins, *Black Feminist Thought;* and Gloria T. Hull and Barbara Smith, "The Politics of Black Women's Studies," in *All the Women Are White, All the Blacks Are Men, But Some of Us Are Brave: Black Women's Studies,* ed. Hull, Bell-Scott, and Smith (Old Westbury, N.Y.: The Feminist Press, 1982), xvii-xxxi for a discussion of the politics of language and reform versus transformation in Black women's studies.

[6] For representative works that employ international and comparative perspectives see *Africana Women's Studies Series,* vols. 1-4 (Atlanta, Ga.: Atlanta University, Africana Women's Center, 1985); Carole Boyce Davies and Elaine Savory Fido, *Out of the Kumbla: Caribbean Woman and Literatue,* (Trenton, NJ.: Africa World Press, 1990); Davies and Anne Adams Graves, *Ngambika: Studies of Womm in African Literature* (Trenton, N.J.: Africa World Press, 1986); Beverly Lindsay, *Comparative Perspectives of Third World Women* (New York: Praeger, 1980); and Filomina Chioma Steady, *The Black Woman Cross-Culturally* (Cambridge, Mass: Schenkman, 1981); Selwyn R. Cudjoe, ed., *Caribbean Women Writers: Essays from the First International Conference* (Amherst: University of Massachusetts Press, 1990).

[7] See Elsa Barkley Brown, "Mothers of Mind," *SAGE* 6, no. l (Summer 1989): 4-11 for a detailed discussion of the role of multiple voices in her own scholarship.

[8] Davies credited Hortense Spillers with the phrase "politics of mention." Bell-Scott's use of negotiated interpretation as a strategy is informed by Abigail Stewart, "Toward an Inclusive Feminist Strategy for Studying Women's Lives" (Paper delivered at The Study of Individual Lives, Radcliffe College, Cambridge, Mass., 11 May 1990).

[9] The relationship of Black women's studies to social activism and personal growth is considered also in Hull and Smith, "The Politics of Black Women's Studies." The Black Women's Voices Project is co-directed by Ruby Sales and Janet Sims-Woods; for more information contact Ruby Sales, 3032 Gentain Court, NE, Washington, D.C. 20017. The National Black Women's Health Project was founded by Byllye Avery: for more information contact NBWHP, 1237 Gordon Street, SW, Atlanta, GA 30310. For information on the *Sage*/student internship program, contact Jacqueline Jones Royster, Comprehensive Writing Program, Spelman College, Atlanta, GA 30314, also see n. 3.

[10] Hull and Smith, "The Politics of Black Women's Studies," xxv.

11. Black Women's Studies: The Interface of Women's Studies and Black Studies (1992)

The most significant reforms in American higher education over the past two decades have come as a result of the Black Studies and Women's Studies[1] movements. Less well known but also important has been the development within the past several years of a new field of study—Black Women's Studies—which emerged in part because of the failure of Black and Women's Studies to address adequately the unique experiences of Black women in America and throughout the world. In the first publication on this newly emerging discipline called *Black Women's Studies*, the editors, all three of whom were solid Black Studies scholars, attempted to define the new concept, trace its development, and provide a rationale for its existence:

> Women's studies courses ... focused almost exclusively upon the lives of white women. Black studies, which was much too often male-dominated, also ignored Black women. Because of white women's racism and Black men's sexism, there was no room in either area for a serious consideration of the lives of Black women. And even when they have considered Black women, white women usually have not had the capacity to analyze racial politics and Black culture, and Black men have remained blind or resistant to the implications of sexual politics in Black women's lives.[2]

It is important to understand the context out of which this first interdisciplinary anthology in Black Women's Studies emerged and without which it could not have been produced. The most noteworthy developments in Black Women's Studies (though this designation was not in use) came from a relatively small but ever-expanding group of women scholars who had been teaching and doing research on Black women for at least twenty years. Many probably would have considered themselves Black Studies scholars. The pioneering work of educator Anna J. Cooper, who wrote *A Voice from the South: By A Black Woman of the South* in 1892, has the distinction of being the first scholarly publication in what now we would call Black Women's Studies. The publication of Toni Cade's *The Black Woman* in 1970, the first anthology of writings by and about Black women, was significant because of the value it attached to hearing the distinct voices of Black women themselves as they analyzed a number of contemporary issues. Two years later, Gerda Lerner's documentary history *Black Women in White America* (1972) underscored the importance of treating the experiences of Afro-American women as distinct from those of white women and Black men.[3]

Several other pioneers in the newly emerging field of Black Women's Studies were historians Rosalyn Terborg-Penn and Sharon Harley, whose anthology (also a first) *The Afro-American Woman: Struggles and Images* (1978) contains original essays which treat Black women's experiences from a historical perspective. Terborg-Penn's bibliographic essay "Teaching the History of Black Women" contains an exhaustive listing of the secondary sources available in Black women's history.[4] Similarly, the work of La Frances Rodgers-Rose and Filomina Chioma Steady, both of whom edited the first social science anthologies on Black women, has been critical as far as sociological and anthropological approaches to the study of Black women are concerned.[5]

Attempts to celebrate the existence of a distinct Black female literary tradition in America, which can be traced further back in time, also fall under the rubric of Black Women's Studies because they acknowledge the politics of sex as well as the politics of race in the texts of Black women writers. This celebration has taken place in two phases. The first phase is characterized by efforts to document that such a tradition exists. Frances Collier Durden's master's thesis, "Negro Women in Poetry from Phillis Wheatley to Margaret Walker" (Atlanta University, 1947), is probably the first work that falls into this category. One of the earliest doctoral dissertations to analyze the Black female literary tradition (which is different from examinations of images of Black women in literature) is Beatrice Hom Royster's "The Ironic Vision of Four Black Women Novelists: A Study of the Novels of Jessie Fauset, Nella Larsen, Zora Neale Hurston and Ann Petry" (Emory University, 1975). Sharyn Skeeter's "Black Women Writers: Levels of Identity" (*Essence*, May 1973) is better known and reached a broader audience.

The second phase was ushered in by the publication of Mary Helen Washington's scholarly article "Black Women Image Makers" (*Black World*, August 1974). Moving beyond the descriptive approach of Skeeter, she argued that Black women writers are a distinct group not only because of their long history but because unique themes recur in their works. The introduction to her pioneering anthology *Black-Eyed Susans: Classic Stories By and About Black Women* (1975) contains a more detailed analysis of these major themes. Alice Walker's essay "In Search of Our Mother's Gardens: The Creativity of Black Women in the South" (*Ms.*, May 1974) is perhaps the most eloquent and poignant account of the Black woman artist ever written. It should be mentioned also that Walker designed the first course on Black women writers, which she taught in 1977 at Wellesley College. Another publication in the second phase was *Sturdy Black Bridges: Visions of Black Women in Literature,* edited by Roseann Bell, Bettye Parker, and Beverly Guy-Sheftall (1979), which was credited with being the "first book-length critical work devoted to a 'minority' literature."[6]

The second phase is distinguished also by the emergence of Black feminist literary criticism, notably Barbara Smith's and Deborah McDowell's groundbreaking work[7] and Barbara Christian's *Black Women Novelists: The Development of a Tradition, 1892-1976* (1981), the first full-length study of the novels of Black women. The publication of Gloria Wade-Gayle's *No Crystal Stair, Visions of Race and Sex in Black Women's Fiction* (1984) links her to a small but productive body of Black feminist critics who "analyze the works of Black female writers from a feminist or political perspective."[8] Wade-Gayle's outstanding contribution to Black Women's Studies is that she provides a coherent conceptual framework for understanding what it has meant to be Black and female as this experience is portrayed in the literature of Black women of the mid-twentieth century. Her use of two central metaphors — the narrow space and the dark enclosure — to illuminate the double burden of race and sex, which is unique to Black women, is stunningly perceptive. She describes three circles, asserting boldly:

> In one circle white people, mainly males, experience influence and power. Far removed from it is the second circle, a narrow space in which black people, regardless of sex, experience uncertainty and powerlessness. And in this narrow space, often hidden but no less present and real, is a small dark enclosure for black women only. It is in this enclosure that black women experience the unique marks of black womanhood.[9]

The most valuable theoretical work in Black Women's Studies is bell hooks' controversial monograph, *Ain't I A Woman: Black Women and Feminism* (1981), which is a long overdue examination of the complexity of Black womanhood from the perspectives of Black women themselves. The major strengths of the book are its delineation of the impact of sexism on the lives of Black women; its analysis of the devaluation of Black womanhood, both historically and contemporaneously; its discussion of the persistent racism of the women's movement, and its careful treatment of the involvement of Black women in struggles to achieve equality for women even when they were discouraged from doing so by various segments of the white and Black communities. hooks' major contribution both to Black Studies and Women's Studies, however, is the theoretical framework she provides for analyzing what it has meant to be a Black woman in America. In her chapter on "Sexism and the Black Female Experience," for example, she advances the thesis that slavery, a reflection of a patriarchal and racist social order, not only oppressed Black men, but it defeminized slave women as well. Though scholars have emphasized the impact of slavery on Black men, which focuses in large part on the theory of the emasculation of the slave male, hooks and other Black feminist scholars argue that it is imperative that historians and other researchers begin to pay more attention to the impact of sexual exploitation on slave women. Furthermore, it is important to point out that Black women were not permitted to conform to the dominant culture's model of True Womanhood in the nineteenth century, just as the Black male was unable to act out the majority culture's definition of "true manhood." hooks' more recent book, *From Margin to Center: Feminist Theory* (1984), is a brilliant critique of contemporary feminist theory from the perspective of a Black feminist and illustrates in a provocative manner how a Black Studies and Women's Studies perspective can provide profound insights about the nature of female experience.

Until the emergence of Black Women's Studies, most of the research on Black women, excluding the work on Black women writers, focused on their roles within the Black family, especially the role of the Black matriarch, a persistent theme in Black Studies scholarship.[10] A second area of research has focused on the public lives of notable Black women such as Sojourner Truth, Harriet Tubman, Mary Church Terrell, and Mary McLeod Bethune. Part of the motivation for this "great Black women in history" approach that characterizes much of the Black Studies work on Black women is simply to record the fact that Black women were indeed present in history. In her analysis of research priorities in Black Women's Studies, Patricia Bell Scott has argued that there should be "more examinations of the black and female experience that are sensitive to the ways in which racism and sexism bear upon black women."[11] While such approaches to the study of Black women are appropriate, a major problem that continues to confront the Black Women's Studies scholar, whose primary challenge remains exploring the intersection of race, gender, and class, is the difficulty of arriving at theoretical frameworks which will enable one to understand the complexity and diversity of the Black female experience throughout the world.

According to Gerda Lerner, the major conceptual framework for studying American women has been provided by feminist scholars who, using the women as minority group model (the minority group model has been frequently used by Black Studies Scholars as well),[12] see women mainly in terms of their oppression and their struggles to overcome it. The shortcomings of this widely used minority group model to explain the history of American women have been analyzed by historian William Chafe, who has written of both Black and women's history. His major points concerning the problematic nature of the analogy between race and sex are that the collective oppression of Blacks, especially the physical abuse they have suffered, is substantially greater than that of white women; that there is physical distance between whites and Blacks, whereas white women live in close contact with white men, which gives them greater access to the sources of power than is the case with Black women; and that white women as a group are not as conscious of their oppression as are blacks.[13] The major weakness in this analogy between women and Blacks, which Chafe also argues, is that it obscures the critical differences between Black and white women, the major one being that Black women suffer the double burden of racism and sexism, which makes them a unique group in American society. Moreover, Black women have not had the so-called benefits of being female; they have not been sheltered, protected, or idealized by their men to the extent that was possible for white women. More importantly, because of the thoroughly entrenched and therefore persistent racial caste system which defined relations between Blacks and whites (and relegates Blacks to a subordinate position), the oppression of Black women links them to Black men rather than to white women. Finally, the economic realities of the Black community have forced Black women to participate in the labor force to a greater extent than white women.

This brief summary of the weaknesses of the Blacks/women parallel, which Chafe and others have discussed, points to a major problem that confronts the Black Women's Studies scholar, which is not as thorny an issue for Black Studies and Women's Studies scholars. If women do form a distinct social group, as some feminist scholars argue, how does one formulate a conceptual framework that takes into consideration race and its interaction with gender (and class) in the case of Black women's experience? A number of conceptual issues arise when one considers the race/gender nexus in this context. Is it possible, given the rigidity of the racial caste system, to perceive American women as a distinct social group? Since Black women belong to a minority group, can one reject completely the minority group model when conceptualizing them as a group? What happens to the minority group model when one considers that, despite their subordination to whites, including women, Black men are in a position to exercise power over black women because of the benefits which accrue to them because of their gender? Are the bonds of womanhood sufficiently strong to counteract the racial barriers which separate Black and white women, or does race override gender in most interactions between these two groups?

Though theoretical problems are inherent in Black Women's Studies, scholars in this field are in a unique position because of their ability to explore the intersection of race, sex, and class as experienced by Black women in ways that are impossible for other segments of the population. They are also in a position, as Black Studies scholars always have been, to challenge accepted scholarship. The study of Black women, for example, renders invalid many of the generalizations which abound in the historiography of American women and are considered "universal." An example from the introduction to *Root of Bitterness*, a documentary social history of American women, will illustrate this point. Here Nancy Cott states that most of the late-nineteenth-century women who initiated significant social welfare activities in cities did their work while unmarried or widowed, and one thinks immediately of Jane Addams and nods in agreement. Cott then speculates that these educated women were unable to reconcile the demands of the nuclear family with their newly defined roles, so they evaded the problem by remaining single. When one recalls the history of Black women during this same period (as one familiar with Black Studies would), one thinks of Lugenia Bums Hope, Ida Wells Barnett, and other middle-class, educated, married Black women who performed pioneering social welfare activities when racial uplift preoccupied the Black elite. A critical question for the Black Women's Studies scholar (which might not be raised by the conventional Black Studies scholar) is why these Black women were better able to juggle the roles of wife, mother, and career than their white female counterparts. For example, Ida Wells Barnett, determined not to give up her public life, carried her baby Charles (and nurse) along with her to women's conventions and political campaigns. He became such a fixture at the National Association of Colored Women's meetings that on one occasion he was elected Baby of the Association.[14] In order to explain why Black women's lives diverged from white women's lives in this respect, it would be helpful to consider the special historical experiences of Blacks, the particulars of the women's lives, and the sociology of sex roles.

Another generalization in women's history is that women can be compared to other minority groups because their physical characteristics make them easily identifiable and, therefore, they can be "singled out from the others in the society in which they live for differential and unequal treatment."[15] The case of Lucy Parsons renders invalid even this seemingly indisputable fact. Lucy is the relatively obscure "invisible" Black woman who was married to Albert Parsons, one of the anarchists accused of the Haymarket bombing in 1886 and later executed.[16] Because Lucy refused to acknowledge her racial identity (she pretended she was of mixed ancestry, mainly Indian) after her marriage, she becomes "invisible" as a Black person. That is, her name is mentioned on numerous occasions in histories of working women (because of her life-long struggle to alleviate their plight) and in histories of radical movements, but her race is ignored, as Lucy would have preferred. She therefore is missing from Black history. She is missing from "general" histories because of her sex, for it is presumed that her only significance was that she was the wife of Albert Parsons. She is missing frequently even from women's histories because her anarchist activity was out of the mainstream of nineteenth-century women's activities such as suffrage, settlement, and club work, which have attracted more of the historians' attention.

Thus, despite Lucy Parsons' persistent and dedicated struggle to improve the lives of the working class (before and after her husband's untimely death), which can be documented because of her many publications and because her activities were followed in newspapers throughout the country, she mainly appeared in footnotes before the publication of Carolyn Ashbaugh's study, which rarely appears on Black Studies reading lists. That very little about her life prior to her marriage (except that she was an ex-slave born in Texas) was uncovered by her biographer is indicative of the "invisibility" of Blacks during slavery, one of the most difficult periods of study for the Black Women's Studies scholar. Though Lucy is certainly easily identifiable as a woman, she avoids the "differential and unequal treatment" that she would have experienced as a Black by passing and denying her minority group status. She, therefore, escapes the indignities that members of her own race suffer even though she is female because, in effect, she becomes white. As a member of the dominant race, despite her gender, she does not suffer the differential and unequal treatment which proponents of the race/sex analogy argue is universal among Blacks and women.

There is exciting and challenging work yet to be done in Black Women's Studies. Much more is needed in the area of reconceptualizing Black Studies and Women's Studies so that the history, experiences, and cultures of Black women will be more effectively taught and studied, thereby enabling both disciplines to reflect more accurately the complexity of experiences of Blacks and women throughout the world. *But Some of Us Are Brave* provided a needed shot in the arm for the expansion of Black Women's Studies on college campuses throughout the nation. The birth of *SAGE: A Scholarly Journal on Black Women* in 1984, which is edited by Patricia Bell Scott, Beverly Guy-Sheftall, Jacqueline Jones Royster, and Janet Sims Wood, and is housed at Spelman College's Women's Research and Resource Center, is a concrete manifestation of the "coming of age" of Black Women's Studies. Numerous periodicals and journals are continuing to produce special issues on Black women. Approximately fifty dissertations on Black women with a variety of subjects have been listed with University Microfilms since 1970 compared with less than ten prior to that time. The ultimate challenge, however, is for Women's Studies and Black Studies scholars to recognize that Black women's history is, in fact, women's history and Black history. Such a perspective would render Black Women's Studies unnecessary or at the very least redundant over the long run.

NOTES

[1] For a comprehensive examination of women's studies generally see Marilyn J. Boxer, "For and About Women: The Theory and Practice of Women's Studies in the United States," *Signs*, 7 (Spring 1982): 660-96.

[2] Gloria T. Hull, Patricia Bell-Scott, and Barbara Smith, eds, *All the Women Are White, All the Blacks Are Men, But Some of Us Are Brave: Black Women's Studies* (Old Westbury, New York, 1982), pp. xx-xxi. Subsequent references will refer to this source as *But Some of Us Are Brave.*

[3] Recent publications in Black women's history are Dorothy Sterling, ed., *We Are Your Sisters: Black Women in the Nineteenth Century* (New York, 1984); Paula Giddings, *Where and When I Enter: The Impact of Black Women on Race and Sex in America* (New York, 1984); Jacqueline Jones, *Labor of Love, Labor of Sorrow: Black Woman, Work, and the Family from Slavery to the Present* (New York, 1986); Bettina Aptheker, *Women's Legacy: Essays on Race, Sex, and Class in American History* (Amherst, 1982); Angela Y. Davis, *Women, Race, and Class* (New York, 1981); and Deborah Gray White, *Ar'n't I A Woman? Female Slaves in the Plantation South* (New York, 1986).

[4] *The History Teacher*, 13 (February 1980): 245-50.

[5] See La Frances Rodgers-Rose, ed., *The Black Woman* (Beverly Hills, California, 1980) and Filomina C. Steady, ed., *The Black Woman Cross-Culturally* (Cambridge, Mass., 1981).

[6] Cheri Register, "Literary Criticism," *Signs*, 6 (Winter 1980): 270.

[7] See Barbara Smith, "Toward A Black Feminist Criticism," Conditions: Two (October 1977): 27-28 and Deborah McDowell, "New Direction for Black Feminist Criticism," *Black American Literature Forum*, 14 (October 1980): 153.

[8] McDowell, "New Directions," p. 156.

[9] *No Crystal Stair*, pp. 3-4.

[10] See W.E.B. DuBois' *The Negro American Family* (Atlanta, 1908); E. Franklin Frazier's *The Negro Family in the United States* (Chicago, 1939); and Daniel Moynihan's *The Negro Family: A Case for National Action* (Washington, D.C., 1965) for a discussion of the black matriarch theory. Critics of this theory include Robert Staples, "The Myth of the Black Matriarchy," *The Black Scholar*, 1 (January/February 1970): 8-16, and Andrew Billingsley, *Black Families in White America* (Englewood Cliffs, N.J., 1969).

[11] *But Some of Us Are Brave*, p. 89.

[12] The women as minority group analogy was developed in 1951 by Helen Hacker. See her "Women as Minority Group," *Social Forces*, 30 (October 1951): 60-9.

[13] William Chafe, *Women and Equality* (New York, 1977), pp. 45-8.

[14] Dorothy Sterling, *Black Foremothers*, (Westbury, N.Y., 1979), pp. 97-8.

[15] "Louis Wirth, "The Problems of Minority Groups," in *Man in the World Crisis*, ed., Ralph Linton (New York, 1945), quoted by William Chafe, *Women and Equality*, p. 4.

[16] See Carolyn Ashbaugh's *Lucy Parsons: American Revolutionary* (Chicago, 1976), for the most comprehensive account of Parsons' life.

12. Reconstructing a Black Female Intellectual Tradition:

Commentary on Harold Cruse's *The Crisis of the Negro Intellectual* (1994)

In the introduction to the 1984 edition of Cruse's *The Crisis of the Negro Intellectual,* Bazel Allen and Ernest Wilson III place this pioneering text within a grand tradition of landmarks in African American intellectual history—Du Bois's *The Souls of Black Folk,* Alain Locke's *The New Negro,* Carter G. Woodson's *The Mis-Education of the Negro,* and E. Franklin Frazier's *Black Bourgeoisie.* Included within this role call are other distinguished black male writers/thinkers—Richard Wright, Ralph Ellison, James Baldwin, Amiri Baraka, and, more recently, William J. Wilson and Thomas Sowell. Conspicuously absent in this litany of pioneering and provocative landmarks are any works by African American women, an oversight which was inexcusable in 1984 given the emergence in the 1970s of a Black feminist movement, one of whose major objectives has been reconstructing a Black female intellectual tradition too long obscured by all the men being Black and all the women being white.

After reading the 1984 introduction to *The Crisis of the Negro Intellectual* in preparation for these comments, I remembered my first response to reading Cruse in the late sixties while a student at Clark Atlanta University. It was simply this—that there was a major oversight in an otherwise incisive analysis of the failures in black leadership over the preceding three decades or so. Though the women's movement was in its embryonic stages, and though Toni Cade's pioneering text *The Black Woman* was not to be published until three years later (1970), I recall being disappointed at the invisibility of African American women, except for Lorraine Hansberry, who is mostly vilified in Cruse's massive tome on Black intellectuals. I was attempting to write a master's thesis on Faulkner's treatment of women in his major novels without the benefit of feminist literary criticism, but I was beginning to understand how important a gender analysis would be in fresh interpretation of the "masters." I wondered to myself why it would not also have occurred to Cruse that a comprehensive discussion of Black intellectuals should not have been a male discourse. Eventually, I finished the Cruse text and the thesis, got a teaching job, and embarked upon (with a colleague) the arduous task of making visible to my students at Spelman College the forgotten tradition of Black women writers, having discovered that my students' knowledge of the Black literary tradition focused entirely on men. I thought about the Cruse text during those years Roseann Bell and I were working on *Sturdy Black Bridges: Visions of Black Women in Literature* (Doubleday, 1979), a corrective, we hoped, to the notion that only men had written anything worth reading in our communities. Many years later I was to be reminded by Alice Walker, who was a sophomore at Spelman when I was a freshman, that she had not heard of Zora Neale Hurston until after college, a situation which my colleague and I teaching freshman English at Spelman hoped none of our students would replicate.

I thought deeply about the Cruse text again after the Women's Research and Resource Center was founded in 1981 and I was planning a symposium on the Black female intellectual tradition. Two Black women intellectuals who had written pioneering texts were invited to speak—Paula Giddings, author of *When and Where I Enter: The Impact of Black Women on Race and Sex in America,* and bell hooks, author of *Ain't I a Woman: Black Women and Feminism*; they would join Gloria Wade-Gayles and myself, professors at Spelman, in a standing room only crowd of students throughout the Atlanta University Center who were eager, it seemed, to learn about a subject we suspected would be fairly new to them. This was confirmed by what happened at the beginning of our deliberations. hooks asked the students, before she began her formal presentation, to name some Black women intellectuals. To our astonishment, there was absolute silence. I've repeated this question, on occasion, at the beginning of talks I give throughout the country on Anna Julia Cooper, one of the most important nineteenth-century Black women intellectuals, and I continue to be amazed when I sometimes get no response. This happened a few months ago and I thought again about Cruse's text and the difficulty of conceptualizing Black women as intellectuals. We can think of Black women as mothers, church women, activists (à la Harriet Tubman and Sojourner Truth), teachers, even writers, but almost never as intellectuals.

As I reread Cruse's profoundly patriarchal text, I was reminded that while there are insights which are relevant for an analysis of contemporary Black leaders (male), *Crisis* is also in many ways outdated. The overarching paradigm that posits two paths for Black progress—integration and nationalism—is overly simplistic at the turn of the century. The assumption that the Black community is an undifferentiated mass with respect to gender is also passé. We must be as vigilant about understanding sexism and its impact on Black women and men and our communities as we are about understanding racism and classism.

In other words, we must struggle to eradicate the twin evils of racism and poverty. Gender must become as important as race as an analytic category in our analyses of the work of Black intellectuals, male and female. A gender analysis of the work of Lorraine Hansberry by Cruse would have rendered her a more exciting figure, particularly with respect to her use of feminist themes in *Raisin.* We will continue to distort the intellectual history of African Americans if we fail to include the work of our womenfolk who have consistently provided some of the most passionate and insightful analyses of what it means to be Black and female in a patriarchal, capitalist, racist culture.

Black feminist scholars are not the only ones who have written about the erasure of the intellectual discourse of Black women, however. Manning Marable's *How Capitalism Underdeveloped Black America* underscores the critical importance of such a paradigm shift in the writing of African American intellectual history.

> The sexist critical framework of American white history has been accepted by black male scholars; the reconstruction of our past, the reclamation of our history from the ruins, has been an enterprise wherein women have been too long segregated. . . . To understand the history of all Blacks . . . special emphasis is required in documenting the particular struggles, ideals and attitudes of Black women . . . Black male liberationists must relearn their own history, by grounding themselves in the wisdom of their sisters.

Another paradigm shift we must make in subsequent analyses of Black intellectuals is moving away from the assumption that the experiences of Black men can represent the condition of Black people in general. Black male experience is the norm in Cruse, so that Black men become the representative intellects. This masculinist bias renders invisible a host of important intellectual women—Jessie Fauset, Margaret Walker, Anna Julia Cooper, Ida Wells Barnett, to name a few. What is worse, it perpetuates the erroneous belief that important political ideas have sprung from the brains of men only.

Though contemporary Black intellectuals face a host of challenges not anticipated by Cruse—a devastating drug and violence culture within and without our communities, the ascendancy and high visibility of Black neo-conservatives, the impact of mass media, including rap music, on youth culture, a war between the sexes, homophobia, silence about AIDS, and confusion about appropriate strategies for empowerment in the post-civil rights era—it is important to remember Cruse's final warning: "Those who cannot remember the past are condemned to repeat it." As we ponder the future for African Americans, we need all our sages, male and female. We must not repeat the mistakes of yesteryear by silencing or listening to those who hold up half the sky. We must remember Frances E. W. Harper, Anna Julia Cooper, Ida Wells Barnett, Amy Jacques Garvey, Eslanda Goode Robeson, Sonia Sanchez, Angela Davis, as well as Booker T. Washington, William E. B. Du Bois, Frederick Douglass, Marcus Garvey, Paul Robeson, Martin Luther King, Jr., Amiri Baraka, and Stokely Carmichael. *Crisis* revisited would certainly be made stronger by such a crucial paradigm shift.

13. Exploring Difference: Racial and Global Perspectives in Graduate Women's Studies (1998)

Six years ago, I completed a report for the Ford Foundation, "The Status of Women's Studies, 1969-1992,[1] in which I analyzed the development of this new interdisciplinary field over its twenty-three-year history, assessed its current status nationally, and discussed future directions as the new century approached. Since its inception in the late 1960s, women's studies has certainly revitalized the traditional disciplines, especially in the humanities and social sciences, by challenging curricular and pedagogical practice, opening up the canon,[2] blurring disciplinary boundaries, and introducing the social construction of gender as a major focus of intellectual inquiry. At the same time, women's studies was itself being revamped as it gave greater attention to difference, race, the lives of Third World women, and global feminisms. The internationalization of feminist scholarship and the growth of graduate study, especially free-standing women's studies PhD programs, would contribute, I predicted, to the continued transformation of the field both within the United States and around the world.

When I completed the Ford report, there were only five free-standing master's programs in women's studies, one PhD program in women's history (University of Wisconsin-Madison), and three autonomous doctoral programs in women's studies–at Clark University in Worcester, Massachusetts, at Union Institute in Cincinnati, and at Emory University in Atlanta, where as a part-time adjunct faculty member I have been teaching a course on "African American Feminist Thought/Theory" for several years and very recently a course on "Third World Feminisms."[3] In fall 1997, there were still only three free-standing doctoral programs in women's studies in the United States although many are newly approved or in the process of being established.

Given the development of new graduate programs in women's studies, it is especially important to ask whether earlier critiques of undergraduate women's studies by scholars of color, and the new impetus toward global perspectives, are being reflected in the ways these new programs are being conceptualized in various institutional contexts. Are there adequate conceptions of the variety of feminisms around the globe? Are the standard feminist theory courses usually required of doctoral students in women's studies sufficiently inclusive? Are students encouraged to take courses in area studies, Black or Africana studies, diaspora studies, cultural studies, or other ethnic studies, even if these do not employ feminist perspectives, so that the students might have access to a broader range of interdisciplinary scholarship for understanding the global realities of women and their families and gender systems cross-culturally? Are students being exposed to course work that will enable them to understand cross-cultural sexualities and the social construction of masculinities? Will graduate training prepare these students more adequately to theorize the intersections of race, gender, ethnicity, class, and sexuality in the lives of women here and around the globe? Is there a "chilly climate" for students of color or international women in these relatively new graduate programs, or are they sufficiently welcoming of students from a variety of backgrounds?[4] Are faculty of color, whether from the United States or elsewhere, adequately represented within graduate women's studies programs (either as joint appointments, affiliated faculty, or fully budgeted within women's studies) or within other programs or departments at universities which provide graduate certificates or minors in women's studies? Are graduate students with research interests and dissertation topics on women who are not Euro-American and white able to find a sufficient number of faculty members on their respective campuses with the appropriate interest and expertise to guide them adequately?

Although I have not conducted a comprehensive survey of doctoral programs in women's studies (both free-standing and otherwise), as far as faculty and curricula are considered, I am familiar with a range of programs either because I have visited them as a member of an external review team; teach graduate women's studies courses and serve on doctoral committees; have had conversations with a number of faculty members attached to graduate programs with which I am not affiliated; and, on a regular basis, read material (including new proposals for doctorates) generated by programs that offer graduate training. My commentary here will focus on the importance of addressing difference and global issues in the training of students pursuing the free-standing doctoral or graduate certificates or minors in women's studies. My suggestions reflect my own vantage point as a teacher and researcher of the history of women's studies in the academy for nearly twenty years.

First of all, it is imperative that graduate programs make concerted efforts, which should be ongoing, to address issues of difference as fundamental to the viability of their project. One model is apparent at the University of Iowa, which will require that students take courses that would satisfy "diversity" as well as the usual core courses in women's studies.[5] A critically important issue in assessing this model is whether the core courses move beyond the "add and stir" approach with respect to scholarship on women of color within the United States and women from around the world or whether the expectation is that "diversity" is handled in elective courses. It is important to specify that students must take courses that address issues of difference, but this does not mean that core courses in women's studies, especially feminist theory and histories of feminism, are not also important sites for serious attention to the problems of hegemonic Western approaches to feminist discourses in various disciplines. Emory University requires that PhD students take a seminar in feminist theory, and there has been discussion about whether courses such as "African American Feminist Thought/Theory" might satisfy the require ment in addition to the standard feminist theory course. An examination of the syllabus of a graduate seminar at Emory in feminist theory/queer theory, which focuses on gender and sexuality, reveals a Euro-American focus and scanty attention to women of color, raising questions about the need within women's studies contexts more broadly to interrogate the limitations of contemporary queer theory where race and cross-cultural sexualities are concerned. Texts such as *Sites of Desire, Economies of Pleasure: Sexualities in Asia and the Pacific* (edited by Lenore Manderson and Margaret Jolly) reveal the limitations of Western understandings of sexuality and provide a more global exploration of important issues within feminist theorizing about gender and sexuality. Emory indicates that it promotes a comparative and global perspective on the experiences of women in different cultures, races, and classes in its doctoral program; and it is important to articulate how this important goal is achieved. It is certainly the case that such a commitment be reflected in the core program—the required feminist theory seminar and the introductory course on feminist approaches. While this attention to difference might be more *implicit* in the program at Clark University, it is not made explicit in their program descriptions, although conversations with several doctoral students in women's studies affirmed the program's sensitivity to issues of difference in its overall mission.

What follows are my brief recommendations about how doctoral programs in women's studies can practice their commitments to issues of difference in the very design of their programs and their advocacy efforts on campus as they carry out the critically important training of a new generation of scholars for the field. The core feminist theory or history of feminism courses are the most critical sites for the exploration of difference and the disruption of discursive practices which have historically privileged hegemonic Western feminist discourses. Feminist theory and history of feminism courses (sometimes they are the same course) must move beyond the approach taken in Rosemarie Tang's *Feminist Thought: A Comprehensive Introduction* (which traces the development of Western feminism) and include nondominant discourses which demonstrate that indigenous feminisms have characterized various cultures around the globe for hundreds of years. These courses must include Third World feminisms and scholarship on women's movements outside the West. Texts such as *The Challenge of Local Feminisms: Women's Movements in Global Perspective* (edited by Amrita Basu); *Third World Women and the Politics of Feminism* (edited by Chandra Mohanty, Ann Russo, and Lourdes Torres); *Feminist Genealogies, Colonial Legacies, Democratic Futures* (edited by M. Jacqui Alexander and Chandra Talpade Mohanty); *Making Face, Making Soul: Creative and Critical Perspectives by Feminists of Color* (edited by Gloria Anzaldúa); *Opening the Gates: A Century of Arab Feminist Writing* (edited by Margot Badran and Miriam Cooke); *Expanding the Boundaries of Women's History: Essays on Women in the Third World* (edited by Cheryl Johnson-Odim and Margaret Strobel); *Theorizing Black Feminisms* (edited by Stanlie James and Abene Busia); and *Words of Fire: An Anthology of African American Feminist Thought* (edited by Beverly Guy-Sheftall) must be added to feminist theory/history syllabi so that newly trained professors of women's studies will enter classrooms with new knowledge and new ways of teaching about women, gender, sexualities, and feminisms.

Doctoral programs in women's studies can also demonstrate their commitments to difference by actively recruiting women of color for their joint appointments or full-time fully budgeted lines in women's studies or even for the rare chairs in women's studies which a few institutions are privileged to have been awarded. It will be crucial as graduate programs in women's studies continue to proliferate that the common practice of joint appointments be examined and that full faculty lines in women's studies become the more usual pattern of hiring. With its new departmental status and its plans for a doctoral program, Ohio State University is seeking to hire two full-time faculty members within women's studies. The University of Maryland's Women's Studies Department is also able to hire full-time faculty. It is my hope that as women's studies programs gain more control over their tenure lines, then it will be possible to attract more women of color to their ranks.

This is an exciting time in the evolution of women's studies in the academy. Graduate programs in women's studies should ensure the development of a new crop of scholars who will, it is hoped, be better prepared for interdisciplinary inquiry about the global realities of women. If these new graduate programs demonstrate their commitments to engage with difference in tangible ways, then it is possible that women's studies will be truly transformed by the time a new major assessment of the field is undertaken.

Notes

[1] See the abbreviated version of this lengthy consultant's report: Beverly Guy Sheftall (with Susan Heath), *Women's Studies: A Retrospective* (New York: Ford Foundation, 1995).

[2] As of 1995, Emory University, the program with which I am most familiar, had 32 students enrolled and approximately 100 students in the certificate program. In May 1997, five PhD's in women's studies were granted, the largest number ever granted at Emory. Its distinguished speaker series brings a number of women of color to the campus for lectures, and the program has one faculty woman of color with a joint appointment with women's studies and English; she was recently granted an endowed chair. Women's studies also cosponsors with the Program of African American Studies an annual "Intersections of Race and Gender Lecture Series" which brought to the campus, in March 1997, Paula Giddings, research professor of African, African American, and women's studies at Duke University. There are plans for a faculty search for a position in women and development, a joint appointment with anthropology or sociology, which will enhance the program's international component.

[3] See Karen Kidd and Ande Spencer, eds., *Guide to Graduate Work in Women's Studies* (College Park, Md.: National Women's Studies Association, 1994); and Ann B. Shteir, "The Women's Studies PhD: A Report from the Field," *Women's Studies Quarterly* 25 (spring/summer 1997): 388-403, for a discussion of the current status of doctoral training in women's studies. The latter discusses the graduate program in York University in Canada, as well as emerging programs at the University of Iowa, University of Washington, and University of Minnesota. Several other major universities are also proposing doctoral programs. The University of Michigan has a joint PhD in women's studies and English and women's studies and psychology, which began in1994. Several institutions offer PhD minors in women's studies, and a larger number of universities offer graduate certificates in women's studies where the student's home base is in a discipline-based program. None of these discussions of doctoral programs mentions that Clark Atlanta University in Atlanta offers a Doctor of Arts in Africana Women's studies, although I cite this in the Ford Report.

[4] The first student to receive the doctorate in women's studies at Clark University (established in 1992) was an African American, Angela Bowen, who wrote a dissertation on "Audre Lorde, Life and Politics," and is now in a tenure-track position at the University of California at Long Beach. Similarly, among the first two students at Emory to complete the PhD (1995) was an African American woman, Ise Williams, who is now director of the program in Women, Leadership, and Social Change at Agnes Scott College in Atlanta.

[5] Shteir, 399. Although this article alludes to the diversity requirement, it does not discuss how it might be fulfilled.

14. Shifting Contexts: Lessons from Integrating Black, Gender and African Diaspora Studies (2002)

In a special issue of *SAGE: A Scholarly journal on Black Women* on "Africa and the Diaspora" (fall 1996), the editors called attention to the emergence of a new field of study, African diaspora studies, which was in many ways the result of the evolution of Black studies since its beginnings in the 1960s.[1] In 1979, many of the world's leading scholars and Africanists assembled at Howard University for the First African Diaspora Studies Institute. The publication of *Global Dimensions of the African Diaspora*[2] was one of the most important results of that historic conference because it provided new conceptual frameworks for the study of African peoples around the globe. For purposes of the conference, the African Diaspora was defined as "the voluntary and forced dispersal of Africans at different periods in history and in several directions; the emergence of a cultural identity abroad without losing the African base, either spiritually or physically; the psychological return to the homeland, Africa."[3] The African diaspora includes both "continental Africans" as well as "descendant Africans" (Blacks dispersed in the New World). Four years later, the Association of Black Women Historians sponsored a conference at Howard University on "Women in the African Diaspora: An Interdisciplinary Perspective" because of the lack of women participants at the earlier Howard conference and inadequate attention to women's experiences in teaching and research about the African diaspora. *Women in Africa and the African Diaspora,* edited by Rosalyn Terborg-Penn, Sharon Harley, and Andrea Benton Rushing (conference co-conveners), underscored the importance of the newly evolving field of women and African diaspora studies (also called Black women's studies or African diaspora women's studies). The new scholarship aimed to foreground gender issues within the fields of Black or Africana studies, which had historically been focused on men or insensitive to the intersection of race, class, and gender in the lives of African peoples.[5]

Our curriculum development project at Spelman College—Women and African Diaspora Studies—has had two major goals: reconceptualizing the women's studies program so that it will be more comparative, more global; and gendering African diaspora studies, which has historically been more sensitive to race, class, and geographical region than it has been to gender and sexuality issues.[6] The faculty has also found it necessary, like other scholars studying women around the globe, to problematize the binary of biological sex and social gender, which has been a fundamental conceptual paradigm within Western women's studies teaching and research. A basic limitation of the sex/gender binary can be underscored by an analysis of the experiences of African women in particular cultural contexts and at various historical moments.

Multiple Challenges from One Text

In a groundbreaking anthropological text by Ifi Amadiume, *Male Daughters, Female Husbands: Gender and Sex in an African Society,* Western feminist scholars can find a useful analysis surrounding the situation of Igbo women in Nigeria during the precolonial era.[7] In this text, Amadiume asserts the flexibility of gender constructs among the Igbo, where women can become husbands in woman-to-woman marriages and where, as daughters within their lineage groups, their age or birth order significantly influences their experience of what it means to be female. Amadiume offers evidence that the Western preoccupation with the status of wife obscures the important role of daughter among West African women. The tendency on the part of Western scholars to examine primarily the conjugal household in other cultural contexts misrepresents the complex institution of family within the sub-Saharan African context, for example, where women have multiple roles and statuses beyond that of wife.

Early on, conceptualizing the category "woman" was regarded as relatively unproblematic in Anglo-American feminist theory construction since the conceptual distinction between biological sex and social gender was critical to an understanding of human experience. In fact, the separation of sex and gender has constituted a basic conceptual framework in Western women's studies. A basic limitation of this sex/gender binary can be underscored by an analysis of the experiences of African women in a particular precolonial context, as Amadiume's anthropological work on the Igbo underscores.

My experience as a women's studies professor in graduate classes is that it has frequently been unsettling for "seasoned" women's studies students within the U.S. academy to have some of their basic conceptual frameworks challenged by moving outside Western cultural contexts. A primary example is the tendency of U.S. students to read woman-to-woman marriages as examples of lesbian partnerships on the African continent. In Amadiume's

Male Daughters, Female Husbands, there is a discussion of woman-to-woman marriages that is frequently very difficult for Western students to process (unless they've been exposed to anthropology classes) because they employ their familiar notions about marriage as they attempt to understand the institution of marriage, broadly speaking, in other parts of the world. Lesbian students are frequently very disturbed by Amadiume's introduction, which they label heterosexist (and worse) because she challenges Western feminists, including Audre Lorde, who interpret woman-to-woman marriages as an illustration of lesbianism in the African context. Though Amadiume explains the cultural context in which woman-to-woman marriages occur among the Igbo, many women's studies students critique the text for its silences about, rather than a discourse on, sexuality, its refusal to acknowledge that the women in these marriages could in fact be practicing lesbian sex, and her lack of an analysis of the nature of female friendships in the polygamous cultures she studies.

Prominent African feminist scholar/activist Malara Ogundipe-Leslie identifies areas of research that need to be undertaken without the ethnocentric biases that have characterized analyses of African women in the past: "Some gender issues are not yet receiving the intellectual attention they should. Too many silences persist in the area of human sexuality in Africa. Sexual orientation is certainly one area that has not been opened up for research or discussion ... The experiences of sexual orientation in traditional arrangements require discovery still."[8] It is certainly the case that it is also necessary to probe issues of sexuality in cultural contexts that constitute the African diaspora (the Americas, Latin America, the Caribbean, Europe, and Africa). Such an investigation represents a particular challenge since the discourse on sexuality outside the United States has been more limited than discussions about sexuality within this country. It is also the case that some cultures consider public discourse about sexuality to be inappropriate.

There are disciplinary biases as well. Women's studies students who may not have had an anthropology course also critique Amadiume's text because it does not employ interdisciplinary women's studies frameworks, though it is clear that *Male Daughters, Female Husbands* is solid anthropological scholarship that attempts to disrupt the ethnocentrism of Western studies of African women, including that generated by white feminist scholars.

I am not suggesting, however, that there are easy answers in classrooms that address cross-cultural issues or that there is one correct way to approach complicated questions. There are still many silences, many gaps in our knowledge about gender constructs outside the United States. There is considerable debate among scholars, for example, about the status of women in precolonial Africa and the impact of colonialism on the situation of women. The emergence of African feminist scholarship calls into question the discourse about women within the contemporary context as well.

Moving Beyond U.S. Categories of Identity

Other contentious issues have emerged in our exploration of the implications of gendering the field of women and African diaspora studies. It is necessary to interrogate traditional racial categories within and outside the United States. Racial categories familiar within this country are somewhat useless in a consideration of what we would call racial/ethnic women outside it. Borrowing U.S.-based racial categories, for example, to analyze the experiences of women in the African diaspora, which includes the Caribbean, South America (especially Brazil), Canada, and the United Kingdom, would render invisible the complexity of racial constructs outside the United States. It is sometimes the case that Caribbean faculty, with intimate knowledge of the history of South Asians and their relationships with persons of African descent in many parts of the Caribbean, especially Trinidad, find it difficult to conceptualize South Asians as "black," which is a racial category that is useful in the black British context. Many other contentious issues arise when North American students and faculty confront different discourses about race in assigned texts. For example, Molara Ogundipe-Leslie asserts that she does not see herself as "black" or use this language to describe other African women and asserts that there are cultural contexts in which ethnicity, nationality, age, and class are more important categories for understanding identity formation. She, for example, refers to herself as an African, Yoruba, middle-aged, middle-class woman.[10] There are no references to her racial identity in these descriptors. She goes on to say, as well, that she does not refer to herself as "a black woman." When a few of my African American students read this particular essay, they asserted what I would call ethnocentric biases when they accused Leslie of being in denial of her "blackness." In other words, it was difficult for them to transcend African American or pan-African political imperatives, which insist that people of African descent proudly espouse a "black identity" as one way of resisting the hegemony of a Western racial discourse associating "blackness" with a broad range of pejorative attributes.

And finally, the problem of using Black nationalist versus Afrocentric versus African feminist versus African American feminist frameworks in the study of women of African descent is a vexing one. In this regard, a number of contentious issues remain around linguistic categories, especially Third World/First World. There is some hostility among non-U.S. Black women about the use of the category Third World, which some perceive to be a derogatory category, even when women of color within the United States and around the world embrace this terminology as a political category that is useful in discourse on global feminisms. Nor have debates been resolved about the relevance of the term "feminism" for women who are not white and middle class. Alice Walker's counter discourse on "womanism" provided an alternative terminology for Black feminists in the early 1980s when many African American women, as well as other women of color within the United States, were raising angry voices about their marginalization or erasure from mainstream white feminist discourse. Walker introduced the term "womanist" in her collection of essays, *In Search of Our Mothers' Gardens: Womanist Prose,*[12] not as a rejection of the term "feminist," which is often how her statement is interpreted, but as a way of broadening the concept to include a range of perspectives. In fact, she asserts that "womanist is to feminist as purple to lavender," which suggests that womanism is a deeper, more intense form of feminism.[13] Walker's use of the term "womanist" underscores a particular, culturally specific way in which African American women conceptualize resistance to cultural norms of many kinds. Consider Walker's dismissal of normative categories: "A woman who loves other women, sexually and/or nonsexually. Appreciates and prefers women's culture, women's emotional flexibility . . . and women's strength." Womanists are not narrowly focused on women's liberation: "Committed to survival and wholeness of entire people, male *and* female. Not a separatist, except periodically, for health." Her concept of "womanism" (from the Black folk expression "womanish," which mothers use to describe feisty or "outrageous" female children) captures the legacy of struggle that Black women collectively inherit as a result of our particular history in the United States. Writes Walker: "Traditionally capable, as in, 'Mama, I'm walking to Canada and I'm taking you and a bunch of other slaves with me.'" Though the term "feminism" continues to be contested and controversial within many black communities, students and some faculty are often surprised by the growing body of gender discourse generated by women on the continent and throughout the African diaspora who employ the term "feminism" and who make an effective argument for our need to examine indigenous feminisms in many cultural contexts outside the West.[14]

This new feminist scholarship by African women, as well as women of African descent in Europe and the Americas, is critically important for understanding the experiences of women in different regions of the world and in helping to dismantle the hegemony of Western (white) feminist analytical frameworks. These emerging and evolving African diasporic feminist frameworks have the potential for transforming both African diaspora studies and women's studies. I am also hopeful that the required feminist theory courses in most women's studies programs in the United States and the required introductory courses in African American or Africana studies will begin to take into consideration feminist discourses outside the West. This will certainly make for more contentious classrooms, but it will also surely provide a more textured, more complicated analysis of the meanings of race, gender, and sexuality here and around the globe.

NOTES

[1] Black studies, also called Afro-American studies, African American studies, and Africana studies, emerged in the 1960s as a response to black students' demands for a more inclusive and relevant curriculum within higher education during the social upheaval of the Civil Rights Movement. This interdisciplinary academic field called attention to Eurocentric biases in the construction of knowledge and the erasure of the histories, cultures, and experiences of African peoples within the U.S. academy.

[2] See Joseph E. Harris, ed., *Global Dimensions of the African Diaspora* (Washington, D.C.: Howard University Press, 1982).

[3] Editorial, *SAGE: A Scholarly journal on Black Women* 3, no. 2 (fall 1986): 2.

[4] Rosalyn Terborg-Penn, Sharon Harley, and Andrea Rushing, eds., *Women in Africa and the African Diaspora* (Washington, D.C.: Howard University Press, 1987).

[5] A number of publications have appeared since *Women in Africa and the African Diaspora,* many of which are comparative studies of women of African descent throughout the diaspora.

[6] The culminating activity of our Ford Foundation project was an invitational conference on Women and African Diaspora Studies (May 29-30, 1998), during which four commissioned papers were presented: Rosalyn Terborg-Penn, "The State of the Field of Women and African Diaspora Studies"; Rhoda Reddock, "Black Women in the Anglophone Caribbean"; Angela Gilliam, "Black Women in Brazil"; and Carole Boyce Davies, "Claudia Jones: Anti-Imperialist, Black Feminist Politics."

[7] Ifi Amadiume, *Reinventing Africa: Matriarchy, Religion and Culture* (London: Zed Books, 1997).

[8] Molara Ogundipe-Leslie, *Re-Creating Ourselves: African Women and Critical Transformations* (Trenton, NJ.: Africa World Press, 1994), 15.

[9] Recent publications, especially the scholarly work of African women, are particularly useful in this regard: Ogundipe-Leslie, *Re-Creating Ourselves;* Amadiume, *Reinventing Africa;* Gwendolyn Mikell, ed., *African Feminism: The Politics of Survival in Sub-Saharan Africa* (Philadelphia: University of Pennsylvania Press, 1997); Juliana Makuchi Nfah-Abbenyi, *Gender in African Women's Writing: Identity, Sexuality, and Difference* (Bloomington: Indiana University Press, 1997); Chikwenye Okonjo Ogunyemi, *Africa Wo/Man Palava: The Nigerian Novel by Women* (Chicago: University of Chicago Press, 1996). See also the creative/ political work of Professor Osonye Tess Onwueme, especially her play, *Tell It to Women: An Epic Drama for Women* (Detroit: Wayne State University Press, 1997), which critiques Western feminism from the vantage point of rural African women and "is the first dramatic text from Africa to break the literary silence on issues of homosexuality," according to Ngugi wa Thiong'o who has written an excellent foreword to the play (p. 9). The earlier work of Filomena Steady, ed., *The Black Woman Cross-Culturally* (Cambridge, Mass.: Schenkman, 1987) and

African-American anthropologist Niara Sudarkasa on African family structures are also useful.

10 Ogundipe-Leslie, *Re-Creating Ourselves,* 218.

11 See Chandra Talpade Mohanty, Ann Russo, and Lourdes Torres, eds., *Third World Women and the Politics of Feminism* (Bloomington: Indiana University Press, 1991), for a useful discussion of these issues.

12 See Helen Charles, "The Language of Womanism: Re-thinking Difference," in *Black British Feminism: A Reader,* ed. Heidi Safia Mirza (London: Routledge), 278-97, for a lengthy analysis/ critique of Walker's concept of womanism, from the perspective of a black British critic.

13 Alice Walker, *In Search of Our Mothers' Gardens: Womanist Prose* (San Diego: Harcourt Brace Jovanovich, 1984), xii. See also Chikwenye Ogunyemi, "Womanism: The Dynamics of the Contemporary Black Female Novel in English," *Signs* 11.1 (1985), in which she indicates that she "arrived at the term 'womanism' independently" (p. 72). There have been a range of responses to Walker. Some black women reject the use of the term "feminist" altogether because of its exclusive association with white women and prefer the term "womanist." This includes a group of self-defined African-American "womanist" scholars doing pioneering work in theology such as Jacquelyn Grant. There are black women, such as bell hooks and others, who prefer the term "feminist" though they continue to critique Western feminism. For hooks, in *Talking Back: Thinking Feminist, Thinking Black* (Boston: South End Press, 1989), "the term 'womanist' is not sufficiently linked to a tradition of radical political commitment to struggle and change" (182). Ogundipe-Leslie (*Re-Creating Ourselves,* 207-41) uses the term "stiwanism," an acronym for Social Transformation Including Women in Africa, to describe feminist discourse in Africa and its cultural specificity.

14 See Safia Mirza, ed., *Black British Feminism*; Heidi Safia Mirza, *Young, Female and Black* (London: Routledge, 1992); Jayne O. Ifekwunigwe, *Scattered Belongings: The Cultural Paradoxes of 'Race,' Gender,* Nation (London: Routledge, 1998); Irene A. d'Almeida, *Francaphone African Women Writers: Destroying the Emptiness of Silence* (Gainesville, Fla.: University Press of Florida, 1994); Carole Davies and Anne Adams Graves, eds., *Ngambika: Studies of Women in African Literature* (Trenton, NJ.: Africa World Press, 1986); Stanlie M. James and Abena P.A. Busia, eds., *Theorizing Black Feminisms: The Visionary Pragmatism of Black Women* (London: Routledge, 1993); Juliana Makuchi Nfah-Abbenyi, *Gender in African Womens Writing; Awa Thiam, Speak Out, Black Sisters: Feminism and oppression in Black Africa* (London: Pluto Press, 1986); Terborg-Penn et al., *Women in Africa and the African Diaspora*; Beverly Guy-Sheftall, ed., *Words of Fire: An Anthology of African American Feminist Thought* (New York: New Press, 1995).

15. Conquering the Black Girl Blues (with Lani Valencia Jones) (2015)

The complex and busy nature of women's lives inevitably has an impact on their mental health. Domestic burdens of child bearing and caretaking, combined with work–life balance, all create difficult environments in which women are expected to cope. In addition to experiencing these typical domestic and work challenges, black women in particular also endure "multiple" oppressions associated with racism, sexism, classism, and heterosexism (Grote, Bledsoe, Wellman, & Brown, 2007; Kwate, Valdimarsdottir, Guevarra, & Bovbjerg, 2003; Thomas, Witherspoon, & Speight, 2008). Black women report experiences of alienation, isolation, and denigration in association with their identified "isms" (Boyd-Franklin, 1991; Jones & Warner, 2011; C. B. Williams, 2005; Woods-Giscombé & Black, 2010). In an effort to manage stressors associated with their complex and demanding roles as well as their experiences of gender oppression, many women seek out mental health services that are empowerment focused and women centered. Feminist therapy is one such mental health service.

Feminist therapy is the practice of mental health informed by feminist political philosophies and analysis, and incorporates the psychology of women (Miller, 1986), developmental research (Gilligan, 1982), cognitive–behavioral techniques (Worell & Remer, 2003), multicultural awareness (Comas-Díaz & Greene, 1994), and social activism (Brown, 2010) in a systematic platform. The principles of feminist therapy assert that social inequality between genders is a root cause of mental health problems among women (Greene, 1997). Feminist therapy acknowledges that sex roles, female socialization, and women's minority status in a patriarchal society are sources of psychological difficulties. The historical backdrop of the feminist movement and the different waves of feminism provide a context for understanding how feminist therapy has been adapted in the field of mental health.

With women gaining voices and visibility through their activism in the 1960s, feminists began to challenge existing societal gender biases. As feminist therapy began to evolve, the civil rights movement and the Stonewall rebellion also were forthcoming, all combining to form an atmosphere that triggered change in human rights (Marecek, 2001). Feminists formed unique avenues of advocating for their agenda through activism, politicization, and consciousness-raising. In fact, early models of feminist therapy were patterned after consciousness raising groups, which provided a vehicle for exploring women's experiences of sexism and discrimination, as well as the creation of a platform for social and political activism (Enns, 2012).

In the early 1970s feminist therapy emerged as one of the responses to second wave feminism, which among many issues was focused on the guaranteeing of economic and social equality and full humanity, regardless of gender. The imbalance of power and its impact on the behavior of men and women has served as the focus of traditional feminist therapy (Cammarat & Larsen, 1988; Marecek & HareMustin, 1991). Feminist therapists began to draw attention to the damage women suffered in traditional, patriarchal structures of the therapeutic process. They criticized the imbalance of power in the male therapist–female client relationship, in which the man is seen as the expert and the woman must conform to patriarchal norms of gender roles. Feminist therapists argued that a woman's self-concept, identity formation, and overall emotional well-being were overlooked or ignored in previously established therapeutic models. As an alternative, they advocated for gender-neutral and sensitive approaches that put gender and power at the center of the therapeutic process (Brown, 2010). For this reason, many feminist therapists are also engaged in social activism to affect policies and structures outside of the therapy office to improve the quality of life for all citizens.

Whereas feminist therapy has become a viable treatment option for women and men, having risen dramatically from receiving almost no attention to a position of considerable popularity, of concern is the lack of attention to the integrated realities of black women in the practice of and research on feminist therapy. Scholars argue that feminist therapies have historically excluded and devalued the experiences of black women and that there have been misguided interpretations of their realities at the conceptual, theoretical, and methodological levels (Brown, 2010; Fulani, 1988; Jackson & Greene, 2003). In particular, feminist therapies have been criticized for their limited focus on the cultural context of white middle-class women and the exclusion of women of color and other oppressed groups such as black women (Brown, 2010; ComasDíaz, 2011; C. B. Williams, 2000). The argument is that these practices often reinforce the same racial discrimination and sexist denigration that have often brought black women into treatment. Hence, we arrive at a place in the 21st century where the field of social work and other mental health fields are faced with the critical task of providing culturally relevant services to women who are routinely ignored by the dominant feminist movement.

A number of black feminist scholars and practitioners have challenged universalizing, hierarchical, and dualistic limitations of feminist therapy to be more inclusive of race, class, and sexual orientation in the development and utilization of black feminist perspectives (Boyd-Franklin, 1991; Fulani, 1988; Greene, 1997; Jackson & Greene, 2003; Mays, 1985; C. B. Williams, 2000). Black feminist therapists adopted an urgent mandate to address all forms of marginalization and discrimination simultaneously, instead of privileging gender issues alone. Furthermore, black feminist therapists advocated for therapeutic processes and methods that reflect the psychological and multiplicative oppressions faced by women within their social—cultural contexts (Sparks & Parker, 2000). These are processes and methods that offer more complex conceptualizations of gender and its intersections of difference and incorporate a fundamental understanding of black women's historical, sociocultural, familial, and developmental heterogeneity.

Such therapeutic methods as outlined by Fulani and black feminist practitioners would not only help black women to reconstruct negative self-images constructed by patriarchal therapeutic ideologies, but also assist them in consciousness-raising regarding their socially constructed identities and to reject socially induced shame and degradation. Hence, the incorporation of culturally specific therapeutic practice perspectives that raise consciousness and foster resilience and empowerment among black women will serve to decrease psychosocial stressors and promote positive coping strategies (Boyd-Franklin, 1991; Greene, 1997; Jones & Ford, 2008; Woods-Giscombé & Black, 2010). With few connections between black feminism and therapy present in the social work practice literature, we suggest that a black feminist perspective may be a useful starting framework for understanding the multiplicative impact of black women's oppression on their psychological well-being.

A crucial component of black feminism is the identification and rectification of gaps that address the life concerns and possible futures of black women; hence the purpose of this article is to address the aforementioned existing gap in the feminist therapy literature. We hope that this article will stimulate more debate and discussion on the mental health status of black women and lead to development of culturally responsive treatment initiatives and policies that place black feminist ideologies at their core.

Literature Review

Black Feminist Thought

Guy-Sheftall's work on black feminist thought (1986, 1995) has informed a black feminist approach to therapy and mental health services. The argument that African American women confront both a "woman question and a race problem" (Cooper, 1892, p. 134) captured the essence of black feminist thought in the 19th century and has reverberated among intellectuals, journalists, activists, writers, educators, artists, and community leaders, both male and female, for generations. Although feminist perspectives have been persistent and important components of the African American literary and intellectual traditions for generations, scholars have focused primarily on its racial overtones. This tendency to ignore long years of political struggle aimed at eradicating the multiple oppressions that black women experience resulted in erroneous notions about the relevance of feminism to the black community during the second wave of the women's movement. Rewriting black history using gender as one category of analysis should render obsolete the notion that feminist thinking is alien to black women or that they have been misguided imitators of white women. An analysis of the feminist activism of black women also suggests the necessity of reconceptualizing women's issues to include sexuality, poverty, racism, imperialism, lynching, welfare, economic exploitation, sterilization abuse, decent housing, and a host of other concerns that generations of black women foregrounded.

Black feminism is not a monolithic, static ideology, and there is diversity among African American feminists, but certain premises are nevertheless constant: (a) black women experience a particular kind of oppression and suffering in the United States—one that is racist, sexist, homophobic, and classist—because of their multiple identities and their limited access to economic resources; (b) this "multiple jeopardy" has meant that the problems, concerns, and needs of black women are different in many ways from those of both white women and black men; (c) black women must struggle for black liberation and gender equality simultaneously; (d) there is no inherent contradiction in the struggle to eradicate sexism and racism as well as the other "isms" that plague the human community, such as classism and heterosexism; and (e) black women's commitment to the liberation of black people and women is profoundly rooted in their lived experience.

In 1977, the Combahee River Collective, a group of mainly black lesbian feminists such as Audre Lorde, Pat Parker, Margaret Sloan, and Barbara

Smith released a statement that attempted to define black feminism, as they saw it (first published in Eisenstein, 1978). The collective's work was grounded in a feminist perspective, addressed homophobia, and called for sisterhood among black women of diverse sexual orientations. A fundamental belief of theirs was that "black women are inherently valuable and that our liberation is a necessity not as an adjunct to somebody else's but because of our need as human persons for autonomy" (Eisenstein, 1978, p. 2). Furthermore, they argued that sexual politics are as pervasive in black women's lives as are the politics of class and race, and because race, class, and gender oppression often operated simultaneously in black women's lives, it is often difficult to separate them. Underscoring their affinity with black men, however, they felt linked to them in their common struggle against racism at the same time that they felt that black women must often struggle with black men over the issue of sexism.

Collins's (1990) landmark *Black Feminist Thought* identified the fusion of activism and theory as its distinguishing characteristic and analyzed the core themes outlined by Guy-Sheftall (1995). These core themes of analysis are identified by Collins as (a) the interlocking of race, class, and gender oppression in black women's personal, domestic, and work lives; (b) the necessity of re-creating positive self-definitions and rejecting denigrating, stereotypical, and externally imposed controlling images (mammy, matriarch, welfare mother, whore), both within and without the black community; and (c) the need for active struggle to resist oppression and realize individual and group empowerment (Collins, 1990). The Collins text would further establish, along with Bambara's (1970) *The Black Woman* and hooks's (1999) *Ain't I a Woman,* a continuous black feminist intellectual tradition going back to the publication of Cooper's (1892) *A Voice from the South.*

Black Women and Mental Health: Service Needs and Utilization Issues

Over the past two decades, the importance of culturally congruent services has gained support from federal initiatives that have focused on advancing research that addresses racial and ethnic minority health and mental health disparities. Specifically, these strategies have included career development programs for underrepresented groups; strategic plans; requirements for enrolling minorities in clinical trials; and, most recently, the establishment of the National Center on Minority Health and Health Disparities, which has recently been renamed the National Institute on Minority Health and Health Disparities. The salience of these initiatives for improving services for black women is underscored by epidemiologic data about the disproportionate burden of stress-related illnesses, such as cardiovascular disease, depression, and anxiety (Artinian, Washington, Flack, Hockman, & Jen, 2006; Grote et al., 2007; Kwate et al., 2003; Thomas et al., 2008). However, when black women seek out professional mental health services, research indicates that they are less likely than white women to obtain professional care (Alegría et al., 2002; Jackson & Greene, 2003); they are more likely than others to have reached a crisis point; are more likely to be misdiagnosed (Carrington, 2006); and may delay or withdraw from treatment early because their ethnic, cultural, or gender needs go unrecognized or mistreated (Blazer, Hybels, Simonsick, & Hanlon, 2000). One consistently highlighted shortcoming is that therapeutic treatment models are culturally inappropriate or inadequate to meet their specific needs (Greene, 2000; Jones & Warner, 2011). Alegría and colleagues (2002) argued that mental health systems and treatment models are based on racist patriarchal concepts of mental health, and new models must be developed to accommodate the pressing needs of women across all racial backgrounds. The treatment and prevention of psychosocial distress among black women requires practitioners to make use of strategies that are based on culturally congruent, positive mental health paradigms that stress the strengths of the clients and recognize the deficits in the environment (Jones & Warner, 2011; Thomas et al., 2008; Woods-Giscombé & Black, 2010).

The field of social work has progressively given attention to the needs of diverse groups through the cross-cultural practice literature, with the intention of rethinking practice frameworks and adapting existing practice models to serve women and people of color (Comas-Díaz, 2011; Lum, 2010; Sue & Sue, 2013). In short, cross-cultural practice efforts equip practitioners with cultural knowledge about race, gender, and class aimed at increasing cultural literacy to improve the level of understanding that mental health practitioners bring to their work with clients from different cultures (Husband, 2000). Although this attention is a step in the direction toward cultural sensitivity, it overlooks the importance of developing and relying on practice interventions that reflect the lived experiences of black women.

Black Feminisms as an Emerging Mental Health Treatment Perspective

The emphases on black women's historical struggles, the "personal is political," and on empowerment and social change have been at the core of black feminist theoretical frameworks. These principles represent themes that emerge from black feminist literature, research, and the lived experiences of black women in the United States and resonate with the work of black feminist practitioners in the field (Greene, 1997; Jones, 2008; Vaz, 2005; C. B. Williams, 2005). Black feminist therapists question the application of traditional mental health theories and methods applied to black women, positing that the approaches lack congruence with their life experiences. Black feminist therapeutic perspectives are offered as an alternative to traditional mental health treatment that often views black women as "other" and whiteness, maleness, heterosexuality, and middle-class status as the norm, which resulted in biased psychological frameworks, perspectives that consistently fail to acknowledge experiences that differ from dominant patriarchal perspectives (Jackson & Greene, 2003). According to Comas-Díaz (2011), a feminist therapist must have an understanding of the culture of each of his or her clients as well as knowledge regarding gender role standards for members of that cultural group and should adapt techniques accordingly. This perspective recognizes different ways of seeing black women's reality from a positive standpoint and helps to forge a greater understanding of their strengths, resilience, and struggles. The use of black feminism as a philosophy in therapy intentionally acts as a strategy that gets to the heart of the inequalities suffered by black women.

Black feminist practitioners and scholars note that the use of these perspectives in therapy appreciates and reflects an integrated analysis of race, gender, sexuality, class, and other "isms," offering a lens through which to view the multiplicity and simultaneity of oppressions and emotional struggles that black American women experience (Bowleg, Huang, Brooks, Black, & Burkholder, 2003; Coleman, 2006; Collins, 1990; Eisenstein, 1978; Jackson & Greene, 2003; King, 1988; Thomas et al., 2008). They advocate for theories and practice interventions that assist black women in sorting out their personal struggles from the structural constraints of racism, sexism, classism, and homophobia and move from models of pathology to those of risk, reliance, and wellness. Postulating that therapeutic interventions developed from a black feminist perspective must help black women recognize how the internalization of stereotypes and negative notions of black womanhood contribute to their negative psychological symptoms (for example, depression, anxiousness, low self-esteem, and decreased sense of mastery and control) (Jackson & Greene, 2003; Jones & Warner, 2011; King, 1988; C. B. Williams, 2005). This unique form of therapy allows black women to be liberated from internal psychological distress and societal barriers and promotes skills that assist them to be self-actualizing in their goals, their willpower, and their way power.

Black feminist therapeutic analysis and interventions of race, gender, and class role analysis; sexual identity; consciousness raising; exploration of power imbalances; social action; and empowerment are key modes of change in the therapeutic process (Greene, 1997; D. S. Williams, 1993). In working therapeutically with black women, it is essential for practitioners to help them, regardless of the presenting problem, to build skills to resist negative cultural messages and thereby alleviate their psychiatric symptoms. That may include assisting black women in identifying gender role expectations and messages that influence their attitudes and behaviors, teaching constructive assertiveness and active coping skills to assist in overcoming perceived barriers, assisting in understanding how societal and political forces affect their mental health dilemmas, and encouraging social and political action against all oppressions. Following this logic, black women's greater likelihood of suffering from mental health difficulties may be an inevitable result of the many conflicts these women face as they navigate multiple roles and identities in a patriarchal system of domination. According to C. B. Williams (2005), black women's depression and other difficulties should be seen as an outgrowth of multiple conflicting socially defined roles and identities and that a true understanding of the nature of depression in this population is best gained from reshaping the therapist's views from one of pathology to one of risk and resilience.

Explanations and efficacy as to how black feminist perspectives are integrated into the ongoing dialogue of therapy are limited; however, there are numerous conceptual examples of black feminist thought in the context of healing and psychological recovery that appear in the mental health literature (Boyd-Franklin, 2010; Comas-Díaz & Greene, 1994; Greene, Boyd-Franklin, & Spivey, 2013; Guy-Sheftall, 1995; Jackson & Greene, 2003; Jones & Warner, 2011; Taylor, 1998). Specifically, practice frameworks regarding the utility of black feminist perspectives in mental health and substance abuse treatment can be found in the literature. To highlight a few, Roberts, Jackson, and Carlton LaNey (2000) discussed the use of a black feminist therapeutic approach that assists drug-abusing black women to explore the negative controlling images of "mammy," "matriarch," "welfare mother," and "Jezebel." Using consciousness raising, a key construct of black feminist perspectives in treatment, women were able to gain an understanding of these negative societal images and participate in a redefinition of the self as a source of empowerment in recovery. In a similar but independently developed framework, C. B. Williams (2000) presented black feminist therapeutic techniques of consciousness raising and empowerment to assist women in drawing connections between their everyday life difficulties and the historical experience of African American women. She advocated for an integrative approach to working with black women through an examination of the psychological, social, and cultural context surrounding their search for wellness. Using the superwoman schema and strong black woman script frameworks, Woods-Giscombé and Black (2010) focused on black women's unique stress experiences affected by "strength" obligations (for example, emotional suppression, extraordinary caregiving, and self-care postponement), suggesting the use of culturally derived mind–body interventions that emphasize a gender-role analysis, another key construct of black feminism. Woods-Giscombé and Black offered an analysis of socially and culturally ingrained gender roles and reframed strength from a stance of weakness to a place of empowerment. Jones and Warner (2011) examined the efficacy of an evidence-based, culturally relevant intervention grounded in black feminism and psychosocial competence perspectives to reduce depressive and stress symptomatology; decrease externality of locus of control; and increase active coping among black women in shelter, substance abuse, and mental health programs.

The following vignette is offered as an example of the use of a black feminist perspective in a group therapy program titled Claiming Your Connection. Key black feminist features of the intervention are (a) the incorporation of accurate cultural knowledge and attention to the multiple cultural influences of black women's mental health, (b) systematic focus on and discussion of cultural themes to enhance engagement, and (c) discussion of the psychological implications of oppression (racism, sexism, classism, heterosexism) to heighten black women's awareness of psychosocial dynamics that often contribute to depression and psychosocial stressors.

Case Vignette

Lola is a 32 year old African American woman, a mother of two, separated from her spouse; she recently lost her job as a vice president of development at a technology firm. At intake she stated, "I committed myself to my job, I gave them three miserable years of my life, and they told me in a five minute meeting that they were moving in a different direction." She reported poor sleeping and eating patterns, tearfulness, decreased energy, and decreased concentration over the past few months.

At the start of the group, Lola rarely participated in group conversations without prompting and did not offer feedback to the other participants. The third session of the group program focused on the role of stress and coping in the lives of African American women. During this session the group leader provided a definition of psychological stress. The group leader then asked the members to identify their emotional and physical reactions to stress. The group members listed several reactions, such as "I've lost my patience," "I can't breathe," "I am overwhelmed," "I am exhausted," "I get irritable," "I am eating too much," and "I'm having a nervous breakdown." The group leader asked members to identify possible stressors related to them as black women. Lola abruptly stated,

> Since our first meeting y'all been whining about how your boss treats you, you're always letting this shit get in your way, you'll need to bulldoze down your issues and the people in your way. You have no control over these negative things that happen.

Group members glared at Lola, with disappointment and annoyance. A participant responded, "If you were perfect, you wouldn't be here." The group immediately responded with agreement.

This statement opened up the floor for Lola to engage in further disclosure. Lola stated, "Have you ever been in love with a man who didn't love you, so you looked for love in your work? Have you ever been stripped of your hard work and dedication, and not one soul to confide in? When you experience these things, come see me." Group members listened attentively as Lola told her story, filled with rejection and pain. Lola's story was rooted in the unfortunate internalized tradition that says that African American women must be "strong" in the face of adversity and accept life's ups and downs as the products of their unalterable destiny. In breaking the group's silence and providing support for Lola's story, the group leader asserted,

> Societal attitudes and biases can negatively influence a person's self-esteem and limit opportunities, resulting in a sense of powerlessness, suffering, and psychological symptoms. An important part of our work here is identifying our strengths and positive ways in which we can cope with daily life adversities. One way is through support of one another, so we'll start that here. Let's back up and identify the external stressors that we are reacting to, and in turn cause us pain.

As harmful beliefs and judgments are identified, and feelings of anger and disappointment are worked through, greater self-confidence, acceptance, and satisfaction in life are experienced both personally and in the relationships between group members. The group leader concluded by saying, "We must work towards liberating ourselves from deep sadness, using this group as a forum to become connected with our feelings and tell our stories. If you can tell your story, we can help each of you." By the end of the session, the group members began to understand, identify with, and support Lola. Lola became less defensive and more open to receiving feedback from the group for the remainder of the program. The support offered by the group gave Lola and the other members tangible tools for addressing such issues as stress and internalized oppression.

Conclusion

As underscored here, it is clear that little inquiry exists on feminist therapy and black women in mental health treatment. Just as feminism has been compelled to develop a more inclusive discourse, acknowledging the full array of diversity among women, and the impacts of oppression on women, mental health therapy will need to similarly evolve. A black feminist perspective challenges the prevailing notion in therapy that gender is the only salient category of oppression and insists that experiences of white women cannot be generalized in the development of therapeutic treatment strategies for black women. The challenge in the 21st century is to put black feminist theory into action in mental health practice.

A black feminist perspective reflects an integrated analysis of race, gender, sexuality, and class in therapy and offers possibilities for working with black women and other women of color from a holistic framework. It offers practitioners a useful method of providing services from a strengths-based perspective, in contrast to traditional models regarding the prognostic course and treatment of trauma, stress, and coping among black women. An important goal of practitioners is to attend to both individual and societal stressors, especially those influenced and exacerbated by experiences of oppression, in an effort to promote positive mental health outcomes among black women. These goals posit a practical perspective for assisting black women in the healing of psychological and social damages of racism, sexism, and other forms of oppression that often obstruct self-actualizing behaviors. When this progress is made, feminist therapeutic interventions may become more useful in assisting black women to heal and recover.

References

Alegría, M., Canino, G., Ríos, R., Vera, M., Calderón, J., Rusch, D., & Ortega, A. N. (2002). Inequalities in use of specialty mental health services among Latinos, African Americans, and nonwhite Latinos. *Psychiatric Services*, 53, 1547–1555.

Artinian, N. T., Washington, O. G., Flack, J. M., Hockman, E. M., & Jen, K.L.C. (2006). Depression, stress, and blood pressure in urban African American women. *Progress in Cardiovascular Nursing*, 21, 68–75.

Bambara, T. C. (1970). *The black woman: An anthology.* New York: Washington Square Press.

Blazer, D., Hybels, C., Simonsick, E., & Hanlon, J. T. (2000). Sedative, hypnotic, and antianxiety medication use in an aging cohort over ten years: A racial comparison. *Journal of the American Geriatrics Society*, 48, 1073–1079.

Bowleg, L., Huang, J., Brooks, K., Black, A., & Burk holder, G. (2003). Triple jeopardy and beyond: Multiple minority stress and resilience among black lesbians. *Journal of Lesbian Studies*, 7, 87–108.

Boyd-Franklin, N. (1991). Recurrent themes in the treatment of AfricanAmerican women in group psychotherapy. *Women & Therapy*, 11(2), 25–40.

Boyd-Franklin, N. (2010). Incorporating spirituality and religion into the treatment of African American clients. Counseling Psychologist, 38, 976–1000.

Brown, L. S. (2010). *Feminist therapy.* Washington, DC: American Psychological Association.

Cammarat, L. P., & Larsen, C. C. (1988). Feminist frameworks for psychotherapy.In M. A. Dutton Douglas & L. E. Walker (Eds.), *Feminist psycho therapies: Integration of feminist systems* (pp. 12–36). Norwood, NJ: Ablex Publishing Corporation.

Carrington, C. H. (2006). Clinical depression in African American women: Diagnoses, treatment, and research. Journal of Clinical Psychology, 62, 779–791.

Coleman, M. A. (2006). Must I be a womanist? *Journal of Feminist Studies in Religion*, 22, 85–96.

Collins, P. H. (1990). *Black feminist thought: Knowledge, consciousness, and the politics of empowerment.* Boston: Unwin Hyman.

Comas-Díaz, L. (2011). Multicultural approaches to psychotherapy. In J. Norcross, D. Freadheim, & G. I. Vandenboss (Eds.), *History of psychotherapy: Continuity and change* (2nd ed., pp. 243–267). Washington, DC: American Psychological Association.

Comas-Díaz, L., & Greene, B. (1994). Overview: Gender and ethnicity in the healing process. In L. Comas Díaz & B. Greene (Eds.), *Women of color: Integrating ethnic and gender identities in psychotherapy* (pp. 185-193). New York: Guilford Press.

Cooper, A. J. (1892). *A voice from the South: By a black woman of the South.* Xenia, OH: Aldine Printing House.

Eisenstein, Z. (Ed.). (1978). The Combahee River Collective statement. In *Capitalist patriarchy and the case for socialist feminism* (pp. 362-371). New York: Monthly Review Press.

Enns, C. Z. (2012). Feminist approaches to counseling. In E. M. Altmaier & J. C. Hansen (Eds.), *Oxford handbook of counseling psychology* (pp. 434-459). New York: Oxford University Press.

Fulani, L. (1988). *The psychopathology of everyday racism and sexism.* New York: Haworth Press.

Gilligan, C. (1982). *In a different voice: Psychological theory and women's development.* Cambridge, MA: Harvard University Press.

Greene, B. (1997). Psychotherapy with African American women: Integrating feminist and psychodynamic models. *Smith College Studies in Social Work,* 67, 299-322.

Greene, B. (2000). African American lesbian and bisexual women. *Journal of Social Issues,* 56, 239-249.

Greene, B., Boyd-Franklin, N., & Spivey, P. B. (2013). African American lesbians and gay men in couples relationships: Threats to intimacy and considerations in couples psychotherapy. In K. M. Helm & J. Carlson (Eds.), *Love, intimacy, and the African American couple.* New York: Routledge.

Grote, N. K., Bledsoe, S. E., Wellman, J., & Brown, C. (2007). Depression in African American and white women with low incomes: The role of chronic stress. *Social Work in Public Health,* 23, 59-88.

Guy-Sheftall, B. (1986). Remembering Sojourner Truth: On black feminism. *Catalyst,* 1, 54-57.

Guy-Sheftall, B. (1995). *Words of fire: An anthology of African American feminist thought.* New York: New Press.

hooks, b. (1999). *Ain't I a woman: Black women and feminism.* Boston: South End Press.

Husband, C. (2000). Recognising diversity and developing skills: The proper role of transcultural communication. *European Journal of Social Work,* 3, 225-234.

Jackson, L. C., & Greene, B. A. (2003). Review of psychotherapy with African American women: Innovations in psychodynamic perspectives and practice. *Psychoanalytic Quarterly,* 72, 524-526.

Jones, L. V. (2008). Preventing depression: Culturally relevant group work with black women. *Research on Social Work Practice,* 18, 626-634.

Jones, L. V., & Ford, B. (2008). Depression in African American women: Application of a psychosocial competence practice framework. *Affilia,* 23, 134-143.

Jones, L. V., & Warner, L. A. (2011). Evaluating culturally responsive group work with black women. *Research on Social Work Practice,* 21, 737-746.

King, D. K. (1988). Multiple jeopardy, multiple consciousness: The context of a black feminist ideology. *Signs,* pp. 42-72.

Kwate, N.O.A., Valdimarsdottir, H. B., Guevarra, J. S., & Bovbjerg, D. H. (2003). Experiences of racist events are associated with negative health consequences for African American women. *Journal of the National Medical Association*, 95, 450-460.

Lum, D. (2010). *Culturally competent practice: A framework for understanding diverse groups and justice issues* (4th ed.). Pacific Grove, CA: Cengage Learning.

Marecek, J. (2001). Disorderly constructs: Feminist frameworks for clinical psychology. In R. K. Unger (Ed.), *Handbook of the psychology of women and gender* (pp. 303-316). New York: John Wiley & Sons.

Marecek, J., & HareMustin, R. T. (1991). A short history of the future: Feminism and clinical psychology. *Psychology of Women Quarterly*, 15, 521-536.

Mays, V. M. (1985). Black women and stress: Utilization of self-help groups for stress reduction. *Women & Therapy*, 4(4), 67-79.

Miller, J. B. (1986). *Toward a new psychology of women.* Boston: Beacon Press.Roberts, A., Jackson, M. S., & CarltonLaNey, I. (2000). Revisiting the need for feminism and Afrocentric theory when treating African American female substance abusers. *Journal of Drug Issues*, 30, 901-918.

Sparks, E. E., & Parker, A. H. (2000). The integration of feminism and multiculturalism: Ethical dilemmas at the border. In M. M. Brabeck (Ed.), *Practicing feminist ethics in psychology* (pp. 203-224). Washington, DC: American Psychological Association.

Sue, D. W., & Sue, D. (2013). *Counseling the culturally diverse: Theory & practice* (4th ed.). New York: John Wiley & Sons.

Taylor, J. Y. (1998). Womanism: A methodologic framework for African American women. *Advances in Nursing Science*, 21, 53-64.

Thomas, A. J., Witherspoon, K. M., & Speight, S. L. (2008). Gendered racism, psychological distress, and coping styles of African American women. *Cultural Diversity and Ethnic Minority Psychology*, 14, 307-314.

Vaz, K. M. (2005). Reflecting team group therapy and its congruence with feminist principles: A focus on African American women. *Women & Therapy*, 28(2), 65-75.

Williams, C. B. (2000). African American women, Afrocentrism and feminism: Implications for therapy. *Women & Therapy*, 22(4), 1-16.

Williams, C. B. (2005). Counseling African American women: Multiple identities—multiple constraints. *Journal of Counseling & Development*, 83, 278-283.

Williams, D. S. (1993). *Sisters in the wilderness: The challenge of womanist godtalk.* Maryknoll, NY: Orbis Books.

Woods-Giscombé, C. L., & Black, A. R. (2010). Mindbody interventions to reduce risk for health disparities related to stress and strength among African American women: The potential of mindfulnessbased stress reduction, loving kindness, and the NTU therapeutic framework. *Complementary Health Practice Review*, 15, 115-131.

Worell, J., & Remer, P. (2003). *Feminist perspectives in therapy empowering diverse women* (2nd ed.). New York: John Wiley & Sons.

Part IV

HBCUs

16. Black Women and Higher Education: Spelman and Bennett Colleges Revisited (1982)

No history of women's education in America would be complete without the Spelman and Bennett stories. However, the histories of higher education for women usually focus narrowly on the "seven sisters." Such authoritative treatises as Thomas Woody's classic *A History of Women's Education in the United States,* Louise Shutz Boas' *Women's Education Begins: The Rise of Women's Colleges,* and Mabel Newcomer's *A Century of Higher Education for American Women,* are similar in their failure to include even a footnote on Spelman and Bennett Colleges, the nation's oldest and best-known colleges for Black women.

Despite increased interest during the past decade in a number of topics relating to women, including women's education, the history of higher education for Black women has been grossly ignored by those documenting the history of education for women in America.[1] Recently, however, Patricia Bell Scott, in a ground-breaking article entitled "Schoolin' 'Respectable' Ladies of Color ...," has analyzed in a cogent manner the most critical issues surrounding the history of Black women's higher education. She also traces the development of educational institutions for Black women from the early efforts of Myrtilla Miner, a white woman who established in 1851 in Washington, D.C., a teachers' training school for Black girls (later known as District of Columbia Teachers Colleges-Miner Branch and finally became part of the University of the District of Columbia), to the emergence of Spelman and Bennett Colleges. Similarly, a bibliographical essay on academic women in the South, which appears in *Stepping Off the Pedestal* (See Bibliography) reviews the major sources available on the history of higher education for women and includes a section on Black women.[2] However, the history of the Black woman's contribution to education in general remains to be written, despite the numerous primary and secondary sources now available to scholars.

This article will highlight the impact that Spelman and Bennett Colleges have had on educational opportunities for Black women. There will also be a brief discussion of selected Spelman and Bennett alumnae and their roles in the larger community. Special attention is given, near the end, to Dr. Willa Player (Bennett's first woman president), who still has the distinction of being the only Black woman to have headed a Black woman's college.[3] And, finally, the article contains an extensive bibliography which includes material that focuses entirely on Black women and higher education or that contains information on the subject.[4]

Though the majority of Black women have been educated in co-educational institutions,[5] single-sex colleges for Black women, all of which have been located in the South, have provided unique educational experiences for those women who have chosen through the years to attend Bennett, Spelman, Barber-Scotia, and Huston-Tillotson University. Bennett, founded as a co-educational school in 1873 in the basement of St. Matthew's Methodist Episcopal Church in Greensboro, North Carolina, became a college for women in 1926 mainly as a result of the Women's Home Missionary Society's desire to enlarge its educational program to Black women. Spelman, founded in 1881 by Sophia Packard and Harriet Giles in the basement of Friendship Baptist Church in Atlanta, Georgia, has always been for women only.[6] Barber-Scotia and Huston-Tillotson were initially for women, but later became co-educational.

High on the list of priorities at both institutions has been the training of Black women for leadership roles, though the training of teachers was their earliest mission. The extent to which Spelman and Bennett have been successful in this regard is apparent if one considers only a few of their outstanding alumnae whose roles as policy makers and managers deserve special mention. This very special sisterhood of Spelman and Bennett graduates was certainly nurtured in environments which stressed the importance of Black women serving their communities and the nation. President Florence Read of Spelman alludes to the kind of education that was stressed at both institutions and what was expected of their daughters:

> This must be the spirit that motivates Negro education, particularly the education of Negro women, who must go forth from college and share to the full with their fellows what they have gained. It is not enough that a woman shall become a self-contained, economically independent, and completely rounded individual. Neither is it sufficient that she shall have developed her taste for the good things in life and acquired skills in the arts. If the college has succeeded in its purpose, she will be not only willing but eager to share her gifts and use her newly acquired skills to better the lives of all those within the reach of her influence. And by that strange paradox which is the profoundest truth yet discovered or revealed, it is thus that her own life will reach its richest fulfillment.[7]

A large number of Spelman and Bennett alumnae certainly have lived up to these ideals, and they include: Selena Sloan Butler, who established the first Black parent-teacher association in the country and later founded the

National Congress of Colored Parents and Teachers; Georgia Rooks Dwelle, founder of Dwelle Infirmary, an obstetrical hospital in Atlanta, which was the first of its kind for Black women in the South; Ludie Clay Andrews, founder of the training School for Colored Nurses at Grady Memorial Hospital; Dorothy Brown, a graduate of Meharry Medical College and a practicing surgeon in Nashville; Atty. Marian Wright Edelman, founder of the Children's Defense Fund of Washington, D.C., and the first Black woman to head Spelman's Board of Trustees; Maxine Atkins Smith, executive secretary of the Memphis branch of the NAACP and a key member of the Board of Education for the Memphis city schools; Dr. Eleanor Ison Franklin, first woman to obtain a top-level administrative post at the Howard University School of Medicine when she was appointed Associate Dean for Administration; Thelma Davidson Adair, professor of education at Queens College in New York, and the first woman to serve as president of Black Presbyterians United; and finally, Atty. Glendora McIlwain Putnam, a member of the Board of Trustees of the Boston Conservatory of Music, a member of the Massachusetts Bar, the Federal Bar, and the Supreme Court Bar, and former chair of the Massachusetts Commission Against Discrimination.

Though women's colleges traditionally have been less resistant than coed colleges to placing women in high-level administrative posts and in hiring women faculty, only recently have Spelman and Bennett (though to a lesser degree) begun to practice what they preached in terms of placing Black women in leadership positions on their campuses, though they certainly always encouraged their students to seek such positions in the larger society. It was not until the mid-seventies that a woman became the dean of the college at both institutions, even though females had constituted well over half the faculty for a much longer period.[8] At Spelman, all the division chairs presently are Black women while Bennett has two male and two female division chairs. Bennett's top-level administrative staff consists of only two women (which includes the President, Dean of the College, Director of Planning, Dean of Student Affairs, Director of Development, Business Manager, Special Consultant to the President, and Registrar) consists of only two women, while Spelman's top administrative staff (which includes similar positions) consists of primarily women, all of whom are Black. President Donald Stewart must be credited for the increase in the number of Black women as high-level administrators at Spelman.

Black female college presidents, even at Black women's colleges, have been extraordinarily rare, which reflects the persistent male control of Black institutions generally. When Dr. Willa Player became president of Bennett College in 1955 (after having been a teacher of French, director of admissions and vice president in charge of instruction there), she became the first Black woman to head a college for Black women. Spelman has been headed by several white women and two Black men.[9] During her almost eleven years of service to Bennett, Dr. Player, a nationally known educator, demonstrated superb leadership skills, and during her tenure Bennett was admitted to membership in 1957 to the Southern Association of Colleges and Schools, being one of the first fifteen Black four-year colleges to be admitted.

Though some would argue that separate colleges for women are presently an anachronism, it seems reasonable to assume that Spelman and Bennett will continue to provide for the special educational needs of Black women in ways that co-educational institutions do not. Both institutions, for example, are in the forefront of curriculum development in women's studies on Black college campuses, mainly as a result of their historic commitment to the education of women, especially Black women. Bennett has an interdisciplinary women's studies program which includes a number of women's studies courses and a wide range of informal programs and seminars that explore the female experience. Spelman has recently established an interdisciplinary women's studies minor, though the College's involvement in sponsoring seminars and conferences on issues relevant to Black women is considerably older. Even as early as 1944, for example, Spelman was the site of a "Conference on Current Problems and Programs in the Higher Education of Negro Women," during which representatives of several Black colleges focused on directions for the post-war education of Black women.

Bennett's Women for Leadership Roles in International Service is just one of the newly established programs at the College which illustrates its continual efforts to provide for the special needs of women. Similarly, the newly established Women's Research and Resource Center at Spelman (the first of its kind on a Black college campus) is the most recent example of the College's commitment to the educational development of Black women. The Center will conduct research on Black women, sponsor outreach activities to women in the community, and develop courses in women's studies, especially Black women's studies. Both colleges have also seen a need for collecting books and other material on Black women; the development of the Afro-American Women's Collection at Bennett was initiated during the early 1940s and the Margaret Nabrit Curry Collection on Women opened as part of the Quarles

Library at Spelman in 1970. Both colleges also have an impressive archive, which is indispensable for the scholar who would chronicle the history of Black women's education in this country.

The Spelman and Bennett families continue to affirm the value of separate colleges for women and recognize the unique role that Black women's colleges must play in the continuing saga of women's education in America. Spelman and Bennett are indeed very special places for Black women to pursue an education. As President Donald Stewart observed in his inaugural address at Spelman:

> . . . Spelman and institutions like it provide a unique environment which is supportive of female leadership roles in our society . . . Coed schools . . . tend to be male dominated. It is the presence of high-status women faculty and administrators in women's colleges that help develop strong identities and positive self-images on the part of female students.[10]

Notes

[1] Exceptions to this generalization would be the pioneering work of Jeanne Noble (see Bibliography) and more recently Patricia Bell Scott (see Bibliography), as well as a number of graduate students, primarily Black women, who have chosen the subject of Black women's education for theses and doctoral dissertations (see Bibliography).

[2] In addition to exploring issues involved in studying various aspects of the higher education for Black women in the South, this section of the article also suggests a series of questions to which future scholars might address themselves.

[3] Barber-Scotia in Concord, North Carolina, which was founded for Black women in 1867, has had a Black female president but only after the college became co-educational. Two historically Black co-educational colleges have also been headed by Black women---Bethune-Cookman (founded by Mary McLeod Bethune, who was president from 1904-1942) and Frelinghuysen University of Washington, D.C., (whose president was Anna J. Cooper from 1930 to 1941).

[4] I was assisted by Eleanor Hinton Hoytt, assistant professor at Atlanta University in the School of Library and Information Studies, in the preparation of the Bibliography. Ms. Hoytt and I also co-authored the section on Black women in the bibliographical essay mentioned earlier and which appears in *Stepping Off the Pedestal: Academic Women in the South.*

[5] The first Black woman to receive a college degree, Mary Jane Patterson, also attended a co-educational institution, Oberlin College, from which she graduated in 1862. Since it was more economical to educate Black men and women together, because of a limited number of resources available for the establishment of Black institutions after Emancipation, single-sex institutions were atypical in the Black community.

[6] Florence Read's history of Spelman College and *Spelman: A Centennial Celebration* (see Bibliography) are the only published accounts of a Black women's college. No formal history of Bennett College exists. Willa Player presents the needs and experiences of Bennett's graduates in her 1948 Columbia Teachers College dissertation (see Bibliography).

[7] "The Place of the Women's College in the Pattern of Negro Education," *Opportunity,* 15 (September 1937), 270.

[8] Before 1920, the majority of teachers at Spelman were white females, though there were a few Blacks. During the 1920s and 1930s, however, Blacks became more prominent on the faculty. In 1925, Margaret Nabrit Curry, a 1924 Spelman graduate, became the first Black to join the College faculty.

[9] Following the announcement of Dr. Donald Stewart's appointment to the Spelman presidency in 1976, dramatic efforts were taken by some students and faculty to block the appointment of a man to succeed Dr. Albert Manley. It was felt that the time had come for Spelman to have its first Black female president. See G. O'Brien, "Five Campuses Hit by Protest," *The Chronicle of Higher Education,* May 3, 1976, p. 4.

[10] *Spelman Messenger,* November 1976.

Black Women and Higher Education: Selected Bibliography

Books

Alexander, William T. "Women's Higher Education," in *History of the Colored Race in America,* 1887, reprinted by Negro Universities Press, 1968.

Brawley, James P. *Two Centuries of Methodist Concern: Bondage, Freedom and Education of Black People.* New York: Vantage Press, 1974.

Brown, Hugh Victor. *A History of the Education of Negroes in North Carolina.* Raleigh: Irving Swain Press, 1961.

Burroughs, Nannie. *Making Their Mark.* Washington, D.C. The National Training School for Women and Girls, n.d.

Carroll, Constance, "Three's a Crowd: The Dilemma of the Black Woman in Higher Education" in *But Some of Us Are Brave,* ed. Gloria Hull et al. Old Westbury, New York: Feminist Press, 1982.

Culp, D. W. *Twentieth Century Negro Literature,* Toronto: J. L. Nichols and Company, 1902.

Daniel, Sadie Iola. *Women Builders.* Washington, D.C.: Associated Publishers, 1970.

Dannett, S. *Profiles of Negro Womanhood.* Vol. 1, Chicago: Educational Heritage, 1966.

Fletcher, R. A. *A History of Oberlin College.* Vol. II. Ohio: Oberlin College, 1943.

Flexner, Eleanor. *A Century of Struggle.* Cambridge: Howard University Press, 1959.

Fuller, Edmund. *Prudence Crandall: An Incident of Racism in 19th Century Connecticut,* Wesleyan University Press, 1971.

Furniss, W. Todd and Patricia Graham, eds. *Women in Higher Education. Washington,* D.C.: American Council on Education, 1974

Guy-Sheftall, Beverly and Jo Moore Stewart. *Spelman: A Centennial Celebration.* Delmar, 1981.

Harley, Sharon and Rosalyn Terborg-Penn, eds. *The Afro-American Woman. Port Washington,* New York: Kennikat Press, 1978.

Hutchinson, Louise Daniel. Anna J. Cooper, *A Voice from the South.* Washington: Smithsonian Institution Press, 1981.

Holmes, Dwight Oliver Wendell. *The Evolution of the Negro College.* New York: Bureau of Publications, Teachers College, Columbia University, 1934.

Lerner, Gerda, ed. *Black Women in White America: A Documentary History.* New York: Random House, 1972.

Malcolm, S. et al. *The Double Bind: The Price of Being a Minority Woman in Science.* Washington, D.C.: American Association for the Advancement of Science, 1976.

Montgomery, Winfield Scott. *Historical Sketch of Education for the Colored Race in the District of Columbia,* 1807-1905. Washington, D.C.: Smith Brothers Printers, 1907. National Institute of Education. *Conference on the Educational and Occupational Needs of Black Women.* Washington, D.C.: NIE, 1978.

Noble, Jeanne. *The Negro Woman's College Education.* New York: Columbia University Press, 1956.

O'Connor, Ellen. *Myrtilla Miner: A Memoir and the School for Colored.* Miami: Mnemosyne Publishing Co., Inc., 1969.

Range, Willard. *The Rise and Progress of Negro Colleges in Georgia, 1868-1949.* Athens: University of Georgia Press, 1951.

Read, Florence. *The Story of Spelman College.* Princeton: Princeton University Press, 1961.

Sicherman, Barbara and Carol Hurd, eds. *Notable American Women.* Cambridge: Harvard University Press, 1981.

Silene-Yates, Josephine, "Afro-American Women as Educators," in *Women of Distinction,* ed. Lawson S. Scruggs, 1893.

Spivey, Donald. *Schooling for the New Slavery: Black Industrial Educational, 1868-1915.* Westport, Connecticut: Greenwood Press, 1978.

Stringer, Patricia S. and Irene Thompson. *Stepping Off the Pedestal: Academic Women in the South.* New York: The Modern Language Association of America, 1982.

Sutton, Virginia Ann. *The Early History of Bennett College.* Winston-Salem, N.C.: The Author, 1969.

Washington, Josephine Turpin. "Higher Education for Women" in *Women of Distinction.* ed. Lawson A. Scroggs., 1893.

PERIODICAL LITERATURE

The Belle Ringer. Bennett College. Greensboro, N.C., 1970-

Berry, R. M. F. "Southern Training School for Colored Women," *Good Housekeeping,* 53 (October 1911), 562-63.

Black, Watt. "Education in the South from 1820 to 1860 with Emphasis on the Growth of Teacher Education." *Louisiana Student,* 12 (Winter 1973), 1,617- 29.

Breit, Ruth et al. "A Symposium, Our Living History, Reminiscences of Black Participation in NAWDAC," *Journal of NAWDAC,* (Winter 1979), 3-13.

Bruce, Josephine D., "What Has Education Done for Colored Women?" *Voice of the Negro,* July 1904), 294-98.

Carnegie, M. E. Lancaster. "Nurse Training Becomes Nursing Education at Florida's A & M College." *Journal of Negro Education,* 17 (Spring 1948), 200-04.

Chivers, Walter. "The Founding of Spelman College—A Challenge to Negro Women." *Spelman Messenger,* 59 (May 1943), 7-10.

Cochran, Anne S. "The Development of Teacher Education at Morris Brown College." *Journal of Negro Education,* 16 (Spring 1947), 146-57.

Coles, Anna B. "The Howard University School of Nursing in Historical Perspective." *Journal of the National Medical Association,* 61 (March 1969), 105- 118.

Cooper, Anna J. "The Higher Education of Women," *Southland,* 2 (April 1891), 186-202.

____"The Higher Education of Women," in *A Voice From the South by a Black Woman of the South.* Xenia, Ohio: The Adine Printing House, 1892.

Doughty, R. "The Black Woman in School Administration." *Integrated Education,* (July/August 1977), 34-47.

Eagleston, Oran and Eleanor Bell. "The Values of Negro Women College Students." *Journal of Social Psychology,* 22 (Nov 1945), 149-54.

Friedman, Lawrence J. "Racism and Sexism in Antebellum America: The Prudence Crandall Episode Remembered." *Societas,* 4 (Summer 1974), 211-27. Harper, R. N. "Matrimonial Prospects of Southern College Women." Journal of Heredity, 21 (1930), 29-33.

Jones, David. "The War and the Higher Education of Negro Women." *Journal of Negro Education,* 11 (July 1942), 329-37.

Kittrell, Flemmie. "Home Economics at Bennett College for Women." *Southern Workman,* 60 (1931), 381-84.

Laney, Lucy. "The Burden of the Educated Negro Woman." Paper read at Hampton Negro Conference, No. 3, July, 1899.

Leffall, Dolores C. and Janet I. Sims. "Mary McLeod Bethune—The Educator: Also Including A Selected Annotated Bibliography." *Journal of Negro Education,* 45 (Summer 1976), 342-59.

Marteena, C. "A College for Girls," *Opportunity,* 16 (1938), 306.

Moore, Malvin E. "Mainstreaming Black Women in American Higher Education." *Journal of the Society of Ethnic and Special Studies,* V (Spring-Summer 1981), 61-69.

Noble, Jeanne. "Negro Women Today and Their Education." *Journal of Negro Education,* 26 (Winter 1957), 15-21.

Ostlund, Leonard A. "Occupational Choice Patterns of Negro College Women." *Journal of Negro Education,* 26 (Winter 1957), 86-91.

Parsons, M. "Mount Holyoke of the South." *Home Mission Monthly,* 1908.

Read, Florence, "The Place of the Women's College in the Pattern of Negro Education." *Opportunity,* 15 (September 1937), 267-70.

Scott, Patricia Bell. "Schoolin' "Respectable" Ladies of Color: Issues in the History of Black Women's Higher Education." *Journal of NAWDAC,* Winter 1979, 22-28.

Shadron, Virginia, Eleanor Hinton Hoytt, Margaret Parsons, Barbara Reitt, Beverly Guy-Sheftall et al. "The Historical Perspective: A Bibliographical Essay," in *Stepping off the Pedestal* (op. cit.), pp. 145-170.

Slowe, Lucy. "Higher Education for Negro Women." *Journal of Negro Education,* 2 (July 1933), 352-58.

____"The Colored Girl Enters College: What Shall She Expect?" *Opportunity,* 15 (1939), 276-279.

Small, Miriam R., "Prudence Crandall: Champion of Negro Education." *New England Quarterly,* 17 (December 1944), 506-29.

Spelman Messenger. Atlanta: Spelman College, 1885.

Stevens, B. S. "The Development of Stronger Womanhood." Paper read at Hampton Negro Conference, No. 2, July, 1898.

St. Clair, Sadie, "Myrtilla Miner: Pioneer in the Teacher Education of Negroes." *Journal of Negro History,* 34 (1949), 30-45.

"Talented Negro Women." in *Graduates of Predominantly Negro Colleges, Class of 1964,* by Joseph H. Fichter, Public Health Service Publication No. 1571, p. 77-101.

Tapley, Lucy. "Our Negro Colleges-Spelman Seminary." Opportunity, I (April 1923), 16-17. "Spelman College," *Atlanta Historical Bulletin,* I (May 1930), 38-56.

Taylor, Lois. "Nurse Education at Hampton Institute." *Opportunity,* 22 (Spring 1944): 83, 100.

_____. "Social Action at Bennett College" *Opportunity,* 20 (January 1942), 8-10.

Terrell, Mary C. "History of the High Schools for Negroes in Washington," *Journal of Negro History,* 2 (1917), 252-66.

Thorpe, Jack. "A Plea for Social Justice for the Negro Woman." Occasional papers, No. 2, Negro Society for Historical Research, 1912.

Trenholm, H. Councill. "The Role of the Negro Teacher's College in Post-War Reconstruction." *Journal of Negro Education,* 11 (July 1942), 412-22.

Trigg, Frank. "Bennett College," *Southern Workman,* 5 (February 1926), 84-5.

Wesley, Charles. "Graduate Education for Negroes in Southern Universities." *Harvard Educational Review,* 10 (January 1940), 82-94.

Wormley, S. Smith. "Myrtilla Miner," *Journal of Negro History,* 5 (1920), 448-57.

Theses and Dissertations

Bolton, Ina. "Problems of Negro College Women Graduates." PhD dissertation, Univ. of Calif., 1948.

Butcher, Beatrice. "The Evolution of Negro Women's Schools in the United States." Master's thesis, Howard Univ., 1936.

Carter, Mary M. "The Educational Activities of the National Educational Association for College Women, 1923-1960." Master's thesis, Howard Univ., May, 1962.

Cash, R. Singleton. "A Follow-up Study of the Graduates of Spelman College for the years 1947-58." Master's thesis, Atlanta Univ., 1960.

Cuthbert, Marion. "Education and Marginality: A Study of the Negro Woman College Graduate." PhD dissertation, Teachers College, Columbia Univ. 1942.

Demons, Leona Marie. "Graduates of Spelman, Clark and Morris Brown College Who Have Earned Doctoral Degrees." Master's thesis, Atlanta Univ., 1965.

Gordon, Ruth L. Hill. "Differential Value Patterns of Black and White Women in Higher Education." PhD dissertation, U.S. International Univ., Calif, 1974.

Lane, Cecilia Scott. "The Place of Home Economics in the Curriculum for Women of Houston College for Negroes." Master's thesis, Iowa State College, 1937.

McDowell, Ruth Doris. "Beliefs About Sex Among College Women and the Sources of Their Information." Master's thesis, Atlanta University, 1949.

Patterson, E. H. "The Work of the Methodist Episcopal Church in Establishing and Maintaining Schools in the South for Negroes, 1866-1892." Master's thesis, Univ. of Chicago, 1940.

Payne, N. Joyce. "The Status of Black Women in Education Administration." PhD dissertation, Atlanta Univ., 1975.

Perkins, Linda. "Fanny Jackson Coppin and the Institute for Colored Youth: A Model of Nineteenth-Century Black Female Educational and Community Leadership 1837-1902." PhD dissertation, University of Illinois at Urbana Champaign, 1978.

Phillips, Ollie. "Higher Education for Negro Women in Alabama." Master's thesis, Fisk, 1939.

Player, Willa. "Improving College Education for Women at Bennett College." Teachers College, Columbia, 1948.

Porter, Ruth. "The Health Program for Women Students in Southern Colleges." Master's thesis, Univ. of Calif., 1937.

Robinson, Florence Ann. "A Study of the Occupational Choices of the Negro Women of the Senior Classes in Atlanta Colleges, 1940-1941, in Relation to Possible Employment." Master's thesis, Atlanta Univ., 1941.

Robinson, Omelia. "Contributions of Black American Academic Women to American Higher Education." PhD dissertation, Wayne State, 1978.

Smothers, James. "Socio-Economic Status and Academic Achievement of College Women, North and South." Master's thesis, Fisk, 1947.

Taylor, Annie Alford. "The Current Status of Black Women in American Higher Education Administration." PhD dissertation, Arizona State, 1977.

REFERENCES

Chambers, Frederick. *Black Higher Education in the United States, A Selected Bibliography on Negro Higher Education and Historically Black Colleges and Universities.* Westport, Conn.: Greenwood Press, 1978.

Sims, Janet L. (comp.). *The Progress of Afro-American Women: A Selected Bibliography and Resource Guide.* Westport, Conn.: Greenwood Press, 1980. (Chapter on Education).

17. Educating Black Women Students for the Multicultural Future (with Kimberly Wallace Sanders) (1996)

The Fourth World Conference on Women held in Beijing was attended by a small delegation from Spelman College that included Glenda Price, provost; Kimberly Wallace Sanders, assistant director of the Women's Research and Resource Center; Evelynn Hammonds, Spelman alumna, assistant professor of the history of science at the Massachusetts Institute of Technology (MIT), and co-convener of the historic Black Women in the Academy conference held at MIT in 1993; and Beverly Guy-Sheftall, founding director of the Women's Research and Resource Center. The Spelman delegation was supported, in part, by the Ford Foundation under the auspices of a new three-year grant, which will enable us to enhance our present women's studies program and better prepare our Black women students for the global, multicultural world of the future in which people of color and women are in the majority.

In 1994, Guy-Sheftall completed a report for the Ford Foundation, which was released in time for the women's conference in Beijing.[1] It is a retrospective on the interdisciplinary field of women's studies since its inception in 1969 to the present, where now more than seven hundred programs exist throughout the United States. A major recommendation of the report is that to facilitate the "global reach" of women's studies and to facilitate greater collaboration between women's studies and area studies or ethnic studies, the Ford Foundation should allocate major funding for programs that would enhance knowledge about gender roles in areas of the world that have been researched inadequately, support scholarship on women and gender in undergraduate curricula of developing or Third World countries, and support the development of the internationalization of women's studies in underrepresented colleges and universities in the United States and institutions that have had a history of involvement with issues relating to race, class, and gender. The Ford Foundation's response was the establishment of a new initiative that would support projects that integrate international scholarship into U.S. women's studies programs and gender research into area or international studies programs.

For us at Spelman, the long trip to Beijing was the culmination of a journey we began in 1981 when we instituted a new women's studies minor that would foreground the experiences of women of African descent nationally and globally. Spelman was a pioneer among historically Black colleges with respect to addressing issues of gender in a major way in its curriculum. In the early eighties, women of color were suspicious of women's studies because of its inadequate attention to race and the experiences of most of the world's women. Many Black women were hostile to feminism because of its primary association with Euro-American women. We hope that the recent book *Words of Fire: An Anthology of African American Feminist Thought* will help to establish that Black women in fact have been in the forefront of struggles for racial and gender equality since the nineteenth century.[2]

The forty-five-minute bus trip between our Beijing hotel and the conference site in Huairou gave us an opportunity to share our experiences in workshops, panels, and plenary sessions. Our conference experience was enriched by our hunger to gather as much information and as many resources as possible to take home with us. As educators, we were struck by the vast opportunities for us to use these resources as transformative tools in the classrooms, as preparation for our students to participate in the fight for women's lives. We returned again and again to the truth that American women of African descent would benefit from a more expansive vision for the twenty-first century.

Spelman students are often so overwhelmed by the negativity directed at African American women that it is difficult for them to take a more global approach to understanding how the media represent women throughout the world. Listening to reports from feminist media-watch organizations from England, Jamaica, Canada, and Chile convinced us that Spelman students would develop a greater sense of themselves as female citizens of the world when they were able to recognize worldwide patterns of negative representation and violence directed against women. While we were moved to learn that twelve British women who were raped were told they looked like "a page 3 girl," referring to the provocative, almost nude models appearing in advertisements on the third page of a British newspaper, and that many Jamaican women are deeply engaged in an often dangerous battle to ban misogynist reggae songs, it was equally significant that these women were familiar with the empirical studies on women in the media in the United States. Clearly there was no indication that their focus was compromised by their assuming that what adversely affected women in their country was related to women everywhere.

In addition to fundamental pedagogical resources, we also found ourselves fascinated by the complexities of the bureaucratic processes for conference resolutions. For many women attending the conference, being surrounded by women, literally moving about in what seemed to be a world of women, was a completely new experience. While the Spelman delegation was accustomed to a female-majority environment, we found that it was impossible not to be both impressed and inspired by the coalitions of women working together to produce the Platform for Action. The controversy over choosing words like "gender" versus "sex," "equity" versus "equality," and "people" versus "peoples" was perhaps the most salient example of how language and culture shape our perceptions of what it means to value women's lives. What often seemed to be a semantic disagreement about wording in the document was clearly a highly charged debate about ideology, cultural representation, and inclusion. As Spelman College moves toward a greater understanding of the subtle and overt heterogeneity of a historically Black women's campus, we will be mindful of the diligence and collaboration necessary for women to work together toward the many plans of action to which we are committed.

Our journey to Beijing confirmed for us that, despite our detractors, we were on the right track in 1981. Women of color, women who were not European or white American, were actually in the majority at the Non-Governmental Organization (NGO) Forum. The issues facing poor women, women in developing countries, and other groups at the margins were at the center of dialogues and debates. Priority issues were equality and power sharing; the eradication of poverty; economic empowerment; human rights for women, with special emphasis on violence against women; and health. We have been told that women who were accustomed to being at the center of such international gatherings in the past were actually frustrated by this reversal.

We returned to Spelman convinced that we must double our efforts with respect to several issues. We need to ensure that students, particularly Black women, leave the college understanding the global economy and its impact on women throughout the world and in the United States; they must understand the impact of structural adjustment in Africa and the Caribbean and the ways in which women pay the price for many of these problematic programs; they must understand women's movements from a global perspective, especially in the African Diaspora, and the many faces of feminism throughout the world. They must analyze how xenophobic nationalisms and religious fundamentalisms at home and abroad affect the body politic, and especially the lives of women. They must understand how patriarchy or gender asymmetry functioned in pre-colonial Africa and postcolonial contexts. They must develop visual literacy for a world saturated with images and dehumanizing representations of the "other," so as not to accept passively all that passes before their own eyes. They must be prepared to participate in the transformation not only of the communities in which they live but, indeed, of the entire world.

In the aftermath of Beijing and the close of the UN Decade for Women, we at Spelman are prepared for a renewal of our commitment to providing students with the best education we can as we approach the end of the century. This means creating space for women throughout the world, many of whom we met in Beijing, to come here for residencies or as visiting professors. It means greater collaboration with universities training women in Africa and other parts of the world that have missions similar to our own. Finally, it means constructing a curriculum that is even more sensitive to the urgencies and realities that confront women and men, not just in our small village, but throughout the world. Our experience in Beijing also certainly underscored the urgency of our responsibility to help improve the lives of millions on the planet still devastated by poverty, war, instability, and despair. We were moved by what we learned about the current state of Black America and the condition of our sisters and brothers on the African continent. There is enormous work to be done, and the trip to Beijing left us energized and anxious to proceed.

NOTES

[1] Beverly Guy-Sheftall with Susan Heath, *Women's Studies: A Retrospective: A Report to the Foundation* (New York: Ford Foundation, 1995).

[2] Beverly Guy-Sheftall, ed., *Words of Fire, An Anthology of African-American Feminist Thought* (New York: New Press, 1995).

18. Shared Governance, Junior Faculty, and HBCUs (2006)

Although there is a large body of scholarship on historically black colleges and universities (HBCUs), their governance practices have been under researched. What little research we have on the topic points to campus climates that are "president-centric" and hierarchical structures that do not encourage faculty governance. Yet my own institution, Spelman College—founded in 1881 and one of only two historically Black colleges for women—has made much progress in faculty governance over the past twenty years. For the past eight years, I have served on the college's faculty council (the equivalent to a faculty senate), first as a member, then as president. During my service, we have probed the barriers or resistance on campus to greater faculty involvement in institutional decision-making, and we have created opportunities for more candid dialogue about shared governance. We are also helping to foster a campus culture that encourages junior and senior faculty alike to become more active in their roles as academic leaders. It hasn't always been easy, and it's still a work in progress, but faculty members, with support from the administration, are exploring more effective, long-term strategies for institutionalizing a new model of shared governance that we hope will be replicated on other campuses of our size, especially at HBCUs.

Although HBCU presidents have traditionally shared less power than their counterparts at many predominantly white institutions, perhaps there has been some justification for that. As James Minor, an HBCU alumnus and higher education scholar at Michigan State University, pointed out in the May-June 2005 issue of *Academe*, the less robust governance structures at HBCUs relate to the fact that "strong presidential leadership ... is partly responsible for the survival and progress of some campuses" in a national climate that has often been hostile to the values HBCUs represent. Faculty governance advocates at HBCUs, myself included, negotiate a difficult terrain in which we respect the best traditions of our institutions and at the same time push to develop more democratic forms of governance, especially those that incorporate junior faculty members into the governance process as early as possible.

On a personal note, I faced a difficult choice in 1976, when I decided, as an untenured faculty member, to join senior faculty members in a protest against the board of trustees over its appointment of another male president of the college. (During the April meeting of the board following the announcement of the new president, several hundred students and a few faculty members kept trustees locked in their board room for more than twenty hours in an effort to persuade them to reconsider the appointment.) The absence of formal faculty governance structures at that point in Spelman's history made the decision to participate in the protest more daunting and risky for junior faculty members; however, faculty were not punished for their actions. This helped to create a climate, I believe, where junior faculty, in particular, could feel more comfortable about challenging the status quo.

Power Sharing

One of the most unusual aspects of the history of shared governance at Spelman is that Johnnetta B. Cole, shortly after she assumed the presidency in 1987, actually encouraged faculty to pursue the establishment of formal governance structures. Given her own history as an outspoken faculty member at the universities at which she had worked previously, especially with the establishment of Black Studies, and given her experience with faculty governance, I am convinced that she believed that Spelman would be a stronger institution if junior and senior faculty became more involved in important decision-making on campus. Her commitment to sharing power with her senior staff and faculty provided an important catalyst for institutional change that would distinguish Spelman from other HBCUs in the 1990s.

Cole appointed a committee of senior and junior faculty members to explore shared governance, and a faculty council was initiated in 1994. Several other changes, such as the appointment of strong provosts, the rotation of department chairs, greater involvement of faculty in departmental matters, faculty input into the capital campaign, and faculty involvement in significant curriculum transformation, also contributed to the evolution of the college.

As a result of these initiatives, Spelman has been moving from a more president-centric culture to one in which shared decision-making about important academic matters—tenure and promotion policies, faculty hiring, the faculty handbook, curriculum review, faculty grievances, and, most recently, program development and review—is more normative. Since the arrival of President Beverly Daniel Tatum in 2002, the faculty council has worked more closely with senior administrators as the shared governance process continues to evolve.

An important recent development has been the formation of a junior faculty caucus, which emerged in 2003 after a faculty member in the

English department expressed frustration during her third-year review about insufficient mentoring. She took action by forming a caucus that assumed responsibility for mentoring junior faculty. In addition to functioning as a support group and organizing forums, the caucus has enabled junior faculty to become more involved on campus, although some still feel marginalized in the governance process.

In his *Academe* article, James Minor reminds readers that "developing an institution-wide definition of shared governance is essential for minimizing misunderstandings about the meaning of and process for making decisions. Communication lapses can arise from an institutional culture that discourages the expression of diverse or dissenting views."

His survey, one of the few studies of faculty governance at HBCUs, revealed that HBCU faculty have significant authority over academic matters such as the curriculum and tenure and promotion policies but less influence over nonacademic matters such as budget priorities, athletics, and the selection of the president. Site visits to campuses in the survey—eighty-eight were included—helped put into context the complex environments in which these institutions have had to operate and the ways their histories have differed from those of predominantly white colleges and universities.

All the campuses Minor examined valued shared governance, but he found a wide gap between faculty and administrators regarding perceptions of the effectiveness of faculty governance. Many respondents indicated that substantive academic decision-making took place in faculty standing committees and departmental committees rather than in faculty senates.

As outgoing president of the faculty council at Spelman, I have taken seriously my role as a faculty leader in working with my faculty colleagues to stimulate college-wide discussions about governance. Here are some of the questions we've considered and that others might ask at their own institutions.

1. What would make decision-making processes more transparent, especially those related to such issues as faculty lines, budget priorities, and the organizational structure within academic affairs?
2. How might we improve communication among campus constituents so as to promote greater collaboration in addressing academic climate issues? One such issue involves the need to provide more opportunities for junior faculty members to assume leadership roles at the departmental and institutional

levels. Doing so at the institutional level is especially difficult because untenured faculty are ineligible for membership on some key committees (the tenure and promotion committee for example). How can we improve communication between the board of trustees and the faculty?

3. How might we engage in more candid dialogue about the systemic barriers to greater faculty involvement in decision making at HBCUs?
4. How might we make the academic mission more central to the way we conduct business and decide important issues that affect all aspects of institutional life?

Given the limited financial resources of HBCUs, economic imperatives frequently dictate academic decisions such as class size, faculty lines, the availability of particular majors or programs, and the nature of faculty appointments. It is difficult, for example, to secure senior faculty appointments, funds for endowed chairs, or even regular full-time faculty positions for important curricular initiatives. The solution has sometimes been greater reliance on part-time faculty, even with core courses or introductory courses in the disciplines. On too many of our campuses, faculty are excluded from decision-making in these matters because they are not involved in budget discussions even at the departmental level.

Faculty leaders at Spelman understand the complexities inherent in tackling these issues. We also believe, however, that high-quality colleges and universities need effective shared governance practices and a palpable commitment to the involvement of faculty in decision-making about all aspects of a college's mission. Because untenured faculty are ineligible for membership on our faculty council, although they serve on other important college-wide governance committees and departmental committees, senior faculty members at Spelman have assumed greater responsibility for ensuring that shared governance is taken seriously. Over the past four years, we have met with relatively little resistance from the administration.

Secret of Our Success

Our success arises from several factors. Over the years, our faculty council has had strong presidents and assertive members who are committed to bringing about long-lasting changes in faculty culture. They have promoted the involvement of faculty, including junior faculty members, in institutional governance. In addition, they have encouraged open discussion of faculty behavior conducive to such involvement, shared with faculty effective governance models at other institutions, and explored how Spelman could become a stronger institution with a more engaged faculty. This project has benefited greatly from the presence of a strong junior faculty caucus and strategic mentoring of junior faculty by engaged senior faculty at the college.

President Tatum reached out to the faculty council when she first arrived on campus in 2002 and continues to meet with the council at least twice a year. When Yvonne Jackson became chair of the board of trustees in 2005, she sought the council's advice and met with the council president. This past spring, the council met with President Tatum's senior staff for the first time to share several concerns, attention to which will certainly result in an improved intellectual climate on campus. Perhaps most important, the Spelman faculty has been engaged as a collective in more focused discussions of shared governance because it has been a major priority of the faculty council over the past several years. Without these sustained dialogues and the vigilance of the council, old patterns would undoubtedly emerge, making faculty governance more elusive.

Ivory Paul Phillips, professor of social science education at Jackson State University, wrote a scathing review of HBCU governance in the July-August 2002 issue of *Academe* in which he said that "on most black college campuses, the budget is considered to be outside the purview of the faculty and the faculty senate."

One of the most promising developments in shared governance at Spelman has been President Tatum's acceptance of a faculty council proposal for a budget committee. The provost will chair the committee, whose members will consist of both senior and junior faculty, including the president of the faculty council. The council will suggest members for the committee, which will convene in fall 2006 and begin deliberating about how to make the budget process more transparent. The committee will also consider resource allocation for academic programming and ways to increase faculty involvement in budget matters. Through this committee, Spelman faculty will engage for the first time in discussions about these matters with senior administrators. To share our experience with other HBCUs interested in more robust shared governance procedures, the faculty council is considering starting a newsletter that, among other issues, would include information about its evolving governance processes.

Faculty Resistance

It will be important for future studies of shared governance at HBCUs to explore a phenomenon that was apparent at Spelman but has not been alluded to in the literature to date. The "sad state of affairs on black college campuses" to which Phillips refers is mostly attributable to administrative resistance to faculty governance. But faculty can resist change as well. Changes in institutional culture often produce discomfort, even tension, among faculty members who have learned how to navigate hierarchical, president-centered environments by negotiating for their needs on an individual or departmental basis with presidents or provosts. Strong faculty senates or faculty handbooks that have clearly defined academic policies may actually work against certain individual or departmental agendas. Assertive, elected faculty leaders may be seen as threats in institutional contexts in which faculty are comfortable with "business as usual." Junior faculty members may find it especially difficult to assume leadership positions and participate in shared governance when senior faculty are unwilling to share power or conduct business differently.

Other generational divides can affect faculty culture and governance reform as well. Senior faculty, for example, may be accustomed to tenure and promotion criteria that de emphasize scholarly research. But many junior faculty members, fresh out of graduate school, will expect to focus on scholarship in addition to teaching and service. Senior faculty may even resist new tenure and promotion guidelines (especially for full professor) more strongly than administrators, resenting what they perceive as reluctance among junior faculty to engage in substantive service on campus in favor of establishing a strong publishing record. These tensions are likely to fester if campuses fail to have candid discussions about them.

Through my experience on the faculty council at Spelman, where I've taught for thirty-five years, I have learned important lessons about shared governance at HBCUs. First, shared governance is worth struggling for, no matter how strong the resistance. In addition, we need to work harder to ensure the involvement of junior faculty members in governance structures. Their involvement is important for their own professional development and benefits the institution in that faculty members who feel included and empowered are easier to retain. Unlike passive junior professors, assertive new faculty members also make excellent role models for students and are more likely to become courageous, engaged senior faculty. Perhaps it is time for us at Spelman to revisit our eligibility requirement for faculty council, especially since resistance has weakened to the idea that various campus constituents might profitably contribute to campus governance.

In the final analysis, assertive, committed, and engaged faculty members are critical to any college's well-being and continued growth, while passive, disengaged, or fearful faculty members contribute to an institution's stagnation and imperil its future. Despite the historical fragility of shared governance at many HBCUs, strong faculty members have helped to make Black colleges and universities what they've become since their beginnings in the nineteenth century. These capable faculty members have dedicated themselves to making their institutions better; resisted authoritarian presidents and provosts; pushed back against timid, deferential colleagues; and promoted positive change on departmental and college-wide committees and faculty senates. As we move forward, the ability of HBCUs to retain talented junior faculty will depend as much on our commitment to developing strong faculty governance processes as on our willingness to reduce teaching loads and increase salaries.

19. Audre Lorde and Spelman College (with Johnnetta Betsch Cole) (2014)

I Am Your Sister: Collected and Unpublished Writings of Audre Lorde, co-edited by Rudolph P. Byrd and the two of us, is a highly selective collection of Lorde's speeches and essays, as well as personal reflections from sister-scholars Alice Walker, Gloria I. Joseph, and bell hooks. The anthology includes, for the first time, reflections on Audre Lorde's connections with Spelman College, the oldest historically Black college for women in the world. Spelman is also the home of the Audre Lorde Papers, which arrived on the campus in 1995 and have been open for scholars since 2009 in the College Archives, which is managed by the Women's Research & Resource Center. A generous grant from the Arcus Foundation in 2005 enabled us to process the papers and host students, faculty, and researchers from around the globe. Audre Lorde's journey to Spelman did not happen as one might have imagined.

In 1976, Ruby Sales, a temporary professor in the history department, a former SNCC organizer, and an aspiring historian, invited Audre to speak at Spelman—without fanfare or institutional support. This was a historic moment from my (Beverly) vantage point as a young member of the English department because she was likely the first out lesbian to speak to students and faculty. Rather predictably, her visit met with some resistance when word circulated that she had spoken openly about sexuality matters.

Audre's return to Spelman in 1988 when I (Johnnetta) invited her to speak not long after I was inaugurated as the College's first Black woman president was certainly a major event. When I arrived at Spelman in 1987, I was told that Audre had visited the campus about a decade earlier, but because she had been coldly received and was the target of homophobia, she had vowed never to return to Spelman. Drawing on our sisterly relationship, I invited Audre to come to Spelman and participate in a series that I called "Speaking at Spelman, Readings at Reynolds." At first, she resisted but finally, perhaps as much to end my persistent asking, agreed to visit the campus in 1988. This time she was warmly and properly received. In many ways the work of the Women's Center, founded in 1981 by Beverly, had been dealing head on with gender and sexuality issues, so there was less hostility to Audre's radical feminist politics.

To be sure, Audre's most cherished gift to the College and future generations of scholars was her decision to give her personal papers and other artifacts to the Spelman Archives, a component of the Woman's Center. Catching the significance of the connection at the 25th anniversary celebration of the Center, which was a symposium on Lorde's legacy, Leslie Feinberg asserted: "It is here at Spelman that words and works of Audre Lorde have found a home. This historically Black college has ensured that her fiery words will never be extinguished." I (Beverly) am convinced that it was Audre's cherished friendship with Johnnetta and her subsequent visit to the Spelman campus that precipitated her decision to deposit her papers here. Her will made provisions for this precious gift, and three years after her death in 1992, Audre's archive arrived at Spelman.

We are convinced that Audre Lorde's life work helped us envision at Spelman a "beloved community" of sisters and brothers who are committed to a world free of all the isms, poverty, religious intolerance, misogyny, and violence. The Lorde papers were the first acquisition in a broader strategy on the part of the Women's Center and President Cole of becoming a major repository for the papers of influential contemporary Black feminist scholars/activists/writers. Professor Alexis de Veaux, who completed a biography of Lorde, *Warrior Poet*, was the first to conduct research in the Lorde Archive, followed by Rudolph P. Byrd, who conceptualized *I Am Your Sister* (2009).

Audre's journey at Spelman had a profound impact on what we would like to call its feminist transformations. The students who enrolled in the first Audre Lorde seminar on campus last year are witnesses to her continued presence on the campus, which we believe Ruby Sales could not have imagined in 1978!!!

20. Breaking Silence (with M. Jacqui Alexander) (2019)

In solidarity with feminist/womanist comrades in *Building Womanist Bridges*, we foreground the important work of eradicating all forms of oppression, including those within our own communities. While historically Black colleges and universities have been necessary bread for our survival since the 19th century, issues of difference around sexuality and heteronormativity have been particularly difficult to navigate. Audre Lorde's prophetic, now vintage, charge serves as a poignant response to the crisis we now face: "It is better to speak knowing we were never meant to survive." Now more than ever as old divisions are being re-ignited in the dismal service of political expediency, we cannot choose silence, nor can we afford to live in silos, cordoned off from one another. Commitment to a survival of wholeness is Alice Walker's elegant framing of the imperative we must embrace at this perilous moment, within and across communities. . . wholeness of an entire people. This commitment requires us to bring the full dimensions of our being to this project we call life as we continually, consistently re-imagine Martin Luther King Jr.'s dynamic vision of building "beloved community" on our campuses—indeed wherever the stubborn traces of injustice reside. Let us not be afraid to say unequivocally: *All* Black lives matter.

Background

In 2006, the Spelman College Women's Research & Resource Center (Women's Center) received a one-year grant from the Arcus Foundation to launch *Breaking the Silence: The Audre Lorde Black Lesbian Feminist Project.* The project was named in honor of Audre Lorde, the most productive and influential Black, lesbian, feminist/writer/activist/educator of the 20th century. This important project, the first of its kind on an historically Black college campus, is part of a larger effort to establish a Lesbian, Gay, Bisexual and Transgender (LGBT) program within the Women's Center at Spelman College. From the outset we also conceptualized the project to be Phase I of a larger project surrounding LGBT issues at historically Black colleges and universities and were pleased to attract major funding from the Arcus Foundation for a three-year project beginning July 1, 2008–*The Audre Lorde Project Phase II, Facilitating HBCU Campus Climates of Pluralism, Inclusivity and Progressive Change.*

The overall objectives of the Audre Lorde Project (Phases I and II) were to increase public awareness and understanding about African American gay and lesbian experiences as well as sexuality issues in the African diaspora; to increase awareness about the marginalization of racial issues in the LGBT movement and Gay and Lesbian Studies or Queer Studies; and to facilitate a climate of institutional change at HBCUs that acknowledges, values, and respects difference.

During Phase I of the Project, we inaugurated the Zami Salon, a series of student-driven activities designed to raise awareness, combat homophobia/heterosexism, and promote a more inclusive environment among students, faculty, and staff of the Atlanta University Center (AUC). This student-led Zami Salon brought LBGT scholars and activists to campus who discussed a variety of issues about their experiences both inside and outside Black communities. For example, Thomas Glave, now professor of English at SUNY, Binghamton, New York, and an award-winning writer, discussed the necessity of interrogating heteronormativity in African Diaspora cultural contexts, particularly Jamaica. Cara Page, National Director of the Committee on Women, Population, and the Environment, presented a workshop entitled "Designer Genes: Queer Conversations on Genetic Technologies." Dr. Layli Phillips, Professor of Women's Studies at Georgia State University (Spelman alumna, Class of '86), announced a gift of $1,000 at the 25th anniversary celebration (2006) of the Women's Center to fund an LGBT student scholarship. In the spring of 2008, the Women's Center arranged for Dr. Phillips to offer a course on "Black Queer Studies" that was an elective for our comparative women's studies major/minor. Based on our survey of gay and lesbian studies curricula at Black colleges and universities, we believe this is the first time that a semester-long, dedicated queer theory course has been offered at one of our institutions. Prominent transgender activist Leslie Feinberg donated her honorarium from the 25th anniversary conference to the scholarship as well. Under the auspices of the Zami Salon, the Women's Center also sponsored the first Spelman faculty "Coming Out Day."

In September 2008, we held a major symposium on the life and work of Audre Lorde in connection with our launching of an endowment campaign for the Women's Center, both made possible by a major leadership gift of one million dollars from the Ford Foundation. During the symposium we also explored a range of topics related to Black LGBT issues among a racially diverse cross-section of academics, activists, and students from the U.S. and globally.

At the core of Phase I of the Arcus project was the processing, digital conversion, archival coding, and public unveiling of the Audre Lorde Papers, the most comprehensive documentation of Lorde's life and work as a Black lesbian feminist writer/activist/educator. The papers were willed to Spelman College by Lorde during Johnnetta Betsch Cole's presidency (1987-1997) and are part of the Special Collections of the Spelman Archives, the research component of the Women's Center. Upon the completion of the processing of the papers by project archivist Brenda Banks, the National Archives Publishing Company was hired to undertake the scanning of items from the Audre Lorde Collection. Reproductions were made of 12,000 pages of correspondence, personal letters, journals, notebooks, unpublished poems, essays, speeches, manuscripts, lecture notes, and photographs. The Audre Lorde papers were officially opened in September 2009.

Also, during Phase I of the Arcus Project, co-editors Rudolph P. Byrd (African American Studies, Emory University), Johnnetta Betsch Cole (President Emeritus, Spelman and Bennett Colleges), and Project Director, Beverly Guy-Sheftall, completed *I Am Your Sister: The Collected and Unpublished Writings of Audre Lorde* (Oxford University Press, 2009). It would have been difficult to complete this important book project without having access to the Audre Lorde Papers, which the Arcus Foundation grant made possible. In her reflections, Johnnetta Betsch Cole discusses her friendship with Lorde and the circumstances surrounding the papers having been gifted to Spelman College; in her epilogue, Guy-Sheftall chronicles the connection between Audre Lorde and Spelman College and her impact on the mission of the Women's Center; and in his introduction Byrd articulates the significance of Audre Lorde in the development of Black feminist studies.

Phase I of the Audre Lorde Project established the Women's Center at Spelman College as a major site for the exploration of Black LGBTQ issues in the academy. As a result of Arcus funding, the Spelman Archives (attached to the Women's Center) is becoming a major repository for the work of contemporary Black feminist scholar/activists. We remain committed to exploring LGBTQ issues in multiple racial/ethnic communities, especially in the African Diaspora, and in stimulating further exploration of these important issues at historically Black colleges and universities. We are also committed to stimulating additional research about LGBT matters at HBCUs. In this regard, one of the most exciting and important aspects of the Arcus Project was reconnecting with Spelman alumnae who had been involved with advocacy around sexuality issues, which included the founding of our first LGBT organization, Lesbian and Bisexual Alliance (LBA). It is now possible to chronicle that early history as well as engage in a more comprehensive analysis of LGBT issues at Spelman, which will be similar when it is completed to Howard University's *Lavender Report*.

According to the testimony of Spelman alumna Wendi O'Neal (Class of '96), Kendra Johnson was the first student to approach then-President Johnnetta Cole in 1992 about chartering an LGBT organization in response to an earlier homophobic incident on campus; at that point there were about eight students who were meeting secretly in the counseling center with a supportive staff member; among them was an out domestic exchange student as well. Wendi (see the new LBA/Afrekete list-serv) attributes events in their own lives, the contentious public debate around gay rights, and the rise of the Christian right's mobilization in Black churches as factors that motivated them to push for a chartered student organization so that they could address the needs of lesbian and bisexual women in the AUC. They called themselves the LBA, the Lesbian and Bisexual Alliance, so that students would know they weren't hiding. The following year only two of them returned, Antonia Randolph and Wendi, the first co-presidents of LBA. Wendi indicates they were able to keep the small organization going with help from friends and allies, especially Women's Center staff. In the fall of 1993, President Cole wrote an open letter to the College community in which she joined the debate about the recently chartered LBA. Her goal was to affirm her commitment to diversity and to help create a "beloved community" at Spelman, including students who marked sexual difference. Excerpts from the letter are reprinted in *Gender Talk: The Struggle for Women's Equality in African American Communities* (2003), which Cole and Guy-Sheftall co-authored some years later.

Given the fragility and size of LBA and the departure of its founding presidents in 1996, the organization might not have survived were it not for Donna Hope, who attended Spelman from 1995 to 1998 and returned to graduate in 2000. Donna was asked to carry the torch and articulates the genealogy of the organization which is still a vibrant entity:

> I admit I was very reluctant! I was in the very intense Dual Degree program with very little free time; LBA had no faculty advisor, no meeting space, and our beloved and progressive Dr. Cole was resigning as President. It wasn't easy, but I was determined to make the LBA thrive. I placed ads in the paper, petitioned several faculty for support, and fliered all around the AUC each week for meetings. I was just making some headway sophomore year when my mother expectedly passed away in January '97. I decided not to take time off but requested a domestic exchange that spring semester at Barnard College. I returned to Spelman my third and final year in fall '97 with bold ideas. I decided that the LBA needed a new name to reflect the

new, fierce, bold, proud, and OUT lesbian/bisexual Spelman sister. I had just read Audre Lorde's *Zami* and Catherine McKinley's Black lesbian anthology, *Afrekete*, and knew that Afrekete was the perfect name. Voila! This rich legacy of Spelman student activism around LGBT issues has not had a public face until the Arcus project, and we are determined to write a more complete history of this important phase in the College's evolution.

Our Howard University liaison, Victoria Diane Kirby, graduate assistant in the Office of the President and author of their *Lavender Report*, shared with us important aspects of their LGBT history as we struggled to make more visible these hidden histories at HBCUs. Howard was the first HBCU to have a recognized LGBT organization on campus as early as 1980 but, like Spelman's, it could be characterized as fragile from the beginning. The first group, Lambda Student Alliance, was recognized by the university as an official student organization and lasted until the mid 1980s. In the 1990s, a new LGBT student group, Oxala, began, but by 1999 it had faded. In September 2000, Sean McMillan and Sterling Washington started a new student group and began the process of having it recognized officially. On October 6, 2000, they met for the first time. Named the Bisexual, Lesbian and Gay Organization of Students at Howard (BLAGOSAH), the group has flourished over the past decade. In 2009, the name BLAGOSAH was officially changed to the Coalition of Activist Students Celebrating the Acceptance of Diversity and Equality (CASCADE).

Kirby also shared with us the variety of ways that Howard University has been in the forefront of LGBT equality since the early 1900s, beginning with its appointment of Professor Alain Locke to the faculty. Locke was not only the first African American Rhodes Scholar but also openly gay. His protégé, Zora Neale Hurston, the co-founder of the *Hilltop*, has been rumored by various scholars to have been openly bisexual, and during the time she was at Howard used, along with a group of other students, *The Caverns* (now Bohemian Caverns) as an early meeting place for LGBT students. Lucy Diggs Slowe, a Howard alumna and its first Dean of Women, had a female partner during her tenure at Howard (See Ruby Nell Sales' commissioned paper). Howard is also seen as the birthplace of the Black Pride Movement, an international movement celebrating the unique experiences of Black people who are same-gender loving (SGL); the first Black Pride celebration was held across the street from Howard at Banneker Field.

Howard alumni, such as Darlene Nipper of the National Gay and Lesbian Task Force (NGLTF) and Sterling Washington of the International Federation of Black Prides (IFBP), started the first Black LGBT churches in Washington,

D.C. and are active in prominent Black and mainstream LGBT organizations according to Howard's *Lavender Report*. In terms of university policy, Howard was the first HBCU to have an anti-discrimination policy designating gays and lesbians as a protected class; it was approved twenty years ago by the Board of Trustees when most HBCUs were unwilling to do likewise. Howard is one of three HBCUs that grants employee health benefits to the spouses of LGBT faculty and staff and has partnered with the Metropolitan Police Department's Gay & Lesbian Liaison Unit (GLLU) to provide LGBT sensitivity training to its campus police. Religious life at Howard has also been inclusive. Bernard L. Richardson, Dean of the Chapel, has selected openly gay assistants and brought LGBT preachers to speak at Rankin Chapel. Dean Pollard of the School of Divinity and its alumni were instrumental in organizing a group of over 100 D.C. ministers and other faith leaders to support marriage equality in the nation's capital. University chaplains Rev. Franklin Vaughn (Anglican/ Lutheran/ Episcopal) and Reverend Frazier (United Methodist) have made their ministries open and affirming, becoming beacons of light for students struggling to reconcile their same-gender affections with their religion. This academic year (2010-2011), the Office of the Vice President of Student Affairs launched an LGBT learning cohort for the entire campus community that served as an important site for discussion of LGBT issues, art, and literature.

Phase II of the Audre Lorde Project—"Facilitating HBCU Campus Climates of Pluralism, Inclusivity and Progressive Change"—is an expansion of Phase I, which focused on Spelman College and the AUC. It engages in research, outreach, and community-led change at ten HBCUs. Our broad goals are to raise awareness, inspire critical dialogue, and explore senior administration-endorsed strategies to facilitate progressive change around inclusivity and difference in a variety of Black colleges and universities. During the first year of the project, we engaged in extensive data gathering and analysis relative to institutional policies and practices at our partnering institutions: Philander Smith College, Morgan State University, North Carolina Central University, Bennett College for Women, Clark Atlanta University, Southern University, Howard University, Fisk University, Morehouse College, and Spelman College. We commissioned a case study of Dillard University during Michael Lomax's presidency because of its LGBT-friendly campus climate and culture, given a set of criteria that we identified. Because of the uniqueness of Dillard during Lomax's presidency, we engaged a consultant to write a report based on interviews with key administrators; we were interested in an analysis of the specific conditions and circumstances that situated Dillard in this unusual place among HBCUs. The consultant we chose was former director of International Programs both at Dillard and Morehouse Colleges and a doctoral student at Clark Atlanta University. Our assumption was that this consultant's report would enable us to ascertain what constitutes a gay-friendly Black college or university so that we would be able to advise and make policy recommendations for other HBCUs more effectively. We used Campus Pride's "LGBTQ-Friendly Campus Climate Index: National Assessment Tool" as our primary instrument for assessing campus cultures at the Black colleges with whom we collaborated.

During the first year of the project, we also wanted to ascertain the nature of already existing projects that might have addressed LGBT issues at HBCUs. In this regard, three important national initiatives were identified: the Human Rights Campaign Foundation's HBCU Program, whose Hype '08 involved ten HBCU campuses; SoulforceQ, whose Equality Rides visited fifteen Black colleges, including Spelman and Morehouse, in the fall of 2008; and Campus Pride, whose collaborative questionnaire we would be encouraging all of our partner institutions to complete and use in the working groups they would form for their own individual assessments of their campus climates. We also commissioned an additional four papers that constitute the intellectual underpinnings of this historic four-year Audre Lorde project. Collectively, the five papers represent the most comprehensive scholarship to date on a broad range of LGBT issues at Black colleges and universities, some of which challenge conventional notions about the nature of homophobia in African American communities or the experiences of Black gay and lesbian faculty in particular institutional contexts.

Much of the work during Phase II focused on cementing our partnership with ten carefully selected HBCUs and hiring the appropriate staff to carry out this challenging but important work. We hired a senior professor, M. Jacqui Alexander (Women's and Gender Studies, University of Toronto), who was Cosby Chair at Spelman (2008-2009), and Aaron Wells, a Hampton University alumnus who served as part-time research coordinator. We also hired Taryn Crenshaw, a Spelman alumna who had assisted with our Zami Salon in Phase I of the Arcus Project; she gathered data about a variety of issues at a range of HBCUs, including curricula matters and institutional practices around gender and sexuality. The primary activities during this year were securing buy-in from our partners, which began by soliciting presidents to partner with Spelman;

conducting campus visits; finalizing the four commissioned papers that would provide the intellectual backdrop for the project; and planning for the culminating activity, which would be a historic summit that focused on HBCUs.

Our campus visits were informed by particular sets of data: 1) pertinent information from the respective college's website (history, mission, diversity programming, curricula, and institutional policies); and 2) the LGBT campus climate index that was developed by Campus Pride. The index scans college campuses to determine their level of LGBT inclusion and engagement or what they call "gay-friendliness." The questionnaire that colleges complete (after registering with Campus Pride) includes a broad range of questions that relate to services and campus climate around issues of inclusion. During campus visits, we met with presidents, provosts, student life professionals, faculty, a broad range of staff, and students. We were attentive in our discussions to whether campuses addressed issues of diversity broadly and the extent to which gender/sexuality issues were perceived to be connected to racial/ethnic, class, or religious diversity. We made use of what we had learned from the Dillard case study, which explored strategies that shifted the usually chilly climate for LGBT persons on campus. The case study turned out to have been an indispensable orienting document for us as we planned our campus visits. We undertook extensive preparations prior to each campus visit. Initially, we contacted presidents and provosts requesting that they designate a campus liaison who would coordinate our visits; in some cases, Project Staff identified campus liaisons based on our having already worked with them in Women's Center projects. We stressed the importance of identifying administrators/faculty/staff whose administrative, policy, pedagogical, curricular, or political work bore on dimensions of the Arcus project. Faculty advisors to LGBT student organizations, as well as members of those organizations, were critical during our campus visits. Fortunately, there was widespread enthusiasm for our visits among most of our collaborators. Despite the logistical challenges associated with scheduling all-day visits with a variety of participants (including presidents and provosts), we managed to complete all the visits by the third year of the project. There were only two campuses where we were unable to meet with presidents.

And finally, there are recommendations that we believe will be useful as Black colleges and universities expand their efforts to facilitate campus climates of inclusivity and progressive change. A Luta Continua! The struggle continues.

Curricular Issues

Exploring diversity at HBCUs may seem to be an oxymoron, but only because of the ways that curriculum transformation projects on college campuses have been conceptualized. Nationally these projects assume a predominantly white institution whose students and faculty of color constitute a minority. A main premise of these efforts to bring about a more inclusive curriculum has been that white students have not been prepared to deal adequately with an increasingly multicultural, multiracial world.

Spelman College's Women's Center (in an atypical occurrence within the HBCU context) began its curriculum transformation efforts with a Ford Foundation-funded mainstreaming women's studies project in 1983 ("Curriculum Development in Black Women's Studies"); a decade later, in 1994, it embarked upon another Ford-funded project to infuse diversity in the liberal arts curriculum. As in diversity projects at predominantly white institutions (PWIs), we addressed issues of race/ethnicity, gender, class, religion, disability, and sexuality. In our survey of curricula at other HBCUs during the 1980s, we discovered that while race and class may be dealt with routinely, there are silences about other diversity issues, especially gender and sexuality. When Spelman initiated a Women's Studies minor in 1981, it was the first HBCU to do so; in 1996, it expanded the program to include a major in Comparative Women's Studies, the first and only HBCU with a Women's Studies major. If Women's Studies has been slow to become institutionalized at HBCUs, Gay and Lesbian Studies is virtually absent, though there has been some attention to sexuality, broadly speaking.

At HBCUs, courses on sexuality have been offered in a variety of disciplines, including social work, sociology, psychology, Women's Studies, family and consumer sciences, the natural sciences, medicine, and theology. In the data-gathering phase of Phase II of the Arcus Project, the Women's Center found that from a random sample of 29 HBCUs, 17 had offered courses with the term "sexuality" in the title and/or course description. Located primarily in the social/behavioral sciences, content on sexuality was typically found in courses like Sex and Gender or Race, Class, and Gender. Human Sexuality, a course that preceded the development of women's studies as a field of study, appears to have been one of the more common courses taught at HBCUs, since ten of the seventeen institutions surveyed had at least one Human Sexuality course, which was offered in various academic departments. Descriptions of the courses varied tremendously. One such course (offered in sociology) described its objectives as follows: "This course surveys the biological and social components of sexuality. Relevant concepts include reproduction, birth control, venereal disease, emotions, etc." Five of the seventeen institutions offered courses in sexuality that were based in women's studies. Only one HBCU (Spelman) offered a dedicated course that narrowed the pervasive analytic distance between Black Studies and LGBT studies by treating explicitly 'queer' scholarship. The syllabus for this Special Topics in Women's Studies course, "Black Queer Studies," appears in the Appendix.

Faculty at five of our partnering institutions spoke about integrating LGBT content (some more than others) in their courses in Philosophy, Sociology, Political Science, Women's Studies, Religion/Theology, Performance Studies, and in a cluster of courses at one institution called, Platinum by Design. In two other cases, faculty were in the process of developing new LGBT courses, one on queer theory at the graduate level in English. Our assumption that the humanities might have been a vibrant place for LGBT curricular engagement turned out to be misplaced in most cases. In a few instances we found that it was possible to teach James Baldwin—one of the most iconic 'gay' authors—without interrogating his sexuality. Audre Lorde, a Black lesbian icon and writer, seems not to have been taught routinely in English departments, including in African American literature courses. No HBCU offered LGBT studies as an academic major, minor, concentration, or certificate program although, because of student advocacy, one of our partnering institutions is in the process of working with consortium schools to construct a possible major or minor. This same institution sponsors what is referred to as an "LGBT learning community/cohort" that is called "To Be Young, Gifted, Black and Gay." It is offered as a seminar course, but without course credit. It appeared that our partnering campuses did not carry a significant number of LGBT-inclusive books and periodicals on sexual orientation in their libraries, though one bookstore seems to have moved in that direction.

In the absence of LGBT Studies, the intellectual and emotional space for students to wrestle with gender and sexuality as social constructs is understandably circumscribed. In contexts where same-sex sexuality remains taboo, presumably supported by religious dictates that mark it as such, pervasive ideas about heterosexual morality or heteronormativity usurp the place of curricular engagement in ways that make it difficult for LGBT students to locate themselves within a robust intellectual legacy. Additionally, the absence of curriculum helps to perpetuate the myth that LGBT orientation is a lifestyle, one of individual choice, therefore personal, therefore private, and therefore unworthy of scholarly pursuit. One chair of a history department noted, "The curriculum is failing us in regard to sexuality and gender ... it is disappointing."

An unexpected issue turned out to have been the question of Black faculty living closeted lives, at least on campus. While we must be wary of attempts to collapse identity into scholarship, the pervasive pattern of closeted Black faculty may account for the dearth of LGBT curricular offerings. In those instances where there was LGBT content in courses, they were taught mostly by white faculty who were "out." In one case, however, an out Black lesbian faculty member shared that she had designed a Black queer course, but no students enrolled. In one faculty discussion, one semi-closeted junior faculty member disclosed that he was dissuaded from offering courses on sexuality by the chair of his department, whom he thought to be gay. Here is an instance where the boundaries of the heteronormative are being actively maintained by heterosexual and homosexual alike. When on other occasions we asked (presumably heterosexual) faculty why they believed their LGBT colleagues might be reluctant to be out or to offer LGBT courses, they cited "fear of institutional backlash," of being seen as "controversial." Junior faculty expressed concern that being out "would result in refusals around tenure and promotion." One faculty focus group summed it up in this way: "Don't Ask Don't Tell" is the same policy for professors; most faculty are not out; the idea here is that LGBT people must not be too flamboyant; it will be seen as unprofessional, lead to political backlash ... damage professional development. Faculty feel they shouldn't get into the conversation in the classroom around sexuality ... because it will be easier for their lives; better for their reputation; and new faculty are advised not to do this. Departmental committees may not give you the green light when a faculty member wants to introduce a course on queer/gender issues and might say, 'this is not the type of course that we want here.'"

No discussion of academic life would be complete without some mention of the type of classroom culture that obtains in the conflictual arrangements of silence, religious taboo, invisibility of LGBT students, closeted Black faculty, and an overall climate that enforces heterosexuality. Incidents of homophobia in the classroom figure prominently in alumni accounts of their experiences at HBCUs, though less so in our discussions with students about academic life. Students nonetheless did reference incidents of homophobia in the classroom during which their LGBT status was used to mark negative difference, a matter to which we return later. The point here is not really about whether Black faculty use the classroom as the site for coming out, but, rather, about whether the scholarly silence around sexuality forestalls a series of critical conversations that mark the territories of Blackness, gender, sexuality, class, nationality, and pedagogy.[1] In such a situation, it becomes easy to believe that these very topics are "unspeakable" and therefore lie outside the boundaries of theoretical and intellectual inquiry. In the same way that the absence of Black Studies/Black history rendered 'American' history incomplete, so, too, the absence of Black LGBT studies renders Black Studies similarly incomplete. Perhaps ultimately, the absence might well be ostensible, in the sense that that which is queer is always already contained within Black and always gestures rupture and possibility. Related to these varied engagements with LGBT Studies, we found that Women's Studies courses, including courses on Black women, played an important role in the intellectual and political preparation of students at HBCUs. During our campus visits we observed a notable difference in intellectual/analytic skills between those students who had been exposed to Women's Studies as an academic discipline and those who were not. Students who had enrolled in Women's Studies courses, even in the absence of LGBT studies, were more likely to be conscious of the politics and history of their campuses in relation to matters of gender and sexuality and as a result were more likely to view these matters not as private, individual concerns but as public, culturally constructed, and ultimately amenable to intervention. The interplay between the local and the global provided them with a vocabulary to understand themselves and the world at the same time that they were engaged in critical scholarship about feminism and sexuality.

LGBT Student Life

Directors and staff at the Offices of Student Life who deal in an immediate way with the day-to-day realities of LGBT students made several important observations about their experiences. One director with close to three decades of experience framed the general problem in these terms: "One of the challenges we have here is that we are taking young people from much larger adaptive environments and putting them into a microcosm (HBCUs) that hasn't caught up with the real world." They noted a marked increase in intimate partner violence for both LGBT and heterosexual students over the number of years they were employed at a given HBCU and outlined the ways that gender perceptions shaped the degree to which heterosexual students embraced ally relationships with their LGBT peers. They knew of situations where vocal LGBT students felt that they had been singled out, silenced, or were involved in organizations that had been refused a charter. Gay male students have been told in the classroom to "put some bass in their voice." They commented as well on the kind of distortions that result from gender imbalances and uninterrogated ideas of masculinity. In one instance where women students outnumbered men, it was men, "gay men [who] tended to assume more leadership positions."

Most often, Offices of Student Life were focal places for LGBT programming though there were two instances in which proactive Women's Centers also assumed that role. These offices sponsored diversity workshops and panel presentations and otherwise assisted in organizing training for Safe Zone programs. Faculty, students, and staff complete Train the Trainer workshops to become Safe Zone facilitators by agreeing to serve as a campus resource. The goal of Safe Zone is to provide a network of persons who would be "understanding, supportive and trustworthy if a sexual minority student or employee need[ed] help, advice, or just someone to talk with." Still, in many instances, administrators sounded the urgency of designing structural mechanisms for gathering data about the experiences of LGBT students and developing tailored programs. One director of an Office of Student Life put it flatly, "There is simply no institutional capacity to do the strategic work we know needs to be done."

The dire need for tailored programs is evident in complaints by student life staff that they could not identify proactive and consistent programming that their offices had undertaken to shift the culture of silence at their respective schools or attend effectively to the incidents of violence that had occurred among students. While they knew of some of the more egregious and public incidents of violence at HBCUs, such as suicide, an attack on a gay student by members of a school's marching band, and the beating of a male student with a baseball bat, there seemed to be an implicit sense that they were not those institutions. Somehow, then, egregious violence was something that occurred elsewhere. As is the case at PWIs, LGBT students are severely harmed, attacked and harassed *for* their sexual orientation on HBCU campuses; they have been the survivors of hate crimes, and some have harmed themselves. On the same day that we visited one campus, LGBT students learned that a lesbian student, who had only a few months earlier withdrawn from the university, had taken her own life. Admittedly, this incident occurred after she had withdrawn, but there has been one reported incident of suicide at an HBCU, and students revealed in conversations with us that they, too, had considered suicide. What this suggests is that HBCUs are indeed microcosms of the national picture with respect to violence. It is important to remember that, nationally, Black LGBT youth are nearly 35 percent more likely than other youth to be homeless or commit suicide, even though they are a mere one percent of the overall youth population.[2] While the term "hate crime" rarely surfaced in our discussions of violence against LGBT people, it would be useful to introduce the concept in future discussions of campus violence on HBCU campuses. Much like violence in the larger society, these incidents of violence might well be flash points that signal certain ruptures in the social systems of gender-sex at schools. It is thus another area that requires deeper investigation.

From students in our focus group discussions, mostly with LGBT organizations, we heard a variety of disturbing occurrences: that LGBT students drop out or transfer when campus pressures become psychologically unbearable; that they experience peer pressure to acknowledge their racial identity but not their sexual orientation; that they have experienced homophobia in the classroom; that they have been harassed by faculty with apparently little recourse as policies that prohibit sexual harassment do not routinely include harassment on the basis of gender identity; that they live in fear of being ostracized; that they have struggled with coming out on campus; that they have heard whisperings about the presumed damnation of their souls because of their sexual orientation; that "butch" women have been dubbed "the aggressives" by virtue of how they look and what they wear; that lesbians have been told they are "too cute to be lesbian;" that gay men have been told that "sissies are not real men." There were two instances in which students were required to adhere to a "dress code" and codes of "appropriate attire." Though LGBT students in the case of the latter were divided on the intent of the policy, they were nonetheless the most vocal opponents of the policy on campus. More work will need to be done to determine whether the focus on looks and dress works to displace engagement with other issues that pertain to gender and sexuality.

On campuses where loyalty to race dovetailed closely with hetero-masculinity, students believed it was "easier to be out as a lesbian than as a gay man"; while in other co-ed contexts, they felt that "heterosexual women accepted lesbians far more easily than heterosexual men accepted gay men." Other campuses seemed less polarized and polarizing. In the absence of student organizations, especially on small campuses, one out LGBT student can bear the onus of all that signifies LGBT on that campus, assuming a level of hypervisibility and taking on a level of extra work that borders on danger. Some LGBT students live on campuses where their student handbooks prohibit them from "showing affection," and others revealed that they feel compelled to hold administrators accountable for "creating a hostile environment." All these experiences can be understood as violence of different kinds.

But perhaps the most consistent area of collective student discontent about academic matters pertained to epistemic violence, the erasure of LGBT knowledge and ways of knowing, evidenced in the absence of focused LGBT curriculum across different disciplines. It was often difficult for students to identify LGBT courses. They also alluded to closeted faculty and administrators whom they believed perpetuated the culture of silence and therefore made it difficult to be held accountable by virtue of their remaining in the closet. For them, closeted Black faculty meant that, in most instances, advisors to their organizations were white. A white gay faculty member on one of the campuses captured the dilemma this way: "Students have said to me that one of the hardest things on this campus is that there are no role models who are out and proud ... the fact that they have an old white guy as their LGBT advisor speaks volumes ... I was hired as an openly gay man in my department and I can say that it is easier being an out white man than it is for my Black colleagues ... When I brought up LGBT issues in 1999, there was a multitude of really concerning responses, from total ignorance to really hateful remarks; there is much less of that these days. I've seen students lead the way on this issue."

Indeed, LGBT students and their allies are the catalyst for change at HBCUs. Political organizing on the part of LGBT students at our partner schools is one clear indication that gender-sex systems are being publicly contested and renegotiated despite the cost. But there is also substantial benefit in the sense that political organizing assists in building a collective consciousness among LGBT students that reduces the tendency to individualize social injury. Some organizations are of long standing—two decades and more—while others have been formed recently. Where organizations were small and embattled, they experienced the arm of the administration as long and retaliative. They experienced "being pushed around a lot." On some campuses, strong cultures of heteromasculinity conspire to keep gay men away from LGBT organizations, in which case such organizations tend to be small and comprises mostly lesbians. Such cultures can produce a certain amount of homophobic polarization among students, as this statement indicates: "As a heterosexual male, I would not join ... LGBT groups ... [They] promote segregation. They are promoting themselves ... segregation is an inevitable result." This occurred on the very campus where we noted the hypervisibility of the single lesbian student. The comment helped explain the failure of events that she almost singlehandedly organized: "I organized this event *Gay Questions, Straight Answers* ... sides were set up for the gay side and a straight side ... nobody from the straight side came out to support us, only some high school students that were brought in by another woman from off campus." Aware of the costs of her own hypervisibility, she yearned for an organization: "If we had a gay/straight alliance on this campus, it would give people a place to go so they could come out; it would help lines of communication."

In all but four of our partner schools, students had important experiences in building vibrant organizations. Thus, the LGBT student organizations with whom we held focus group discussions comprise approximately 23 percent of all LGBT student organizations among HBCUs. While their missions vary, SafeSpace at Morehouse, CASCADE at Howard, B.R.I.D.E. at Bennett, RAINBOW SOUL at Morgan State, COLORS at North Carolina Central, and Afrekete at Spelman all agree on the importance of combating "heterosexism and homophobia," on providing "support and company," on building a "safe, respecting and affirming campus," and on creating relationships with allies. They have lobbied administrators and their peers for LGBT programs and curricular interventions, which they believe will benefit the entire campus. They understand that misogyny and patriarchy undergird and prop up heterosexism, therefore the slogan, "No More No Homo," at one campus, and they have likened sexual injustice to racial injustice: "Is Gay the New Black?" In collaboration with faculty and offices of Student Life, they have organized for "Dinner After Sex," and have sponsored film series. They have created magazines, set up e-portals to facilitate quick and easy communication, and have documented their lives. They have joined fraternities and sororities, sometimes in tense ways and sometimes in ways accommodative to them. They have staged days of silence on their campuses to coincide with 10 April, the National Day of Silence.[3] SafeSpace and Afrekete worked collaboratively in the Atlanta University Center to sponsor their first Pride Week at Spelman College (November, 2009). Among other events in November 2010, the second Pride Week, they featured "a drag fashion show ... to normalize concepts of gender and gender expression that have been deemed 'alternative' by mainstream society." They have also worked collaboratively and in conjunction with Equality Ride, a project of SoulforceQ, "a traveling forum that gives young adults the chance to deconstruct injustice and the rhetoric that sustains it." Our campus visit to Howard coincided with Cascade's celebration of 30 years of LGBT student organizing on its campus; there we read its *Lavender Report,* written by Victoria Kirby, a model for other HBCUs interested in chronicling their LGBT history. LGBT students have called for a variety of changes on their campuses: "resource centers with paid dedicated staff" to serve as the springboard for conferences, symposia and research; the establishment of "safe space;" clearly articulated and consistently visible non-discriminatory LGBT policies; LGBT training for faculty, staff, health professionals, police officers, and residence hall directors; active LGBT recruitment; substantive LGBT presence at Open Houses and New Student Orientation; signage for gender-neutral/family bathrooms."

Much of LGBT student organizing has come about in the wake of campus violence and in closely aligned partnerships with organizations such as the National Black Justice Coalition (NBJC), Campus Pride, and the Human Rights Campaign (HRC). The HRC began its HBCU initiative in 2001 in response to an incident in which the founder of an LGBT student organization was threatened with a gun as he walked on campus with his boyfriend; he was later attacked on campus. HRC intervened on behalf of the gay student and since that time has worked closely with LGBT student organizations at 22 HBCUs.[4] They also maintain their Equality Forward Research Project/Resource Guide to coming out for African Americans. They provide resources, assist students in chartering their organizations, identify advisors, engage in succession planning, and organize student empowerment sessions as well as dialogues on sexuality.[5] In 2009, HRC worked in concert with members of Rainbow Soul to launch a letter writing campaign in support of the Employment NonDiscrimination Act (ENDA) that prohibits workplace discrimination on the basis of sexual orientation and gender identity. HRC teamed with CASCADE to present a panel titled, "Legalize Gay: A Dialogue on Race, Faith and Marriage." [6]

Working at the intersection of various identities of "race/ethnicity, gender, religion," Campus Pride offers resources and programs in conjunction with some HBCUs. Its Voice and Action National Leadership Award grew out of a scholarship program for HBCU students, Camp Pride Summer Leadership Camp, which is based on a social justice model of leadership development. It is under the auspices of this leadership camp that JeShawna Wholley (2011), past president of Spelman's Afrekete, was recognized in 2011 as the first African American awardee.[7]

In 2010, The National Black Justice Coalition, which works at the confluence of civil rights and LGBT rights, placed HBCUs at the heart of its work. Among other projects they have "provided leadership opportunities to HBCU students from around the country to participate in the 2010 "OUT on the Hill," an NBJC conference that brings Black LGBT leaders to Washington, D.C., to hold members of the Congressional Black Caucus accountable for taking on these questions. They have also met with twelve senior level administrators at HBCUs on the climate issues that are the subject of our campus visit and were instrumental (along with HRC) in highlighting HBCU visibility at the National Coming Out Day at the White House.[8]

Generally, all these organizations have brought legitimacy to the concerns of LGBT students on our campuses. One outstanding question remains about how to make inroads and create a ripple effect with other HBCUs who have not yet begun to consider these questions. Very recently, the Human Rights Campaign has created a partnership with the United Negro College Fund to explore ways to reach additional HBCUs. Out of 103 HBCUs, 26 have LGBT student organizations.

LGBT Recruitment and Retention Efforts

To be explicit about LGBT recruitment and retention of students suggests that institutions have been simultaneously explicit about the range of policy and program matters that shape the cultural and academic lives of LGBT communities. We were unable to find such explicit policies. As administrators at HBCUs shy away from being known as a magnet for LGBT students, citing at times pressure from alumni, it is left up to students to use the mechanisms at their disposal to recruit other students to build a critical mass. Gay friendliness is oftentimes a determination that students make, and they tend to make that determination not so much based on the existence of policy, but on numbers, on the presence of a few, yet important faculty and administrator allies and based on vibrant student organizations.

LGBT Policy Inclusion

In our review of their public documents, we found that nine of our partner schools prohibit discrimination based on sexual orientation and include the words "sexual orientation" as part of a list of other possible categories of discrimination such as race, color, national or ethnic origin, religion, sex, age, marital status, and disability or physical challenge. Three schools explicitly prohibit discrimination on the basis of gender identity by including the words "gender identity" in their policy, and one school explicitly outlawed discrimination on the basis of HIV status. Perhaps the most inclusive of all these statements of nondiscrimination indicated that the school was "committed to ensuring equal opportunity without regard to race, color, national or ethnic origin, sex, actual or perceived gender, age, religion, creed, disability, sexual orientation, gender identity and expression, genetic information or parental, marital, domestic partner, civil union, military or veteran status."

Three of our participating schools offer health insurance coverage to their employees' same sex partners. As posed on the questionnaire, the query asked: What other benefits does your campus offer equally to both opposite-sex spouses of employees as well same-sex partners of employees? The options listed twelve possible benefits ranging from dental and vision insurance to tuition remission for spouse/partner and employee discounts. From a lengthy discussion on one of our campuses as part of the LGBT working group on LGBT issues convened by the President, we learned that in some instances certain benefits were not included in any employees' compensation packages while others would require negotiations with health insurance companies. A benefit such as tuition remission for spouse/partner/dependents, for instance, bears on larger legal questions about whether LGBT persons are prohibited from adopting dependents, from marriage, and from registering/claiming domestic partnership. This is one major area where clarification and ongoing discussion will be most needed. Access to this information also emerges as an area of concern. In one of our faculty discussions and in conversation with one director of human resources at the same institution, it was revealed that although same-sex partner benefits were provided, the information had not been made public. The director of HR immediately noted that it was an omission and promised a correction. The correction has since been made. However, in light of the varied accessibility of printed materials that would send a clear signal about LGBT inclusion to all segments of the campus community and the concern voiced by some, mostly senior, administrators about outside perception of their schools as havens for lesbians and gay men, a question emerges about whether the inconsistency of visible materials contributes to the self-presentation of the school as heteronormative. In some instances, we observed a gap between a vision of inclusion at the senior level of the institution and implementation that would have been evidenced, for instance, in proactive strategies to train faculty and administrators about what LGBT policy inclusion would entail for themselves, the students whom they served as well as the larger campus climate.

LGBT Support and Institutional Commitment

Questions about diversity in higher education have gained widespread attention over the last two decades, so much so that there is perhaps no institution in higher education today whose intellectual culture has not been shaped by it. But diversity means different things, and while it has been pervasive both as ethos and as practice, these meanings shift within and across campuses and disciplines, depending on the play of social demographics and political will. Notably, HBCUs have been missing from these national debates about diversity.

One of the pivotal questions we posed in focus groups on various campuses had to do with public conversations about diversity, whether they had been undertaken, what had been the impetus for them and whether sexual orientation or sexual diversity figured as important constituents of those conversations. According to one Vice President for Academic Affairs: "When I first got here five years ago, we didn't have the infrastructure for diversity programming ... the majority of diversity work was around food, music, and fashion. Most student activities are centered around Homecoming since we are a traditional HBCU." That situation has certainly changed, but most of our partnering schools revealed that more deeply contextual conversations about diversity would be of enormous benefit to their institutions.

In many instances where inclusive discussions about diversity had occurred, they came in response to incidents of physical violence against LGBT persons. They have taken the form of mandated workshops and professional training that engaged the multidimensionality of diversity. Such workshops are critical not only for building sensitivity but also for opening the analytic parameters of a way of thinking, a new consciousness about diversity that is not exclusionary and that can imagine all different kinds of people within its ambit. For campuses that are in the early stages of building awareness and instituting critical dialogue on matters of sexual orientation and campus culture, these workshops are foundational to establishing a learning curve. But the question arises: Where does sensitivity training end and implementation begin? Is there a sustained institutional commitment to move ahead of the moment of acute crisis or preempt it by adopting practices and programs that anchor the multidimensional *experience* of diversity?

Support for and commitment to these understandings of sexual orientation as diversity can be demonstrated in the following ways: assigning full-time professional or dedicated staff to address the unique needs of LGBT students and continuing the ongoing work of legitimating sexual diversity on a campus-wide basis; creating a student resource office that provides gender and sexuality information; creating a safe zone, a web of visible people on campus who identify openly and therefore publicly as allies for LGBT concerns; establishing a standing committee that advises the administration on all dimensions of diversity; facilitating the creation of an LGBT alumni group within the existing alumni organization; providing gender neutral/single occupancy restroom facilities in various buildings throughout the campus. One could imagine in such a context senior level administrators utilizing gender– and sexuality-inclusive language both in spoken and written statements about diversity in ways that legitimate the existence of actual programs and the building of new understandings of identity. These are some of the underlying assumptions that the Council for Advancement of Standards in Higher Education (CAS) adopted in a widely disseminated document that deals with the imperatives of establishing targeted programs and services that can reverse the disproportionate harassment, discrimination, and hostility that LGBT students face on our campuses.[9]

When asked to gauge the climate in one of our joint administrator/faculty focus group discussions, one chaplain responded: "We do not have a climate." He went on to explain that one piece of work that needed to be undertaken on his campus was the deconstruction of religious belief systems and that in those instances where religion was a firm part of the "cultural narrative" of an institution, the task of deconstructing those belief systems was an uphill battle. "How does one establish a climate?" he asked. "How do we get from point A to point B?" These are critical questions considering the strong links many HBCUs have with the churches from which they originated. In one instance, we found an HBCU president who initiated a blog, "Time for HBCUs and the Black Church to Talk about Sex." In 2011, the school hosted its first Sex Week, "its goal [being] to provide a forum for frank and honest dialogue among the students, faculty and staff ... to promote healthy behaviors and good decision making with regard to sex ... The topics included STD and HIV education, sexual harassment and Christian relationships." [10] Still a certain silence persists.

Many faculty and administrators attributed the continued silence and taboo around talking sex, sexuality, and sexual orientation to the pervasiveness of Christianity in campus cultures and the more dominant Biblical interpretations that promote a conservatizing ethos by branding homosexuality as sin and a 'lifestyle' to be condemned and converted rather than as a minoritized identity formation that needs to be engaged. But data from the Centers for Disease Control confirm that both Black heterosexual and LGBT people of color are disproportionately affected by HIV, thus making it an ethical imperative for HBCUs to provide sex-positive and inclusive information that is clearly missing from the larger society.[11] Now, as part of a small but growing movement within Black religious communities to re-examine their beliefs and move toward the affirmation of LGBT people, prominent ministers have also visited campuses and addressed questions of homophobia and heterosexism head on.[12] We found that chaplains have an important role to play in reframing the language of 'worship' and 'prayer' to be inclusive of multiple belief systems; in advancing plausible Biblical explanations for some of the thorniest theological issues that pertain to sexuality such as the fall of Sodom and Gomorrah (interpretations that do not reside in the 'sin' of 'homosexuality,' but rather in 'inhospitality'); and, where possible, participating in coalitional strategies between the university and wider community. One such strategy was undertaken in Washington D.C., in which the Divinity School of one of our partners worked collaboratively with LGBT groups in the area on the successful passage of same-gender marriage.[13]

LGBT Housing and Residence Life

Questions about the creation of inclusive housing environments for LGBT students pertain to an area which requires attention at HBCUs. On our partner campuses, there seemed to be no formal mechanisms to match LGBT students with LGBT-friendly roommates in their application for student housing, though in many instances students were free to choose their roommates; or to provide for gender-neutral, single-occupancy rest rooms; or to install individual showers to protect the privacy of transgender students. Housing and residence life staff noted that training on LGBT issues was insufficient for the task that confronted them and that oftentimes they worked without formal mechanisms in place. It is in this context that dorms become the flashpoint for the fractures and unevenness in the campus response to the growing and visible presence of LGBT students. Proximity, intimacy, friendship, and the sheer dailyness of living push competing sexual anxieties to the fore in ways that provoke dormitories to become living incubators of things denied and unexplored.

There are several sexual cultures that reside oftentimes uncomfortably in the tight space of the dorm and that therefore make interpersonal relationships especially fraught. Students are required to adhere to the etiquette of shared living, but they are also bound, especially in single-sex contexts, by sexual codes for visitation and the like. In those instances in which heterosexual coupling takes place between and among schools that are in close proximity to one another, both administrators and faculty report a marked increase in both intimate partner violence and physical violence among women in particular, as they compete for the same male partner. At times the details of relationships were posted on Facebook and other social media causing women to experience a double shame—the shame of violence as well as the shame of compromising sexual exposure. But there were also instances reported to us in which off campus partners were physically abusive to their student partners who lived in the dorms. And there is evidence as well of partner violence among the smaller, yet growing numbers of LGBT students.

Increasingly, LGBT students are refusing to inhabit the closet or to choose silence as a way of living. In a context in which they are made to be hyper visible, they are thus targeted by heterosexual students. Residence life staff sometimes referenced several reasons why LGBT students were targeted: perceived loud and aggressive behavior on the part of LGBT students; the fact of an LGBT student being unapologetically out; and presumed favoritism, where requests for friendly rooming choices by LGBT students were perceived by heterosexual students as an unfair bending of rules. Paradoxically, this latter form of reverse heterosexism has reared its head on single-sex campuses where heterosexual students claim disproportionate injury. Some administrators were of the view that if rooming choices were made on the basis of sexual orientation, it would open the door for sex in dormitories to become the norm. Central to this claim, however, is the assumption that two LGBT students living together is motivated by sex. It is another claim that operates in the wider society as well in ways that circumscribe the possibilities of kinship, support, and chosen family in which LGBT people engage. These arrangements could potentially open the door for deepened conversations about different family configurations, about sex, and about the complicated sexual cultures that these generations of youth inhabit. As the packed rooms at fora such as Dinner After Sex 1 & 11 and Sex Week indicate, *all* students stand to benefit from such conversations.

LGBT Campus Safety

All our partner campuses, like other campuses in the country, are mandated under the terms of the Clery Act to have clear procedures for reporting and processing complaints, bias incidents, and hate crimes.[14] But as one president put it, "Federal regulations such as the Clery Act require certain things of us, but to move from regulations to intentional programmatic efforts is a whole other thing." During our campus visits, we did not collect information on specifically LGBT-related incidents as hate crimes. Yet, concerning one publicized case, we learned that one incident that could have been recorded as a hate crime was reported instead as "disorderly conduct."[15] The significance here lies in the naming and the use of specific language that could assist in the development of procedures and response structures for "LGBT bias incidents and hate crimes." As one of its HBCU campus initiatives, Campus Pride has developed a Stop the Hate initiative that involves the training of public safety staff in strategies to monitor and prevent incidents of bias and hate crimes against LGBT people.16

LGBT Counseling and Health

From a survey of websites, there were no counseling centers on our partner campuses that promoted and advocated for services that address the unique needs of LGBT students. They do not make specific mention of serving the needs of LGBT students as there are no targeted support services for coming out and addressing LGBT concerns in relationship to those multiple dimensions of diversity that institutions vow to protect in their statements of non-discrimination. In follow-up correspondence with one of our partner institutions, however, we found out that the university had created an Empowerment Committee that was being led by a member of that university's Counseling Center. Located within the department of Student Health and Counseling Services, its purpose "is to provide a venue for faculty, staff, students, and community partners to develop and implement support services to the LGBT community on campus." The committee is currently working on the following initiatives: i) assessing the university climate for readiness regarding [specific] services for the LGBTQ community; ii) assessing the current needs of the LGBTQ community; iii) developing "inclusive" outreach materials during health awareness screening activities; iv) developing culturally competent peer educators within Student Health and Counseling Services; and v) increasing professional cultural competency within the division of Student Affairs by means of in-services regarding LGBTQ support services."[17]

While no formal mechanisms appear to have been established to train staff and increase their sensitivity to meet the needs of LGBT students, individual counselors, however, by virtue of their own professional training, counsel LGBT students who seek their services. At one school, the counseling center was at the forefront of a major outreach effort to LGBT students that ultimately served as the catalyst for the formation of their student organization. In one focus group discussion with administrators, we learned that another school had pioneered a sensitive model of HIV testing and services for counseling that in the words of the counselor "created an environment where students knew they could bring their concerns and knew that they would be cared for;" while at another institution, one student noted, "we can't get birth control on campus and health services will only test for STDs if you have symptoms." Given what has been reported about the incidence of violence of different kinds, including violence against LGBT persons, services for survivors and perpetrators of homophobia, bi, and transphobia, and those that address domestic and relationship violence are critical in getting to the underside of the causes of such violence and in implementing strategies to reduce it. The large absence of designated counselors was one of the reasons students cited for not using counseling centers as a place to address their problems.

In an overall context where silence prevails and where violence has occurred, students reported a complex of emotional and psychic responses to coming out: confusion, shame, loneliness, anger, and fear of being ostracized by their families and their peers. Some have considered suicide. It is a long and difficult process to come to the point of asking, as one lesbian student did: "Should I stuff who I am in the closet because I'm simply trying to get an education at a university that happens to be in the Bible belt?" This refusal to continue to stuff oneself, to come into oneself, to move in and out and beyond the boundaries of the closet requires scrutiny, intentional support, advocacy, and visible safe space services that send a clear signal to LGBT students that institutions care about what matters to them as LGBT persons.

Conclusion

The major goal of this advocacy project was to raise awareness and engage in critical dialogue with various segments of the campuses of ten HBCUs on climate issues that shape the experiences of LGBT communities. In several cases we were informed that this was the first time the conversations our Arcus Project had initiated had taken place on their campuses, especially among high-level administrators, faculty, and staff. Underlying both the questions we posed and the discussions that were generated was a tacit adoption of the essence of the epigraphs with which we began this book. We are referring to Audre Lorde's trenchant insight: "it is not those differences between us that are separating us. It is rather our refusal to recognize those differences, and to examine the distortions which result from our misnaming them and their effects upon human behavior and expectation." And the equally trenchant recognition of Rev. Dr. Martin Luther King, Jr.: "(We are) caught in an inescapable network of mutuality, tied in a single garment of destiny. Whatever affects one directly, affects all indirectly ..." Thus, this project has placed the valuing and respecting of difference at the center of institutional transformation at HBCUs. What affects LGBT communities affects everyone.

We know from the higher education literature that both campus climate and campus culture play a formidable role in students' educational success, in the scholarly achievement of faculty, and in the productivity of all employees.[18] We know as well that the cultures of racial justice, which HBCUs have intentionally cultivated, are, in large measure, responsible for our success in educating and matriculating high-quality graduates and undergraduates. We are now at a crucial juncture where a new challenge awaits us–that of creating cultures on our campuses in which academic excellence, inclusion, and equity are at the forefront of our institutional imperatives. If the color line was, as W.E.B. Du Bois so wisely predicted, the problem of the 20th century, attending to multiple dimensions of difference and our inescapable mutuality are the problems or rather the opportunities of the 21st. They are the cognates for structuring some of the most vibrant educational communities imaginable.

NOTES

1. Bryant Keith Alexander, "Embracing the Teachable Moment: The Black Gay Body in the Classroom as Embodied Text," in E. Patrick Johnson and Mae G. Henderson, eds. *Black Queer Studies: A Critical Anthology,* London, Durham: Duke University Press, 2005, p. 261.

2. Department of Health and Human Services, Task Force of the Secretary on Youth Suicide, 1989, Washington, D.C.

3. The National Day of Silence is now being annually held on the third Friday of April.

4. www.hrc.org/hbcu.

5. Email correspondence with Donna Payne, Associate Director of Diversity, HRC, March 2011.

6 http://hrcbackstory.org/2010/04/race-faith-and-marriage-equality-dialogue-at-howard-university.

7. www.campuspride.org; email correspondence and conversation with Shane L. Windmeyer, Executive Director/Founder Campus Pride, March, 2011.

8. Email correspondence and conversations with Tarrance Laney, resource person, National Black Justice Coalition, March 2011.

9. CAS Professional Standards in Higher Education, "The Role of Lesbian, Gay, Bisexual, and Transgender Programs and Services: CAS Contextual Statement," Washington, D.C. 2000 and 2010; www.cas.edu.

10. See http://newsone.com/newsone-original/newsonestaff2/time-for-hbcus-and-the-black-church-to-talk-about-sex/ Dr. Walter Kimbrough, President of Philander Smith College, February, 2011.

11. CDC. Subpopulation Estimates from the HIV Incidence Surveillance System– United States, 2006. MMWR 2008;57:985-9.CD.C.. Prevalence and awareness of HIV infection among men who have sex with men–21 cities, United States, 2008. MMWR 2010; 59:1201-7. Hall I, Song R, Rhodes P, et al. Estimation of HIV incidence in the United States. JAMA 2008; 300: 520-9; See also, Office of National AIDS Policy, National HIV/AIDS Strategy. Washington, D.C.: Office of National AIDS Policy, 2010. Available at http://www.whitehouse.gov/administration/eop/onap/nhas. Accessed November 1, 2010.

12. http://www.theroot.com/views/black-church-and01lgbt-community

13. For this discussion, see Howard University's unpublished *Lavender Report;* See E. Patrick Johnson, *Sweet Tea: Black Gay Men of the South*, for a compelling account of the ways in which Black gay men weave their day to day lives into the church. For an expansive and moving treatment of the varied spiritual lives of Black same-gender loving people, see G. Winston James and Lisa C. Moore, *Spirited: Affirming the Soul and Black Gay/Lesbian Identity,* Washington. D. C: RedBone Press, 2006. And in that vein, Randy P. Conner and David Hatfield Sparks, *Queering Creole Spiritual*

Traditions: Lesbian, Gay, Bisexual and Transgender Participation in African-Inspired Traditions in the Americas, New York: Harrington Park Press, 2004.

14. The Clery Act requires higher education institutions to collect crime data, report, and disseminate this information to the campus community and to the Department of Education. The Act is intended to provide students and their families around the country with accurate and complete information about the safety of colleges and universities in the United States. To comply with the Clery Act, the Office of Public Safety is responsible for compiling and reporting specified crime statistics and certain referral information for the campus, on a monthly and/or annual basis, to the U.S. Department of Education (USDE), the (relevant state's) Bureau of Investigation, and the Metropolitan Police Department (MNPD). In addition, the Office of Public Safety is responsible for publishing the University's policies pertaining to crime prevention and awareness on the campus. This overview of the terms and regulatory procedures of the Act is reproduced on many campuses. The Act clearly states that in compiling statistics colleges and universities "must indicate whether a specified crime is a hate crime." See also Federal Register 22314 et seq, April 29, 1994. Also, Title 34, Code of Federal Regulations.

15. The Matthew Shepherd and James Byrd, Jr. Hate Crimes Legislation of 2009 underscores this point as it specifically addresses crimes that are motivated by a victim's "actual or perceived gender, sexual orientation, gender identity or disability."

16. Conversation and email correspondence with Shane L. Windmeyer, Executive Director/Founder Campus Pride, March 2011.

17. Email correspondence with Chimi L. Boyd-Keyes, Director, Women's Center, North Carolina Central University, March, 2011, and our Arcus campus liaison.

18. See A. Kezar and P.D. Eckels, "The Effects of Institutional Culture on Change Strategies in Higher Education, *The Journal of Higher Education,* vol. 73 (222): 435-460; see also Shawn R. Harper and Marybeth Gasman, "Consequences of Conservatism: Black Make Undergraduates and the Politics of Historically Black Colleges Universities," *The Journal of Negro Education,* (Fall 2008) 77(4):336-351.

21. Challenges and Possibilities at HBCUs after the COVID-19 Pandemic

Reinvesting in Vital Institutions, with Kimberly M. Jackson **(2021)**

Historically Black colleges and universities (HBCUs), founded in the nineteenth century, are well-known for empowering students to become leaders and change agents. HBCUs have varying demographics, but all are centrally focused on ensuring the academic success of students of color. Among our 101 institutions are colleges and universities public and private, urban and rural, large and small, thriving and struggling, and single-gender and coeducational, awarding degrees ranging from the associate's to the doctorate.

Historically, HBCUs have produced 50 percent of Black teachers and doctors and 80 percent of Black judges. They continue to graduate the largest percentage of African American students with degrees in science, technology, engineering, and mathematics. According to the National Science Foundation, Spelman College has produced the highest number of Black women doctoral recipients in science and engineering. Xavier University of Louisiana and Howard University have been the top producers of African American medical school graduates. HBCUs deliberately focus on brokering access to STEM through a variety of policies, practices, and activities. Howard University now has the distinction of having graduated the first woman vice president in the nation's history. Other outstanding alumni and alumnae include Toni Morrison, Thurgood Marshall, Martin Luther King Jr., Oprah Winfrey, Common, Stacey Abrams, Rosalind Brewer, Andrew Young, Levi Watkins Jr., Jesse Jackson, Samuel L. Jackson, and Chadwick Boseman.

The continued relevancy of HBCUs has generated academic inquiry for more than a decade. Some believe that HBCUs are an outmoded vestige of segregation and cite opportunities for African Americans now to attend all institutions of higher education. Increased access for African American students to the full range of colleges and universities has, for many, become an argument to dismantle HBCUs. Between 2010 and 2018, HBCUs experienced a 10 percent decrease in enrollment, according to the National Center for Education Statistics. However, applications and enrollments have increased at some HBCUs among international and Latinx students over the past four years as well as among Black students, perhaps as a result of the current political climate concerning structural racism. In this regard, an increase in hate crimes, including racist police violence, has been cited as a possible explanation for increased HBCU enrollments. Walter Kimbrough, president of Dillard University, attributes this increase at forty HBCUs to what he calls the "Missouri Effect"—racial harassment of Black students at majority (predominantly white) institutions.

At HBCUs around the nation, the COVID-19 pandemic has pushed administrators to think more strategically about their institutions in the wake of perhaps the most daunting challenge to face higher education in the twenty-first century. In many ways, it is the best of times and the worst of times. On the one hand, millions in much-needed philanthropic dollars have made their way to Black colleges in the aftermath of the killing of George Floyd by Minneapolis police in May 2020. On December 12, 2020, Congress finally passed the HBCU Propelling Agency Relationships towards a New Era of Results for Students (HBCU PARTNERS) Act following decades of lobbying efforts by HBCU advocates. Certain federal agencies are now required annually to explain how HBCUs can compete more effectively for contracts and grants. On the other hand, only a handful of Black colleges have endowments that exceed $200 million; inequitable federal and state funding continues; our students, coming from households that on average earn considerably less than the median white family income, must secure larger federal, state, and private loans than many non-HBCU students, resulting in substantially greater debt upon graduation; and graduation rates in 2019 were reported to be only 35 percent compared with 60 percent for all higher education institutions. Chief among the various factors contributing to differential graduation rates is the large number of low-income and first-generation Black students at HBCUs, who face daunting financial and other challenges that make graduating from college in four years more difficult.

A year after the start of the pandemic, HBCUs are struggling to make difficult decisions about reopening and cope with daunting shortfalls in critical tuition and room and board revenue resulting from enrollment drops and campus closures. While students focus on preserving their GPAs with pass/fail requests, connecting with their peers, or wanting to walk across the stage at sometimes-canceled in-person graduation ceremonies, administrators have been forced to prioritize the health and safety of students and their workforce. These additional financial and operational burdens have forced many institutions to shift to crisis-management mode. HBCUs are among the estimated half of US colleges and universities facing financial crises, with effects that will likely linger beyond the pandemic. Significant declines in federal funds for HBCUs and rising college tuitions have also forced many HBCUs to the brink of financial disaster.

And yet, for many African American students, HBCUs remain irreplaceable. In a recent article in *Inside AAMU,* "House Not a Home without Students: HBCUs and COVID-19," Alabama A&M University student Aayana Ingram powerfully captures the importance and uniqueness of Black colleges: "These institutions are not just institutions of knowledge for students but their home." Testimony from a graduating student and student government association president underscores both the challenges and the possibilities facing HBCUs: "COVID-19 has affected the experience and the community of HBCUs drastically. However, the worldwide pandemic has brought HBCUs even closer together virtually. We are reaching out to each other to share ideas on how we can cater to students across universities. We are doing everything we can to keep the students involved, engaged, and entertained."

Despite having shut down temporarily in March 2020, many HBCUs had no choice but to allow students, faculty, and staff to return to campus in August, despite increased COVID-19 cases in their states. Closing campuses for even one semester surely would have severely hindered their ability to reopen the following year, given the reliance of HBCUs on tuition and room and board for financial sustainability.

They did their best to keep students safe. Many of these Black colleges applied for federal assistance to create COVID-19-testing hubs. Institutions that chose to reopen their campuses for instruction in the fall 2020 semester applauded their students for compliance with social-distancing and mask-wearing requirements and reported lower COVID-19 infection rates than predominantly white institutions. However, there has been limited reporting of data on COVID-19 at HBCUs and limited information about campus protocols surrounding frequency of testing, quarantining on campus, and contact-tracing implementation. Faculty members on many campuses are frustrated by inadequate technology upgrades for remote instruction; the digital divide among students and between tenure-line and non-tenure-line faculty must be addressed. Faculty see continuing challenges associated with the lack of adequate training for hybrid, asynchronous, and synchronous teaching; uncertainty about the health and well-being of their faculty and staff colleagues as well as students; and an overall unease about the rush to reopen or stay open in the spring 2021 semester, given the increased numbers of COVID-19 cases and deaths in their respective cities and states. They are also keenly aware that African Americans have borne a heavier burden than the rest of the population since the beginning of the pandemic. While students overwhelmingly share a desire to return to their campuses as soon as possible, they are also anxious about what they perceive to be less than optimal planning on the part of administrators with respect to a broad range of safety issues. For example, in spring 2021, Spelman College, whose pre-pandemic enrollment was 2,100, brought back a small number of students to campus using a low-density model (350 students or less). And, although the campus has instituted a "reset and pause" period (five days of rest for those students living on campus), mandatory COVID-19 tests including weekly rapid tests for students and staff, and extensive town-hall meetings, students and parents remain concerned about care available for students and staff when someone becomes ill, the cleaning and ventilation of campus buildings, the adequacy of food services, plans for contact tracing, and services for mental health. However, the desire of students to connect to unique campus cultures and to their peers appears to be outweighing their anxiety about returning to campus, given their reasons for having chosen to attend an HBCU in the first place: community and a sense of home.

HBCUs face compelling and difficult questions in a post-pandemic era. How will they evolve and adapt to the serious financial burdens that are likely to linger or worsen, especially at more fragile institutions? The influx of millions of dollars from wealthy donors over the past several months has landed at only a handful of institutions, most of which are the least financially at risk. What is the likelihood that institutions can ensure safety for students, faculty, and staff returning to campus and to dormitories? How can HBCUs handle their serious financial challenges if post-pandemic enrollments continue to drop? While the pandemic is certainly not responsible for all of the enrollment and retention challenges at HBCUs, it definitely has exacerbated them. The socioeconomic status of African American families as well as their more serious health issues have also exacerbated the pandemic's impact in our communities.

An urgent question for administrators and faculty members at HBCUs to ponder remains: What have we learned about ourselves—our strengths and liabilities—during the past year? Because the COVID-19 crisis amplified deeply rooted inequities in education, we are at a turning point. HBCUs are critical to the higher education landscape, providing more reliable safe havens for students through housing, food security, health-care access, and mental-health support. State and federal agencies must reinvest in and reprioritize funding for HBCUs and other colleges that do the brunt of the work in supporting Black and brown students. Faculty at HBCUs should be recognized as they continue to be extraordinary teachers and advocates in places where students enter with serious financial and other challenges. HBCUs will need compassion and resources to address the ongoing impact of the COVID-19 crisis on Black and brown students in the years to come. They must continue to plan, prepare, train, equip, and organize for disasters; design and offer a model for sustainable tuition and fees; increase financial stability through alternative funding revenue streams; substantially increase endowments with more aggressive fundraising among philanthropists and other individual donors (including alumni and alumnae) and foundations; implement alternative and effective teaching models when in-person teaching is not an option; recruit more competitive, affluent international students; and close the digital divide. We are confident that serious attention to these challenges on our campuses will result in a reimagining of our futures and recommitments to what we do best. Increased and substantial philanthropic dollars for urgent racial equity projects in the aftermath of highly publicized anti-Black violence, especially the murders of Breanna Taylor and George Floyd by police, are also signs of hope.

22. Building the House You Want to Live and Teach In

How Women's Studies Nurtured Radical Transformation at Spelman College (2022)

I have always been committed to Black, feminist education: but sometimes you have to create the college you want to teach at. Let me explain.

When I graduated from Spelman College in 1966 at the height of the civil rights movement, I reflected upon the kind of professional life I wanted to craft, though, as for many young people, the details of this portrait were fuzzy and out of focus. I spent a year at Wellesley College studying literature and then returned to Atlanta for a master's degree in English at Atlanta University (now Clark Atlanta University or AU).

By this time, at the urging of my mother, I understood that I wanted to be a college professor. My uncle was the president of Alabama State University, so I went there after AU for my first job (a path that might astonish young people entering the market today).

But after two years, my then-husband, who taught economics, decided to attend law school at Emory University. We returned to Atlanta, and I began a non-tenure track position in the English department in 1971. Shortly after I began teaching the required first-year composition and World Literature courses, I began to realize that the Eurocentric, Christian-centered, male-dominated, conservative college that I had left in 1966 was as yet unaffected by the vast changes brought about by the civil rights movement, and it was then that I made a critical decision for my career. Even though I was an untenured professor I decided that I would position myself as a "radical" teacher who would try and disrupt some of the "mis-education" of the curriculum, which at the time mirrored the traditional higher education curriculum throughout the United States.

I am now certain that I had been impacted significantly by my immersion in academic feminism. I had written a master's thesis on "Faulkner's Treatment of Women in His Major Novels" at Atlanta University. At the same time, I participated in a consciousness raising group, organized by a member of the National Black Feminist Organization founded in 1972, that met regularly at the nearby public housing project. Committed to transformation concerning issues of race and gender, I designed the first women's studies classes in the

English Department, and perhaps at the College more broadly: "Images of Women in Literature," "Images of Women in the Media," and two mini-courses on "Black Women Writers."

In 1976, five years after I began teaching at Spelman, I made the most difficult decision of my academic career: playing a role in the lock-up of the Board of Trustees because of their decision not to appoint the first Black woman president of Spelman. Since its founding in 1881, the college had had a number of white women, and one Black male as president, so this was an opportunity for historic change.

It was the first week of April, which is when the Board of Trustees always met in the student center on campus. Because I was untenured, and students were also involved in the protest, I knew that I could, and probably would, lose my job. But I also knew that if I survived and was allowed to remain at Spelman I would continue to practice what I had been preaching to the students who chose to join the small band of faculty engaging in positive social and institutional change. I also vowed to myself that I would continue my oppositional stance with respect to faculty and curriculum development around gender and sexuality issues and faculty governance.

Spelman didn't have to look far to see where I stood, since it was during this time that I also published my first book—the coedited, first anthology of Black women's literature, *Sturdy Black Bridges: Visions of Black Women in Literature* (1979). It was also becoming clearer what I needed to do institutionally: make Black feminism visible. So, although we failed to prevent the hiring of the male Dr. Donald Stewart in 1976, although I was still untenured in 1981 (ten years after arriving at Spelman), I decided to leave the English Department and establish the Women's Research and Resource Center.

For me, "teaching while Black" had come to include creating the institutional structures and reforms that made my pedagogy possible, and that's the 1987 struggle, almost ten years after the lock-up protest, that resulted in Spelman finally hiring our first woman president, Johnnetta Betsch Cole. This time, I chose to work under the radar with a particular Board member in perhaps one of the most contentious episodes in Spelman's recent history. The Board was divided. Johnnetta was not our risk-averse faculty's choice, but I knew that if the Board made the wrong decision in this case, the future of Spelman as a progressive, feminist-aspiring institution would be in peril, along with my ability to stay there.

So, I decided to marshal all of my Black feminist energies and knowledge, and, with visiting history professor Paula Giddings, became a collaborator behind the scenes by drafting documents for a few Board members that would help to make the case for Cole as our first Black woman president. The resistance to her presidency in various circles was connected to why Spelman needed Dr. Cole: her radical political commitments. Prior to entering Spelman's presidential pool, as a professor at other universities, Dr. Cole publicly opposed the 1983 United States invasion of Grenada, she had traveled to Cuba, and was committed to the women's movement and feminism.

I am pleased to say that it worked: the Board made the difficult decision, in the aftermath of contentious debates on campus, to appoint Dr. Cole. Sometimes, when you fight for something you believe in, you win.

But I want to bear witness to what I think have been the consequences of the radical stances I, and a few others, chose to take at Spelman as we fought for institutional transformation during this juncture in its evolution. We were the first historically Black college with a women's studies program, a women's research center, and an LGBT project. Then, the public protest that a few faculty and students waged in 1976 made it possible, over a decade later, for Johnnetta Cole to be appointed president of Spelman.

That presidency, I would argue, helped to transform Spelman in ways that would be difficult to imagine now that it is no longer the conservative institution I first worked at. Dr. Cole supported, with resistance among many alumnae, the first LGBT student organization on campus. She enhanced the intellectual climate on campus, was openly feminist in her stances, and invited guest speakers such as Audre Lorde, Sonia Sanchez, Mari Evans, Angela Davis, Anita Hill, and Alice Walker.

Dr. Cole was certainly the kind of feminist role model that our students had never experienced in the president's office. In the ground-breaking Black Women's Studies anthology, *All the Women Are White, All the Blacks Are Men, But Some of Us Are Brave* (1993), co-editors Gloria T. Hull, Patricia Bell Scott, and Barbara Smith call for something that still doesn't exist in most colleges and universities. But we have managed to craft at Spelman's Women's Center an autonomous Black feminist space or institute as an alternative to mainstream academic cultures, one that constantly attends to the intersection of race, gender, class, and sexuality in various contexts.

Such a place is not just for faculty: it is a site where student activist leadership is welcomed and nurtured. It was, for example, women's studies students at Spelman who mounted the protest against music star Nelly. Their opposition to misogynist images of Black women in music videos garnered national and international attention and is featured in Byron Hurt's 2006 documentary about masculinity, *Hip Hop: Beyond Beats and Rhymes.* It is a site where LGBTQ and questioning students feel at home and are introduced to Black Queer Studies. It is a place where our most politically engaged students get energized around a range of issues. It is a place where students, not just our women's studies students, are intellectually engaged in exciting interdisciplinary discourse about white supremacy, HIV/AIDS, heteropatriarchy, racialized health disparities, homophobia in Black communities, among many other critical societal issues. It is a place where women from around the globe, especially from the Global South, gather in feminist solidarity to work on urgent issues facing persons of African descent, no matter where they live, and craft important collaborative projects.

Along this journey, the Center also supported me. I did get tenure, write the books I wanted to write, teach the courses I wanted to teach, engage in the work off campus that brings me tremendous joy, and collaborate with the most amazing group of women on the planet. What I am most pleased about, however, is that the decision to teach and agitate at Spelman, achieve my own dream of teaching Black feminist studies at an HBCU, and be an "out" radical professor means that I have been able to contribute to the development of a new generation of young feminists who will go out in the world as leaders and agitators no matter what spaces they find themselves in.

I want to end with a praisesong for just one of our daughters, Leana Cabral, a 2006 graduate and a member of radical philosopher Amilcar Cabral's family, because she illustrates the powerful impact of women's studies classes and programming at Spelman. When she enrolled in my introductory women's studies class as a sophomore, despite having come from a politically active family, she was shy. Uneasy about the radical gender politics of the class, she also wasn't sure whether she would stay at Spelman because of its overall conservatism.

But this is how transformation happens. Cabral left for a year, but she returned as a women's studies major, enrolled in my feminist theory class, and became one of the behind-the-scenes strategists for the Nelly protest. In her role as convener for the Feminist Majority Leadership Alliance on campus, she helped to craft the strategy for the Atlanta University Center Consortium (AUC) anti-rape campaign, which put her in a contentious relationship with senior administration and some students. During her senior year, Cabral also wrote a brilliant thesis, under Professor Patricia McFadden's tutelage, which was a feminist critique of three revolutionary giants in the struggle for Black liberation—Frantz Fanon, Amilcar Cabral, and Kwame Nkrumah.

There is no question in my mind that without radical Black feminist professors, it will not be possible to transform the academy, reinvigorate a transnational women's movement, or enable the emergence of a new generation of sister/comrades like Leana Cabral. And without transforming our structures and knowledge, we cannot have those scholars. Women's Studies does that, and continues to provide an important site for the transgressive pedagogies, research and activism that shaped me, shaped Spelman, and in which I hope to be engaged for the rest of my professional career.

Part V

Celebrating Black Women

23. | The Women of Bronzeville (1979)

An obvious difference between Gwendolyn Brooks and male writers such as Richard Wright and Ralph Ellison who have used the urban environment as the setting for their works is the greater amount of attention she devotes to the experiences of females. While women are not absent from Wright's or Ellison's ghetto worlds, they remain background figures who are of secondary importance, at best, to the central actions of their novels. Like Ann Petry, Brooks focuses on the impact of the urban experience on females as well as males. Her gender identity as well as her racial identity have molded her vision of the city. Though this aspect of her work has been generally ignored by critics, occasionally one can find comments about the value of the insights she has gained as a result of her gender.

> . . . The life of women, particularly Negro women, and the life of Negroes, particularly those who have grown up since World War I in the North, where America's big towns are, figure prominently in Miss Brooks' poetry. Moreover, it does seem true that she is a woman writing, although not in the manner of the damned mob of scribbling women who so distressed Hawthorne---nor because of any mysterious and occult woman's intuition which seems to guide her inner labors . . . Miss Brooks is a woman, and yet not one in an ignoble way. . . . There is a general way in which women do tend to know women and also a general way in which they tend to know men, largely because our culture makes it so. Miss Brooks, whether she is talking of women or men . . . constantly speaks as a woman. . . .[1]

Though one might disagree with this assessment of her as a woman writer, it is difficult to ignore her numerous portraits of the women who inhabit Bronzeville,[2] the setting for much of her poetry.

Like Richard Wright, she explores the tragic aspects of black ghetto life, but she also probes beneath the surface in order to illuminate those areas of the slum dweller's life which often go unnoticed and should not be seen as ugly or horrifying. Ironically, then, her poems reveal both the destructive and the nurturing aspects of the black urban environment. Brooks's paradoxical vision is perhaps best revealed in a statement which appears in the appendix of her autobiography concerning her plans for *In the Mecca*.

> . . . I wish to present a large variety of personalities against a mosaic of daily affairs, recognizing that the *grimiest* of these is likely to have a streak of sun.
> In the Mecca were murders, loves, lonelinesses, hates, jealousies. Hope occurred, and charity, sainthood, glory, shame, despair, fear, altruism.
>
> (*Report from Part One* pp.189-90)

A central paradox of her composite portrait of Bronzeville is the ability of its residents to transcend, if only temporarily, the sordid conditions of their lives. They are not dehumanized or paralyzed by the poverty which engulfs them. It is against this backdrop of Brooks's overall vision of Bronzeville that her images of urban women as they appear in selected poems from *The World of Gwendolyn Brooks* will be examined. Though a discussion of the urban women in *In the Mecca, Riot,* and *Family Pictures* will not be included, it would be interesting in a more comprehensive study of Brooks's women to compare the images projected in her pre-1967 poems with these later ones.

The diverse nature of Brooks's females enables her to reveal the many facets, complexities, and paradoxes of the urban black experiences. They range from the death-in-life figure of a woman in "obituary for a living lady"[3] to the life-in-death figure of a woman in "the rites for Cousin Vit." The unnamed woman in the first poem (based on a person Brooks knew well)[4] is the antithesis of Cousin Vit. Though she was a "decently wild child" and as a girl was "interested in a brooch and pink powder and a curl," as a young woman she would not permit sexual contact between herself and the man with whom she had fallen in love. She continued to wait by the windows in a "gay (though white) dress," and finally decided to say "yes," though by this time it was too late because he had found a woman "who dressed in red." Though red traditionally has negative connotations where women's dress is concerned, here it is being used positively to contrast the latter woman's *joie de vivre* with the lack of it in the main character; her purity and paleness of spirit (which the white dress symbolizes) cause her to be rejected. Here Brooks has taken the conventional "scarlet woman" figure usually associated with the corrupt, sinful city and transformed her into a positive, vital force. After mourning for a long time and "wishing she were dead," the woman in white turns to religion and away from the world of the flesh.

> . . . Now she will not
>   dance
> And she thinks not the thinnest thought of any type of
>   romance
> And I can't get her to take or touch of the best cream
>   cologne. (pp.18-19)

Cousin Vit, on the other hand, has lived an exciting, full life and even in death refuses to be confined.

> . . . it can't hold her,
> That stuff and satin aiming to enfold her. . .
> . . . Even now, surmise,
> She rises in the sunshine. There she goes,
> Back to the bars she knew and the repose
> In love-rooms and the things in people's eyes.
> Too vital and too squeaking. . . (p. 109)

She has tasted much of life's pleasures and sorrows. Disappointments have not caused her to withdraw from life and miss out on its more pleasant aspects.

> Even now she does the snake-hips with a hiss,
> Slops the bad wine across her shantung, talks
> Of pregnancy, guitars and bridgework, walks
> In parks or alleys, comes haply on the verge
> Of happiness . . . (p.109)

She has taken chances in order to find joy. Ironically, she seems more alive in death than the living woman in the previous poem. One critic has commented on her and other women in Brooks's poems who are to be admired for attempting to get the most out of their basically narrow and drab lives.

> Whatever her shortcomings, Cousin Vit has asserted her pagan self without asking questions or whining. It may be that she, Sadie, and others like them, girls who "scraped life/with a fine-tooth comb," girls who seize their love in hallways and alleys and other unconventional places—it may be that these carefree souls have a deeper understanding of the modern scene than any of their sedate sisters and friends. Perhaps they are the only ones who do understand.[5]

"Sadie and Maud" (alluded to in the previous quote) deals with two sisters whose contrasting approaches to life are somewhat analogous to the women discussed in the two previous poems. Sadie, like Cousin Vit, has gotten out of life all it has to offer, despite her limited resources.

> Sadie scraped life
> With a fine-tooth comb.
>
> She didn't leave a tangle in.
> Her comb found every strand.
> Sadie was one of the livingest chits
> In all the land. (p.16)

Though she bore two "illegitimate" daughters and shamed her family, she has left her offspring a rich heritage—her fine-tooth comb—so that they will presumably also squeeze as much joy out of life as possible. She does not have wealth to leave them but she leaves them something perhaps equally valuable. Maud, on the other hand, who followed the more conventional path and went to college, is, at the end of the poem, alone and like a "thin brown mouse." Like the unnamed woman in "obituary for a living lady," she has followed society's rules, but her life has lacked the vitality and fullness which makes one's existence meaningful.

Brooks also explores the impact of poverty on the lives of her women characters. "the mother" deals with a poor woman who has had a number of abortions and who experiences anxiety and anguish as a result of these decisions. In the appendix of her autobiography Brooks refers to her as "hardly your crowned and praised and customary Mother; but a Mother not unfamiliar, who decides that *she* rather than her World, will kill her children."[6] Accepting full responsibility for her "crime," she nevertheless remains ambivalent about her actions and exactly what she has done. Though she realizes that she has shielded her unborn babies from the harsh realities of the life they were sure to lead, she also admits having stolen from them whatever joys they might have been able to experience. She wonders if she had that right.

> . . . if I sinned, if I seized
> Your luck
> And your lives from your unfinished reach,
> If I stole your births and your names,
> Your straight baby tears and your games,
> Your stilted or lovely loves, your tumults, your mar-
>   riages, aches, and your deaths,
> If I poisoned the beginnings of your breaths,
> Believe that even in my deliberateness I was not de-
>   liberate. (p 5)

Throughout the poem, one has the feeling that if circumstances had been different, if she had been able to provide adequately for them, they would have been allowed to live. Ironically, it was her deep concern for them as well as her own situation, which caused her to have the abortions.

> Believe me, I loved you all.
> Believe me, I knew you, though faintly, and I loved, I
>   loved you

All. (p.6)

She knew perfectly well what their fate would have been.

You will never neglect or beat
Them, or silence or buy with a sweet.
You will never wind up the sucking-thumb
Or scuttle off ghosts that come.
You will never leave them, controlling your luscious
sigh,
Return for a snack of them, with gobbling mother-eye. (p.5)

Though George Kent criticizes the poem for failing "to convey the attitude of the author toward her subject—the several abortions of the mother,"[7] there is no question in my mind nor probably in the minds of women who have had abortions for similar or even other reasons where Brooks's sympathies lie.

"when Mrs. Martin's Booker T." contains a contrasting portrait of a mother and provides another view of the black urban resident. The code of behavior to which she adheres is more conventional. Mrs. Martin is disgraced by her son Booker T., who "ruins" Rosa Brown when he impregnates her before marriage. She is embarrassed to the point that she cannot face her community, so she moves to the other side of town and renounces her son. The intensity of her feelings is revealed in the simile "He wrung my heart like a chicken neck." The only cure for her damaged pride would be for her son to marry Rosa—"But tell me if'n he take that gal/And get her decent wed." Her strong sense of honor and decency will not permit her to condone behavior which reflects badly on the family. "Good" people marry when babies are on the way. It may also be that Mrs. Martin insists on marriage because she does not want Rosa and her illegitimate child to experience the hardships which usually befall those in their situation.

We also get glimpses into the lives of female ghetto dwellers in other poems from *A Street in Bronzeville* and *The Bean Eaters.* Though their world is drab and ordinary, and sometimes even fraught with danger, they go about their daily lives accepting their plight and somehow managing to survive. In "the battle" the persona (probably Hattie Scott, since this poem belongs to that series) would like to believe that she would have behaved differently from Moe Belle Jackson, who, after being beaten by her husband the night before because of a domestic quarrel, probably arose the next morning and continued with business as usual.

I like to think
Of how I'd of took a knife
And slashed all of the quickenin'
Out of his lowly life.

But if I know Moe Belle,
Most like, she shed a tear,
And this mornin' it was probably,
"More grits, dear?" (p. 39)

In "when I die" (from the same series) there is a similar acceptance of the realities of life, no matter how unpleasant. An unnamed female, again presumably Hattie, imagines that when she dies, there will be no fanfare but simply "one lone little short man/Dressed all shabbily." Her husband or boyfriend will bring his cheap flower—"He'll have his buck-a-dozen"—but immediately after the funeral he'll shed his mourning clothes and wipe away his tears. sources? She also has no illusions about what will happen next—"And the girls, they will be waitin'/there's nothin' more to say." She does not romanticize him or their relationship. In "the murder"[8] a mother must face the tragic death of her barely one-year-old son which was caused by his brother, who "with a grin/Burned him up for fun." She may also have to live with a guilty conscience for the rest of her life because it might not have happened had she been there.

No doubt, poor Percy looked around
And wondered at the heat,
Was worried, wanted Mother,
Who gossiped down the street. (p.22)

There is no explanation for Brucie's behavior, which is even more terrifying.

No doubt, poor shrieking Percy died
Loving Brucie still,
Who could, with clean and open eye,
Thoughtfully kill. (p.22)

Despite their frustrations and limitations, however, happiness does penetrate the lives of the Bronzeville women, though it has to be found in small things. The woman in "patent leather" is thrilled at having a man whose hair is so slick, black, and straight that it looks like patent leather. Though the other men "don't think he's such/A much" because of his shrill voice and "pitiful" muscles (unmasculine traits as far as they are concerned), she "strokes the patent-leather hair/That makes him man enough for her" (p. 13). Similarly, the woman in "when you have forgotten Sunday: the love story" experiences extreme pleasure on Sundays when she is able to stay in bed late with her mate and forget about the cares of the week. She remembers ordinary matters such as how he reacted to interruptions during their love-making sessions, how long they stayed in bed, and what they finally had for dinner. Though their apartment is tiny and unappealing, and they don't eat exotic meals, they are still able to enjoy each other on this one day of the week when their usual problems don't intrude.

> . . .we finally went in to Sunday dinner,
> That is to say, went across the front room floor to the
> ink-spotted table in the southwest corner
> To Sunday dinner, which was always chicken and
> noodles
> Or chicken and rice
> And salad and rye bread and tea
> And chocolate chip cookies— (p.20)

Though this seems to be all she has to look forward to, she's happy.

> Or me sitting on the front-room radiator in the limping
> afternoon
> Looking off down the long street
> To nowhere,
> Hugged by my plain old wrapper of no-expectation
> And nothing-I-have-to-do and I'm-happy-why?
> And if-Monday-never-had-to-come— (p.20)

Although life in Bronzeville is seldom without frustrations, its inhabitants do experience moments, however temporary, when they are glad to be alive.

Other urban poems reveal the plight of the dark-skinned or kinky-haired girl because of the color prejudice within the black community. Since this problem (discussed in detail in an article mentioned below) is shared by black women no matter where they live, it will not be dealt with in detail here, though a discussion of Brooks's images of women generally would include a thorough analysis of such poems as "the ballad of chocolate Mabbie," "Ballad of Pearl May Lee," "Jessie Mitchell's Mother," and selected poems from *Annie*

Allen. Beauty parlors are a crucial part of Bronzeville as they are in other black environments, and a critic explains their significance.

> The worship of "good" hair naturally suggests the importance of beauty parlors in Bronzeville. They tend to become miracle-working shrines to which the dark girl goes in search of beauty. . . . They know that it is tough to be "cut from chocolate" and to have "boisterous hair" in a land where "white is right." To be black is to be rejected. . . .[9]

"at the hairdresser's" contains a portrait of a black girl who is almost ecstatic over the passing from the vogue of long hair. Her short hair, which Madam Walker's and Poro Grower could not help, is no longer a problem now that the "upsweep" is in style. She no longer has to feel inferior to the girls with long hair.

> GIMME an upsweep, Minnie,
> With humpteen baby curls.
> 'Bout time I got some glamour.
> I'll show them girls. (p.37)

Brooks's urban world is also inhabited by older women who have a different kind of struggle. The persona in "A Sunset of the City" can be seen as a victim of a modern, urbanized environment, not necessarily Bronzeville, where close family ties have broken. She is resentful as she approaches middle age because of the way she is now treated by her children, husband, and lovers.

> Already I'm no longer looked at with lechery or love.
> My daughters and sons have put me away with marbles
> and dolls,
> Are gone from the house.
> My husband and lovers are pleasant or somewhat polite
> And night is night. (p.337)

"Night is night" rather than a time for fun and adventure as it was when she was younger. Not only is it "summer-gone" where the seasons are concerned, but she is also approaching the winter of her own life. She is like the flowers and grass which are personified.

> The sweet flowers indrying and dying down,
> The grasses forgetting their blaze and consenting to
> brown. (p.337)

She sees herself as a hopeless woman whose needs are no longer satisfied in her cold, empty house.

There is no warm house
That is filled with my need.

I am cold in this cold house this house
Whose washed echoes are tremulous down lost halls. (p. 338)

Like old furniture, she is "dusty," and now "hurries through her prayers," since they seem useless. She contemplates suicide as an alternative to a numb existence where she would do nothing, feel nothing, and desire nothing. This death-in-life quality has been seen before in one of Brooks's women. The poem ends on a pessimistic note with her concluding that Fate has played a cruel joke on her. One critic sees this poem as "another indication of the spiritual bankruptcy of our times," of "the meaninglessness of modern living," and "our loss of faith."[10] While the poem can be seen as having a universal theme, its central purpose should not be overlooked—the revelation of the inner turmoil of a woman as she faces a critical point in her life. The nature of the frustration she feels is in many ways different from what a man growing old would experience, yet similar.

Often Brooks's older women are seen in their relationships with their husbands, though these portraits tend to be less sharply focused than the ones which include a female figure only. In "the old marrieds" she explores, among other things, the negative impact of cramped ghetto quarters on a couple's relationship. Although the possibilities for romantic love have been perfect on this day, they are unable to communicate with each other because of circumstances beyond their control.

And he had seen the lovers in the little side-streets.
And she had heard the morning stories clogged with
 sweets.
It was quite a time for loving. It was midnight. It was
 May.
But in the crowding darkness not a word did they say. (p.3)

One would surmise that though it is dark, they still do not have the privacy desired for intimate contact. So, they remain silent. One might also conclude that the passage of time has caused their relationship to deteriorate to the point where it is impossible to express love.

In "The Bean Eaters," which also deals with an older married couple, Brooks explores the effect of poverty on their lives. They, like others in Bronzeville, attempt to make the most of their economic deprivation.

> They eat beans mostly, this old yellow pair.
> Dinner is a casual affair.
> Plain chipware on a plain and creaking wood,
> Tin flatware. (p.314)

Though they go about their daily lives in an almost mechanical manner, they refuse to give up.

> Two who are Mostly Good.
> Two who have lived their day,
> But keep on putting on their clothes
> And putting things away. (p.314)

Their memories, some of which are unpleasant, keep their lives from being totally meaningless.

> Remembering, with twinklings and twinges,
> As they lean over the beans in their rented back room that
> is full of beads and receipts and dolls and cloths,
> tobacco crumbs, vases and fringes. (p. 314)

Though the couples in these two poems do have companionship, life seems to be just something to be endured, though the latter poem gives a more positive portrayal of the mates having endured together.

Without the perspective of the black woman writer, certain aspects of life in the urban ghetto would possibly remain hidden. Brooks explores not only what it is like to be poor and black and male but also what it is like to be poor and black and female. She treats the relationships between males and females and the joys and frustrations which women experience in a way that is different from her male counterparts. The female images she creates reflect her personal experiences with black women, her observations of them in the community, and her general knowledge of their history in this country. These images are as varied as the human types present in any community.

Her poems present a more realistic view of the diversity and complexity of black women than the stereotypes (matriarch, whore, bitch, for example) which have persisted in other literary works by black and white artists alike. The lack of uniformity in her portraits of black women would contradict the notion that there is a monolithic black woman. There are females in her poems who commit adultery ("the vacant lot") and are sexually inhibited ("obituary for a living lady"); they are aggressive ("Mrs. Martin's Booker T.") and passive. (Maud of "Sadie and Maud"); they are extraordinary (Madam Walker of "southeast corner") and ordinary ("Mrs. Small"); they are exploited (un-named women in "The Sundays of Satin-Legs Smith") and protected (young girl in "a song in the front yard"). They dream in the midst of adversity ("Callie Ford" and "hunch-back girl: she thinks of heaven") and they wallow in despair ("A Sunset of the City"). Though they share a common environment and heritage, they are still presented as individuals with different priorities and values, different levels of tolerance for misery, and different ways of dealing with problems. The major portion of Gwendolyn Brooks's work does indeed reflect, among other things, an intense awareness of our identity as black women and an unusual insight into the problems we face.

Notes

1. Blyden Jackson and Louis D. Rubin, *Black Poetry in America: Two Essays in Historical Interpretation* (Baton Rouge: Louisiana State University Press, 1974), p. 82.

2. In a 1967 interview with Illinois historian Paul Angle, which appears in Brooks's autobiography, *Report from Part One*, pp. 160-61, she says that Bronzeville was not her own title but was "invented" many years ago by the *Chicago Defender*, a black newspaper, to refer to the black community.

3. *The World of Gwendolyn Brooks* (New York: Harper & Row, 1971), p. 18. Further references to individual poems are from this edition.

4. Gwendolyn Brooks, *Report from Part One* (Detroit: Broadside Press,1972), p.154.

5. Arthur P. Davis, "Gwendolyn Brooks: Poet of the Unheroic," *CLA Journal*, 7 (December 1963), 118.

6. Brooks, *Report from Part One*, p. 184.

7. George Kent, "The Poetry of Gwendolyn Brooks," Part II, *Black World*, October 1971, p.38.

8. Brooks says in *Report from Part One* that this poem was also based on a real-life situation except that the mother was really working instead of gossiping down the street. She adds, "I guess I did her an injustice there" (p. 154).

9. Arthur Davis, "The Black-and-Tan Motif in the Poetry of Gwendolyn Brooks," *CLA Journal*, 6 (December 1962), 95-97.

10. Davis, "Gwendolyn Brooks: Poet of the Unheroic," p. 117.

Bibliography

Brooks, Gwendolyn. *Report from Part One.* Detroit: Broadside Press, 1972.

Davis, Arthur P. "The Black-and-Tan Motif in the Poetry of Gwendolyn Brooks." *CLA Journal*, 6 (December 1962), 90-97.

"Gwendolyn Brooks: Poet of the Unheroic." *CLA Journal*, 7 (December 1963), 114-25.

Jackson, Blyden, and Rubin, Louis D. *Black Poetry in America: Two Essays in Historical Interpretation.* Baton Rouge: Louisiana State University Press, 1974.

Kent, George. "The Poetry of Gwendolyn Brooks." Part I. *Black World,* September 1971, pp. 36-71.

-----. "The Poetry of Gwendolyn Brooks." Part II. *Black World,* October 1971, pp. 36-71.

Miller, Jeanne-Marie. "Gwendolyn Brooks-Poet Laureate of Bronzeville, U.S.A." *Freedomways*, 10 (1970), 63-75.

Parker, John. "Saga of the Bronzeville Community." *CLA Journal*, 4 (September 1960), 59-61.

The World of Gwendolyn Brooks. New York: Harper & Row, 1971.

24. | Warrior Women: Art as Resistance (1996)

We ought to stop thinking we have to do the art of other people. We have to create an art for liberation and for life.

Elizabeth Catlett, 1971

After I decided to be an artist, the first thing that I had to believe was that I, a black woman, could penetrate the art scene and that I could do so without sacrificing one iota of my blackness, or my femaleness, or my humanity.

Faith Ringgold, 1985

Every time I think about color it's a political statement. It would be a luxury to be white and never to think about it.

Emma Amos, 1993

Two of the most significant events in recent United States history—the civil rights and women's movements—have had a profound impact on contemporary African American women artists. While considerable attention has been paid to the racial politics of the image-making of black women artists and their role in the black arts movement, they have been absent, for the most part, in histories of black feminism and the development of the feminist art movement. In her groundbreaking essays on "Afrofemcentrism" and "Black feminist art-historical discourse," artist and critic Freida High Tesfagiorgis articulates a unique method for analyzing black women artists which simultaneously considers the politics of race, class, gender, and sexuality.[1] This black feminist critique is long overdue, she argues, because "much of what has been written lies within the history of African American art, is secondary to male production, and for the most part is without critiques of class, gender and sexuality ..."[2]

Sculptor and printmaker Elizabeth Catlett comes to mind most immediately in an analysis of black feminist impulses in the visual art of African American artists. Her pioneering 1946-47 series, *The Negro Woman* (fifteen linocuts, later named *The Black Woman Speaks*), challenged the stereotypical, non-heroic treatment of black women, which characterized Western art for decades, by portraying them as strong, beautiful, political, creative, and intelligent. In fact, women of color, particularly ordinary women such as those portrayed in *Tired* (terracotta, 1946), *The Survivor* (linocut, 1983), *Nina* (linocut, n.d.), and *Sharecropper* (linocut, 1968), were the primary subjects of her prints and sculptures. She was unapologetic about her focus on women:

> I don't have anything against men, but since I am a woman, I know more about women and I know how they feel. Many artists are always doing men. I think that somebody ought to do women. . . .I think there is a need to express something about the working-class black woman and that's what I do.[3]

A self-defined feminist, she espoused her commitment to the eradication of the oppression of women, particularly black and Latin American women, whose struggles were different from middle-class white women:

> I am interested in women's liberation for the fulfillment of women; not just for jobs and equality with men and so on, but for what they can contribute to enrich the world, humanity. Their contributions have been denied them. It's the same thing that happens to black people. I think that the male is aggressive and he has a male supremacist idea in his head, at least in the United States and Mexico. We need to know more about women.[4]

Homage to My Young Black Sisters (cedarwood, 1968) is perhaps the most stunning example of her commitment to the empowerment of women. In this magnificent sculpture, which was carved to honor brave young women in the civil rights movement, a woman holds her head high and points her clenched fist toward the sky in an unmistakable stance of defiance. Catlett herself also defied conventional gender roles by becoming the first woman to head the sculpture department at the National School of Fine Arts at the National Autonomous University of Mexico in 1959, which angered the male faculty.

Her political stance with respect to black arts was evident in a historic speech delivered in 1961 at the National Conference of Artists, an organization of art professors in black colleges. It was the beginning of the civil rights movement in the South and the 104th anniversary of the end of slavery in the United States. She spoke on "The Negro People and American Art at Mid-Century," during which she asserted the value of all-black exhibitions and of using black history as subject matter. She also articulated her vision of the political function of black art and the necessity for black artists to express their racial identity, communicate with the black community, and participate in struggles for social, political, and economic equality:

> Whether we like it or not, we, Negro artists, are part of a worldwide struggle to change a situation that is unforgiveable. . . .Children can no longer be denied the right to food, to clothing, and to education . . .we must search to find our place, as Negro artists, in the advance toward a richer fulfillment of life on a global basis. Neither the Negro artist nor American art can afford to take an isolated position.[5]

Painter and quilter Faith Ringgold also fought for the rights of black artists who were marginalized or invisible in a predominantly white male art world. In her extraordinary memoir, *We Flew Over the Bridge,* she describes her own struggles as a mother and wife in the 1960s to become an artist and express her female point of view about the historic era of civil rights and black power. In 1963 her attempts to join the mostly black male artists' group Spiral (the only female member was Emma Amos), headed by Romare Bearden, were unsuccessful, though four years later her first solo show of paintings, "The American People," opened at the Spectrum Gallery and was attended by the "old men of black art."[6] In her *Black Light* series, begun in 1967, she would embrace the "black is beautiful" slogan of the era by creating a new palette which would resist the Western preoccupation with white pigment and substitute black.

> In the painting of *Die,* I had depended upon the bloodsplattered white clothing of the figures to create the contrast needed to express the movement and energy of the riot. I felt bound to its use, having been trained to paint in the Western tradition. But I was now committed to "black light" and subtle color nuances and compositions based on my new interest in African rhythm, pattern, and repetition. In 1971 I described these new works as experiments in toning the light to the blacks, browns, and grays that cover my skin and hair; and the shades of blues, greens, and reds that create my forms and textures.[7]

Nineteen seventy would turn out to be a pivotal year for Ringgold and for black women's cultural and literary history, in part because of the publication of Toni Cade's *The Black Woman,* Shirley Chisholm's *Unbossed and Unbought,* Toni Morrison's *The Bluest Eye,* Alice Walker's *The Third Life of Grange Copeland,* and Audre Lorde's *Cables to Rage.* The second-wave women's movement was also getting underway and Ringgold recalls having been introduced to the movement by lawyer Flo Kennedy in 1967. It was three years later, however, in 1970, that Ringgold became a feminist in order to "help my daughters, other women, and myself aspire to something more than a place behind a good man."[8] She also became seriously involved in the newly emerging women's art movement. In the early 1970s women artists protested their exclusion from museums, mainstream exhibitions, and art history scholarship, and initiated alternative exhibitions and women's galleries for achieving visibility. At the same time, black artists were struggling for inclusion at The Museum of Modern Art (MoMA) by establishing a separate wing for their art and demanding Board representation. Ringgold would become an important figure among both protest groups.

In 1970, the group Art Strike was organized by Robert Morris to protest the American invasion of Cambodia. They also objected to American artists' participation in the annual Venice Biennale, and decided to exhibit at the School of Visual Arts in New York instead. Ringgold and her daughter Michele Wallace, outraged by the proposed alternative exhibition in New York because it included only white male artists, formed Women Students and Artists for Black Art Liberation (WSABAL), which eventually was successful in getting black, Puerto Rican, and women artists exhibited at the "liberated" Biennale, though white women were surprisingly against such a move. During these contentious debates, which now included uncooperative white feminist artists, Ringgold advocated fifty percent women (Michele's mandate) and "open shows," a kind of affirmative action for blacks, especially black women artists who had been discriminated against by the mainstream art world for generations because of a set of criteria for inclusion which favored Euro-American males.

It was also during 1970 that Ringgold joined Ad Hoc, a women's group inspired by feminist art critic Lucy Lippard and Poppy Johnson, which began demonstrations against the Whitney Museum of American Art for its discriminatory practices with respect to women artists; as a result of this agitation, Betye Saar and Barbara Chase Riboud became the first black women to be exhibited at the Whitney Annual (1971). During the same year Ringgold's activism continued with the co-founding (with Kay Brown and others) of Brooklyn-based Where We At, which mounted the first exhibition of black women's artists—"Where We At Black Women Artists."[9] It opened at Acts of Art Gallery in New York and included twelve artists. Ringgold's explicitly feminist art also began in 1970 with a mural entitled *For the Womens House,* which was hung at the Women's House of Detention on Rikers Island, New York. The mural contained eight components which depicted women in traditional and non-traditional roles—as a bus driver, drummer, police officer, basketball player for the Knicks, and even the President of the United States. Begun a year later, her *Feminist Landscape* series, acrylic paintings framed in cloth, captured the forgotten history of black women's resistance by embellishing the landscapes with quotations, "words of fire," of historic black feminists such as Harriet Tubman, Sojourner Truth, Maria Stewart, Anna Julia Cooper, Amy Jacques-Garvey, and Shirley Chisholm,[10] the only living woman in the series. Ringgold explains what motivated her feminist landscapes, initially inspired by Chisholm's bid for the Presidency in 1972, and later, her reading of Gerda Lerner's documentary history, *Black Women in White America,* which further kindled her interest.

> Back in the early seventies black women were in denial of their oppression in order to be in support of their men. This made it very important for me to put the words of these valiant black feminists in my art so that people could read them and be as inspired as I had been.[11]

The Slave Rape series, sixteen tanka paintings done in collaboration with her mother in 1973, was a manifestation of her feminist impulses and her desire to revise African American history with a strong gender focus. This work links her to a group of black feminist scholars who were challenging the invisibility of black women in mainstream white and black scholarship—Toni Cade, Pauli Murray, Barbara Smith, Michele Wallace (whose controversial feminist polemic *Black Macho and the Myth of the Super Woman* [1979] generated a black sexism de bate), Paula Giddings, and others. Angela Davis's landmark essay, "Reflections on the Black Woman's Role in the Community of Slaves," written while she was in a California prison in 1971 on false charges of murder, kidnapping, and conspiracy, unmasked masculine biases in African American political history by calling attention to the erasure or marginalization of women in studies of slave resistance. Davis's radical activism for black liberation also inspired many black women artists including Elizabeth Catlett, whose 1972 serigraph, *Angela Libre*, immortalizes the most well-known African American woman political figure of the contemporary era. Subsequent work by black feminist scholars Darlene Clark Hine, bell hooks, Deborah Gray White, Nell Painter, and Brenda Stevenson underscored the necessity of differentiating between the worlds of enslaved men and women and exploring the intersections of race and gender in the lives of the latter.

The horrendous circumstances that African women endured after being brought in chains to the "New World" in 1619 inspired their yearnings for freedom and made rebellion inevitable. They resisted beatings, breeding, unwanted pregnancies, sexual exploitation by white masters, family separation, and debilitating work schedules. They penned liberation narratives which called attention to their unique situations. In her celebrated antebellum autobiography, *Incidents in the Life of a Slave Girl, Written by Herself* (1861), Harriet Jacobs publicized her sexual vulnerability and stated unequivocally that "slavery is terrible for men; but it is far more terrible for women. Superadded to the burden common to all, they have wrongs, and sufferings, and mortifications peculiarly their own."[12]

Ringgold's first three *tankas* in *The Slave Rape* series, which she describes as some of her most prized pieces because of the work her mother did on them, were *Fear: Will Make You Weak, Run: You Might Get Away, and Fight: To Save Your Life.* They were described as "large, close-up figures of idealized African women struggling against capture and enslavement."[13] She continued this theme of rape and rebellion in sixteen acrylic paintings, "set against an African landscape of flowers and trees,"[14] in which tiny, nude, fleeing women (which underscores their sexual vulnerability and ostensible dehumanization) are portrayed defending themselves against white slave masters, which Ringgold describes with glee:

> In some of the tankas . . . the tiny figures are armed with hatchets and defend themselves. The captor then retreats and is depicted as a fragment of a man, clothed in white pants and boots, running from the scene. . . . "Help: Your Sister" shows two women fighting off their captor. "Fight: To Save Your Life" depicts one woman standing alone wielding a ceremonial hatchet in defense of herself. In "Run: You Might Get Away," a lone woman flees in a desperate attempt to avoid capture.[15]

In a remarkable revision of the slave experience, it is women rather than men who are depicted as rebellious, and slave masters who are rendered powerless in the face of warrior women bent on liberation.

Perhaps the most stunning example of the involvement of slave women in dismantling the "peculiar institution" is the work of abolitionist/military strategist Harriet Tubman (nicknamed Moses), probably the most well-known female slave in the United States, and one of the warrior women who appears in the work of black women artists. Catlett's linocut series on black women for the Rosenwald grant of 1946-47 includes an early example of Tubman's impact in a work called *I'm Harriet Tubman. I Helped Hundreds to Freedom.* This was followed by the more well-known 1953 and 1975 linocuts, *Harriet Tubman* and *Harriet.* In addition to being a successful "conductor" on The Underground Railroad, by which she led more than three hundred slaves to freedom, Tubman was a co-conspirator with John Brown on his ill-fated raid on Harper's Ferry (1859), though illness prevented her from joining him. For three years she was also a nurse, spy, and scout for the Union army. During the Civil War, she led the only military campaign (along the Combahee River in South Carolina with Colonel James Montgomery) ever to be waged by a woman. It resulted in 750 slaves being freed in 1863.

Ringgold would also remember our slave foremothers and countless other rebellious women throughout history in her *Womens Liberation Talking Mask* series, which began to appear in 1973. Inspired by African art, these works included intricate beading and raffia for hair. During this period she also turned to story quilts to counter stereotypes of blacks and women and because she needed to tell stories "not with pictures or symbols alone, but with words." [16] Her first quilt, *Echoes of Harlem*, done in collaboration with her artist mother, Willi Posey, was to be included in "The Artist and the Quilt," a group show of twelve women artists working with twelve quilters.[17] Her narrative quilts, which enabled her to tell the stories of women's lives because they included text as well as painted images, include *Slave Rape Story Quilt* (1985), a bittersweet narrative of a mother and daughter who experience the familiar tragedy of slavery,[18] and *The Purple Quilt* (1986), in memory of the characters in Alice Walker's award-winning novel, *The Color Purple*. The text on the quilt states that the book is a "tribute to all US women (and men) who have survived to tell the story." The quilt contains her "visual conceptions" of the characters (based on her memories of people in the Harlem community) and quotes from the novel, particularly Celie's letters to God. These quilts link her to the black women's literary renaissance of the 1970s and 1980s which has received considerable scholarly attention. As Cheryl Wall indicates, "over the past two decades, Afro-American women have written themselves into the national consciousness. Their work is widely read, frequently taught, and increasingly the object of critical inquiry."[19]

Ringgold's *Women on the Bridge* series, which she began during the late 1980s, is a continuation of her feminist vision of powerful women who resist narrow gender definitions. In her description of the way in which the painted quilt series evolved, her passion for seeing women differently from men, and her insistence that they be portrayed differently than they had been in Western art, is striking:

> It was going to be about women's courage; comparing women with something as monumental as a bridge. It's always constructed by men who get up there and die making it; and I wanted to pit us against that. I had no idea they would be flying ... As I drew my pictures ... I realized the women could not be grounded. But what I ran to my typewriter with was why are you doing women on a bridge? So then I wrote down some things to remember that the bridge idea was significant to me and it would be about women's courage, women doing great, creative, exciting things.[20]

Her feminist activism is also apparent in "The Wild Art Show," an exhibition of over fifty women artists, which she curated for P.S. 1 in 1982.

Ten years earlier, the historic women's gallery A.I.R. (Artists in Residence), had opened in New York, initiated by Barbara Zucker and Susan Williams. This first feminist gallery included among its small group of women artists only one black woman, Howardena Pindell. Eight years later it mounted "Dialectics in Isolation: An Exhibition of Third World Women Artists of the U.S.," which included two African Americans, Beverly Buchanan and Pindell. Like the mainstream feminist movement in general, the feminist art movement was perceived by artists of color to be basically a white middle-class movement. Ana Mendieta made this clear in her introductory essay for the exhibition catalogue, while discussing racism in feminist art circles more broadly. The most extensive treatment of the struggles of artists of color within the feminist art movement appeared in the essay "Social Protest: Racism and Sexism" by Yolanda M. Lopez and Moira Roth. They assert that "despite the many efforts and good intentions of white women in the arena of political art, racial separation and racism existed de facto within the Feminist Art movement from the beginning."[21] For example, in 1973, when Betye Saar curated "Black Mirror," an exhibition about black women artists in the new feminist gallery Womanspace in Los Angeles, she was disappointed at the turnout by her white feminist colleagues and commented, "It was as if we were invisible again. The white women did not support it. I felt the separatism, even within the context of being in Womanspace."[22]

Howardena Pindell, a black woman artist who was active in feminist art circles and was also an associate curator at MoMA, responded to the racism within the women's art movement by creating a twelve-minute video, "Free, White and 21," in which the black narrator (herself) describes the racist experiences she's suffered, all of which are dismissed by a white woman (also portrayed by Pindell) with the response, "but of course, I'm free, white and 21." The video was shown at the "Dialectics of Isolation" exhibition at A.I.R. Pindell also worked tirelessly to expose racism within mainstream art circles[23] and counter the invisibility of women artists of color. This led to her curating "Autobiography: In Her Own Image" in 1988, an important traveling exhibition that showcased and introduced different racial/ethnic women whose work had not been seen before.

A feminist vision is also apparent in the work of painter Emma Amos, who was active in the women's art movement through her association with the feminist art journal *Heresies,* which first appeared in 1977. Though she was a member of Spiral and active in the black arts movement in the sixties, her work on women, black women in particular, was never shown. The male members of the group didn't appreciate Elizabeth Catlett's work, Amos recalls in an interview with bell hooks, and only referred to her as the former wife of artist Charles White.[24] In 1990 Amos would correct this negation of women artists by initiating a series of portraits of women artist friends to present as a legacy to her daughter India on her twentieth birthday. *The Gift* (forty acrylic paintings on paper), inspired by memories of her mother's supportive women friends, is a powerful statement about the creative legacy of women, to which she alludes in an interview with bell hooks:

> They can't X the work out. *The Gift* is not possible to negate. . . .Those women are too powerful to ignore. These friends sat for me as my support, as my mother's friends had supported her. I give them to my daughter India as her support, and I hope anybody who sees them will realize that there's something powerful and strong about women artists, about womanhood.[25]

The Gift includes a dazzling array of artists, critics, and writers including Faith Ringgold, Elizabeth Catlett, Camille Billops, Lucy Lippard, Miriam Schapiro, Kay WalkingStick, Howardena Pindell, Vivian Browne, Moira Roth, and her own daughter, India.

In 1991 she completed the *Women Artists* series, another group of paintings that called attention to women artists and the importance of remembering the history of women. Giza and Faith (acrylic on linen canvas, African fabric borders) memorializes Giza Daniels Endesha, a painter and Amos's former student at Rutgers who died of AIDS; it also includes a self-portrait and a portrait of artist Faith Ringgold. Thalia Gouma-Peterson, who curated a major exhibition on Amos in 1993, comments on this series of paintings in which the artist acts as witness:

> Diagonally across from Amos, an image of the well known African American artist, Faith Ringgold looks at us. This image reproduces one of the portraits Amos did for her series of artist friends, and it too is blown by the wind but, in contrast to the figure of Giza, Ringgold's portrait is anchored to the frame of African cloth. This dignified image is the most reassuring presence in the painting. While the center of the painting, with its allusions to European culture, has collapsed, the two African American artists, Amos and Ringgold, look at each other across the abyss.[26]

Four other paintings in the 1991 series—*Howardena* (intaglio printed silk collagraph, watercolor), *Camille, Remember Me* (silk collagraph), *Have Faith* (silk collagraph, copper), and *Elizabeth Catlett, India and Emma* (intaglio printed silk collagraph, watercolor) feature black women artists. In *Camille, Remember Me* there are three images—Camille Billops, visual artist and filmmaker; a laser transfer photograph of Amos's mother's friends; and a self-portrait of Amos wearing a tee-shirt with the word "artist." It is not surprising that Amos would bear witness to the creative and political work of Billops. With her husband James Hatch, Billops cofounded the Hatch-Billops Collection:

Archives of Black American Cultural History in New York City. Because of its thousands of slides, photographs, and books on black artists it is an important resource and gift to the community. Her important periodical *Artist and Influence* records the ongoing cultural history of African Americans and includes the voices of black artists who are still marginalized within the mainstream art world. *Elizabeth Catlett, India and Emma* pays tribute to the sculptor, Catlett, and includes an image of her onyx sculpture, *Recognition,* which shows two women embracing. The importance of mother/daughter relationships is also emphasized here by the image of Amos's daughter clutching a photograph of her artist/mother.

Political commentary in the traditional and avant-garde art of Joyce Scott, who works in jewelry, fiber, beads, quilts, and performance, is most apparent around issues of race and gender. She examines rape, apartheid, sexuality, defiance of racial stereotypes, body image, and genetic engineering. In 1982 she co-founded *Thunder Thigh Revue* (with Kay Lawal), a multi-media performance piece which was described by Lowery Sims as being about "the pain and passion of being the 'other,' an overweight black woman in this society."[27] She describes her *Race Break* series as being inherently oppositional:

> It speaks to inflexibility. To the unyielding state of affairs for a person of color in the world generally and the U.S.A. specifically. To the unjustness, how it hurts. In fact, all the work, whether written, performed, or visual, addresses the constant fight to be balanced in an existence where your skin tone, weight, or ethnicity, validates your impact. Not your kindness, your need to love and give love in return.[28]

These black feminist artists and many others on the contemporary scene—spiritual daughters of Harriet Tubman and Sojourner Truth—are also warrior women, bearing witness to both the joys and turbulence of being black and female in America. When the history of black feminism is written, it must include the work of contemporary black women artists whose ways of seeing and portraying the world have much to tell us about struggle, resistance, and ultimately triumph.

Notes

1. Stanlie M. James and Abena P.A. Busia, eds., *Theorizing Black Feminisms: The Visionary Pragmatism of Black Women* (New York: Routledge, 1993), p. 240.

2. Ibid., p. 246.

3. Samella S. Lewis, *The Art of Elizabeth Catlett* (Claremont, CA: Hancraft Studios, 1984), p. 102.

4. Ibid., pp. 102-4.

5. Ibid., pp. 97-8.

6. Faith Ringgold, *We Flew Over the Bridge: The Memoirs of Faith Ringgold* (Boston: Little, Brown, 1995), p. 159.

7. Ibid., p. 162.

8. Ibid., p. 175.

9. See Norma Broude and Mary D. Garrard, eds., *The Power of Feminist Art: The American Movement of the 1970s, History and Impact* (New York: Harry N. Abrams, 1994), for a description of the organization, the names of the members, and a photograph, pp. 106-7. This text includes the most extensive coverage of black women in the feminist art movement. Ringgold's *We Flew Over the Bridge* also describes the activities of the organization.

10. See Beverly Guy-Sheftall, ed., *Words of Fire: An Anthology of African American Feminist Thought* (New York: The New Press, 1995).

11. Ringgold, *We Flew Over the Bridge,* p: 196.

12. Jean Fagan Yellin, ed., *Incidents in the Life of a Slave Girl,* Written by Herself (Cambridge, MA: Harvard University Press, 1987), p. 77.

13. Ringgold, *We Flew Over the Bridge,* p. 197.

14. Ibid., p. 198.

15. Ibid., pp. 197-98.

16. Eleanor Flomenhaft, ed., *Faith Ringgold: A 25 Year Survey,* exh. cat. (Hempstead, NY: Fine Arts Museum of Long Island, 1990), p. 23.

17. *Gumbo Ya Ya: Anthology of Contemporary African American Women Artists* (New York: Midmarch Arts), p. 226.

18. See Thalia Gouma-Peterson's insightful analysis of Ringgold's story quilts in Flomenhaft, *Faith Ringgold,* pp. 23-32. See also Gouma-Peterson's "Faith Ringgold's Narrative Quilts," *Arts Magazine,* vol. 61, no. 5 (January 1987): 66-68, for a more extensive discussion of *The Purple Quilt.*

19. Cheryl A. Wall, ed., *Changing Our Own Words: Essays on Criticism, Theory, and Writing by Black Women* (New Brunswick, NJ: Rutgers University Press, 1989), p. 1.

20. Ringgold, *We Flew Over the Bridge,* pp. 11-12.

21. Yolanda M. López and Moira Roth, "Social Protest: Racism and Sexism," in Broude and Carrard, *The Power of Feminist Art,* p. 140.

22. Ibid., p. 152.

[23] See her stunning research on institutionalized racism within prestigious New York museums and galleries, which she presented at Hunter College in 1987 and later published as "Art (World) and Racism: Testimony, Documentation, and Statistics," *Third Text*, vol. 3, no. 4 (Spring/ Summer 1988): 157-62.

[24] See bell hooks, "Straighten Up and Fly Right: Making History Visible," in *Emma Amos: Paintings and Prints*, 1982-92, exh. cat. (Wooster, OH: The College of Wooster Art Museum, 1993), pp. 15-28. The interview is reprinted in hooks's *Art on My Mind: Visual Politics* (New York: The New Press, 1995).

[25] Ibid., p. 21.

[26] Ibid., p. 13.

[27] Lowery Stokes Sims, "Aspects of Performance in the Work of Black American Women Artists," in *Feminist Art Criticism: An Anthology*, eds. Arlene Raven, Cassandra L. Langer, and Joanne Frueh (New York: HarperCollins, 1991), p. 219.

[28] Joyce Scott, *En Masse/Fiber* (St. Louis: St. Louis Gallery of Contemporary Art, 1988), n.p.

AUTHOR'S NOTE

I have written here not as an art historian or art critic, but from my vantage point and training as a women's studies scholar who documents the intellectual, cultural, and political history of black women. I am also interested in the participation of black women in both black liberation movements and feminist movements and have analyzed our erasure in scholarly treatments of both struggles. By locating contemporary black women artists within the broader black feminist movement that began in the nineteenth century and continues to the present, this essay complements the point of view in my book *Words of Fire: An Anthology of African American Feminist Thought.*

25. Elizabeth Catlett: Making What You Know Best (2003)

Art is, and always has been, an expression of the historic conditions of people and should be a part of humanity's cultural wealth. Because I am a woman and know how a woman feels in body and in mind, I sculpt, draw, and print women. . . . I think there is a need to express something about the working-class Black woman and that's what I do. Art can't be the exclusive domain of the elect. It has to belong to everyone. . . . Artists should work to the end that love, peace, justice, and equal opportunity prevail all over the world.

Elizabeth Catlett

One is immediately struck by the abundance and power of female images in Grant Hill's important collection of African American art. From Romare Bearden's *Mother and Child, Morning Gingham,* and *The Evening Guitar,* to Malcolm Brown's *Sophisticated Lady* and *Innocence,* we are compelled to take notice of the woman-centeredness of Hill's collection, whether the artists are male or female. It is tempting to assert that this extraordinary young man was intentional in his acquisition of powerful images of women as a way of celebrating the dignity, beauty, hard work, heroism, and complexity of African American women who have been undervalued and stereotyped in this culture. It is also the case that Black women artists have not received the attention they deserve, so that Hill's appreciation of the compelling sculpture and prints (lithographs) of Elizabeth Catlett, one of the most extraordinary American artists of the twentieth century, compels us to take notice. The art historian and critic Freida High Tesfagiorgis, in a ground-breaking essay on Black women artists, marks the importance of perhaps the most celebrated of Catlett's images of Black women, the series "The Negro Woman" (lithographs, 1946-47), which was later renamed "The Black Woman Speaks": "a landmark in the pictorial representation of Black women for it liberated them from their objectified status in the backgrounds and shadows of white subjects in the work of white artists, and from the roles of mother, wife, sister, other in the work of Black male artists."[1]

The art historian Samella Lewis begins her important study of Elizabeth Catlett, whose grandparents were slaves, with these simple words: "This is a complex person—and a profound art."[2] The writer and art collector Maya Angelou is even more eloquent: "She reads our dreams and fashions them in sculpture, in paintings, in drawings, and words. She boldly uses all media to make public the best of our most private selves."[3] Born in Washington in 1915, Catlett recalls that she wanted to be an artist while she was still in elementary school and that her Dunbar High School teacher, Haley Douglass (a descendant of Frederick Douglass), was influential in her much later development as a sculptor: "What I remember most—and, I guess, when my creativity really began to work—was when we had to carve a bar of soap. I tried carving an elephant. At first I was just timidly chipping off the edges. And then I went home and I remember thinking about it when I was going to sleep, and suddenly I realized just how that little elephant ought to be carved. I went back to school the next day and did it, and I was very pleased with the result. I must have been thirteen at the time, and I still work that way today. If I'm working on something, when I go to bed, I start thinking about it, and I get a direction and a solution."[4]

It was Catlett's matriculation at Howard University (1931-35), which she selected because of its art department (the first of its kind at a historically Black college), that would be the pivotal influence in her development as an artist. At the age of eighty-eight, she continues to produce art and is now celebrated around the world for her accomplishments as well as her passionate commitment to social justice and social change, especially for African Americans and other oppressed peoples. While at Howard she came in contact with Black artists for the first time and studied with extraordinary professors–James Herring, James Porter, James Wells, and Lois Mailou Jones. Majoring in painting, she was introduced to the revolutionary Mexican muralists Diego Rivera, Jose Clemente Orozco, and David Alfaro Siqueiros, and while a student she also experienced a political awakening as she became more knowledgeable about the plight of poor and oppressed people. Her activism propelled her to "stand in front of the Supreme Court building with a hangman's noose around her neck as part of an organized protest against the existing practice of lynching."[5] Political themes such as lynching and later civil rights and Black nationalism would be prominent in such familiar works as *And a Special Fear for My Loved Ones* (linocut, 1946- 47), *Civil Rights Congress* (linocut, 1950), *Watts/*

Detroit/Washington/Newark (linocut, 1970), *Black Is Beautiful* (lithograph, 1970), *Malcolm X Speaks for Us* (linocut, 1969), *Black Unity* (mahogany, 1968), *Political Prisoner* (cedar, 1971), *The Protester* (bronze, 1981), *Homage to the Panthers* (linocut, 1970), and *Homage to My Young Black Sisters* (cedar, 1968), a celebration of women of the Black Power movement and one of her best-known works.

After teaching art in the public schools of Durham, North Carolina, Catlett left for the University Iowa, where she became the first student to earn an M.F.A. degree (in sculpture, 1940). While a graduate student there, she sculpted *Mother and Child* in limestone, which won the first prize for sculpture at the Negro Exposition in Chicago in 1940. Later she studied ceramics at the Art Institute of Chicago and joined the faculty at historically Black Dillard University in New Orleans, where she taught painting and sculpture from 1940 to 1942. In 1945 she was the recipient of a fellowship from the Julius Rosenwald Foundation, which would allow her to complete a series of prints, paintings, and sculptures on the oppression, resistance, and achievements of African American women. The series of fifteen linoleum cuts was collectively entitled "The Negro Woman" (1946-47). Her *Domestic Worker* (lithograph, 1946), produced around the same time, evokes the struggles of hard-working, tired Black women who labor without adequate compensation but who manage to survive the indignities of racial, class, and gender oppression.

Catlett's journey to Mexico for the completion of this ambitious project was to have a transformative impact on her career as an artist and activist, for it was here that she came into close contact with Mexican artists in solidarity with struggles against social, economic, and political oppression. After working with a group of influential printmakers at the Taller de Grafica Popular (Popular Graphic Arts Workshop) in 1946, she decided to live in Mexico and later joined and chaired the sculpture department at the National School of Fine Arts, National Autonomous University of Mexico (1958-76), becoming its first woman professor and sculptor. A year later she established permanent residence in Mexico and married her fellow artist Francisco Mora, whom she had met at the Taller; in 1962 she would become a Mexican citizen after being harassed by the federal government for her political views and even denied entry into the United States for allegedly being an "undesirable alien." After a ten-year hiatus, she was finally given a visa to enter the United States in 1971, enabling her to attend a solo exhibition of her own work at the Studio Museum in Harlem.

Having been greatly influenced by the progressive politics of Mexican artists, she executed prints in which the primary subjects were women and children, workers, freedom fighters, and historical figures. The greatest impact of these works was "their social commitment, direct engagement with the experiences of ordinary people, deliberately accessible style, and choice of medium."[6]

The sculpture in Hill's collection—whether in stone, bronze, or onyx—is representative of the body of Catlett's magnificent sculptural art, which routinely and proudly focuses on the female figure, especially Black women, and the image of mother and child. *Standing Mother and Child* (bronze, 1978), *Mother and Child* (bronze, 1977), and *Mother and Child* (onyx, 2001) evoke memories of Catlett's master's thesis project, the limestone *Mother and Child* (1940) for which she won the first prize at the Negro Exposition. In her thesis statement, "Sculpture in Stone: Negro Mother and Child," Catlett explained her interest in the mother and child figure, which she never abandoned: "The implications of motherhood, especially Negro motherhood, are quite important to me, as I am a Negro as well as a woman."[7] Many years later, she explained why she continues to explore this theme: "Because I am a woman and know how a woman feels in body and mind I sculpt, draw, and print women, generally black women. Many of my sculptures and prints deal with maternity, for I am a mother and a grandmother."[8] The Catlett scholar Melanie Herzog offers her own explanation as well: "She saw this theme as one in which blackness and femaleness intersect. That she grew up in a household where her mother and maternal grandmother were primary presences greatly influenced her consciousness of the maternal as central to female experience. Her mother-and-child images speak of a protective love that is simultaneously tender and fierce, of intergenerational continuity, and of the determination of strong women to hold their families together."[9] Catlett's own description of her creative process involves the use of models and close observation, but perhaps more importantly, the use of her own body: "I take the position that I want to do. It's feeling more visual when I'm working out an idea. So let's say it's a model sitting, leaning on an elbow. I'll sit like that, and I'll feel where the stress and tensions are. . . .I use my own body in working. When I am bathing or dressing, I see and feel how my body looks and moves. I never do sculpture from a nude model .... *Mostly I watch women*" (my emphasis).[10] Hill's collection also includes *Standing Woman* (bronze, 1987), *Reclining Woman* (stone, 2001), *Star Gazer* (bronze, 1997), and *Woman's Torso* (bronze, 1998), as well as portrait heads—*Cabeza Cantando* [Singing Head] (bronze,1960), *Glory* (bronze, 1981), and *Fluted Head* (bronze, 1997)—which capture, as always, the power and beauty of the Black female form. The art historian Richard Powell eloquently captures the transgressive nature of Catlett's portrayals of beautiful Black women who are the antithesis of Eurocentric conceptions of beauty: "In prints created as early as 1946, Catlett raised aspects of Black facial physiognomy—dark skins, coarse and curly hair, broad noses, and full lips—to unprecedented heights of aesthetic contemplation and veneration. Simultaneously, her images of women—as workers, social activists, creative individuals, scholars and intellectuals, and, of course, as mothers—stood in sharp contrast to the often one-dimensional representations of women created by many visual artists."[11] These Catlett prints also reflect the influence of African art, especially West African masks, which we have come to associate with the highly celebrated art she has been producing for over sixty years. Catlett explains her lifelong affinity with her ancestral home: "I look for the relationship between African art which I cannot live without and the relation of that to black people. And I see in their faces and bodies African sculpture. And it's something I've been living with all my life."[12] Hill's collection of Catlett graphics are mostly from the series "For My People" (1992), commissioned by the Limited Editions Club to celebrate Margaret Walker's epic poem "For My People," included in her master's thesis in creative writing at the University of Iowa.[13] Catlett's long-standing friendship with Walker began while they were roommates (they were unable to live on campus because of segregation) at the University of Iowa pursuing graduate study. This limited-edition portfolio, illustrated in collaboration with the celebrated Black woman writer Walker, helps to immortalize Walker's famous poem. The prints which accompany the text of the poem explore themes that are reminiscent of the art Catlett has produced since the beginning of her career, including her first solo exhibition, "Paintings, Sculptures and Prints of the Negro Woman," which opened at Barnett-Aden Gallery in 1947 in Washington. One of the prints, *Singing Their Songs,* recalls the Black women workers in the 1946-47 linocut series, especially *I Am a Negro Woman,* as well as Catlett's well-known linocuts *Sharecropper* (1968) and *The Survivor* (1983).

Elizabeth Catlett is certainly the most prolific, well-known, politically radical and socially engaged African American woman artist of our time. She is still "making what she knows best" in her home in Cuernavaca, Mexico, as one of our most revered elders and warrior women.[14] Passionate still about producing the "people's art," especially for Black people, she leaves as perhaps her most important legacy to all of us her uncompromising celebration of African American women: "Black women have been cast in the role of carrying on the survival of black people through their position as mothers and wives, protecting and educating and stimulating children and black men. We can learn from black women. They have had to struggle for centuries. I feel that we have so much to express and that we should demand to be heard and demand to be seen because we know and feel and can express so much, contribute so much aesthetically."[15]

Grant Hill's art collection is also a celebration of Black women from whom, we presume, he has also learned a great deal. What we see in the faces and bodies of women depicted by Elizabeth Catlett, Romare Bearden, John Biggers, Malcolm Brown, Hughie Lee-Smith, and Phoebe Beasley will remain in our hearts and souls forever.

Notes

Epigraph. Samella Lewis, *The Art of Elizabeth Catlett* (Claremont, Calif.: Hancraft Studios, 1984), is the first monograph on Catlett; Lewis was a student of Catlett at Dillard University in the early 1940s when she chaired the Department of Art. A second monograph, Melanie Anne Herzog's *Elizabeth Catlett: An American Artist in Mexico* (Seattle: University of Washington Press, 2000), is an important contribution to the scholarship on Catlett. This essay's title was inspired by Catlett's painting professor at the University of Iowa, Grant Wood, who advised her to "make what you know best."

1. Freida High Tesfagiorgis, "Afrofemcentrism and Its Fruition in the Art of Elizabeth Catlett and Faith Ringgold," *Sage: A Scholarly Journal on Black Women* 4, no. 1 (spring 1987): 28.
2. Ibid., 1.
3. Lucinda H.Gedeon, ed. *Elizabeth Catlett Sculpture: A Fifty-Year Retrospective* (Purchase, N.Y.: Neuberger Museum of Art, State University of New York, 1998), 8.
4. Ibid.
5. Lewis, *The Art of Elizabeth Catlett,* 11.
6. Herzog, *Elizabeth Catlett,* 5.
7. Ibid., 21.
8. Ibid., 23.
9. Ibid.
10. Ibid., 35.
11. Richard J. Powell, "Face to Face: Elizabeth Catlett's Graphic Work," in *Elizabeth Catlett: Works on Paper,* 1944-1992, ed. Jeanne Zeidler (Hampton, Va.: Hampton University Museum, 1993), 49.
12. Ibid., 42.
13. See Margaret Walker, *For My People* (New Haven: Yale University Press, 1942).
14. See my essay, "Warrior Women: Art as Resistance," in *Bearing Witness: Contemporary Works by African American Women Artists* (Atlanta: Spelman Museum of Fine Art and Rizzoli International, 1996), 39-46.
15. James V. Hatch and Leo Hamalian, eds., *Artist and Influence II* (1991): 14.

Other Sources

Thalia Gouma-Peterson, "Elizabeth Catlett: The Power of Human Feeling and of Art," *Woman's Journal* 4 (spring-summer 1983): 48-56.
Juan Mora, E. C.: *The Work of Elizabeth Catlett.* New York: Third World Newsreel, 1978 (documentary film).
Carolyn Shuttlesworth, ed., *Three Generations of African American Women Sculptors: A Study in Paradox.* Philadelphia: Afro-American Historical and Cultural Museum, 1996.

26. "Rebel Woman" in *Mickalene Thomas: I Can't See You Without Me* (2018)

In the early 1970s, women artists protested their exclusion from museums, mainstream exhibitions, and art history scholarship and called for alternative exhibitions and women's galleries. At the same time, Black artists were struggling for inclusion at The Museum of Modern Art in New York by establishing a separate wing for their art and demanding representation on the museum's board of trustees. Artist Faith Ringgold would become an important figure among both protest groups. In 1970 she joined the Ad Hoc Women Artists' committee, a group inspired by feminist art critic Lucy Lippard and artist Poppy Johnson, which held demonstrations against the Whitney Museum of American Art for its discriminatory practices with respect to women artists. As a result of this agitation, Betye Saar and Barbara Chase-Riboud became the first Black women artists to be exhibited at the Whitney Annual in 1971. During the same year, "Where we At," a collective of Black women artists, was founded following the first exhibition of Black women artists at the Acts of Art gallery in Greenwich Village, New York. Nearly fifty years later, the Brooklyn Museum opened a major exhibition of Black women artists titled *We Wanted a Revolution: Black Radical Women,* 1965-85. As a 2017 review asserted, the exhibition "honors the black women who laid the groundwork for such contemporary artists, activists and artist-activists, whose influence on contemporary feminism and contemporary art is nothing less than cosmic."[1]

Mickalene Thomas comes to mind most immediately among today's Black women artists who carry on the radical tradition of their foremothers. She continues the creative and political work of queer Black women such as Audre Lorde, Cheryl Clarke, and Barbara Smith, who resisted heteronormative scripts in their quest for a more complex rendering of Black womanhood. Thomas also acknowledges the impact of Alice Walker's 1982 novel *The Color Purple*—especially the loving, life-sustaining, erotic relationship between characters Celie and Shug—on her own work and the recurring themes of sisterhood, femininity, sexuality, beauty, and power that appear in her photography, painting, and videos.

In an interview with Antwaun Sargent published on the opening day of her 2016 solo exhibition *Mentors, Muses, and Celebrities* at the Aspen Art Museum, Thomas underscores the significance of Black women bonding. "The inspiration behind the show is mainly love...we look at each other in this sisterhood way and it defines who we are—our sense of confidence, our sense of worth."[2] Here and elsewhere, Mickalene Thomas's artistry provides a powerful, perhaps unparalleled, visual dimension to key Black feminist principles that were captured in the now-canonical 1977 *Combahee River Collective* Statement: "our politics initially sprang from the shared belief that Black women are inherently valuable...We realize that the only people who care enough about us to work consistently for our liberation are us. Our politics evolve from a healthy love for ourselves, our sisters, and our community."[3]

Black feminist impulses in the visual art of African American women have been the subject of a growing body of scholarship that began with Freida High Tesfagiorgis's pioneering essay "Afrofemcentrism and Its Fruition in the Art of Elizabeth Catlett and Faith Ringgold." The Wexner Center's extraordinary, courageous exhibition *Mickalene Thomas: I Can't See You Without Me* is the quintessential manifestation of Tesfagiorgis's concept of "Afrofemcentric" elements in the visual arts, which she describes as a "unique assertiveness-consciousness in Afro-American women."[4] Throughout the exhibition's focus on a new concept of the muse, the viewer is struck by the abundance, fierceness, and eroticism of its Black female images, including Thomas's *Me as* Muse (2016), a multimedia video installation that captures, unapologetically, the artist's own sexuality. We are compelled to take notice of the woman-centeredness of the work because it is so unusual, even in solo exhibitions of women artists. Resisting the hypersexualized Black female bodies of Western art and popular culture, Thomas's depictions of Black female sexuality are fearless and liberating, including the images of her mother, Sandra ("Mama" Bush), her first and most influential muse. The transgressive nature of Thomas's portrayals of beautiful, powerful Black women, who often embody the antithesis of Eurocentric conceptions of beauty, is simply unparalled. The artist captures the meaning of the 1960s mantra Black Is Beautiful, depicting dark skin, natural hair, broad noses, full lips, and sexy thighs and hips in ways that are delightful and alluring.[5]

I am unaware of a more loving and bold tribute to one's mother in any artist's work than the images captured in such paintings as *Mama Bush III: One of a Kind* (2007); *Mama Bush: (Your Love Keeps Lifting Me) Higher and Higher* (2009); and *A-E-I-O-U and sometimes Y (Mama Bush)* (2012); as well as in her first documentary film, *Happy Birthday to a Beautiful Woman* (2012), which collectively introduce the exhibition. Despite their complex relationship, in numerous interviews Thomas testifies to the centrality of her mother to her work as an artist: "I started with my mother and myself"; "I pulled everything I am and do from her"; "The moment I started photographing my mother was the moment my work completely changed."[6] It was her photography professor at Yale, David Hilliard, who had persuaded his student to photograph her mother, and during that process, the artist recalls, she "began to look at her as a person and accept her weaknesses, her failures."[7] In a later interview, with *New York Times Style Magazine* writer/editor Thessaly La Force, Thomas explains what motivated her to move beyond photographing her mother to making a documentary as Mama Bush was battling a terminal illness: "When I photographed her in my studio, we always talked, we had conversations ...they were just for us. This was different. I wanted people to really know her. How did she get to this point? What was her story?...And I wanted to learn about my mother as a person—to separate from my relationship to her as her daughter—and look at her as the human being she was."[8]

The 1991 anthology *Double Stitch: Black women Write About Mothers & Daughters* captures the turbulence and tenderness that characterizes Black mother-daughter relationships at various points during the life cycle. Like Maya Angelou, who wrote its foreword, Thomas was at one point estranged from her mother, with whom she reconnected as a young adult. The stunning beauty of both mothers—Vivian Baxter and Sandra Bush—was a frequent reference by daughters who felt less beautiful. As they witness their mothers approaching death, both Angelou and Thomas are grateful for the lessons they've learned despite painful memories. Reminiscing about her mother's independent spirit, Angelou reflects: "My mother raised me, and then freed me."[9] For Thomas, it was her mother's resilience: "I've always coveted and loved and admired and adored that about her...despite how complicated our relationship was. I may have hated her sometimes because she wasn't the person I wanted her to be, but I loved her stature, I loved her strength—through the end."[10] It is not surprising that Mama Bush was Thomas's first muse, without whom, quite simply, the extraordinary artist who began her journey at Yale might not have emerged or evolved.[11]

Perhaps the most audacious and memorable aspect of *I Can't See You Without Me* is its embrace of the aesthetics of desire. *Artsy* writer (and Thomas's former assistant) Yelena Keller captures, as no one else has, this aspect of Mickalene Thomas's body of work: "Not only do [her] images reclaim the sexuality of the Black female body, but they also provide a voice for the queer Black woman as she is empowered to project and claim her desires."[12] Though Keller is commenting more generally about Thomas's portraits, her most astute reminder certainly applies to this exhibition at the Wexner Center: "Rather than overtly expressing these women's sexual orientation, Thomas more unassumingly inserts a queer gaze into her imagery." As she celebrates her muses—Mama, Maya, Racquel, and other friends, lovers, and collaborators—OUT and queer artist Mickalene Thomas signals a new moment in Black feminist art.[13]

What we see in the faces and bodies of Thomas's women will remain in our hearts and minds forever. They are self-confident, charismatic, glamorous, powerful, independent, resilient, bold, alluring, mischievous, and beautiful. Echoing painter and rebel Frida Kahle in the aforementioned interview with La Force, Thomas reminds us that, like her famous sister/artist, "I paint my own reality." She is articulate and eloquent about the nature of her rebellion as an artist, especially her debunking of harmful, stereotypical portrayals of Black women in art and the media. "By portraying real women with their own unique history, beauty, and background, I'm working to diversify the representations of black women in art....We are not validated until we see ourselves.... Not only are we present, we demand that we be seen, be heard, and be acknowledged."[14] In *I Can't See You Without Me,* Mickalene Thomas continues to challenge and unmask demeaning images of Black womanhood, offering instead compelling alternatives that are impossible to ignore. Her stunning, larger-than-life portraits of Black women mesmerize, delight, and overwhelm us and are a visual testament to the transformational and healing power of art.

NOTES

Mickalene Thomas, quoted In Lisa Melandri, "Points of Origin: An Interview with Mickalene Thomas,"·in *Mickalene Thomas: Origin of the Universe,* ed. Lisa Melandrl (Santa Monica, CA: Santa Monica Museum of Art, 2012). 28.

Cheryl Clarke, "Lesbianism: An Act of Resistance," in *This Bridge Called My Back: Writings by Radical Women of Color,* eds. Cherrie Moraga and Gloria Anzaldua (New York: Kitchen Table: Women of Color Press, 1981), 128-37.

1. Priscilla Frank, "An Exhibition Dedicated to Black Women Artists Is Now on View in Brooklyn," *Huffington Post,* April 25, 2017, https://www.huffingtonpost.com/entry/14-extraordinary-black-women-artistsare-now-on-view-in-brooklyn_us_58fe540de4b00fa7de16bfb3.

2. Antwaun Sargent, "Mickalene Thomas on Muses, Models, and Mentors," *Interview Magazine.* March 9, 2016, https://www.interviewmagazine.com/arttmickalene-thomas.

3. Combahee River Collective, "A Black Feminist Statement," 1977, In *Words of Fire: An Anthology of African-American Feminist Thought,* ed. Beverly Guy-Sheftall (New York: The New Press, 1995), 234.

4. Freida High W. Tesfagiorgis, "Afrofemcentrism and Its Fruition in the Art of Elizabeth Catlett and Faith Ringgold (A View of Women by Women)," *SAGE: A Scholarly Journal on Black Women* 4, no. 1 (Spring 198n: 25-29.

5. Sarah Lewis, "Mickalene Thomas on Beauty," in *Mickalene Thomas: Origin of the Universe,* 8-13.

6. Mickalene Thomas, quoted In Julia Felsenthal, "Mickalene Thomas on Her Photographic Muses," *Vogue,* January 28, 2016, https://www.vogue.com/artlcle/mickalene-thomasmuse-aperture; Thessaly La Force, "Artist Mickalene Thomas on Her Film *Happy Birthday to a Beautiful Woman, Her Mother, and Creativity,*" *Vogue,* February 17, 2014, https://www.vogue.com/article/artist-mickaienethomas-on-her-film-happybirthday-to-a-beautiful-woman-hermother-and-creativity; and Melandri, "Points of Origin," 28.

7. Mickalene Thomas, quoted in Karen Rosenberg, "Mickalene Thomas Rediscovers Her Mother—and Her Muse," *New York Times Magazine,* September 27, 2012, https://www.nytimes.com/2012/09/30/magazine/mlckalene-thomas-redlscovers-hermother-and-her-muse.html.

8. Mickalene Thomas, quoted in La Force, "Artist Mickalene Thomas."

9. Maya Angelou, foreword to *Double Stitch: Black Women Write About Mothers & Daughters,* ed. Patricia Bell-Scott (Boston: Beacon Press, 1991), p. xi.

10. Thomas, quoted in La Force, "Artist Mickalene Thomas."

11. See Jennifer Blessing, "Mother-Muse-Mirror," in *Muse: Mickalene Thomas Photographs* (New York: Aperture, 2015), 147-52.

12. Yelena Keller, "Photographers Who Have Captured LGBTQ Life in the African

Diaspora," *Artsy,* August 16, 2017, https://www.artsy.net/article/artsy-editorial-photographerscaptured-lgbtq-life-african-diaspora. See also her essay "The Overlooked, Radical History of Black Women in Art," *Artsy,* April 28, 2017, which reviews the Brooklyn Museum exhibition *We Wanted a Revolution: Black Radical Women.* 1965-85.

13. See also Derek Conrad Murray, *Queering Post-Black Art, Artists Transforming African-Amer/can Identity After Civil Rights* (London: I. B. Tauris, 2015) and "Mickalene Thomas: Afro-Kitsch and the Queering of Blackness," in *American Art* 28, no. 1 (Spring 2014): 9-15; and also Thomas's images of black women, including transgender people, in Lehmann Maupin's exhibition *She's Come UnDone!* (March 26-May 2, 2009), http://www.lehmannmaupin.com/exhibitions/2009-03-_mickalenethomas.

14. Mickalene Thomas, quoted in Katie Booth, "In Mickalene Thomas's aweinspiring portraits, a meaningful reflection of black women in art," *Women in the World,* January 29, 2016, https://womenintheworld.com/2016/01/29/in-mlckalenethomass-awe-inspiring-portraitsa-meanlngful-reflection-of-blackwomen-in"art/.

27. Coretta Scott King: The Beloved Community Revisted (2025)

Freedom from discrimination based on sexual orientation is surely a fundamental human right in any great democracy, as much as freedom from racial, religious, gender or ethnic discrimination.

Coretta Scott King, 2000[1]

We are all caught in an inescapable network of mutuality, tied into a single garment of destiny. Whatever affects one directly, affects all indirectly.

Dr. Martin Luther King, Jr., 1968[2]

Chronicling less visible aspects of the lives of iconic African American figures, especially the wives of famous men, is a perpetual challenge for scholars, particularly when they embrace controversial causes. In the aftermath of Coretta Scott King's death in 2006 at age 78, it is imperative that researchers begin the difficult task of analyzing, assessing, and making visible to a broader audience the fullness of her political commitments. Re-imagining the lives of famous women is particularly daunting, especially when they transgress gender norms, as did Lorraine Hansberry, Barbara Jordan, Angela Davis, or Alice Walker, to name a few, or they depart in significant ways from their public persona, as was the case with Coretta Scott King.

Accounts of the life of Mrs. King have, regrettably though perhaps somewhat justifiably, tended to focus on her life in relation to her husband. All but a few notable examples, a biography by Mrs. King's sister, Edythe Scott Bagley (with Joe Hilley), *Desert Rose: The Life and Legacy of Coretta Scott King* focus on her life with Martin Luther King, Jr., and less attention is paid to her life after her husband was assassinated in Memphis, Tennessee, in 1968, though she lived another 38 years. While there is some discussion of her anti-war/peace activism, anti-apartheid activism, and women's advocacy, there is no mention of her unrelenting LGBTQ activism. Much of the later chapters of *Desert Rose* focus on "finishing Martin's business," especially building the King Memorial Center, now the Martin Luther King, Jr. Center for Nonviolent Social Change in Atlanta, Georgia, and establishing a national King Holiday, which the U.S. Congress passed in 1983. Though her sister acknowledges Coretta's commitment to social justice issues prior to her meeting Martin, the biography is silent about Coretta's more controversial human rights stances. Another departure from predictable portraits of her life is the work of political scientist Jeanne Theoharis, who included a quote from a friend of Coretta's underscoring her own awareness of the ways in which her activism had been erased: "'I am made to sound like an attachment to a vacuum cleaner...the wife of Martin then the widow of Martin, all of which I was proud to be but I was never just a wife, nor a widow. I was always more than a label'."

Michael G. Long's monograph, *Martin Luther King, Jr., Homosexuality and the Early Gay Rights Movement: Keeping the Dream Straight?* is an example of more recent scholarship that examines more fully the aspects of Mrs. King's life. Indeed, the very first chapter, "'It's Consistent with His Philosophy'," discusses Mrs. King's LGBTQ rights advocacy and chronicles the circumstances leading up to her first formal speech on gay rights at the 1986 Human Rights Campaign gala in New York City, having been invited by Winston Johnson, an Eastern Airlines representative, whom she had met in 1968 and with whom she developed a friendship which resulted in his disclosing his sexual orientation to her many years later. My essay here joins in the effort to portray more fully the depth and complexity of the multiple causes and liberation struggles for which Mrs. King advocated.

One of the most precious legacies of Dr. Martin Luther King, Jr.'s monumental human rights struggle was his articulation of the concept of "the beloved community." In a chapter from his *Stride Toward Freedom* (1958), he explained his commitment to nonviolent resistance and its role in the creation of a beloved community. "At the center of nonviolence stands the principle of love. The nonviolent resister would contend that in the struggle for human dignity, the oppressed people of the world must not succumb to the temptation of becoming bitter...In speaking of love...we are not referring to some sentimental or affectionate emotion....It is love in action... love seeking to preserve and create community...a willingness to go to any length to restore community."[4]

What I want to argue as we continue to celebrate the extraordinary legacy of Martin Luther King, Jr. is that while Coretta Scott King (1927-2006) has been celebrated as a civil rights figure, frequently in the narrowest of terms, her vision of "the beloved community" was bolder and more revolutionary. Certainly, her more radical politics requires the kind of scholarly probing that her popular status as a "professional widow" or "First Lady of the Civil Rights Movement" would not have allowed. Despite her deep Christian faith, it is also the case that her broad-based commitment to human rights situated her outside the mainstream of organized religion and the Baptist church communities in which she was immersed as the wife of a legendary minister. In other words, probing Coretta's radical politics enables us to situate her outside the box of Martin Luther King, Jr.'s wife and then widow in ways that would have been unimaginable prior to her death in 2006. To capture her unwavering commitment to a broad range of social justice issues, it is imperative that we envision Martin's comrade as a freedom fighter in the most expansive sense of that term and that we see her as a progressive and passionate teacher whose classroom was many different audiences.

To understand her life-long progressive political commitments, it is necessary to revisit Coretta's life in the Jim Crow South of Marion, Alabama, and her college days at Antioch College (Class of 1949) in Ohio—long before she met her future husband, Martin Luther King, Jr., while studying to become a concert singer in Boston. First, there was the influence of her supportive parents who stressed schooling and encouraged her to develop positive self-esteem, despite having been told, "one way or another, almost every day of my life, that I wasn't as good as a white child," Coretta recalled.[5] Her mother's subversive message that she be independent was heard by many Black daughters in the South. "You're just as good as anyone else. You get an education and try to be somebody. Then you won't have to be kicked around by anybody, and you won't have to depend on anyone for your livelihood, not even a man."[6] At the private Lincoln High School in her hometown, which had been founded in 1867 by freed slaves and later run by Northern white missionaries, academic rigor and independence were stressed. During her senior year, she heard human rights activist and pacifist, Bayard Rustin, speak during his travels around the country for the Fellowship of Reconciliation, an international, multiracial peace organization; among its members were theologians Reinhold Niebuhr and Howard Thurman, Rufus Jones and Henry Cadbury, founders of the American Friends Service Committee, and Oswald Garrison Villard, grandson of abolitionist William Lloyd Garrison. After her marriage, she would meet Bayard Rustin again at her home when he traveled to Montgomery, Alabama, to help her husband Martin with the pivotal bus boycott. In 1963, Rustin would help organize the March on Washington where King delivered his legendary "I Have a Dream" speech.

Having been raised in the rural Jim Crow South, she had witnessed first-hand the pervasive impact of white supremacy and the violence that it spawned on a regular basis. At age 15 she had seen her home and father's sawmill in Marion, Alabama, burned to the ground on Thanksgiving Day by whites upset with her father, Obadiah Scott (1899-1998).[8] Considered to be uppity by angry white townspeople because of his relative success as a grocery store and later sawmill owner, he endured their wrath because he refused to observe racial norms for second-class citizens.

When asked about how she came to be who she was as an adult, she not only always spoke about the values of her parents and the private Black school she attended in rural Alabama, but she also mentioned the impact of her college experience:

> I went to Antioch College in Yellow Springs, Ohio. Antioch is a college that teaches people how to have a world view. All races and religions were represented there, and it was an excellent education. I had a very broad background in liberal arts, and I had work experience as well. Antioch was about making change in societies, about social change, which was preparing me at that time for the role that I would play later in life.[9]

At Antioch she joined its NAACP chapter, Race Relations and Civil Liberties Committees, and was a student delegate to the founding convention of the Young Progressives in 1948. Described by one of its deans as being "on the cutting edge of radical politics," Antioch politicized Coretta as a young woman in ways that helped to illuminate her adult passions.[10] She was clear about its impact on her development and the ways that it prepared her for civil rights activism later. "Antioch students have long been encouraged to speak out, to challenge orthodoxy, to question authority, to be open to new ideas and to exercise freedom of speech." At Antioch's Reunion Weekend, June 25, 2004 (also its 150th anniversary celebration), she recalled first seeing the monument on campus to its founder, Horace Mann, on which were his words, "Be ashamed to die until you have won some victory for humanity," which became the college's motto. These were President Mann's parting words to the Class of 1859, and Coretta shares with the audience that it was "a challenge I took very seriously, and which became a paramount goal in my life."[11]

Mrs. King always acknowledged the ways that both her upbringing in Marion, Alabama, and her college days at Antioch were responsible for the evolution of her political identity:

> It was here that I was able to continue to build upon and strengthen the values taught to me by my parents and the values I absorbed from my religious training—values such as freedom, equality, justice, peace, love, truth, self-respect, sharing, and forgiveness. These values became alive for me in the Antioch environment where they were tested as I sought to make the adjustment from a rural southern farm

background where I led a segregated life to an integrated, multi-cultural and highly sophisticated environment. It was here at Antioch that I gained a deeper understanding of myself, discovering and accepting my limitations as well as my strengths. Here at Antioch, I gained an understanding of individual differences and how to respect those differences. A strong commitment to the life of service to one's fellow human beings was advocated by Antioch, and this was in keeping with the teachings which were a part of my home and school environments.[12]

The story surrounding Mrs. King's public advocacy of gay rights begins in 1983, the 20th anniversary of the now legendary March on Washington, a story which Michael Long details in his probing, yet controversial book on her husband's views on homosexuality.[13] Early in the planning for the anniversary March on Washington for Jobs, Peace and Freedom, a debate ensued about the inclusion of the National Gay Task Force (NGTF) on its national steering committee. Veteran civil rights activist, DC Delegate, and national director of the 1983 March, Walter Fauntroy, apparently objected, according to Long, to addressing gay rights and inviting a gay speaker.

Frustrated, Gilberto Gerald, acting director of the National Coalition of Black Gays (NCBG), sent mailgrams a week before the March to various organizers, including Mrs. King. When objections continued, gay leaders staged a sit-in at Fauntroy's congressional office, followed by negative publicity, which resulted in a conference call two days before the March—which included Fauntroy, Virginia Apuzzo [NGTF], Joseph Lowery [SCLC], Benjamin Hooks [NAACP], and Mrs. King—and a list of five demands. While the demands were not endorsed, Mrs. King agreed to including a gay speaker and endorsing the Gay and Lesbian Civil Rights Act pending in Congress (initially sponsored by Bella Abzug in 1975). Audre Lorde, Black lesbian poet, spoke briefly on behalf of gay rights at the 1983 anniversary March in D.C. Long credits King with being "the most influential voice in the decision to include an openly lesbian speaker and announce support for the gay civil rights bill before Congress."[14] Not mentioned in Long's narrative about the March on Washington II (1983) is that Gloria Steinem had the honor of introducing Mrs. King to the huge crowds gathered at the Lincoln Memorial that historic day, August 25, 1983. The gathering addressed a broader menu of human rights issues under the rubric "New Coalition of Conscience": civil rights, women's rights, gay rights, labor, peace, nuclear arms, South African apartheid, and disability rights.

Despite resistance, Mrs. King was determined to continue underscoring the connections between civil rights and LGBT rights at the 40th anniversary of the March on Washington. She was also intent on honoring Bayard Rustin, the openly gay civil rights activist who was responsible for organizing the 1963 March.[15] In this regard she invited the National Gay and Lesbian Task Force (NGLTF), the largest LGBT rights organization in the U.S., to take part in the celebration. It was the first time that a gay rights group had been invited to a major civil rights gathering organized by African American leaders. Among the speakers were Matt Foreman, NGLTF's executive director, Phil Wilson, executive director of the Black AIDS Institute, and Mandy Carter, founding board member of the National Black Justice Coalition (NBJC), the only national Black LGBT civil rights organization, whose mission is to fight both homophobia and racism. When Carter spoke, she did so also as one of the co-founders of Southerners on New Ground (SONG), founded in 1993 in Durham, NC, at the NGLTF Creating Change Conference: "As a black woman and a lesbian, I think it's important to not only emphasize equal rights for lesbian, gay, bisexual and transgender people as a whole, but specifically for LGBT people of color as well," she asserted. She went on to say, "It's unfortunate that Bayard Rustin couldn't bring all of his identities to the table in his fight for civil rights. We are not only proud to be a part of this 40th anniversary march, but we are extremely proud to be honoring Bayard Rustin for his work from decades ago."[16] An important component of the celebration was the screening at the Kennedy Center on August 22 of the documentary, *Brother Outsider: The Life of Bayard Rustin* (2003). John D'Emilio signed his then newly released book, *Lost Prophet: The Life and Times of Bayard Rustin* (2003); also released that year was Devon Carbardo's *Time on Two Crosses: The Collected Writings of Bayard Rustin* (2003).

Carter, whose multi-issue, multi-racial, grass-roots activism was catalyzed by her involvement in the SCLC's 1968 Poor People's Campaign, co-founded SONG whose mission was to "build progressive movements across the South by developing transformative models of organizing that connect race, class, culture, gender, and sexuality identity."[17] They were especially interested in integrating work against homophobia into freedom struggles in the South. Probably the most well-known grassroots Black lesbian feminist activist within the national LGBTQ movement in the U.S., she was nominated for the Nobel Peace Prize in 2005. Other LGBTQ groups participating in the anniversary events were the Human Rights Campaign (HRC) and the National Association of Black and White Men Together (NABWMT).

In the aftermath of Mrs. King's death on January 31, 2006, the LGBTQ movement, including the National Black Justice Coalition, the Human Rights

Campaign, National Stonewall Democrats, and NGLTF were effusive in their praise of her work. Matt Foreman is quoted in the *Bay Area Reporter,* February 2006, as saying: "Our community has lost a dear and courageous friend, someone who was there for us when virtually no one else was. From the beginning Mrs. King understood that homophobia is hate and that hate has no place in the Beloved Community that she and Dr. King envisioned for our nation and our world."[18]

Ignored by the media, a small but angry group of anti-gay protesters gathered outside her funeral in Atlanta in 2006, one of whose placards carried the hateful message, "Mrs. King Is In Hell." During her life, she had criticized Black ministers who espoused homophobic sentiments and preached against the inclusion of gay rights in the overall civil rights struggle. When white anti-gay extremists appealed to black voters and black churches to support a repeal of Tampa, Florida's gay rights law, Mrs. King joined forces again with Black lesbian activist Mandy Carter and wrote an influential letter to the African American community in which she encouraged them to see the connections between civil rights and gay rights. Two years later, Black ministers in Miami circulated flyers at Black churches denouncing gay rights. Apparently upset because the flyers included a picture of her husband, Martin, she responded quickly by indicating that if he were alive, he would support gay rights. In an interview March 1987 with actor Redvers Jeanmarie, Bayard Rustin speculated about Martin's views on homosexuality:

> It is difficult for me to know what Dr. King felt about gayness except to say that I'm sure he would have been sympathetic and would not have had the prejudiced view. Otherwise he would not have hired me. My being gay was not a problem for Dr. King but a problem for the movement.[20]

He also explains the circumstances surrounding his resignation in 1960 from SCLC (founded in 1957) in the wake of complaints to Dr. King about his homosexuality and King's endorsing him three years later as deputy with A. Phillip Randolph for the 1963 March on Washington.[21] So while there were sympathizers, Mrs. King was perhaps the first African American civil rights leader of her stature and visibility to speak publicly as an ally on behalf of LGBT rights, which she continued to do until the end of her life.

Considering her atypical stances among civil rights leaders, a compelling question for scholars exploring Mrs. King's political commitments is likely to be—what accounts for her early and persistent advocacy surrounding LGBT issues, especially in African American communities? While the answer to this question is certainly complicated and perhaps difficult to reach closure around, it is important to recall a set of circumstances that may lead researchers to plausible explanations. Because I was aware that Lynn Cothren, an openly gay white male activist, had served for twenty-three years as her Special Assistant, I interviewed him in March of 2011. Prior to the interview, Cothren, then Director of Administration at Girl Scouts USA in New York, shared a number of speeches that Mrs. King had delivered to various audiences around LGBT rights from 1999 to 2002. He joined the King Center in 1982 when he was only nineteen as a part-time employee while studying at the Atlanta Art Institute. Before being tapped to be her assistant, he worked for ten years in the Center's library and archives and with the executive vice president of government and international affairs. While working at the Center, he also volunteered with AID Atlanta, as the HIV/AIDS crisis deepened. While he became known as a young gay activist, he was quick to point out in a printed interview that "I see myself as a human rights activist that specializes, maybe, in queer issues. But I work on all the progressive issues because I believe very strongly that everything is interconnected. Where you see racism and sexism, you'll see homophobia."[22]

In the printed interview and his interview with me in 2011, Cothren recalled how unpopular Mrs. King's decision had been at the King Center: "They weren't thrilled with King's choice of a gay white male to head her office. He would, after all, be accompanying her on most public appearances— she made nearly 200 a year—and therefore be very visible."[23] She remained defiant and, I suspect, her decision to appoint Lynn as her special assistant was also strategic on her part. "Several of her board members and other people were like, 'You don't need that gay white boy traveling around with you,'" Cothren recalled. Mrs. King was very clear. She said, "'I know what I need.' She was very clear about [her need]. 'He does his job and that's what I'm about, not about the fact that he's white or gay.'"[24]

When I asked Cothren about whether he believed he was responsible in a major way for Coretta's passionate defense of LGBT rights because of his own highly visible gay rights activism, he was adamant in his refusal to take major credit.[25] He recalled her progressivism before they met and her having known Bayard Rustin before they met. In the published interview with Jason Michael, he also refused to take credit: "I'll have to quote Dr. King here," Cothren said. "I'd like to say as a man that it was all me, that I brought her, but in a lot of ways she's brought me. And I think we bring each other. I think having someone that's openly gay on your staff, that we talk openly about issues and things has helped. She has learned a lot from me. But she knew gay people before me.'"[26] During our interview, he indicated that perhaps he assisted Mrs. King with the *language* of the LGBT movement but it would be inappropriate for him to assume too much responsibility for her stances in this regard. It seems obvious that Mrs. King's decision to appoint Cothren for her Special Assistant in the first place, given that she had to have known his appointment would be unpopular in certain circles, is another manifestation of her already progressive politics around homosexuality.

Cothren also shared with me a personal essay in which he described his pride as he witnessed her speaking "for the dignity of the LGBT community," over and over again. His greatest moment as Special Assistant to Mrs. King, however, was hearing her speak at the annual Pride Celebration in Atlanta in 1996 to thousands of participants. He alluded to the circumstances surrounding her speech. Because he was on the Board of Directors of the Pride Committee, he decided to decline their invitation for Mrs. King to speak because he didn't want her to feel obligated because of his own close association with the committee. He also knew that she would have no objection to speaking because, as he recalled, he had heard her make these remarks many times:

> My gay and lesbian brothers and sisters . . . stood up for my freedom in Montgomery and Selma, in Albany, Georgia and St. Augustine, Florida and many other campaigns of the movement. Many of these courageous men and women were fighting for my freedom at a time when they could find few voices for their own, and I will always remember and honor their contributions.

Later, when she went over the list of declined invitations, she pulled the Pride invitation out and said to Cothren, "I want to do this one. There is something I want to say." Among the many things she wanted to say was this:

> As my husband, Martin Luther King, Jr. said, 'I have fought too long and hard against segregated public accommodations to end up segregating my moral concerns. Justice is indivisible.' The civil rights movement that I believe in thrives on unity and inclusion, not division and exclusion. All of us who oppose discrimination and support equal rights should stand together to resist every attempt to restrict civil rights in this country . . . Therefore, I appeal to everyone who believes in Martin Luther King Jr.'s dream to make room at the table of brother and sisterhood for lesbian and gay people.

Anxious to continue probing the connections between the civil rights movement and the gay rights movement, I met Winston Johnson, a white civil rights and LGBT rights activist, who shared with me a taped interview connected with Touching Up Our Roots, Atlanta's LGBT History Project.[27] It was produced by Dave Hayward, a veteran gay activist who founded the project with gay activist Berl Boykin in 2002. In the interview, Winston spoke about his relationship with Mrs. King and described his early involvement with the civil rights movement (including the NAACP) long before there was a gay rights movement. He asserted matter-of-factly, "that movement is where our movement got our legs." He believed that it was safe to be white and gay in the civil rights movement in the South but not safe to be out and advocating for gay rights. He was happy about "getting crumbs falling off the civil rights movement" in the early years of the gay rights movement in the South. He indicated that his friendship with Mrs. King began in earnest when he worked at Eastern Airlines (now defunct) as an agent and enabled her on her frequent flights to be upgraded to first class; he shared that she preferred Eastern to Delta because the former, a northern-based airline, treated Blacks better during the 60s than did Delta Airlines. He also shared how his white colleagues at Eastern resented his compassionate treatment of both Martin Luther King, Jr. and Mrs. King. He recalled the day she flew into Atlanta from Memphis, Tennessee, to retrieve his body, on April 5, 1968, the day after Martin was assassinated. Winston shared that on every April 4 after that fateful day in Memphis he took Mrs. King one red rose to her home on Sunset Avenue. He also talked about how he and his partner, Leon Allen, helped her as she struggled to build the Martin Luther King Center for Nonviolent Social Change and establish the national King Holiday.

In 1986, after the Supreme Court upheld the U.S. sodomy statutes, Winston officially "came out" to Mrs. King and enlisted her help in speaking out for equal justice for all. In October 1986, she was the keynote speaker at the New York HRC dinner and was the Atlanta guest of honor in 1988 when Winston and Leon helped bring HRC to Atlanta. Winston's story of helping to bring together the civil rights and the LGBT rights movements was featured in an exhibit at the new National Center for Civil and Human Rights in Atlanta, founded in 2014.

Mrs. King's human rights agenda also addressed the plight of exploited agricultural workers. In a speech, "The Right to a Decent Life and Human Dignity," during which she addressed 2,000 Chicano/a farm workers in California, she voiced her solidarity with the farm workers union and their plight as oppressed people. Because she had worked in the hot cotton fields of Alabama as a child, she understood the grueling life of lettuce farmers. "Although my family owned the land, the system was organized to keep the earning from cotton too low to maintain an adequate subsistence." *(El Malcriado, United Farm Workers' Organizing Committee newsletter, January 1, 1971.)* In December 1970, she visited Cesar Chavez, leader of the movement to organize Mexican American farm workers, who was in jail in California in connection with the lettuce workers' strike.

Her commitment to human rights was all-encompassing, unrelenting, and hard hitting. She lifted her voice against apartheid in South Africa, excessive military spending, environmental pollution, the ravages of global poverty, a proposed constitutional amendment banning gay marriage, and the wars in Vietnam and Iraq. In a speech for the Architects of Peace project in 1968, she articulated her own vision of the beloved community:

> We should dare to dream of a world where no child lives in fear of war or suffers the ravages of militarism. Instead of spending more than two billion dollars a day on the arms race, as the governments of the world do now, we must invest in human and economic development, so that no one has to live in poverty. . . .Let's dare to dream of a Beloved Community where starvation, famine, hunger, and malnutrition will not be tolerated because the civilized community of nations won't allow it.[28]

Scolding Congress on a regular basis for investing in questionable military actions, she believed that the U.S. would be better served if resources were expended for improved schools, college tuition support, and training programs for at-risk youth. Her strident anti-war messages and her pacifism were a constant theme in her speeches to college audiences. Speaking to the Antioch College graduating class of 1982, she asked, "Isn't it strange how the leaders of nations can talk so eloquently about peace while they prepare for war . . . there is no way to make peace while preparing for war." Upset about the proliferation of nuclear weapons and unchecked militarism, she reminded them of the extraordinary cost of such militarism:

> The nuclear arms race breeds insecurity and fear the world over and is a shameful thief of funds from programs that would enrich our planet. It has been calculated that the cost of one heavy bomber equals thirty modern brick schools, or two fully equipped hospitals; that the cost of a single destroyer would provide new homes for 8,000 people; and that a single fighter plane would pay for half a million bushels of wheat."[29]

And, finally, her prophetic message: "A nation that continues year after year to spend more money on military defense than on programs of social uplift is approaching spiritual death."[30] Thinking globally, she urged the wealthy nations of the West to cancel Africa's "immoral, unjust" debt—350 billion dollars and growing. Recalling the United States' shameful slaveholding history, she argued: "America owes Africa far more than Africa owes America, and the time has come for America to begin repaying this debt."[31] For Mrs. King, struggles to bring about "the beloved community" involved eliminating this new form of financial colonialism among countries "that have been exploited for far too long." She continued to advance a human rights agenda and the viability of all struggles to end oppression throughout her life and, like her husband, Martin, dreamed of a world that would be free of poverty, racism, violence, and war. Deploying an intersectional approach, she always insisted that these evils were interrelated. Speaking to the Antioch student body in 1994, she would also reaffirm her expanded vision of the beloved community:

> I am glad to see that Antioch today shares the conviction that diversity is not just about securing broad racial representation and greater opportunity for people of color. Diversity means students and faculty of varied religious, ethnic and age groups should also be well represented and respected on campus. The same is true for gay and lesbian people, people with disabilities and people from low-income families.[32]

Having experienced, first-hand, the viciousness of hate crimes which her husband's assassination represented in 1968, it is not surprising that she reached out to the parents of Matthew Shepard the day after he was brutally murdered in Wyoming for being gay.

Given her advocacy surrounding ending violence against gays, it is also not surprising that during an acceptance speech for the Circle of Hope Award (Metropolitan Community Church and Foundation) in San Francisco, November 22, 2002, she would convey her sadness surrounding a highly publicized homophobic crime at Morehouse College, her husband's alma mater, that occurred a few weeks earlier on November 3.[33] On that day, Aaron Price beat a fellow student, Gregory Love, with a baseball bat in a dorm shower that resulted in a fractured skull. According to the *Atlanta Constitution* in an article "Assault Conviction, But No Hate Crime," Bill Montgomery recounts that Price was taking a shower in the dormitory when Love looked into the stall, staring at him. The two exchanged curses after which Price left the shower and returned with a baseball bat. Love, who insisted he was not gay, testified that as Price was beating him, he screamed, "Faggot, you're gay, gay . . . I hate these Morehouse faggots."[34] A year later Price was convicted of aggravated assault and aggravated battery and sentenced to ten years for each count, to run concurrently. For Mrs. King, it was ironic that Morehouse College, which prepares Black men like her husband for important leadership roles, would be a site for such violence and human rights violations:

> MIt is particularly sad to me when I hear black people making homophobic comments or undermining the human rights of people because of their sexual orientation. One young man was recently beaten with a baseball bat at Morehouse College, allegedly as a result of another student's homophobia. If this can happen in Martin Luther King, Jr.'s alma mater, which takes justifiable pride in preparing students for leadership in all areas, it can happen anywhere.[35]

When she analyzed the failures of our democracy and its profound social ills, she blamed, among other factors, male-dominant political institutions. Five months before the 2004 presidential election, she spoke at Antioch's 150th anniversary and urged the students to vote in large numbers, especially since Ohio was a key swing state; she also reminded them that their precious votes might actually decide the election between Bush and Kerry. As important, she insisted, was electing women to public office: "Today, women hold only about 13.6 percent of the seats in the U.S. Congress and 22.4 percent of the seats in the fifty state legislatures. America has no shortage of capable and committed women, and the time has come for women to take their rightful places in the legislative halls of America."[36] Her steadfast belief in the importance of women's roles in social transformation was a recurring theme in her speeches. Only two months after her husband's assassination in 1968, she spoke during the Poor People's Campaign at the Lincoln Memorial in June and boldly asserted that it was time for "a solid block of women power to fight the three great evils of racism, poverty, and war."[37] At the 13th Annual Creating Change Conference of the National Gay and Lesbian Task Force in Atlanta in 2003, she also argued, even more controversially, for more "lesbian and gay office holders as well."[38]

She was also ahead of her time with respect to her early involvement in the peace movement. In one of the earliest testimonies to Coretta Scott King's importance as a political figure in her own right, Alice Walker recalls having met her when she was a first-year student at Spelman College in 1962. A group of Spelman students were going to the World Youth Peace Festival in Helsinki that summer and were encouraged by their adviser, a white peace activist from California, to meet Mrs. King, who, along with other Black women in Atlanta, had supported the students financially. Coretta was preparing to attend a Women's Strike for Peace in Geneva, Switzerland, where she would be a delegate to the Seventeen Nation Disarmament Conference. Three years later, Mrs. King would join a picket line for Americans for a National Nuclear Policy in front of the White House to express her opposition to the Vietnam War and urge negotiations to end it.

In *An Easy Burden*, the autobiography of pastor, activist, advisor to King, former executive director of SCLC, and US ambassador to the United Nations Andrew Young, Young includes a chapter on "War and Poverty," in which there is an extended discussion of Martin Luther King, Jr.'s evolving position on the Vietnam War. Young acknowledges Coretta's impact on Martin's anti-war views and tells us that Martin declined to participate in peace demonstrations early on but often asked her to go in his stead. He is very explicit about Mrs. King's pacifism and her influence earlier on Martin's anti-war stances:

> "She had joined Americans for a National Nuclear Policy in a picket line in front of the White House in 1985.... Coretta had a long association with the peace movement, going back to her student days at Antioch College in Ohio, when she was active in Women's Strike for Peace. Philosophically, Coretta was a pacifist. In fact, her intellectual understanding of nonviolence and her deep personal commitment influenced Martin in the development of his own views."[39]

At the end of 1966, he began to be openly critical of the War and was discouraged by the SCLC Board from continuing to do so. In 1967 he accepted an invitation to be a keynote speaker at the massive anti-war march April 14 at United Nations Plaza, having also been encouraged by peace activist Dr. Benjamin Spock and Buddhist monk Thich Nhat Hanh to join the anti-war movement. However, Andrew Young encouraged him to choose another forum for his first major anti-war speech. So, on April 4, 1967, with the help of the group Clergy and Laity Concerned about Vietnam, he spoke at Riverside Church; Young declared the speech to be "one of the finest and most important of his career."[40] Martin also spoke at the UN march and rally at which over one million were in attendance.

Three years after Martin Luther King's assassination, Alice Walker would interview Mrs. King at her home on Sunset in Atlanta in 1971. Among many issues surrounding feminism, Walker was also curious about why Black women seem to be antagonistic toward the women's liberation movement. Mrs. King's response was insightful and illuminates clearly her own notions of feminism while also underscoring, liberated or not, Black women's unique struggles and character: "When you think of what some black women have gone through, and then look at how beautiful they still are! It is incredible that they still believe in the values of the race, that they have retained a love of justice, that they can still feel the deepest compassion, not only for themselves but for anybody who is oppressed; this is a kind of miracle, something we have that we must preserve and must pass on."[41] Perhaps anticipating her own future, she told

Walker that women have a unique role to play in freedom struggles, "Women, in general, are not a part of the corruption of the past, so they can give a new kind of leadership, a new image for mankind."[42] She also believed that "if women become irrevocably involved in social issues, they will find themselves powerful as activists *and* as women." [43] In other words, the road to liberation for women is not an individual quest, but rather "their involvement in the struggle for change and social justice."[44] For Mrs. King, then, to be liberated, to become powerful as a woman, meant becoming a freedom fighter, a person who takes a stand against injustice no matter who the victim might be. While we know that Martin didn't address women's rights, she told Walker that they talked frequently about the importance of organizing women and that she regretted that he didn't address women's issues. It would not be far-fetched to assume that if her husband had not died at 39, before the women's movement evolved, that she would have perhaps persuaded him to advocate on behalf of women and to make better use of "the woman power that we had" in much the same way that she persuaded him to embrace an anti-war agenda. Her connection with the women's movement included hosting the National Organization of Women's second convention in Atlanta, Georgia, and serving as a commissioner on President Carter's National Commission on the Observation of International Women's Year led by Bella Abzug. On what would have been her husband's 50th birthday, Mrs. King highlighted the ongoing struggle to make his birthday a national holiday, as well as the less well publicized drive to pass the Equal Rights Amendment (ERA). She always attended the annual brunch of the National Congress of Black Women founded by C. Delores Tucker, a civil rights and women's rights activist. In May 1966, Dr. King was among the first recipients of Planned Parenthood Federation of America's Margaret Sanger Award. Accepting the award for him because of his work in Chicago, Mrs. King said that there was a "striking kinship between our movement and Margaret Sanger's early efforts in the birth control movement."[45]

In 1977, a group of progressive activist women in Boston, who called themselves the Combahee River Collective (founded in 1974), crafted a manifesto that articulated what it meant to be Black feminists: "We are actively committed to struggling against racial, sexual, heterosexual, and class oppression and see as our particular task the development of integrated analysis and practice based upon the fact that the major systems of oppression are interlocking."[46] Their Black feminist manifesto was consistent with Coretta Scott King's vision of the beloved community and her evolving commitment to women's rights, gay rights, and human rights more broadly. In 1978, she spoke at a national NOW Conference, having been an early member of their Board of Directors, and urged women to stay the course no matter how difficult the battle: "So let us continue to work together, because when we are together there is a kind of strength that we get from each other, and when we are right, as we are, then we certainly will win our cause."[47] Her parting words are relevant today in the wake of right-wing attacks on all that feminists care about: "My sisters, let us walk together, and don't get weary."[48]

When the grand narrative of civil rights, women's rights, and gay rights is rewritten, it will be a more extraordinary history when the pantheon of women warriors is expanded. Coretta Scott King will join her fallen sisters—Anna Julia Cooper, Ida Wells Barnett, Claudia Jones, Lorraine Hansberry, Audre Lorde, June Jordan—whose collective battles against *multiple* forms of oppression have been as inspirational, as compelling, as transgressive, as the more celebrated icons of various human rights movements. When we retell the story of Black women's radical activism in the 20th century, we can finally embrace Coretta Scott King as the truly revolutionary figure she was already becoming as a college student in Yellow Springs, Ohio, seventy years ago. When we explore her capacious concept of "the beloved community," we will appreciate her embrace of a broader range of liberation struggles and her more radical vision for a new world.

Notes

[1] King, Coretta Scott, Opening Plenary Remarks, 13th Annual Creating Change Conference, National Gay and Lesbian Task Force, Atlanta, Georgia, November 9, 2000. Available at: https://queerrhetoric.wordpress.com/2010/05/21/remarks-at-creating-change-in-2000/ (Accessed August 30, 2022). A useful source for Mrs. King's speeches is "The Power of African American Women, Disk 9: A Coretta Scott King Special," Available at https://archive.org/details/pra_powerofafricanamericanwomen_9 (Accessed August 30, 2022). A few weeks after Dr. King's death, she spoke for him at an anti-war rally in New York's Central Park (using some of the notes pulled from his pockets), "Ten Commandments on Vietnam," Available at https://www.americanrhetoric.com/speeches/corettascottkingvietnamcommandments.htm (Accessed August 30, 2022). A surprising source on Mrs. King is "Coretta Scott King," FBI Records: The Vault. Available at http://vault.fbi.gov/Coretta%20Scott%20King/. (Accessed August 30, 2022).

[2] King, Martin Luther, Jr. Martin Luther King's last speech (at Ebenezer Baptist Church), "A Christmas Sermon on Peace and Nonviolence," December 24, 1967. Broadcast as part of the Massey Lectures on CBC. Reprinted in *Trumpet of Conscience*, (Boston: Beacon Press, 1968). Audio of this sermon is available here: https://www.youtube.com/watch?v=8pSojeyMY8c(Accessed August 30, 2022). Quoted material occurs at 7mins, 17 seconds.

[3] Jeanne Theoharis, "Coretta Scott King and the Civil-Rights Movement's Hidden Women," special KING issue, *The Atlantic*, April, 2018. Available online: https://www.theatlantic.com/magazine/archive/2018/02/coretta-scott-king/552557/(Accessed August 30, 2022). See also her book, *A More Beautiful and Terrible History: The Uses And Misuses of Civil Rights History* (Boston: Beacon Press, 2018).

[4] Martin Luther King, Jr., *Stride Toward Freedom: The Montgomery Story, and Where Do We Go from Here: Chaos or Community?* (Harper & Brothers, 1958). pp. 92-94.

[5] Coretta Scott King, Speech at American Academy of Achievement gathering, Washington DC, 1999. Portions of this speech are available online: https://achievement.org/achiever/coretta-scott-king/#interview (Accessed August 30, 2022). Quoted remarks at 16 mins.

[6] Coretta Scott King, *My Life with Martin Luther King*, (New York, Henry Holt, 1969), p. 34.

[8] See Adam Jones, "Scott Family House Holds Place in History, Hearts," *Tuscaloosa News*, January 18, 2004. Available online: https://www.tuscaloosanews.com/story/news/2004/01/19/scott-family-house-holds-place-in-history-hearts/27856771007/ (Accessed August 30, 2022).

[9] Coretta Scott King returned to Antioch College June 26, 2004 to receive the Horace Mann Award. See the *Dayton Daily News*, June 26 2004 for coverage of her visit and excerpts from her acceptance speech. In 1966, Mrs. King accompanied her husband

to Antioch where he delivered their 113th commencement speech; an assassination attempt was planned during the visit which was not carried out. See *Dayton Daily News*, February 11, 1966.

[10] Ibid.

[11] Ibid.

[12] Coretta Scott King Commencement Address, Antioch College, June 26, 1982, pp. 2-3, LCP.

[13] See Michael G. Long's Martin Luther King Jr., *Homosexuality and the Early Gay Rights Movement: Keeping the Dream Straight?* (New York, NY: Palgrave, 2012).

[14] Ibid., p. 15

[15] For a discussion of Bayard Rustin's role in the civil rights movement and the controversies surrounding his sexuality, see various biographies, especially John D'Emilio, *Lost Prophet: The Life and Times of Bayard Rustin* and the film, *Brother Outsider: The Life of Bayard Rustin,* by Nancy Kates and Bennett Singer. See also *Time on Two Crosses: The Collected Writings of Bayard Rustin,* edited by Devon W. Carbado and Donald Weise (Cleis Press, 2003), especially the section on Gay Rights which includes "From Montgomery to Stonewall" (1986) and "The New 'Niggers' Are Gays." See also *I Must Resist: Bayard Rustin's Life in Letters*; ed., Michael G. Long (San Francisco: 2012) and the essay in this volume, "The Civil Rights Identity of Bayard Rustin" by Devon Carbado and Donald Weise. President Obama awarded the Medal of Freedom to Bayard Rustin posthumously in November 2013.

[16] See CSpan Video of the 40th Anniversary event, August 23, 2003. For more information about Carter, see long interview with Stephen McKiernan at https://omeka.binghamton.edu/omeka/tems/show/862#

[17] See website, https://southernersonnewground.org/, for Southerners on New Ground (SONG), an LGBTQ social justice organization founded in 1993 and headquartered in Atlanta, Georgia. (Accessed August 30, 2022).

[18] Matt Foreman, a LGBTQ rights lawyer and activist, was executive director of the National Gay and Lesbian Task Force from 2003 until 2008. Quoted in Roger Brigham's "Gays Mourn death of Coretta King", *Bay Area Reporter,* February 2, 2006. Available Online:https://www.ebar.com/story.php?ch=obituaries&sc=&sc2=&id=247601 (Accessed Aug 30, 2022).

[19] See Michael Long's Martin Luther King Jr., *Homosexuality and The Early Gay Movement,* especially Chapter 2, "'He Did Not Take a Bullet for Same-Sex Unions': Bernice King's March Against Same-Sex Marriage," pp. 25-36.

[20] Quoted in Devon Carbado and Donald Weise's *Time on Two Crosses,* p. 292

[21] See the introductory chapter of Carbado and Weise's *Time On Two Crosses* for a lengthy discussion of the saga, especially Congressman Adam Clayton Powell's role.

[22] Interview by Jason Michael, "Lynn Cothren: In the Shadow of a Civil Rights Icon," p. 1, *Between the Lines,* April 5, 2013. Online: https://pridesource.com/article/lynn-cothren-in-the-shadow-of-a-civil-rights-icon/ (Accessed August 30, 2022). Historian Michael G. Long also interviewed Cothren in February 2010 whom he described as

"another individual who served a catalytic role in connecting Coretta Scott King to the gay rights movement" (Long, p. 10). Cothren also shared with him copies of some of Mrs. King's speeches on a range of issues surrounding gay rights, including violence against gays and lesbians, homophobia, and HIV/AIDS, without which it would have been more challenging to make the main arguments in Chapter 1of Long's *Martin Luther King Jr., Homosexuality and the Early Gay Movement.*

23. Jason Michael, "Lynn Cothren: In the Shadow of a Civil Rights Icon," April 5, 2013: https://pridesource.com/article/lynn-cothren-in-the-shadow-of-a-civil-rights-icon/ (Accessed August 30, 2022).

24. Ibid.

25. Cothren served as Chair of the Program Committee for the 40th anniversary March on Washington, August 23, 2003. He was also on the Board of Directors and past Chair of the Atlanta Pride Committee. He was a board member of the National Gay and Lesbian Task Force, Fund for Southern Communities, Atlanta Lambda Center, and Georgia Equality Project.

26. Quoted in Jason Michael, "Lynn Cothren: In the Shadow of a Civil Rights Icon": https://pridesource.com/article/lynn-cothren-in-the-shadow-of-a-civil-rights-icon/ (Accessed August 30, 2022).

27. See the website for Georgia's LGBT Story Project: https://www.touchingupourroots.org/

28. Michael Collopy, and Jason Gardner (Eds), *Architects of Peace: Visions of Hope in Words and Images* (Novato, CA: New World Library, 2000), p. 18. Also available online: Santa Clara University Markkula Center for Applied Ethics website: https://www.scu.edu/mcae/architects-of-peace/King/essay.html (Accessed August 30, 2022).

29. Coretta Scott King, Commencement Speech at Antioch College, Yellow Springs, Ohio, June 26,1982, LCP.

30. Ibid.

31. Coretta Scott King speech at Antioch College, June 26, 2004, LCP.

32. Ibid.

33. The Metropolitan Community Church and Foundation was in the forefront of advancing human rights for LGBT people of all races and supported poor and homeless people in San Francisco as well.

34. Paul Donsky, "College Beating Stirs Up Concerns: Morehouse Sophomore Charged in Bat Attack," the *Atlanta Constitution*, November 12, 2002. Text also available on HBCUsports.com: https://www.hbcusports.com/forums/threads/morehouse-sophomore-charged-in-bat-attack.13451/(Accessed August 30, 2022).

35. See, "Address by Coretta Scott King, Circles of Hope Dinner," November 22, 2002, LCP (Lynn Cothren Papers), Metropolitan Community Church and Foundation, Palace Hotel, San Francisco, California. For an exhaustive list of Mrs. King's gay rights speeches, see Long, Chapter 1, Footnotes, pp. 156-160. The remainder of the Mrs. King's speeches here are also from the LCP. Many are also available on YouTube.

36. Coretta Scott King Speech, Antioch College's 150th Anniversary, 2004, LCP.

37. Coretta Scott King Speech, Poor People's Campaign, Washington DC, 1968, LCP.
38. Coretta Scott King Speech, National Gay and Lesbian Task Force, Atlanta 2003, LCP.
39. Andrew Young, *An Easy Burden: The Civil Rights Movement and the Transformation of America* (New York: HarperCollins, 1996), p. 424.
40. Ibid. p. 428.
41. Alice Walker, "Coretta: Revisited," in In Search of Our Mothers' Gardens: Womanist Prose (New York: Harcourt Brace Jovanovich, 1983), p. 153
42. Ibid.
43. Ibid., p. 152.
44. Ibid.
45. Coretta Scott King Speech, "Family Planning—A Special and Urgent Concern by the Rev. Martin Luther King, Jr.," Planned Parenthood, May 5, 1966, https://plannedparenthood.org. Prior to reading Dr. King's speech, she spoke in support of Margaret Sanger and said, "Because of her dedication, her deep convictions, and for her suffering for what she believed in, I would like to say that I am proud to be a woman tonight." See Michele Goodwin's essay, "The Forgotten Reproductive Justice Legacy of Dr. Martin Luther King," Ms., January 18, 2021, in which she discusses the landmark speech on reproductive and civil rights that Dr. King would have delivered about the issue of unwanted pregnancies upon acceptance of Planned Parenthood's award for his support of family planning. Mrs. King accepted the award on his behalf and read his acceptance speech.
46. "A Black Feminist Statement," Combahee River Collective, reprinted in *Words of Fire: An Anthology Of African-American Feminist Thought* (New York: New Press, 1995), pp. 232-240.
47. Coretta Scott King speech, National Organization for Women (NOW), 1978. LCP.
48. Ibid.

Works Cited

"A Coretta Scott King Special." (Collected Speeches) *The Power of African American Women,* Disc 9. Pacifica Radio Archives. Available at http://www.archive.org/details/pra_powerofafricanamericanwomen_9(11 August 2011).

Carbado, Devon and Donald Weise, eds., T*ime on Two Crosses: The Collected Writings of Bayard Rustin,* Cleis Press, 2003

Lynn Cothren Personal Papers (LCP). Copies of Mrs. Coretta Scott King's speeches that were shared with me are available in his unpublished personal papers. See also Jason Michael, "Lynn Cothren: In the Shadow of a Civil Rights Icon," Between the Lines, May 13, 2004 (http://pridesource.com

Donsky, Paul, "College Beating Stirs Up Concerns: Morehouse Sophomore Charged in Bat Attack," *The Atlanta Constitution,* November 12, 2002.

Foreman, Matt. *Tucson Weekly Observer,* February 2006.

King, Coretta Scott, *My Life with Martin Luther King, Jr.* New York: Holt, 1969, and Coretta: My Life, My Love, My Legacy (with Reverend Dr. Barbara Reynolds) Henry Holt & Co, 2017.

King, Coretta Scott. Opening Plenary Remarks, 13th Annual Creating Change Conference, National Gay and Lesbian Task Force, Atlanta, Georgia, November 9, 2000.LCP

———, Speech at Reunion Weekend, Antioch College, *Dayton Daily News,* June 26, 2004. LCP

———, Speech at Antioch College, 1994, LCP

"Address by Coretta Scott King, Circles of Hope Dinner, LCP

"Remarks by Coretta Scott King, Human Rights Campaign Gala Dinner and Awards Ceremony, February 8, 1998, Los Angeles, CA, LCP

"Remarks by Coretta Scott King on Accepting the "Honoring Our Allies Award,'" National Gay and Lesbian Task Force Annual Awards Ceremony, September 15, 1997, Washington, DC, LCP

———,Commencement Speech at Antioch College, Yellow Springs, Ohio, June 26, 1982, LCP

King, Martin Luther, Jr. *Stride Towards Freedom: The Montgomery Story.* New York: Harper, 1958.

———. "A Christmas Sermon on Peace" (1967), Ebenezer Baptist Church, in his *The Trumpet of Conscience,* Beacon Press, 2011.

Long, Michael G., Martin Luther King Jr., *Homosexuality and the Early Gay Rights Movement: Keeping the Dream Straight?* (New York, NY: Palgrave, 2012).

Michael, Jason, "Lynn Cothren: In the shadow of a civil rights icon," p. 1, *Between the Lines,* May 13 2004, http://pridesource.com.

Walker, Alice, "Coretta: Revisited," in I*n Search of Our Mothers' Gardens: Womanist Prose* (New York: Harcourt Brace Jovanovich, 1983).

Young, Andrew, *An Easy Burden: The Civil Rights Movement and the Transformation of America.* Baylor University Press, 1996.

28. | Loving bell hooks (2022)

. . . dissidents are anchored to revolutionary possibilities that demand both intellectual discipline and irrepressible courage to speak the unspeakable, to stand alone if necessary, and to accept the material and emotional consequences of tramping over hegemony's "holy" ground.

Antonia Darder, 2011

Moving from silence into speech is for the oppressed, the colonized, the exploited. . . a gesture of defiance that heals, that makes new life and new growth possible. It is that act of speech, of "talking back," that is no mere gesture of empty words, that is the expression of our movement from object to subject—the liberated voice.

bell hooks, *Talking Back: Thinking Feminist, Thinking Black,* 1989

I am reminded while reading Antonia Darder's riveting anthology *A Dissident Voice: Essays in Culture, Pedagogy, and Power* of teachers, scholars, activists, feminists, colleagues, and dissidents who emerged from marginalized/racialized communities in the U.S. and impacted my intellectual life in significant ways—none more so than bell hooks, with whom I shared a forty-year friendship. It is important to embrace the dissident women among us so often maligned and misunderstood. For four decades, bell hooks's dissenting voice, in her writing and teaching, has been loud and unrelenting, beginning with the publication of her first book, *Ain't I a Woman: Black Women and Feminism,* followed by, to name a few: *Feminist Theory: From Margin to Center; The Will to Change: Men, Masculinity, and Love;* and *Teaching to Transgress: Education as the Practice of Freedom.* One of the most prolific and radical contemporary Black feminist scholars/critics, bell hooks's *Talking Back: Thinking Feminist, Thinking Black* provides a portrait of a dissident Black intellectual whose untimely death at 69 in December 2021 generated perhaps the most commentary that I recall ever having read when a Black woman writer departs. This is how she explains her choosing the name bell hooks and the legacy of her dissident great-grandmother:

> I was a young girl buying bubble gum at the corner store when I first really heard the full name bell hooks. I had just "talked back" to a grown person. Even now I can recall the surprised look, the mocking tones that informed me I must be kin to bell hooks—a sharp-tongued woman, a woman who spoke her mind, a woman who was not afraid to talk back. I claimed this legacy of defiance, of will, of courage, affirming my link to female ancestors who were bold and daring in their speech. . . . bell hooks as I discovered, claimed, and invented her was my ally, my support. (hooks 1989)

My friendship with Gloria Watkins (she was not yet the well-known bell hooks) began at the 1981 National Women's Studies Association (NWSA) conference in Storrs, Connecticut, during which Audre Lorde delivered a ground-breaking, hard-hitting keynote speech, "The Uses of Anger: Women Responding to Racism," in which she spoke about the racism of white women. It was the same year that the Women's Research and Resource Center at Spelman College was founded. At NWSA Gloria (bell hooks) was promoting her first book, *Ain't I a Woman* and introducing herself to this academic feminist gathering.. We shared a dormitory room, talked all night the first day we met—about the whiteness of the women's liberation movement in the U.S. and NWSA—and continued to talk until her untimely death. I did not realize then why we spent all night that first night talking in my dorm room and why we would continue talking for the next four decades. Later I came to realize it was our memories of dissident women in our families and our passionate connection to feminist politics.

The first feminist I ever knew was my mother. Though she would not have used this term, her words and deeds were undeniably feminist. I have no explanation for this since Ernestine Varnado Guy was born in Canton, Mississippi, in 1919, to a stay-at-home mom and a traditional Baptist minister. Frustrated as a math teacher in the Memphis public schools, she chose to work in the male-dominated field of accounting in the business office of a Black college where her brother-in-law, Dr. Levi Watkins, Sr., was President. Her love of mathematics and work choices occurred long before the contemporary women's liberation movement in the U.S. advocated for gender equity in the workplace or the need for girls to have greater access to STEM disciplines. When I was in the eighth grade, she left my father and moved with her three daughters around the corner to live with her parents. While she never fulfilled her professional goal of becoming a CPA—probably because of the demands of being a single mom—she always preached to her daughters the importance of pursuing one's dreams even if they remain elusive.

The most memorable example of my mom's loud resistance to race and gender scripts, probably like bell hooks's namesake, took place in 1958 when I was in the ninth grade and the Memphis public schools were controlled by white men. Bothered by conventional gender norms that positioned females as, first of all, homemakers, she petitioned school authorities to waive their home economics requirements for girls and demanded that I take typing, which was reserved for juniors and seniors who were presumably headed for clerical jobs. Males were required to take auto mechanics and shop. This act of defiance on my mother's part sent several clear messages to me: that learning to be a homemaker was not as important as preparing for a career; that the skills of a typist would be more useful to a college-bound student; and that Black women could resist white patriarchal authority, even in the Jim and Jane Crow South. Her petition was granted, so I may have been the first Memphis public school girl to escape obligatory homemaking classes. Following the example of my mother, I developed the habit of "talking back" which girls were discouraged from doing, as was the case with Gloria.

What I came to cherish about the embrace of a dissident, feminist identity I learned from reading and talking endlessly to Gloria/bell, which began that night at NWSA. Like another dissident scholar/activist Angela Davis and the architects of the Combahee River Collective statement, bell hooks emerges from a robust African American Left tradition which is anti-capitalist, anti-imperialist, and critical of patriarchy, wherever it rears its head. Near the beginning of *Talking Back*, bell acknowledges Davis's impact on her as a young, evolving dissident:

> ["When I was a young soldier for the revolution."] Angela Davis spoke these words. They moved me. I say them here and hope to say them in many places. This is how deeply they touched me—evoking memories of innocence, of initial passionate commitment to political struggle. (hooks 1989, 10)

bell hooks's transgressive writings would have a significant impact on my evolving scholarship. In her first monograph on Black women and feminism, she makes the surprising point that nineteenth-century white female reformers harbored more intense racist attitudes toward Black women than they did toward Black men, which is ironic in light of the "bonds of womanhood" thesis which many other white feminist historians advanced in their attempts to explain alliances between Black and white women in various reform movements. Hooks argues that it was fear of contamination and sexual competition that caused white women to resist cooperation with Black women, including in women's mobilizations during the so called "first wave" of the women's movement:

> . . . black men were more accepted in white reform circles than black women. Negative attitudes toward black women were the result of prevailing racist-sexist stereotypes that portrayed black women as morally impure. Many white women felt that their status as ladies would be undermined were they to associate with black women. No such moral stigma was attached to black men. Black male leaders like Frederick Douglass, James Forten. . .and others were occasionally welcome in white and social circles. . . . Given. . . the history of white male sexual lust for black females

> we cannot rule out the possibility that white women were reluctant to acknowledge black women socially for fear of sexual competition. . . . White women saw black women as a direct threat to their social standing—for how could they be idealized as virtuous, goddess-like creatures if they associated with black women who were seen by the white public as licentious and immoral? (hooks 1981, 130-131)

In her second book, *Feminist Theory: From Margin to Center* (1984), now widely used in Women's Studies classes, there is a hard-hitting analysis of the insensitivity of Women's Studies programs in the early years to race, class, and ethnicity, and a biting critique of racist writings by white feminists: "White women who dominate feminist discourse, who for the most part make and articulate feminist theory, have little or no understanding of white supremacy as a racial politic, of the psychological impact of class, of their political status within a racist, sexist, capitalist state" (4).

If I could speak to Gloria/bell one more time, I would tell her what it meant to share a long friendship with a "dissident." Observing her and reading her feminist books, as well as having the example of my mother and her great-grandmother, I found it easier to resist stifling gender norms in both my personal and professional lives as they related to appropriate behavior for "good," "lady-like" women. I journeyed to distant and unfamiliar places, wore the clothes I wanted to wear, wrote the books I wanted to write, studied the transgressive Black women I wanted to be like (Lorraine, Alice, Angela, Audre), took unpopular stances, refused to be quiet in public, risked being misunderstood, chose the friendships and partnerships I desired, advocated loudly for my passions. Fears I might have harbored about being too aggressive, the stereotypical "angry Black woman," or gender non-conforming had to be abandoned. I am fortunate to have lived the life I wanted to live. Like so many of us, I am grateful for her example.

References

hooks, bell. 1981. *Ain't I a Woman: Black Women and Feminism.* Boston: South End Press.

_____. 1984. *Feminist Theory: From Margin to Center.* Boston: South End Press.

_____. 1989. *Talking Back: Thinking Feminist, Thinking Black.* Boston: South End Press.

Part VI

Friendships

29. | Tribute to Rudolph P. Byrd (2011)

I am not exactly certain when I met Rudolph Byrd, but it was surely here at Emory University within the context of our similar work and commitments as professors and our desire to forge closer bonds between Emory and Spelman College. We somehow knew we were kindred spirits from the very beginning, but I'm not sure we understood why at first. Over the course of our more than twenty-year journey as colleagues, our lives intertwined in ways that I am just beginning to unravel. We co-founded the Alice Walker Literary Society because of our love and respect for one of the most compelling and important writer/activists of the 20th century. Some of our happiest times together were when we were with Alice; one of the most satisfying moments in his short life was when she decided to deposit her precious papers at Emory. I want to thank Provost Earl Lewis for his critical role in the acquisition. I can still recall our trip to Berkeley, California, with Randall Burkett, during which Rudolph whispered to me over and over how ecstatic he was, and how we gave ourselves permission over drinks when we returned home to recall every moment of this three-year saga. When we left the restaurant that night, I got one of the best hugs of my life!! And then there were our long years of work co-editing *Traps: African American Men on Gender and Sexuality* and, with Johnnetta Cole (who couldn't join us today), co-editing *I Am Your Sister: Collected and Unpublished Writings of Audre Lorde.* Johnnetta wanted me to share what we wrote in the dedication: "We dedicate this book to the friendship the three of us enjoy. It is a friendship that keeps us on each other's minds and in each other's hearts, gives us permission to critique each other's work, and is strengthened by the belief we share with Audre Lorde that " 'it is not difference that immobilizes us but silence.' "

My second most prominent set of memories is our frequent late-night conversations about his vision for the James Weldon Johnson Institute. There was a sense of urgency, I believe, because Rudolph knew that he didn't have all the time in the world. He spoke candidly about every aspect of his illness, up until the very end of his eleven-year battle with cancer. During our last ride together, we left the Emory clinic (after he'd finally been prohibited from driving) with his sister Meardis, who had been instructed, in very precise language, to make a pickup from one of his favorite restaurants. He grew impatient while we sat in the car and instructed me to call her cell phone to see what was taking so long. To get his mind off the ticking clock, I mentioned an upcoming Anita Hill event, and he said calmly but skeptically, "I hope I'll still be around then." And to ease my own pain, I said, "Of course, Rudolph, we'll go together."

In my acknowledgments at the beginning of *Traps,* I ended by saying, "If I had a son, I would wish that he were like Rudolph. From him I have learned how precious is a male friend." For his disloyalty to patriarchy, his deep connections to women, his self-identification as a male feminist, his love of African American literature and art, his capacity for friendship across all kinds of difference, his tenacity and humor and grace in the face of unrelenting suffering, his passion for justice, his discipline and ability to get things done, and his appreciation of a perfect martini and a beautiful garden, I am forever grateful.

A final quick whisper to Rudolph: you would be very pleased with the exquisite work, since your departure, of your sister/friends Cecelia and Ingrid, the Cathedral of Christ the King memorial mass, the perfect (as you would have demanded) Tuesday night Johnson Medal Awards ceremony, and this Emory gathering of your family, friends, colleagues, and students who love and miss you deeply. Henry is in good hands with all of us. May you rest in peace.

30. | Love Note to Toni (2014)

Dear Toni:

Over the past fourteen years, we have gathered in March (Women's History Month) at the Women's Center's annual Toni Cade Bambara Scholar-Activism Conference to remember and celebrate your extraordinary life and legacy as a radical Black feminist writer/filmmaker/activist/visionary. So every year, beginning in 2001, I have penned a brief love note—a praisesong—as I reflected on our friendship and your profound impact on my intellectual/political development. It all began in 1974, four years after you published *The Black Woman*, which is now a Black feminist canonical text that is still read, revered, and kept in print!!! Your preface to the anthology and your essay "On the Issue of Roles" are as timely, as urgent, as brilliant, as provocative as they were in 1970, and I include them in my Feminist Theory class every spring. Your twelve-point "blueprint" for liberation and description of the work we must do as "revolutionary" Black women is unparalleled. I just pulled my tattered copy off my bookshelf and reread out loud my favorite lines from "Roles," which are: *Revolution begins with the self, in the self; We'd better take the time to fashion revolutionary selves, revolutionary lives, revolutionary relationships;* and *Not all speed is movement!!!* As a teacher, I also like, *Mapping out a building takeover when your term paper is overdue and your scholarship is under review is not revolutionary.* And I still laugh about, *Ain't no such animal as an instant guerrilla.*

I still remember, as if it were yesterday, coming to your home in 1974 in Atlanta—very nervous, very inexperienced, very intimidated—for my interview with you, which was published in my first book (with Roseann P. Bell) as "Commitment: Toni Cade Bambara Speaks." You will be happy to know that your dear friends Linda Janet Holmes and Cheryl A. Wall reprinted the interview as "Toni Cade Bambara: Black Feminist Foremother" in their extraordinary book *Savoring the Salt: The Legacy of Toni Cade Bambara,* and I wrote a new introduction for it. In that introduction, I wanted to capture the profound impact you had on young Black women like myself (and bell hooks), who were perceived to be race traitors because of our embrace of feminism at a time when the "F" word was being demonized. You may remember that when I asked you—rather naively—whether it was a dilemma for you to be both a feminist and a warrior in the race struggle, you responded, with such ease: *I don't find any basic contradiction or any tension between being a feminist, being a pan-Africanist, being a black nationalist, being an internationalist, being a socialist, and being a woman in North America.* When you shared with me your involvement in what we would now call a global women's movement, I was stunned, especially when I learned that a year later you would travel to North Vietnam, having been invited by their Women's Union, with a delegation called the North American Academic Marxist-Leninist Anti-Imperialist Feminist Women!!!

When I left your home at age 28, where I met your young daughter Karma Bene for the first time, I desperately wanted to be like you—bold, self-assured, down-to-earth, funny, brilliant, sophisticated, a world traveler, comfortable in my own skin, connected to Black communities, unapologetically feminist. Forty years later, I can't imagine who I would have become, Toni, were you not in my life, even after you left us.

Five years after you joined the ancestors, the Women's Center called your name and honored your work. We celebrated with your friends, comrades, students, community organizers, professors, filmmakers, writers, agitators, and your daughter, Karma Bene Bambara Smith, and her growing family. We are deeply indebted to Karma for the precious gift of your personal papers, which she donated in 2004 to the Spelman College Archives, and the Women's Center manages them. Linda Janet Holmes helped persuade her that Spelman would be a good home, and you will be pleased to know that your papers are in good company, since we also have the papers of sister-warriors Audre Lorde and Johnnetta Cole. You will also be pleased with *A Joyous Revolt,* Linda's newly released biography of you, which is a love offering to the world!!

Finally, you remain with us in very profound ways, and I see you every time I enter the space!!! Susan J. Ross's individual photograph of you hangs in the Center, as well as the group photo of Black women writers who gathered for Johnnetta Cole's inauguration as the first Black woman president of Spelman in 1987. The Toni Cade Bambara Collective students meet almost every Friday; scholars come from all over the place to visit your papers; a documentary by your brother/friend Louis Massiah is in the works; I smiled visiting with him and Karma a few weeks ago in the Archives, as we viewed some of your amazing tapes, and I was able to see you and hear your voice again; a book signing of the Holmes biography will take place on Friday in the Women's Center Meeting Room.

I would never have been able to imagine on that beautiful spring day in Atlanta when you greeted me at your back door that you would stay with me forever. The Center loves you deeply.

In gratitude and friendship,
Beverly

31. | Letter to Dr. Levi Watkins, Jr. (2020)

April 11, 2020

Dear Cousin Levi,

On the fifth anniversary of your death, which occurred April 11, 2015, I decided to write an Open Letter to you so that I could capture in writing what I have been thinking about since your abrupt death on the operating table as your Johns Hopkins Hospital heart surgeon colleagues attempted to revive you from a stroke you suffered a few hours earlier at dinner after speaking to medical students. While I have been pondering, remembering, and learning more about your accomplishments as a heart surgeon and activist at Hopkins and elsewhere, this is a personal note rather than a reflection on your extraordinary professional life which I witnessed up close. When cousin Annie Marie called me at 3 am that morning after the failed surgery to let me know you didn't make it, I knew I would pen a note to you, even if only I would ever read it. Unfortunately, I have also written about friends I lost since your death, but this was the most heart-wrenching.

Our mothers, Ernestine Varnado Guy and Lillian Varnado Watkins, were sisters and best friends, and before your family moved back to Montgomery when we were in the eighth grade, we spent lots of time on the S. A. Owen Junior College (now LeMoyne-Owen College) campus in Memphis where my mom worked in the business office and your dad, Dr. Levi Watkins, Sr., was Founding President (1952-1959). Mom had left her frustrating public school math teaching job for a different career as an accountant. During summers, from Monday through Friday, she would drop me and sisters, Carmella and Francine, at your home with your mom, whom we called Aunt Wynn, and her six children, and pick us up after work, a job she thoroughly enjoyed, working, as she did, for her brother-in-law, Uncle Levi. Those summers were some of the best years of my pre-college days. One of my fondest memories is of all of us swimming in the Owen College pool and eating hot dogs and baked beans for lunch at your home. I also remember cousins Marie and Pearl's exceptional piano playing in the living room, Teannie (Doristine) and I talking incessantly, and you, Donald, and James trekking across campus to empty the garbage while us girls were assigned dishwashing duties. I also recall our obligatory Sundays at Metropolitan Baptist Church (Owen College was named after our pastor) and my request to exchange places with Teannie for the rest of the day so I could spend more time at your home. My fondness for the Watkins home and Teannie's fondness for mine was captured when on Sundays after church we would beg our moms to "exchange places." I would go home with Aunt Wynn and Teannie would go home with Aunt Stine. While I found Uncle Levi to be very serious and stern, I also wondered quietly what compelled him to his presidential office seven days a week, including holidays, and why he was so committed to his job at this new, small Black college. I also remember how my mom loved going to work in the business office, especially with her boss, Mr. Peterman, and figuring out how to manage their tight budget. Like your dad, I saw a similar passion with her work at Black colleges, which I found compelling though mysterious at the time. I think my later commitment to Black colleges might have been influenced by my observing Uncle Levi and my mom. I was sad when your family moved back to Montgomery which ended our daily summer visits at the Watkins home. When Uncle Levi decided to return to Alabama State University in 1959 (he would become President in 1962), I remember that last night in Memphis at our grandparents' home. Upstairs, with only a few hours left, you and I said good-bye and shed tears—away from the rest of our kinfolks. That night was the saddest I can recall of those seven years of the family's time together in Memphis because I realized that life as I had experienced it was over—eating Sunday dinner at the Watkins home because I had "exchanged places" with Teannie; listening to Uncle Levi describe the challenges facing private, resource-poor Black colleges; watching and experiencing Aunt Wynn's mothering and disciplining of the nine of us, especially you, Donald, and James; hanging out with Pearl and sharing secrets; watching Marie's studying and seriousness as a high school student and wondering if I could follow suit!!

Growing up in the Jim and Jane Crow South with educated family members, including teachers, we knew we would go to college, but we didn't know that higher education would consume our professional lives, our passions, and our evolving connection with each other as adults. Our maternal grandfather, Rev. Willie Louis Varnado, went to Alcorn College (Lorman, Mississippi) and sent his five children (including both our moms) to Lane College. Your father graduated from Tennessee State University in 1933 and my father from LeMoyne College; both were born in 1911, in Montgomery, Kentucky, and Memphis, Tennessee, respectively. What we didn't know growing up, which was the case with much of our extended family history, was that granddaddy had been pastor (1919-1924) of Mount Helm Baptist Church (later Farish Street Baptist Church) in downtown Jackson, Mississippi, the oldest Black church in the city, which was founded in 1835 when a few enslaved Blacks began worshipping in the basement of white First Baptist Church. We didn't know that Jackson State University (formerly Jackson College) had been housed briefly at Mt. Helm. I learned about the church's amazing interracial history while writing this letter. I am also recalling that granddaddy was at Mason Temple in Memphis on April 3 (the night before King's death), when King delivered his "I've Been to the Mountaintop" speech. When I came home from Spelman in May, granddaddy described in detail that night and stressed that King knew his days were numbered, so to speak. Now I am thinking about your long relationship with both Martin and Coretta King, which began in Montgomery when your family were members of Dexter Avenue Baptist Church. I remember attending with your family during my visits from Memphis.

You and I graduated from high school in 1962; you headed to Tennessee State University, your father's alma mater, and I headed to Spelman, which my mom had chosen, though my first preference was Howard University. Because I had graduated from high school at 16, she preferred the sheltered environment of Spelman for her shy, underage daughter. Four years later, in 1966, we both graduated with honors. You headed to Vanderbilt Medical School, its first Black medical school student, and I headed to Wellesley College for a fifth year of study. My mom thought it was time for me to leave the South and experience a multiracial environment for the first time, since I had spent my entire life in the South. Over the course of your medical school years and training at Johns Hopkins, our friendship deepened, especially with my frequent visits to Baltimore. I recall your sharing with me the racial indignities you experienced at both Vanderbilt and Hopkins, which both angered and saddened me. A memory you shared that I will never forget was what happened while you were a medical student at Vanderbilt on the night of Martin Luther King's assassination. Shockingly, some Vanderbilt medical students (presumably) attached to your dorm door a nasty note expressing their joy at his death and, more amazingly, smeared feces on your door! Much later, when Vanderbilt invited you to join their Board of Trustees at the medical school, you shared with them that horrific experience and remarked about the irony of your journey from medical student to Board member.

Our family ties were critical to our evolving friendship, but they are not the whole story. While we were first cousins who grew up together in a closely bonded family, there were other explanations for our deep connection. We were also both academics, came of age during the civil rights movement, were committed to eradicating racism, and talked politics endlessly on the phone since I was in Atlanta and you in Baltimore. We met and got to know each other's friends and partners. Because you were non-judgmental and open, I could share whatever I pleased about my personal life. We talked about our decision not to marry (in your case) and not to remarry (in my case) or why we chose not to have children. I cherished our straight talk because you were my closest male friend; Rudolph was my second closest. Not sure I ever told you how much I appreciated your coming to spend a day with me in Atlanta following the brutal attack of a former boyfriend. We didn't talk much that day. I picked you up from the airport; we spent the day on Blvd. Granada, the scene of some of the worst days of my life. I shared only a little with you because I could see how sad you were. I also knew that you were unable to understand on any level why this had happened to me. Now I could explain!! After taking you back to the airport, I returned home and remembered all the ways in which you had been PRESENT for me. I deeply appreciated having you in my life and I hope you knew that.

Over the last few months of your life, you tried to prepare me for what you must have known—that we would not grow older together. You were 69 and I was 67. This saddened me, though you assured me that you were not afraid to die and that you had lived a good life and had accomplished all you wanted. This made me happy, and I hoped when the time came for me that I would find the peace that you had. You predicted that you would die before me, though I argued with you about your timeline!! You told me, emphatically, that you would die of heart disease and that you wanted to be cremated and have your ashes scattered in the water behind your condo. Now I realize that you had done your own diagnosis. I did remember during those difficult conversations that during Rudolph's last year battling cancer you advised me to spend as much time with him as possible, which I tried to do. I also remember your sharing with me in 1978 that mom would not survive her breast cancer and you were right; she died two years after the diagnosis. You also advised me to prepare a will and shared with me the details of yours. I followed your advice, reluctantly.

Finally, I want to tell you that I have missed you every day over the past five years. I have longed for our almost daily long-distance telephone calls. I have missed our conversations about medical matters, including those of my friends and our family. I have missed our relationship talk and your advice!! I have missed our political talk about racism and the state of the country. I have missed our laughter and your funny stories about everything!!! I am happy NOW that you didn't experience a debilitating illness which I have witnessed up close, painfully, with several friends. I cherish even more the family time we were able to spend together and know how fortunate we were to have been raised by Ernestine and Aunt Wynn, in particular, and also our fathers and grandparents.

I am finally at peace with your absence. I understand the decisions you made about your health challenges. I hope you are pleased with the decisions I made about the financial resources you made available to me, especially at Spelman College. You will be pleased to hear that I have reconnected with an old friend of ours and that your friend George has written your powerful life story.

Love you,
Beverly

32. Remembering Professor Peter Agbor-Tabi (2021)

In 1983, Dr. Peter Agbor-Tabi became the first recipient of the prestigious Fulbright scholar-in-residence in International Economics at Spelman College, the oldest historically Black college for women, founded in Atlanta, Georgia, in 1881. When he arrived on campus in September, I had left the English Department where I had been teaching since 1971 and had become Founding Director of the Women's Research & Resource Center (1981). What I remember upon meeting him for the first time on campus, by accident, was his quiet, reserved, dignified demeanor, the perpetual smile, and the seriousness with which he was pursuing his academic career. I also recall vividly our long conversations during the year he spent at Spelman about the academic life he imagined for himself when he returned home. As we were heading to the airport in Atlanta for his trip home after a year-long stay at Spelman, I imagined I would not see Peter again but that he would have a brilliant, distinguished career as an educator/college professor and perhaps university president. However, during the subsequent thirty-two years, we managed to stay in contact over the telephone and, on a few occasions during his visits to the U.S. to see family, meet in person. I followed his exceptional career mostly from a distance and was not surprised at the high-level university and political appointments he garnered over time. During our occasional telephone calls, he would speak modestly about his professional accomplishments. As a result, I resorted to reading about his new and more challenging appointments over the years and wondered how he was navigating the complexities of his increasingly more visible political career. Not surprisingly, he rarely spoke about the ups and downs of his public life, and it was only after his death that I came to realize what some of his accomplishments and controversies had been as Chancellor and Cabinet member.

What we didn't know about when Peter became a resident faculty member at Spelman in September of 1983 was he was only 33 years of age in his already distinguished academic career. In 1972 he obtained the Certificat d'Etude Francaise from the University of Dijon, France, and in 1975 graduated from the Department of Bilingual Letters and Linguistics at the University of Yaoundé. Determined to continue his academic pursuits, he traveled to the U.S. and obtained a master's degree (1978) and the PhD in Political Science and

International Relations (1982) from the University of South Carolina, where he met his wife Deborah, also of South Carolina, with whom I have maintained a connection since she returned home to the U.S. An unusual feat was his having completed both the master's and doctoral degrees in the demanding discipline of political science in a very short amount of time, which was a testament to his discipline, determination, and brilliance. His master's thesis was entitled "NGOs, a Threat to IGOs: LONRHO and the OAC;" and the title of his dissertation was "The Delivery of Foreign Aid: A Study of United States Bilateral Aid in Cameroon." Not surprisingly, upon his return home after leaving Spelman, he became lecturer at IRIC (International Relations Institute of Cameroon). Within a short time, he became Deputy Director and in 1988 was promoted to Director of IRIC. Three years later, in 1991, he was made Chancellor of the University of Yaoundé, having garnered the attention of President Biya. Always the scholar, he continued to publish, including an article "Cameroon and the UDEAC," published in *Internationales Afrikaforum*, vol. 22, number 3, 1986, and "International Law and Functional Integration: The East African Community Revisited," which appeared in *The African Review*, vol. 26, no. 21/2, 1989.

When I learned of Peter's death in April 2016, I was sad and surprised, not realizing he had been ill, but also at peace as I reflected upon several decades of a close collegial friendship. I thought about the heart attack he suffered during the second semester of his Spelman visit from which had he thankfully totally recovered. I remember calling my heart surgeon cousin, Dr. Levi Watkins Jr., and asking him to speak with Peter about what he could expect in the aftermath of that health challenge at such a young age. I am assuming that over the years Peter took good care of himself. I remember our last telephone conversation during which he spoke about how exhausted he was, which I now realize in retrospect was probably the result of leukemia. Knowing what a workaholic he was, I simply encouraged him to get more rest and take a much-needed vacation. In his usual manner, he laughed quietly, probably with that broad smile, without responding. I also marveled at his extraordinary academic and political career. I knew Peter as an intellectual, not a politician, though I was aware of his political ambitions. I read his excellent dissertation-inspired book that was published in 1984 by University Press of America, *Bilateral Assistance in Africa: The Case of Cameroon*. His academic interests included international assistance, international transfer of technology, employment, migration, ethnic party politics, women in development and in higher education (a serious interest of mine as well), student unrest in higher education, and colonization. I recall him asking me, during one of our telephone conversations, to send him articles on how universities handled student unrest in the U.S. around a variety of issues, though I didn't realize at the time that this had been a personal issue for him at the university.

I am pleased for this opportunity to reflect upon my friendship with Peter and the professor/politician I came to admire and respect, though mostly from a distance, over many years. I wish I had been able to have one more conversation with him, including about the political landscape in Cameroon, so that I could have shared with him how much our friendship had meant to me, and how much I had learned from him about post-colonial West Africa in general from the lens of a political scientist. I would have told him that I had no idea about the stresses he had endured in his university and political life. I would have also told him how surprised I was that he had kept his promise to me that day in Atlanta as we headed to the airport, which was simply that he would stay in touch. Finally, I would say that I intended to stay connected to Deborah, who had visited at my home in Atlanta once, and maybe even get to know his children.

Rest in peace, Peter.

33.| Letter to Alice Walker **(2021)**

Dear Alice:

When Professor Tillet (Salamisha) asked me to write the afterword to her book, I decided to respond with an open letter to you rather than the conventional expository text. I wanted to celebrate the epistolary genre which you so brilliantly mastered in *The Color Purple.*

Alice...wise, free, gentle, fierce, passionate, courageous...I am grateful for the gift of your friendship, your persistent resistance to injustice, and the stunning artistry of your life and writings.

1961: Atlanta, Georgia, your first year at Spelman College. I would join you a year later. You were inspired by both Martin Luther King Jr. and Coretta Scott King. You met her during your first year at Spelman prior to your attending the World Youth Peace Festival in Helsinki. Not many of us were aware of Coretta's long history as a peace activist, which began when she was a student at Antioch College. I am happy you included your essay "Coretta King: Revisited" in your collection of essays *In Search of Our Mothers' Gardens: Womanist Prose* as well as your praisesong, "Choice: A Tribute to Dr. Martin Luther King, Jr.," in which you recall having seen him on television in 1960 when Hamilton Holmes and Charlayne Hunter were the first African Americans to desegregate the University of Georgia. A frequent visitor to Dexter Avenue Baptist Church in Montgomery, Alabama, when I visited my mother's sister and her family, I remember his Sunday sermons. On reading your words, I wondered in what ways he had impacted me: "At the moment I first saw him, he was being handcuffed and shoved into a police truck. . . . He displayed no fear, but seemed calm and serene, unaware of his own extraordinary courage. His whole body, like his conscience, was at peace. At the moment I saw his resistance I knew I would never be able to live in this country without resisting everything that sought to disinherit me and I would never be forced away from the land of my birth without a fight."

You were taught by Professor Howard Zinn, who, upon his dismissal from the College in 1963, quoted from your student essay in his open letter to the Spelman Board of Trustees, faculty, students, alumni, and President Manley. Anticipating your own legacy as a writer, this was your concluding paragraph in your essay "On Djilas and Kolakowski": "Every country should have a Kolakowski, someone who questions the unanswerable, but who nevertheless prods the people into thinking before they act. 'Will it be possible to formulate a general principle of regulating the mutual relationship between our knowledge of historical necessities and our moral convictions? Between the world of being and the world of values?' These are the questions which were voiced by Polish skepticism after the Stalinist era. Do not they apply to all countries and all societies for all time?"

The last sentence of Zinn's open letter leaves its readers with one of the most precious memories of a teacher: "A student who thinks and writes like this deserves nothing but the best."

It is likely that Zinn and your Spelman "sisters," including me, were unaware of your history growing up in Eatonton, Georgia, and having not experienced "the best." In "Lest We Forget: An Open Letter to My Sisters Who Are Brave," which you circulated March 21, 2008, to several of us (45 years after Zinn's open letter) in the midst of the Obama/Clinton race for the Democratic nomination, you described the dehumanizing world of Jim and Jane Crow that was also familiar to me even though I was born in 1946 in urban, Memphis, Tennessee:

> When I was born in 1944 my parents lived on a middle Georgia plantation that was owned by a white distant relative, Miss* May Montgomery. (She explains later that "during my childhood it was necessary to address all white girls as "Miss" when they reached the age of twelve.) She would never admit to this relationship, of course, except to mock it. . . .My parents and older siblings did everything imaginable for Miss May. They planted and raised her cotton and corn, fed and killed and processed her cattle and hogs, painted her house, patched her roof, ran her dairy, and, among countless other duties and responsibilities, my father was her chauffeur, taking her anywhere she wanted to go at any hour of the day or night. She lived in a large white house with green shutters and a green, luxuriant lawn: not quite as large as Tara of *Gone with the Wind* fame, but in the same style. We lived in a shack without electricity or running water, under a rusty tin roof that let in wind and rain. Miss May went to school as a girl. The school my parents and their neighbors built for us was burned to the ground by local racists who wanted to keep ignorant their competitors in tenant farming. . . .When I look back, this is part of what I see. I see the school bus carrying white children, boys and girls, right past me, and my brothers, as we trudge on foot five miles to school. Later, I see my parents struggling to build a school out of discarded army barracks while white students, girls and boys, enjoy a building made of brick. We had no books; we inherited the cast-off books that "Jane" and "Dick" had previously used in the all-white school that we were not, as black children, permitted to enter.

When you reflected upon the historic election that would result in the first Black president, you shared what you wanted for the country and what I also wanted, and remembered your influential teacher:

> I want a grown-up attitude toward Cuba, a country and a people I love; I want an end to the embargo that has harmed my friends and their children, children, who, when I visit Cuba, trustingly turn their faces up for me to kiss. I agree with a teacher of mine, Howard Zinn, that war is as objectionable as cannibalism and slavery; it is beyond obsolete as a means of improving life. I want an end to the on-going war immediately and I want the soldiers to be encouraged to destroy their weapons and to drive themselves out of Iraq. I want the Israeli government to be made accountable for its behavior towards the Palestinians, and I want the people of the United States to cease acting like they don't understand what is going on. All colonization, all occupation, all repression basically looks the same, whoever is doing it.

Three years later (June 2011), when I joined a women of color delegation to occupied Palestine, I thought about your bravery (in words and deeds) and remember sharing my experiences with you at your home in Philo, California. I still remember your attentive smile as I described one of the most transformative weeks of my adult life. I felt that the sisterly bond between us for nearly 50 years had been strengthened and that we would remember that afternoon on your couch at Temple Jook for a very long time. I also remember us on that same couch watching joyously and sadly (with Rebecca) on your laptop Tracy Heather Strain's Lorraine Hansberry documentary *Sighted Eyes/Feeling Heart* before it was released a few months later on PBS in January 2018.

1970: I haven't seen you since you left Spelman at the end of your sophomore year for Sarah Lawrence College in 1967. I am teaching English at Alabama State University, a year before I return to Spelman's English department in 1971. During that momentous year, I read your first novel, *The Third Life of Grange Copeland*, and Toni Morrison's *The Bluest Eye* (the first two novels by Black women writers that I began teaching at Spelman) as well as Toni Cade Bambara's *The Black Woman.* I didn't know it at the time but while you were teaching a course on Black Women Writers at UMass Boston in 1972, I was preparing to teach a mini course on Black Women Writers in our Department of English. Years later, 1980, Barbara Smith, co-editor of *But Some of Us Were Brave*, shared with me your syllabus when I visited her at Simmons College to talk about my ideas for establishing a Women's Center at Spelman. I and my department colleague Roseann P. Bell were determined, after reading yours and Morrison's work, to make visible the critically important but largely invisible Black women's literary tradition that began in the mid-19th century. The result was *Sturdy Black Bridges: Visions of Black Women in Literature*, the first anthology of Black women's writing, which was published by Doubleday in 1979. When the first draft of *Bridges* was completed in 1976, you had over the previous decade published two volumes of poetry, a collection of short stories, and two novels. Because of your extraordinary impact on African American letters and young Black women, we approached Mary Helen Washington, a pioneering critic, who submitted the insightful and loving "An Essay on Alice Walker." In her opening sentences of a lengthy essay, she captured your genius: ". . .it is clear that the special identifying mark of her writing is her concern for the lives of black women. . .her main preoccupation has been the souls of black women." And then she shares your own words, spoken during an interview with John O'Brien in 1973, which attest to your ongoing commitment to "exploring the oppressions, the insanities, the loyalties, and the triumphs of black women." When I reread Mary Helen's pioneering Black feminist essay, I thought of Celie, your protagonist in *The Color Purple* (not yet born), who embodies your faith in Black women's capacity for healing and transformation: "she sees the experiences of black women as a series of movements from women totally victimized by society and by the men in their lives to the growing developing women whose consciousness allows them to have control over their lives."

I read from cover to cover of the first issue of *Ms.* magazine and became a lifetime subscriber. Perhaps the most impactful piece on me and countless other Black women was your now canonical essay, "In Search of Our Mothers' Gardens: The Creativity of Black Women in the South," which appeared in the May 1974 issue. I read "In Search of Zora Neale Hurston" in the 1975 issue and your second novel *Meridian* a year later. When you were on the 1982 cover of *Ms.* magazine (the fiction issue), I was determined to read *The Color Purple.* I saw the controversial Spielberg-directed movie in 1985, attended the mesmerizing world premiere of the musical adaptation at the Alliance Theater with you and friends in 2004 and a year later on Broadway.

Throughout our celebrations of your remarkable literary achievements, it was impossible to imagine the venom that would be unleashed surrounding the publication and film release of *The Color Purple.* I read with deep sadness the scathing reviews by Black men and women—critics and laypeople alike. Over coffee, at conferences, in living rooms, and classrooms, I also was buoyed by conversations among Black women who spoke about the truths you had dared to make visible. When I pondered which writing of yours I wanted to include in *Words of Fire: An Anthology of African-American Feminist Thought* (1995), I recalled your counter discourse on "womanism," which had provided alternative terminology for Black feminists during a time when many women of color were raising angry voices about their marginalization or erasure within mainstream white feminist discourse. But I settled finally on "In the Closet of the Soul," the final essay in my anthology (in the section on "Discourses of Resistance"), which you included in your collection *Living by the Word* in 1988. It provided a passionate counterargument to those angry voices within the Black community in particular who had raged against *Purple* because of its so-called negative treatment of Black men, its incest theme, and embrace of lesbian love. The essay was originally a letter you wrote in 1986 in response to a question about your reaction to criticisms of the character Mister, whom you tell us you deeply love, certainly not for his brutality and oppression of women but because "he went deeply enough into himself to find the courage to change. To grow." In this regard you remind us, which I think we may have forgotten, that not only are we descendants of slaves but also descendants of slave OWNERS!! I wanted you to have the last word in *Words of Fire* because you capture, eloquently and succinctly and unapologetically, why we have committed to feminist/womanist liberation, in words and deeds, without fail, since the early 1800s: "It has been black men (as well as black women and Native Americans) who have provided in this culture the most inspiring directions for everyone's freedom. As a daughter of these men I did not hear a double standard when they urged each person to struggle to be free even if they intended to impart one. When Malcolm said, Freedom, by any means necessary, I thought I knew what he meant. When Martin said, Agitate nonviolently against unjust oppression, I assumed he also meant in the home, if that's where the oppression was. When Frederick Douglass talked about not expecting crops without first plowing up the ground, I felt he'd noticed the weeds in most of our backyards. It is nearly CRUSHING to realize there was an assumption on ANYONE's part that black women would not fight injustice except when the foe was white."

In your postscript, you expose the despicable attacks of the organization, Blacks Against Black Exploitation of Blacks in the Media, even during the filming, and remind us that it is women loving women in *Purple* that also accounts for the Black community's trashing of your work.

Here we are...58 years since I met you... with our memories, our stories, our hopes. With thirty+ books and a Pulitzer Prize, you are beloved here and around the globe for your writing, your activism, your unrelenting commitment to justice, and for always being yourself. You are a gift, Alice, to the universe because of your wisdom, truth-telling, generosity, reverence for the earth and all its inhabitants, and your deep knowing about what we need to do to keep ourselves and our communities healthy and whole. Even in the midst of toxic realities (war, poverty, racism, genocide, violence against women, cruelty to children and animals), you have never lost faith in the idea that "anything we love can be saved." On our campuses, we teach your poetry and novels and essays, craft Alice Walker seminars, call your name, share with students your journeys to Brooklyn, Boonville, Rwanda, the Congo, Gaza, and home to Eatonton, Georgia.

Salamisha Tillet's *In Search of the Color Purple* is a gift to the universe that painstakingly, meticulously, and lovingly describes all there is to know about the evolution of the novel, its characters, and its adaptation for film and the stage. It is a personal testimony to its healing properties and how it saved and helped to shape Salamisha's journey to wholeness. It beckons your critics to revisit their own rage and the sadness it generated. I hope Black women's suffering is made more legible in the retelling of the story of your "masterpiece." What I know for sure is our evolving bonds... with Gloria, Valerie, Ti, Salamisha, Scheherazade, Mickalene, and Raquel...were sparked by you!! We love Celie and Shug and Sophia and Nettie and, of course, *The Color Purple.*

In struggle and joy,
Beverly

Part VII

Interviews

34. Whither Black Women's Studies? Interview with Evelynn M. Hammonds (1997)

EH: I want to start with a set of questions about women's studies programs. Among the goals that informed the founding of women's studies programs was the integration of women into the existing curriculum. Whether that meant changing the disciplines, rethinking theoretical and analytic approaches, or adding new knowledge about women to ongoing research and teaching projects, the point was to have women included in every branch of knowledge. Has that been accomplished at historically black colleges? Are they operating on a different timeline at these institutions? Are there specific and different issues that women's studies has to address on these campuses versus predominantly white ones? How would you characterize the mission of women's studies at a black women's college? What are the barriers you've encountered in establishing your program? What are your successes?

BG-S: The first thing that I would say is that Spelman has been unique in the commitment that it's made to the establishment of the Women's Studies Program. It is still the case that we are the only historically black college with an undergraduate women's studies program. Atlanta University has a doctorate in African women's studies, but since its merger with Clark College it has kept the doctoral program without an undergraduate option. There are some historically black colleges with a smattering of women's studies courses here and there, but I don't think that there are any that have either a women's studies minor or major, which we at Spelman just passed in the fall of last year. It is still the case that women's studies with respect to coherent programs are just not cropping up at historically black colleges, despite thirty years of agitation on the part of women's studies folk, and I think that there are several reasons for that. One, there is a paucity of interdisciplinary programs in general in these colleges, even, for example, with respect to African American studies. And there is still the assumption that women's studies is not critical to the education of students at historically black colleges. It is also the case that there just hasn't been a critical mass of faculty willing to struggle over a number of years to get a program going without adequate resources. Overall, these efforts are really struggling. The advantages that we have had at Spelman are first, administrative support, and second, external funding.

EH: Do you think that there has been an integration of knowledge about women into the traditional disciplines at historically black colleges?

BG-S: Not to any substantial extent. I'm making this assertion on the basis of my knowledge about curricula from examining catalogs but also from anecdotal reports from faculty at historically black colleges. I have a number of contacts, including the people I met recently when I cotaught a comparative women's studies seminar at NYU with Professor Chandra Mohanty (of Hamilton College). Many faculty from historically black colleges were in that seminar and most of them acknowledged the absence of women's studies either as separate courses or in terms of mainstreamed courses. There are some pockets at particular places. For example, at Howard University in the history department you certainly have a women's studies presence and maybe to some extent in English, but I would say that probably it is still the case in 1997 that women's studies has not been mainstreamed into traditional disciplines in any significant way.

EH: How would you characterize the mission of women's studies at a black women's college?

BG-S: At a black women's college as opposed to a historically black college in general?

EH: Well, both.

BG-S: I believe that any undergraduate college in 1997, including historically black colleges, ought to have reflected in their curriculum important new scholarship on women that's been emerging in the last thirty years, particularly as it relates to women of African descent, women of color, and women in the diaspora (the Americas, the Caribbean, and Europe). This should be done at the most fundamental level in order to have students understand the entire range of human experience. I would also add that this is critical, perhaps even more critical at historically black colleges because there's been such a preoccupation with race and not sufficient attention paid to gender. The addition of women's studies in these colleges would be correcting an imbalance in the way that we transform curricula with respect to race at majority institutions. Dealing with race and gender issues at historically black colleges is extremely important.

EH: Can you say something about the specific barriers that you encountered at Spelman in establishing the program and also from your experience in the NYU seminar this past summer?

BG-S: The first barrier was the assumption that because we were and are a women's college, that we were already by definition doing this work— which of course would be incorrect. The second barrier, and this would have been clearer in 1981 more than fifteen years ago, was the tremendous discomfort about an explicitly feminist curriculum at historically black colleges. The assumption was that feminism was not relevant to black folk. There was also some resistance to what was perceived to be a radical political feminist agenda which was perceived to have nothing to do with traditional disciplinary scholarship. The assumption also was that women's studies would cripple black students by not providing them a traditional, acceptable education and that somehow we were disadvantaging them. In other words, I think there was even greater sensitivity at historically black colleges about providing students with something that was perceived to be "off color." As a result, far too few black students have been exposed to women's studies courses. The situation has changed somewhat over the years; however, the fact that women's studies in general has paid inadequate attention to issues of race and class has also limited the participation of black students. In addition, in many women's studies courses, white students express hostility in discussions about race and class in ways that black students find unsettling.

EH: How would you characterize your successes then?

BG-S: We were able to overcome these barriers because we had a friendly administration that recognized the importance of women's studies, particularly after President Johnetta Cole arrived in 1987. In addition, we always had supportive provosts, both in Donald Stewart's administration and in Cole's with Barbara Carter, Ruth Simmons, and Glenda Price. So we didn't have administrative resistance, which is not the case in many historically black colleges, where the leadership has been predominantly male. The other advantage we had from the very beginning was external funding, much of which came from the Ford Foundation, which meant that we had sufficient external financial support to really do the kind of faculty development on campus that I think was necessary for the curricular transformation. Finally, over time we began to get a critical mass of faculty and students who were very interested in women's studies courses as well.

EH: There's been this extensive critique about identity politics both within and outside of the academy. The argument is that programs like women's studies have institutionalized political agendas, which you referred to when you were talking about some of the barriers at historically black colleges. It has been suggested that these political agendas perpetuated rather than ended discriminatory treatment of women because the programs are often cast as victim studies. Is this a problem for black women's studies? Or is the problem somewhat different in that women's studies is perceived to be aligned with feminism and feminism is perceived as "white"? As a result, is the question of identity politics posed in terms of "feminism" vs. "nation/ black community"—expressed in neonationalist rhetoric which argues that black women don't need to study/research or critically interrogate their position as women separate from the concerns of the "race"?

BG-S: I think that people who identify with black women's studies are aware of, and in opposition to, the victim studies orientation of traditional Western feminist approaches to understanding women's experience. Black women's studies, almost from its inception, wanted to theorize about the oppression of women of African descent but also wanted very much to talk about the ways that black women resisted. Black women's studies consciously and very explicitly wanted not to construct a discourse that primarily emphasized black women's victimhood. At the same time though, black women's studies' advocates were up against the notion that black women were in fact not oppressed and had not been victimized. So we had to find a balance between the two premises because within African American communities there's the notion that black women have not been victimized at all, particularly vis-à-vis black men. This was the difficult balance that black women's studies had to negotiate. I think we have done a pretty good job of both emphasizing the multiple oppressions that black women face, but also we have emphasized the issue of resistance and the need to interrogate the different ways black women experience patriarchy.

EH: What about the question of feminism?

BG-S: I think that black women's studies has as one of its main contributions its reconceptualization of feminism. It has not rejected feminism, but we have said that it needed to be expanded, broadened, and made more sensitive to the issues of race and to global questions with respect to constructions of womanhood outside the United States, around the world. I think black women's studies really reinvigorated and reconceptualized feminism in such a way so that now it is not a narrow, culturally specific manifestation of one group of women's experiences.

EH: I agree that black women's studies has been successful in pluralizing women's experiences, but do you still see a tension in talking about the need to critically interrogate the position of black women vis-à-vis the concerns of "the race" especially when it has been said, pejoratively perhaps, that "the race" is really a code for the concerns of black men?

BG-S: I agree with your assessment of this persistent dilemma, which may also explain why it is that you don't have adequate women's studies curricula at historically black colleges. Or in publications that black people produce. I still think that there's the assumption that teaching African American studies means primarily dealing with racial questions.

EH: Yes, so do you think that identity politics and the whole question of difference as it's characterized in women's studies programs in predominantly white institutions—is the same kind of problem that women's studies faces in the historically black college context?

BG-S: I don't think so. I think that one of the problems that women's studies faces at white colleges is an inability to deal with difference, and here I'm talking primarily about white faculty and white students. There's still tremendous reluctance on the part of women students of color, particularly African American women, to come into women's studies at white institutions, to literally bring their bodies to the court. That is not the same problem that you have at historically black colleges. In other words, we get students into women's studies courses at Spelman because they are not assuming that when they enter the courses they're going to be about white women or taught only by white faculty. The problem that we have at Spelman is that there are many students who are uncomfortable or hostile to feminism. They think our courses are about feminism, which they find uncomfortable because they see it as something that is going to make it difficult for them to have relationships with men.

EH: What about the difference in terms of other women of color or the difference of sexuality or sexual preference?

BG-S: With respect to those questions, black women's studies is still dealing with various problems. In my experience in teaching women's studies at Spelman, the questions of sexuality are probably the most contested and result in the most tension and the most difficulty in the classroom. I think that's because there's so little in the curriculum otherwise that helps students to understand sexuality beyond what they already know. They've had very little discourse which helps them to analyze sexuality in an intellectual and analytical manner, so they're just coming at it with their personal belief systems, like most college students, with their personal values that haven't been subjected to any rigorous analysis. This remains a big problem. With respect to other women of color, there is a lack of information or misinformation about other peoples of color, particularly in the United States. We have to spend a lot of time discussing the fact that black people are not the only group of people who have had difficulties with race in this country or the world.

EH: Now it's often talked about that women's studies in the United States has been successfully institutionalized, although everything you have just said about what has happened in historically black colleges suggests that is not the case in all institutions. Institutionalization of women's studies, as you've pointed out, is at a very different point in historically black colleges. Given that there are your program and others, including the one at Howard, how are they perceived from abroad? I ask this because I think that American women's studies is perceived to be very well established, very well funded, very well supported. Do you think your program and Howard's are seen in this way? For example, I remember when a student of Philomena Essed's came over from Holland to do interviews for her dissertation on black feminism. When she visited me and Fran White at Hampshire College, she said she was looking for the black feminist institute. She believed from reading a number of anthologies and other books on black women's studies that have been widely translated that it must have had an institutional location here in the States. Fran and I laughed somewhat ruefully, but that exchange along with many others gave me the impression that there's this idea that black women's studies is as well established in the United States as women's studies more generally.

BG-S: Let me say two things quickly. First of all, I think that even the question about the institutionalization of white women's studies is a complicated one. I think that in some ways, despite the fact that there are over six hundred women's studies programs in the U.S. academy, women's studies is still institutionally fragile, in the sense that most women's studies programs are without their own faculty lines and have inadequate budgets and very little control over their curricula because they depend on departmental courses or joint appointments. There've also been in recent years a tremendous backlash and some tightening of resources, so that, though women's studies is visible and has had a tremendous impact, it may not be the case that it is institutionally strong in the sense that we think about traditional departmental studies. It is still the case that even if they are fragile, black women's studies probably has almost no institutional strength.

EH: Yours is still a program—not a department?

BG-S: Yes, it's still a program. Ours functions more like a department, but the program is how it is instituted. Structurally, it is not quite as fragile for the reasons I discussed earlier. However, I think that could quickly change. It helps that our women's studies program is in an institutional home (the Women's Center) where it functions more like a department, though it's still problematic because we don't have any faculty lines. My faculty line is still in the English department. There are no prominent black women's studies programs in the United States. And I think it's also fair to say that most well-established African American studies programs do not have even what I would call a serious black women's studies concentration. You might assume that since the institutionalization of black women's studies has not happened within women's studies it is happening within African American studies. Yet this is not the case. As you know, before Elsa Barkley Brown left the University of Michigan, she and other faculty there were working on a gender concentration within African American studies. If they had succeeded, this would have been tantamount to mounting a black women's studies component within that program. Currently, there are no major African American studies programs with a focus on gender. On the other hand, another potential site for the institutionalization of black women's studies is within women's studies programs with a significant number of black women faculty. The University of Maryland's women's studies program, because of the presence of so many black women faculty, certainly has this potential. If black women's studies has a future, in terms of institutionalization, I think it is in those women's studies programs like Maryland's because the difficulties in developing autonomous black women's studies programs are so severe.

EH: I want to take that up in a second, but what about the question of perceptions from abroad?

BG-S: Oh, I think that you're right. The assumption about the strength of black women's studies has no relationship to the reality. But you can also understand why there would be that perception because of the huge popularity of black women writers (mostly novelists) outside the United States—which prompts people to think that there's a cultural context that produces those writings, but it's not in women's studies or the academy by and large. The reception of these books also speaks to the popularity of black feminism outside the United States, which supports the assumption that it is institutionalized within the American academy—which it's not.

EH: Does the popularity of black feminist writings make a demand on black women's studies programmatically to try to address questions about women of color in the diaspora? In other words, when you engage in conversations with other women of color from around the world, as you do when you participate in Andrée McLaughlin's International Cross-Cultural Black Women's Studies Institute, do you have to represent black women's studies as being engaged programmatically with the broader concerns of women in the diaspora?

BG-S: Absolutely. Black women's studies can't be narrowly focused on the United States.

EH: I would argue that's somewhat different from white women's studies. It is not always forced to have that engagement.

BG-S: Right. I think that black women's studies is much more inherently, or at least potentially, global because it is interested in black women's experiences all over the world. As early as 1981, with the publication of Filomena Steady's edited volume *The Black Woman Cross-Culturally,* black women's studies has tried to address the experiences of women on the African continent and in the diaspora, especially in the Caribbean.

EH: Let's return to the question of integrating women's studies into the curriculum more broadly. There's a lot of debate going on right now about whether or not women's studies programs should change their names to feminist studies or gender studies . . . and people are talking about the advantages and disadvantages of such a change. You were just speaking about the integration of black women's studies into African American studies. Would an emphasis on gender rather than women make that integration more possible?

BG-S: I'm one of the people who believe that women's studies ought to keep the name women's studies. I think the whole debate about gender studies is mostly a political one, and I also see a problem with the name feminist studies. If we change to feminist studies, we will face more problems among persons of color.

EH: Well, a change to feminist studies also narrows women's studies.

BG-S: It also narrows it. That's right. I think that women's studies is sufficiently generic and also keeps in the forefront that it emerged from a political movement that began twenty or thirty years ago that's still in progress.

EH: What about gender studies?

BG-S: First of all, I think that women's studies is inherently gender studies. Women's studies claims that it uses gender as a major category of analysis—so therefore to me it's already gender studies. Now that women's studies is moving more toward interrogating constructions of masculinity, I don't think we have to change the name for gender to remain a primary focus. I believe women's studies has already been primarily interested in gender—which has been the major critique by women of color. It hasn't been sufficiently concerned about issues of race and class. I don't think the problem is gender.

EH: I also wanted you to think about this question in light of the position taken by Mamphela Ramphele in her essay "Whither Feminism?" [initially given as a response on a panel at the "Transitions, Translations, Environments: Feminisms in International Politics" conference held at the Institute for Advanced Study at Rutgers in 1995]. In the essay, Ramphele argues, quite persuasively I thought, that feminists need to outline a new vision of gender equity and to directly confront the oppression of men by patriarchy. I thought she specifically put this challenge to African American feminists to address and produce a theory of power.

BG-S: I found her essay problematic, or maybe I could agree with her if she's mostly thinking about the South African context. I think it would be very difficult for me to argue that patriarchy has had as detrimental an impact upon men as it has had on women, which I think she basically says. I could agree, and I think she is probably one of the people who noted early on, that racism has had a very profound impact on white people in ways that we don't think that much about. (James Baldwin also made this point, much earlier.) I don't think, however, that it means racism has had the same impact or as devastating an impact as it has had on black people. And I think that she actually says that.

EH: Well, I agree with you, but I also think that in the positive reading of it from my perspective, it's her insistence that we need to think about the next step. I think she was speaking specifically to the South African context: now that they're in the place of making a new society, they've got to think about gender equity in a new way and therefore take into account the oppression of black African men by white men.

BG-S: What she does not mention in that essay is the oppression of black South African women by black South African men. I think that's the part that was missing. Her premise can be tested in the African American case, but African American feminists have also argued that black men have been complicit in the oppression of black women, and I don't see that in her equation. She also doesn't address the serious problem of violence against black women in South Africa by black men. That is one of the ways the patriarchy has also impacted South African men.

EH: Yet, you don't think she goes far enough in her analysis.

BG-S: No. I agree with her—that it certainly is the case that women of African descent are as concerned about black men as they are about themselves.

EH: Her point raised for me the ongoing difficulties that black feminists have had in confronting patriarchal attitudes within black communities. I think of the problems we encountered in the group of black feminists, largely academics, when we were drafting a black feminist response to the Million Man March. Or earlier when we responded to the Anita Hill/Clarence Thomas hearings. We had real problems trying to talk about male power. And maybe we don't want to go so far as to call it patriarchy, but I felt there was an urgent need to figure out some way to theorize the power that men of color have over women of color. In other words, don't we as black feminists have to find a way to theorize race and gender at the same time?

BG-S: I absolutely agree with that. One of the comments Ramphele makes is that black women want to understand the behavior of black men. I think that this should be a focus of black women's studies, to really look at issues of black masculinity. When we talk about black men, we usually discuss how they have been disempowered racially, but we don't talk about their gender. We race black men, but we don't gender them. This is a critical issue that black feminist scholarship mut address.

EH: In a sense what you're saying is that black women's studies has fallen into the same trap that women's studies has more broadly, in conflating gender with women and thus failing to adequately theorize race *and* gender. As a result, you are arguing that the issue of black male power has to be considered under the rubric of black masculinity.

BG-S: Right. I put it under black masculinity and patriarchy. Which I think, speaking about the future, should be a key area within African American studies as well, which it currently is not.

EH: But hopefully the integration of gender into African American studies might bring that conversation into being. What other issues do you most worry about in terms of the future of women's studies?

BG-S: I continue to worry about the inability of women's studies to deal—in appropriate ways—with issues of race and difference, particularly difference in a cross-cultural context. I don't think women's studies does a good job of addressing women's issues outside the West. Those issues are not always related to race. It could be religion; it could be all kinds of issues, though race continues to be a problem. Also, the persistent white face of women's studies in the United States continues to be a problem. There just are not enough faculty of color within women's studies. The problem is equally dismal within African American studies. The hostility to feminism and to black feminism in black studies is as strong as it was ten years ago, I suspect—with a few exceptions in places where black women and a few black men in black studies are actually self-identified as people who use feminist frameworks. I continue to worry about the hostility to black feminism within African American studies and the continued domination of that field by men hostile to feminism.

EH: What about affirmative action rollbacks?

BG-S: This is going to be devastating with respect to black students' access to white institutions. Think about the situation in Texas, where the affirmative action guidelines in place at the University of Texas have been overturned by recent court orders. Also, the latest data from California show a decline in admissions of students of color as a result of affirmative action rollbacks. The other thing is that the assault on affirmative action also confirms for many black people that race is still the primary problem that black people face, which provokes even more resistance to foregrounding gender.

EH: You hear black people arguing that race is still primary because white conservatives are not going after programs to prevent gender discrimination.

BG-S: And they also see white women as successful.

EH: Yes, but I think that perception only highlights the way in which gender is misunderstood, if not ignored, by some black people. Affirmative efforts to end gender discrimination are seen as only benefiting white women, not black women or women of color. This is precisely why, as you've already suggested, it is critical for black women's studies to engage the intersection of gender and race. Finally, what do you dream about for black women's studies? You know you have to end up with a comment about your vision for the future of black women's studies.

BG-S: The thing that still keeps me committed to this is that I am absolutely certain that women's studies has the capability of transforming black students so that they can develop a radically different lens by which to view the world, one that allows for a more complicated, more nuanced, and more ambiguous view that ultimately would support a deeper intellectual curiosity. Women's studies can force these students to question their values and the ways in which they have been socialized, which I think would produce students who are more critical, more willing to engage in activist projects that would propel them out of the classroom and that would push them out of their "comfort zone" to engage a broader range of questions instead of having a narrow focus on race. My visionary statement is that women's studies can radicalize students of color and help them see the world in very different ways than they saw the world before they entered a women's studies class. Especially around issues of sexuality. I taught one of the first women's studies courses in the English department at Spelman in the mid-seventies. I've been doing this for over twenty-five years, and I am as excited about the women's studies classroom as when I began.

35. Toni Cade Bambara: Black Feminist Foremother (2008)

In 1974, Toni Cade [Bambara] had recently moved to Atlanta and was one of the first persons with whom my departmental colleague Roseann Bell and I consulted when we began conceptualizing our anthology, *Sturdy Black Bridges: Visions of Black Women in Literature,* which would be the first collection of black women's literature in the African diaspora.[1] Bambara's now-classic text *The Black Woman* (1970) had been in print only four years. I also felt strongly that Bambara's contribution to the development of contemporary Black feminism, feminist theory, and women's studies had not been adequately documented by scholars, though it is the case that *The Black Woman* has begun to garner the attention it deserves in mainstream narratives of American feminism.[2]

When I think of the beginnings of women's studies, especially Black Women's Studies, not necessarily academic feminism, I think of Toni Cade Bambara, whose anthology *The Black Woman* was as important in the development of this new interdisciplinary field as Kate Millett's pioneering and more celebrated *Sexual Politics,*[3] though Bambara's work has rarely been seen in this context by white feminists. *The Black Woman* was significant because of the value it attached to hearing the distinct voices of black women, arguing that our experiences were different from both black men and white women. Cade's work preceded by two years Gerda Lerner's influential 1972 documentary history, *Black Women in White America,* which is often erroneously cited as having ushered in Black Women's Studies. Frustrated with the priorities of the new women's movement, which was in process during the writing of her preface, Bambara asserted, "in the whole bibliography of feminist literature, literature immediately and directly relevant to us wouldn't fill a page."[4] By "us," she meant black and other Third World women, for example, sisters in Vietnam, Guatemala, Algeria, and Ghana.

Rather than simply complaining, she advocated a radical agenda for women's studies and the women's movement (inseparable, from her vantage point), which if it had been taken seriously, or even noticed, would have altered the course of "second-wave feminism" within and without the academy. Her plan was to:

> set up a comparative study of the woman's role as she saw it in all the Third World nations; examine the public school system and blueprint some viable alternatives; explore ourselves and set the record straight on the matriarch and the evil Black bitch; delve into history and pay tribute to all our warriors from the ancient times to the slave trade to Harriet Tubman to Fannie Lou Hamer to the woman of this morning ... interview the migrant workers, the quilting bee mothers, the grandmothers of the UNIA[4] . . .outline the work that has been done in the area of consumer education and cooperative economics ... provide a forum of opinion from the YWCA to the Black Women Enraged; get into the whole area of sensuality, sex; chart the steps necessary for forming a working alliance with all nonwhite women of the world for the formation of, among other things, a clearinghouse for the exchange of information.[5]

Commenting on the profound impact of Toni Cade's ground-breaking anthology on her own "revolutionary feminism many years later," bell hooks also captures the significance of *The Black Woman* for other black women like me who, in the early 1970s, were claiming feminism as a legitimate vehicle for understanding black life, and who were working within the academy to transform it:

> Singlehandedly, *The Black Woman* placed black women at the center of various feminist debates. "On the Issue of Roles" ... was one of the first essays on feminist theory that looked at the interlocking relations between race, sex, and class. It legitimized looking at black life from a feminist perspective ... it helped to create an intellectual climate where feminist theory focusing on black experience could emerge. Without the publication of this anthology, later feminist works focusing on black life might never have been written.[6]

Toni Cade Bambara would have as well a profound impact on my own career as a feminist scholar/activist. Because of the historical significance of *The Black Woman* and her importance as a writer, educator, feminist critic, and community worker, the interview with Toni was critical to the vision of *Sturdy Black Bridges,* my first publication. Roseann and I believed it was imperative to mark the visionary thinking of early Black feminist scholar/activists such as Toni Cade who would continue to have a powerful impact on younger women like myself and bell hooks. When I inquired about the possibility of black and other Third World women forming alliances around the eradication of both race and gender oppression, Toni revealed her involvement in what we would now call a global women's movement. A year later (1975) she would travel to North Vietnam having been invited by their Women's Union with a delegation called the North American Academic Marxist-Leninist Anti-Imperialist Feminist Women. She believed that feminist movements should not be narrowly focused on the evils of patriarchy but rather on eliminating all oppressions, including that experienced by the colonized Third World and poor people in the United States. She also bemoaned a missed moment in the early 1960s when what she called a national black women's movement could have been multicultural and multiethnic if African American women had joined Puerto Rican women and Chicanas "who shared not only a common condition but also I think a common vision about the future." In her usual prophetic fashion, she also anticipated that in the last quarter of the twentieth century African Americans would begin to forge critical ties with other communities of color, which, she believed, was also critical for white women involved in the women's liberation struggle in the United States. When I asked her whether it was a dilemma for her to be both a feminist and a warrior in the race struggle, which for some black women and men was an oxymoron, she asserted unequivocally, "I don't find any basic contradiction or any tension between being a feminist, being a pan-Africanist, being a black nationalist, being an internationalist, being a socialist, and being a woman in North America." This was precisely the message many of us young black feminists needed as we found ourselves increasingly under suspicion with respect to our race loyalty. She also pointed us in new directions as she envisioned an updated version of *The Black Woman,* which would include position papers from the Women's Caucus of Student Non-Violent Coordinating Committee (SNCC), the Women's Caucus of the Black Panthers, and the Third World Women's Alliance. There would also be writings from "the campus forces, the prison forces, tenants' groups, and most especially from the migrant workers and sharecroppers of the Deep South." Clearly, her vision of women's liberation was sensitive to class differences and suspicious of monolithic conceptions of womanhood. She was also aware of the perils of exclusion and warned against the marginalization of particular women who were as critical to an understanding of the female condition and the history of women's resistance to oppression globally as were middle-class Euro-American women.

In an interview with Louis Massiah, "How She Came by Her Name," Toni reveals the genesis of *The Black Woman,* which began in 1968 while she was teaching at City College's Search for Education, Elevation, and Knowledge (SEEK) Program. Her initial goal was to collect position papers from black women in civil rights organizations such as SNCC, Congress of Racial Equality (CORE), and the Black Panther Party, who were "taking brothers to task for their foolishness," but their response was, "No, this is in-house stuff. We are not interested in going public."[7] After discovering how difficult it was to convince publishers to publish books about black women, she abandoned the working papers idea and decided that she would create an anthology that would prove that there was indeed a market for black women's work so that more of their writings would appear in print. Within the second month of its hitting the bookstores, *The Black Woman* went into a second edition! Her insistence that it cost less than a dollar and be able to fit in your pocket turned out to have been a stroke of marketing genius.

In the preface to *Deep Sightings*, which was edited by Toni Morrison, her former editor, and published after Bambara's untimely death, Morrison speculates about whether her sister-friend realized how brilliant at writing fiction she was. I continue to wonder whether Bambara fully realized how profoundly she had impacted young black feminists-in-the making through the example of her unconventional life and utter clarity about the evils of white supremacy, misogyny, capitalism, stereotypical gender roles, as well as sexism within African American communities. In the *New York Times* obituary, Bambara is heralded as "a major contributor to the emerging genre of black women's literature, along with the writers Toni Morrison and Alice Walker." Her friend and film collaborator, Louis Massiah, captured her transgressive spirit with the eloquent observation, "She made revolution irresistible." Her vision of radical black struggle was deeply feminist and critical of its patriarchal, heterosexist paradigms:

> we are just as jammed in the rigid confines of those basically oppressive socially contrived roles. For if a woman is tough, she's a rough mamma, a strident bitch, a ballbreaker, a castrator. And if a man is at all sensitive, tender, spiritual, he's a faggot. And there is a dangerous trend observable in some quarters to program Sapphire out of her "evil" ways into a cover-up, shut-up, lay-back-and-be-cool obedience role ... She is being encouraged—in the name of the revolution no less—to cultivate "virtues" that if listed would sound like the personality traits of slaves ... Perhaps we need to let go of all notions of manhood and femininity and concentrate on Blackhood.[8]

The creative, political, and critical work of Toni Cade Bambara certainly made feminist revolution irresistible to many young black women over the past four decades. Her bold, unwavering commitment to liberation struggle, and her hard-hitting, incisive prose inspired a new generation of warrior women. We speak her name and honor her memory.

Beverly Guy-Sheftall [BGS]: Would you describe your early life and what caused you to start writing?

Toni Cade Bambara [TCB]: I can't remember a time when I was not writing. The original motive was to try to do things that we were not encouraged to do in the language arts programs in the schools, namely, to use writing as a tool to get in touch with the self. In the schools, for example, writing, one of the few crafts we're taught, seems to be for the purpose of teaching people how to plagiarize from the dictionary or the encyclopedia and how to create as much distance from our own voice as possible. That was called education. I'd call it alienation. You had to sift out a lot, distort a lot, and lie in order to jam the stuff of your emotional, linguistic, cultural experience into that form called English composition.

The original motive for writing at home was to give a play to those notions that wouldn't fit the English composition mold, to try and do justice to a point of view, to a sense of self. Later on, I discovered that there was a certain amount of applause that could be gotten if you turned up with the Frederick Douglass play for Negro History Week or the George Washington Carver play for the assembly program. That talent for bailing the English teachers out created stardom, and that became another motive.

As I got older, I began to appreciate the kinds of things you could tap and release and learn about self if you had a chance to get cozy with pencil and paper. And I discovered that paper is very patient. It will wait on you to come up with whatever it is, as opposed to sitting in class and having to raise your hand immediately in response to someone else's questions, someone else's concerns.

I don't know that I began getting really serious about writing until maybe five years ago. Prior to that, in spite of all good sense, I always thought writing was rather frivolous, that it was something you did because you didn't feel like doing any work. But in the last five or six years I've come to appreciate that it is a perfectly legitimate way to participate in struggle. That writing, sharing insights, keeping a vision alive, is of value and that is pretty much the motive for writing now. Although I can't really say I have a motive for writing now. I'm compelled. I don't think I could stop if I wanted to.

BGS: Do you remember the very first story you wrote and the circumstances surrounding it?

TCB: No, no. I was really little. I'm talking about kindergarten. Sometimes even now, a line will come out that will take me back to some utterance made in a story or poem I wrote or tried to write when I was in pink pajamas and bunny slippers. It's weird. I've been in training, you might say, for quite a while. Still am.

BGS: Were you conditioned by your family members to assume a traditional female role? I'm asking this because of the number of black female children in your fiction who do not conform to American society's notion of what is "proper" female behavior.

TCB: I think within my household not a great deal of distinction was made between pink and blue. We were expected to be self-sufficient, to be competent, and to be rather nonchalant about expertise in a number of areas. Within the various neighborhoods I've lived in, there was such a variety of expectations regarding womanhood or manhood that it was rather wide open. In every neighborhood I lived in, for example, there were always big-mouthed women, there were always competent women, there were always beautiful women, independent as well as dependent women, so that there was a large repertoire from which to select. And it wasn't until I got older, I would say maybe in college, that I began to collide with the concepts and dynamics of "role appropriate behavior" and so forth. I had no particular notion about being groomed along one particular route as opposed to another as a girl-child. My self-definitions were strongly internal and improvisational.

BGS: Take the little girl in "Gorilla, My Love," a favorite story of mine. Would you say that she was like little girls you grew up with? Does she come out of your personal experience?

TCB: I would say that she's a highly selective fiction. There are certain kinds of spirits that I'm *very* appreciative of, people who are very tough, but very compassionate. You put me in any neighborhood, in any city, and I will tend to gravitate toward that type. The kid in "Gorilla" (the story as well as in that collection) is a kind of person who will survive, and she's triumphant in her survival. Mainly because she's so very human, she cares, her caring is not careless. She certainly is not autobiographical except that there are naturally aspects of my own personality that I very much like that are similar to hers. She's very much like ·people I like. However, I would be hard pressed to point out her source in real life.

BGS: Have women writers influenced you as much as male writers?

TCB: I have no clear ideas about literary influence. I would say that my mother was a great influence, since mother is usually the first map maker in life. She encouraged me to explore and express. And, too, the fact that people of my household were big on privacy helped. And I would say that people I ran into helped, and I ran into a great many people because we moved a lot and I was always a nosey kid running up and down the street, getting into everything. Particular kinds of women influenced the work. For example, in every neighborhood I lived in there were always two types of women that somehow pulled me and sort of got their wagons in a circle around me. I call them Miss Naomi and Miss Gladys, although I'm sure they came under various names. The Miss Naomi types were usually barmaids or life-women, nighttime people with lots of clothes in the closet and a very particular philosophy of life, who would give me advice like, "When you meet a man, have a birthday, demand a present that's hockable, and be careful." Stuff like that. Had no idea what they were talking about. Just as well. The Miss Naomis usually gave me a great deal of advice about beautification, how to take care of your health and not get too fat. The Miss Gladyses were usually the type that hung out the window in Apartment 1-A leaning on the pillow giving single-action advice on numbers or giving you advice about how to get your homework done or telling you to stay away from those cruising cars that moved through the neighborhood patrolling little girls. I would say that those two types of women, as well as the women who hung out in the beauty parlors (and the beauty parlors in those days were perhaps the only womanhood institutes we had—it was there in the beauty parlors that young girls came of age and developed some sense of sexual standards and some sense of what it means to be a woman growing up—it was those women who had the most influence on the writing.

I think that most of my work tends to come off the street rather than from other books. Which is not to say I haven't learned a lot as an avid reader. I devour pulp and print. And of course I'm part of the tradition. That is to say, it is quite apparent to the reader that I appreciate Langston Hughes, Zora Hurston, and am a product of the sixties spirit. But I'd be hard pressed to discuss literary influences in any kind of intelligent way.

BSG: Did you grow up in New York primarily?

TCB: Primarily.

BGS: Let's move to some of your reactions to the literary scene. What would you consider to be some contemporary or past positive images of black women in literature, either by male or female or black or white writers?

TCB: I would define "positive" as usable, characters who can teach us valuable lessons of life, characters who are rounded and who give dimension to the type or stereotype that they are closest to. For example, Sula in the Morrison novel is interesting. She's a champion. She's an adventurer, and she gives up another dimension of the bitch stereotype. She makes us aware of how many people are locked up in that particular cage. Eva, who very much resembles the stereotypic matriarch, is more than that and she too helps us break open that old stereotype and force us to look for qualities, lessons, eclipsed by the stereotypic label. I regard them as positive, for they touch deep. In the contemporary poetry—that is, the poetry that came out of the Neo-Black Arts Movement—there are female personae who are assertive and rounded and they also break open the bitch stereotype for us, so that we find under that label locked-up vibrancy—activists, combatants, the Harriet Tubman heirs, people who come from that championship tradition. That's what I would call positive and in fact there are very few works that are available to us now, say in the last decade, that are not like that. We have very little deadwood in the works that have come out of the sixties and are currently being produced. Very few flat, stupid, useless, and careless portraits.

BSG: Is there a particular black woman writer of fiction who you think best illuminates the black female experience, specifically the double oppression of race and sex?

TCB: No, and I think that's okay. I think if we were designing a course that attempted to project the profile of the contemporary black woman, particularly in respect to double or triple oppression, to someone who did not understand it, it would be necessary to pull out a lot of people because there are a lot of experiences. There is no *the* woman or *the* experience or *the* profile. I would assemble the works of writers like Zora Neale Hurston, Toni Morrison, Carolyn Rodgers, Lucille Clifton, Eloise Lofton, and a good many others and particularly young writers who are coming out of the workshops, in the Southeast particularly, and out of the Berkeley group.

BSG: Do you think the black woman writer has been treated fairly by the critical community, both black and white?

TCB: I have no idea. It's not something I have any comments on because it's not something I generally think about, that is to say, the black woman writer. We know for sure that any cultural product of black people has not been treated intelligently and usefully by white critics. That's one kind of answer. The fact that a good many black women writers do not get into anthologies that are put together by black men is another kind of answer. The fact that black women critics sometimes approach black women's writing as though they were highly particular and had no connection to the group traditions, that's another kind of issue.

I'm not so much concerned with whether black women writers are dealt with fairly but rather with what they're dealing with. And I think the great accomplishment of particularly the poets of the Neo-Black Arts Movement (sister poets) and perhaps to a lesser degree the dramatists, novelists, short story writers, have contributed a great deal toward not only commenting on, correcting, and countering the stereotypic images, but in blasting open a new road, if you will, for younger writers who are coming now: dealing with women who have not been dealt with before, raising issues that have not been tackled before, grabbing hold of a vision that we have let slip and maybe never have laid out in print before. The production itself I find far more interesting than any critical response.

BGS: Near the end of her introduction to *Black-Eyed Susans*, a collection of short stories by and about black women, Mary Helen Washington asserts, with respect to the black woman writer, that "there still remains something of a sacred-cow attitude in regard to black women that prevents exploration of many aspects of their lives . . . There has been a desire," she goes on to say, "to protect and revere the black woman's image." She argues that we need books about black women who have nervous breakdowns, who are "overwhelmed by sex," who are not faithful, who abuse and neglect their children, and so forth. That is, we need stories about "real black women," stories which "interpret the entire range and spectrum of the experiences of black women." Would you agree with her assessment of the black woman writer with respect to these issues?

TCB: I don't approach literature from quite that direction. I think I understand what she's saying, but writing for me is still an act of language first and foremost. I don't know that I need to read a book about a nervous breakdown in order to understand nervous breakdowns or to protect my health. As an act of language, literature is a spirit informer—an energizer. A lot of energy is exchanged in the reading and writing of books and that gets into the debate of whether it is more important to offer a usable truth or to try to document the many truths or realisms that make up the black woman's experience.

I think I see her point and it's all very lovely, but it doesn't concern me, and I'm not altogether sure it's valid or true. It is true that we're so defensive about our detractors, which I think is what one of her points is, that we are not approaching the complexity of ourselves in a fearless way. That is true, but I don't know that the nervous breakdown is what I would argue for. I would argue rather that there is an aspect of black spirit, of inherent black nature, that we have not addressed: the tension, the power that is still latent, still colonized, still frozen and untapped, in some 27 million black people. We do not know how to unleash, we do not even know how to speak of it in a courageous manner, yet. I think that is because we have been so long on the defensive and have invested a great deal of time and energy posturing and trying to prove that indeed we are as clean as they are. Since the sixties, however, a great many of us have been released from that posturing through having dialogues with each other, which is a very radical and new dimension to the dialogue of cultural worker and community. It is in relation to potential that I might argue Mary Helen's general point. Namely, that we are not terribly fearless and courageous and thoroughgoing in dealing with the complexity of the black experience, the black spirit. As a matter of fact, music is probably the only mode we have used to speak of that complexity. But I would argue the point in relation to other aspects of self rather than to nervous breakdowns and the kinds of things that Mary Helen is talking about, which is not to say it has no usefulness, but it doesn't strike me as a priority at all.

BGS: Do you think that the black woman has an advantage or special perspective that may enable her to reveal aspects of the black experience or black spirit to which you refer?

TCB: No, I wouldn't say that black women or children or elders or men or any sector of the community are any more in command of it or in touch with it than any other. I find it interesting in this period, the seventies, that we have begun to embrace within our community (and we can see parallels in the national as well as international community), an interest in holistic healing systems: astrology, voodoo, TM, etc. No, I don't think that any group within the community has any monopoly on that kind of wisdom, a grasp on that new way to prepare for the future.

BGS: Speaking of parallels, have your travels revealed to you how American black and other Third World women can link up in their struggles to liberate themselves from the various kinds of oppression they face as a result of their sexual identity?

TCB: Yes, I would say that two particular places I visited yielded up a lot of lessons along those lines. I was in Cuba in 1973 and had the· occasion not only to meet with the Federation of Cuban Women but sisters in the factories, on the land, in the street, in the parks, in lines, or whatever, and the fact that they were able to resolve a great many class conflicts as well as color conflicts and organize a mass organization says a great deal about the possibilities here. I was in Vietnam in the summer of 1975 as a guest of the Women's Union and again was very much struck by the women's ability to break through traditional roles, traditional expectations, reactionary agenda for women, and come together again in a mass organization that is programmatic and takes on a great deal of responsibility for the running of the nation.

We missed a moment in the early sixties. We missed two things. One, at a time when we were beginning to lay the foundations for a national black women's union and for a national strategy for organizing, we did not have enough heart nor a solid enough analysis that would equip us to respond in a positive and constructive way to the fear in the community from black men as well as others who said that women organizing as women is divisive. We did not respond to that in a courageous and principled way. We fell back. The other moment that we missed was that we had an opportunity to hook up with Puerto Rican women and Chicano women who shared not only a common condition but also I think a common vision about the future and we missed that moment because of the language trap. When people talked about multicultural or multiethnic organizing, a lot of us translated that to mean white folks and backed off. I think that was an error. We should have known what was meant by multicultural. Namely, people of color. Afro-American, Afro-Hispanic, Inda-Hispanic, Asian-Hispanic, and so forth. Not that those errors necessarily doom us. Errors may result in lessons learned. I think we have the opportunity again in this last quarter of the twentieth century to begin forging those critical ties with other communities. It will be done. That is a certainty.

BGS: Do you consider it a dilemma for the black woman today who considers herself both a feminist and a warrior in the race struggle?

TCB: A dilemma? Personally, no. I'm not aware of what the problem is for people who consider it a dilemma. I don't know what they're thinking because it's not as if you're a black or a woman. I don't find any basic contradiction or any tension between being a feminist, being a pan-Africanist, being a black nationalist, being an internationalist, being a socialist, and being a woman in North America. I'm not sensitive enough to people caught in the "contradiction" to be able to unravel the dilemma and adequately speak to the question at this particular point in time. My head is somewhere else.

BGS: Turning to your own writings, you said in your preface to *The Black Woman,* an anthology of readings by contemporary black women published in 1970, that among other evils this country "regards its women as its monsters." Have you seen over the past seven years or so any changes in this country's attitude toward women, especially the black ones?

TCB: The country at large, no. You look at "That's My Mama" and I think it's clear that television program really centers around the son and the activities in the barbershop. That's the most dynamic aspect of that drama. But because the mammy looms so large in the American mentality, is such a durable, persistent psychosexual obsession on the part of white people, male and female, that need demands the presence of the mama figure: on the one hand, a gracious, giving, enduring mammy, but also a Hattie McDaniel sass. Sass as a comic-menace element. The menace element is a white fiction that is meshed into our women, that has to do with their whole "momism" pathology. So they get their thing off in three ways through her: She's useful to keep the "boy" thing going; she's the mother's milk nurturer; plus the "hate mom" white thing can be projected onto her.

I don't know that I have seen any change, by and large, in white America. In terms of black America, there are authors still—I'm thinking of John A. Williams in particular, as well as many other writers who don't come to mind at the moment—who are still a little scary in terms of the assertive black woman, still look at Sapphire as a threat, and who do not come to grips with how the myth functions in American society. The bitch helps justify, for example, hustlers and other collaborators. The presence of the bitch myth also helps those societal restraints that operate on black women, as well as the rest of the community. No, I haven't noticed a change among black male writers either. Ron Milner's women are a change, though.

BGS: If you were to do another anthology of readings by contemporary black women today, what kinds of pieces would you include?

TCB: The papers that I was most concerned with at that time that never got into the book, and those were position papers from the Women's Caucus of SNCC, of the Panthers, of a number of other organizations that eventually did produce papers for publication through Third World Women's Alliance. I was particularly concerned with the evolution of women's groups that had begun as consumer education or single-issue action groups, began studying together and engaging in community organizing and are now, come ten years later, the core network of what will soon become, we hope, a national black women's union. I would include in a new collection writings from the campus forces, the prison forces, tenants' groups, and most especially southern rural women's workers, particularly from the migrant workers and sharecroppers of the Deep South.

Notes

1. See *Sturdy Black Bridges: Visions of Black Women in Literature,* in Roseann P. Bell, Bettye J. Parker, and Beverly Guy-Sheftall, eds. (New York: Doubleday, 1979), 230-249.

2. In my essay, "Other Mothers of Women's Studies," in *The Politics of Women's Studies,* Florence Howe, ed. (New York: Feminist Press, 2000), 216-226.

3. Toni Cade Bambara. The Black Woman: An Anthology (New York: Signet, 1970), 10-11.

4. A body of scholarly literature is now available, which documents the feminist viewpoints of black nationalist women including Amy Jacques Garvey, associated with the Universal Negro Improvement Association (UNIA) founded by her husband Marcus Garvey in Jamaica in 1914 with his first wife Amy Ashwood. See Amy Jacques Garvey's woman's page, "Our Women and What They Think," published in *Negro World,* UNIA's weekly newspaper; Ula Taylor's unpublished dissertation, "The Veiled Garvey: The Life and Times of Amy Jacques Garvey."

5. Toni Cade Bambara. *The Black Woman,* 11.

6. bell hooks. "Writer to Writer: Remembering Toni Cade Bambara," *Remembered Rapture: The Writer at Work* (New York: Henry Holt & Company, 1999), 230-232.

7. Toni Cade Bambara. *Deep Sightings and Rescue Missions: Fiction, Essays, and Conversations,* in Toni Morrison, ed. (New York: Pantheon Books, 1996), 229.

8. Toni Cade Bambara. *The Black Woman,* 102-103.

36. The ROOT Interview: Beverly Guy-Sheftall on Black Feminism

by Akoto Ofori-Atta **(2010)**

As the end of her two-year term as president draws near, Guy-Sheftall sat with The Root *at the 2010 National Women's Studies Association conference to discuss her role with the organization, the importance of black feminism, and the lessons she hopes to pass on to future feminists of color.*

The Root: You've been a part of black feminism from the very beginning. Tell us about where it was then, and where it is now.

Beverly Guy-Sheftall: Coming out of the civil rights era, black feminism was a contentious, debatable, demonized, and divisive notion. It was perceived to be a pro-white, anti-male doctrine that would destroy black families and prohibit unity. I can remember going to all-black gatherings and people asking me whether or not I was a lesbian, because being pro-female translated into a hate for men. Now, though, black feminist thought is very much an important part of a broader women's studies — it would be very difficult to avoid black feminism when speaking about a more general feminism. What's interesting, though, is that black feminism is still very much a suspect politic in black spaces. Despite our progress, it seems that in some hetero-patriarchal paradigms, like black studies and black culture, feminism seems to be less accepted.

TR: So when do you think black feminism cemented its place in scholarship and in the black consciousness?

BGS: I would say it happened in the early '90s, when the anthology *All the Women Are White, All the Men Are Black, but Some of Us Are Brave* was first printed. It was the first cogent and eloquent articulation of black feminist thought. And the title really says it all. That publication made it difficult to ignore black feminist studies. Additionally, there was a proliferation of black women literary scholars — Patricia Hill Collins, Toni Morrison, and others — that helped pave the way.

TR: Is black feminism in your view a visible movement, in comparison with what it was in the 1960s?

BGS: I think it is. The impact of black feminist thinking and writing permeates black communities and culture, even though we may not say it explicitly. One of the things that black feminist thought does is bring attention to the fact that there are no black women on the Supreme Court. Also, any examination of violence against black women is Black Feminism 101, and a testament to its viability.

TR: You came on two years ago as president of the National Women's Studies Association. What was your agenda when you started, and as your term comes to an end, do you think you've accomplished your goals?

BGS: I wanted NWSA to be an inclusive, multiracial, multicultural organization where women of color and their feminisms would not be marginalized. And in looking at the 2010 conference program, you can see that black feminism and transnational feminism are the core of the event, not off to the side. So in that way, I think I've accomplished my goals. The other thing I'm pleased with is the shift in age. I'm struck at how young this year's participants are, so I think that this organization has a very bright future. Truthfully, we were worried. We'd always ask, "Who is going to succeed us?" And as I look around, I no longer see that as an issue.

TR: How can nonacademics and nonactivists gain access to knowledge about black feminism?

BGS: I think that disjuncture between the academy and the community is more blurred when it comes to black feminism, because there are many black feminists who don't confine their work to the academy. People know who bell hooks is. When Ntozake Shange wrote her play, she did that as a community service. When Michelle Wallace wrote *Black Macho and the Myth of the Superwoman,* she did that as a journalist. When Paula Giddings wrote *When and Where I Enter,* she was not in the academy. We need to remember that the pioneering women of this movement often operated outside of the academy and outside of political movements.

TR: Where do black men fit into black feminism? What has been their role?

BGS: We have a generation of young black college men who have been impacted by black feminism. If you pay attention, you'll notice that all the black males that I consider feminists are between the ages of 30 and 45, because they had women's studies classes, were taught by black feminists, and came up in an age where they had black feminist friends and parents. People like Marc Anthony Neal attribute his perspective to having taken classes with Alexis De Veaux. Kevin Powell's analysis of *For Colored Girls* was influenced by his black feminism. Barack Obama was raised by his white feminist mother, so he has an inclusive politic around gender and sexuality.

TR: With the election of Barack Obama, questions about a post-racial America always seem to surface in mainstream media. How does black feminist thought respond to those suggestions?

BGS: We are not post-anything. We still live in a white-supremacist, sexist and homophobic culture. Think back to the presidential campaign, when Michelle was demonized and portrayed as emasculating, so she had to be repackaged. If we were living in a post-racial or post-feminist world, Michelle could be whoever she wanted to be. We don't hear much about her being an educated career woman and lawyer. And look at all the attention we pay to her body — her arms, her bottom, her hair. All that attention is a racialized sexism. So his election really suggested that we still have a lot more work to do.

TR: What do you see as the plight of young black feminists today?

BGS: Dealing with racism and sexism is still at the top of their agenda, but I also see that this generation is consumed with achieving a work-life balance. "How can I study, have a partner, be a mother and have a career all at once?" seems to be an important question for young black women. The second issue I hear, mostly from heterosexual black women, is a deep concern about being un-partnered, which I blame on an overwhelming discourse around this idea that there are no available black men. And to that I say, young black women have got to get rid of the notion that they will not have a fulfilling life if they don't have those things. They also need to expand their notions of what is a desirable partner.

TR: If the progress of the women's movement is any indication, then shouldn't being un-partnered be less of an issue for this generation than it was for yours?

BGS: I am a magazine addict, and if I pick up one more magazine that reads "So- and-so is pregnant," or "So-and-so was the happiest she's ever been during the nine months of her pregnancy," I am going to scream! So in some ways, young women may be more connected to these gender scripts than we were, because marriage and motherhood are at the center of popular discourse. I also think that Christianity and all its messages and norms of marriage and motherhood keep people trapped. Its messages are hard to ignore, so I think that black women really need more models. They don't see women who say, "I chose not to have children and opted out of marriage, and this is why and it was the best decision I ever made in my life." I wish that Oprah would address that, but she doesn't.

TR: What's next for you? And what advice do you give to young black women?

BGS: I hope to write a personal memoir. I chose not to remarry and chose not to have children, and want to tell young feminists that my life has been very fulfilling despite not having those things. And to our future feminists, I say, abandon the scripts you hear and ask yourself, "What kind of life do I want to live?" That is what constitutes liberation — defining your life for yourself

37.

What Would Harriet Do? A Legacy of Resistance and Activism

A Conversation with Barbara Smith and Beverly Guy-Sheftall, Moderated by Paula Giddings[1] (2014)

On March 8, 2013, renowned black feminists Barbara Smith and Beverly Guy-Sheftall were brought together on the same panel, moderated by historian Paula Giddings, in a compelling conversation that closed out the first day of the Harriet Tubman: A Legacy of Resistance Symposium at the University at Albany, SUNY, celebrating the 100th anniversary of Tubman's passing on March 10, 1913. In answering the panel's question, "What would Harriet do?," they addressed the legacy of the famous legend, from how Tubman is remembered to how she is taught (or not taught) to how she might react to the struggles of today, including issues of violence, mass incarcerations, and the election of the first black president of the United States.

Janell Hobson: I want first to introduce our moderator for this session, who will then introduce you to this panel, which is pretty much what I would call a "legends" panel. It is an honor to see all these women here. So, I will start with the first legend, Paula Giddings, professor at Smith College, author of *When and Where I Enter* and the biography *Ida: A Sword Among Lions*. Paula is currently the editor of *Meridians: feminism, race, transnationalism.*

Paula Giddings: It is such a pleasure to be here! When Janell asked me if *Meridians* would be interested in publishing the papers from this extraordinary conference in a special issue, my response took three seconds: Yes! Janell and I have worked together before—she was the guest editor for our special and one of our most popular issues, "Representin': Women, Hip-Hop, and Popular Music," and I know her to be not only an excellent scholar but an efficient, organized, and excellent editor. And I have not been disappointed. The papers have been groundbreaking as they add new dimensions and new ways of thinking about one of the most extraordinary Americans in our history.

I'm thrilled to introduce the panel for this conversation. Barbara Smith just reminded me that we first met in 1974 when I was at Howard University Press and [she was] a book editor at the *National Observer.*

Presently, Barbara is an Albany Common Council member, which means that the city is in good hands. She is a pioneer. Barbara is a founding member of the Combahee River Collective, and a co-founder of Kitchen Table: Women of Color Press. She is the author or editor of four books, including the iconic *But Some of Us Are Brave* and the recently released *Ain't Gonna Let Nobody Turn Me Around: Forty Years of Movement Building with Barbara Smith.* Presently, she is the Public Service Professor at the University at Albany School of Social Welfare.

The next panelist actually got me my first job in academia. That is how long we've known each other, at least since 1984—right after my first book, *When and Where I Enter,* was published. Presently, Beverly is the director of the Women's Research and Resource Center at Spelman College, and she is the Anna Julia Cooper Professor of Women's Studies there. She is also president emerita of the National Women's Studies Association and the author, editor, and/or co-editor of eight books, including *Words of Fire* and *Gender Talk.*

Let's begin, Barbara, with your comments. What does Harriet Tubman's legacy mean to you?

Barbara Smith: I was thinking of how appropriate it is to have this symposium in New York State; I'm sure Janell and others have thought of this as well, because of course this is where Harriet Tubman ended up living, and where she died. Also, New York State, including Albany, was an important stop on the Underground Railroad. As far as Harriet Tubman's legacy [is concerned], I think the main thing is a legacy of struggle and a legacy of activism. I often say that you know that black people, people of African heritage, were instrumental in their own liberation from enslavement because of the fact that we still exist here in great numbers in the United States.

There are a lot of different stories about how the emancipation occurred and why it occurred. One of them is Lincoln. You can see it in the movie; that is one version. But there are other versions. The version that I prefer, because it is the one that is actually accurate, is the one that includes black people's agency in their own liberation and struggle for freedom. And as I just said, it is not necessarily about how many people were able to escape from slavery of the Confederacy; it is not about how many people were able to do that. That was a fairly rare occurrence numerically, but the fact that black people continued to be alive when our lives were completely not valued and that we were always under threat of death for the most minor infractions shows the level of resistance we were involved in and should be involved in still.

Harriet Tubman, of course, is so well known and so revered because of her ability to be proactive at a time of complete danger and of state-sanctioned terrorism. They act like terrorism is something that just started. No. Terrorism has been a part of the United States and what became America as long as we've been here. But the thing is, she is well known because she exercised her capacity as a human being and as a black woman who tried to make things better and different. But as I said, we have a great tradition of that, and I hope we can continue to lift that up in our actions; we'll be talking about that later.

Beverly Guy-Sheftall: Let me just say how thoroughly I have enjoyed all these papers today. I just have to say that Janell and Vivian May were students of mine. I was teaching that first Black Feminist Thought class at Emory, a bit under duress. One good thing that came out of it was the anthology *Words of Fire.* It is quite possible that had I not been trying to teach that course from scratch, that book wouldn't have come into being. I just want to say I am happy to be here today and to have heard the speakers. And how happy I always am to be back with Paula and comrades. We were thinking, Barbara and I, about the circumstances under which we met. I just thought it might be good to share that. We were both English professors at a certain point. I am also a refugee from the English Department, and we were active members of something called The Modern Language Association Commission on the Status of Women. And then when I went on to found the Women's Center at Spelman, Barbara Smith was the first person whom Judy Gebre-Hewitt and I went to talk to in the late seventies.

I think it is fair to say that if you are an African American around my age, or maybe slightly younger, Harriet Tubman was the lone black, female, heroic figure among a huge, robust pantheon of African American men. I think Harriet Tubman was the only black woman who used to get pointed out in Negro History Week, Negro History Month, if you can remember that.

But she was sort of frozen in time. We learned only a few things: she was conductor of the Underground Railroad, and most of us thought that the Underground Railroad was literally underground—nobody really explained what that was. She was the quintessential race woman. We learned very little else about her, other than that she was this larger-than-life figure.

It was much later before any of us realized that she was only five feet tall. What I have been wondering all these years, since having been introduced to Harriet then—and being re-introduced to Harriet through the Combahee Statement—is why is it that radical, transgressive, outlaw black women are gendered male? The image of Harriet Tubman that I can remember over the years was a highly masculinized image. Many of you mentioned that. Why is that?

Is it that we cannot imagine strength or transgression in black women other than in some hyper-masculine form? I think that has happened over time with contemporary black feminists, contemporary black female activists, and so I think Harriet's legacy is extremely complicated. We didn't learn then that she was also a women's rights advocate; that part of her history was erased, in the same way that Frederick Douglass's women's rights activism was erased. So the only thing we could think about Harriet Tubman was her race work. I would say that her legacy is important, but it's also complicated and truncated. This symposium today has gone a long way toward rescuing Harriet from a much too narrow frame. She's gendered male and also asexual. Not manly, but very asexual.

Giddings: Just to add: she was also, as I remember, *silent*. Everyone else had speech. But Harriet didn't. So you can have that figure, and everyone could also provide their own interpretation. But what about the other aspects of her legacy? I remember coming of political age and looking at the freedom rides in the 1960s and remembering that the event was the first time I heard people, young people, talk about how they were willing to die for something. There is a kind of framework of heroism that really goes to that point.

Smith: Her legacy of activism was unswerving. Beverly just made reference to the Combahee River Collective; I don't know if that has been discussed today—I imagine perhaps that it has—but that is why the late twentieth-century black feminist organization in Boston chose the name of the river where she planned and led a military action during the Civil War that liberated at least 750 slaves in South Carolina. I've actually been to the Combahee River for one of those films that never actually got released.

We did an interview with me standing near that beautiful river. But as I said, it is a legacy of struggle and one of the things about struggle is, it is not ever over or finished. Of course, we are looking historically at Harriet Tubman's legacy, but her true legacy is for us to not sit silent and to not be inactive. I think there are so many black women whose names were not necessarily well known, who were in her legacy and in her spirit.

My favorite was Fannie Lou Hamer. Fannie Lou Hamer was the absolute pivot point of the Southern Civil Rights movement, of the entire Civil Rights movement. One of the reasons I hold her memory and legacy so dear is because I got to meet her in the mid-1960s when I had just graduated high school in Cleveland, Ohio, and I was very involved in the civil rights movement as a teenager in Cleveland . . . But even if I had never met her, I would have absolutely lionized and idolized her because her practice was so clear.

I had just finished reading Barbara Ransby's biography of Ella Baker, just as she releases a new book about Eslanda Robeson! . . . They are women whose names are also not well known. [Tubman's legacy] is about *practice*, I believe, and being tenacious and also not being motivated by ego and pettiness and "look how grand and important I am." Black women have held up the race ever since our abduction from our homeland to here, and we have often done it without expecting anything from it except the wonderful treasure of continuing to survive.

Giddings: Do you remember the conversation around Combahee? How you came to that name?

Smith: As usual, I do remember. It was the height of the "second wave" of the women's movement in the United States, and what we observed was that few black women were being taken into account.

So living in Boston during those years, "Sojourner" was already taken. That was the name of a women's newspaper, a really wonderful publication. And there was something called "Ain't I a Woman?" but I had read this wonderful very short biography of Harriet Tubman. It was put out by a leftist press: International Publishers. The book talked about the campaign, the successful campaign on the Combahee River. And I thought, why don't we name ourselves after an *action*, and not just a person?

Guy-Sheftall: I hope some young people in the audience will talk about this. I think it is a real challenge in the contemporary classroom to talk about the legacy of women like Harriet Tubman and make it seem real. You know, this generation is such a visual generation and talking about Harriet is sometimes . . . You get very excited and then you look out and your class is like . . . *(exaggerated dead stare)*. Slavery seems twenty centuries away, so what do you have to talk about to explain an Underground Railroad today? I don't know what they are doing in K–12 in terms of any history. So I showed the Ida B. Wells biography[2] which is very old, but still compelling. I really wish we had more visual material and film. Because I think Harriet is inaccessible and unreachable. She is someone who is so larger than life and so removed. It is really very hard to have Harriet's legacy seem real, and I mean, young people can correct me, but that is my experience in the classroom. We are so excited, and you don't have words or anything but static visuals. Some of my students said she was like their grandma!

Smith: The United States is probably one of the most ahistorical countries on the earth. That is for starters. History isn't valued here. This is the "new world." We are self-reinventors. And history, primarily at the K–12 level, is generally not well taught. The Southern Poverty Law Center did a study recently about how the Civil Rights Movement is taught in K–12 classrooms, and the results were abysmal. Abysmal! And even though, I believe, New York State was among the higher-ranking of the states, the actual score was by no means high. So even the highest-scoring states, as far as how the civil rights material was introduced, wasn't objectively of the highest quality.

I just want to say something we already talked about: Beverly was talking about visuals and not being able to relate to Harriet—that she seemed like someone's grandmother. I mentioned Lincoln already, but we live in the era of *Django Unchained;* these are crazy movies. Lincoln is not particularly crazy, just not accurate. But *Django Unchained* is a crazy movie. And I have to say, I was prepared to really not like it, but I really liked the movie. And I don't want to say why here. You can ask me later. But be that as it may, I knew that I was not witnessing a historical account.

I was thinking when Beverly was commenting about the legacy and reality of Harriet Tubman to our students, I was thinking, how fortunate we are—those in our age range—that we grew up with people whose lives had been touched by slavery. So my grandmother was born in 1886. That was about twenty years after the Civil War ended. Her mother obviously had been enslaved. They never talked about it, but the thing is I just feel that my sister and I got an understanding of racial reality through osmosis. They didn't actually have to talk about it; it was just in the air, you know. I had such a sense of how the world is organized; also, I was growing up during Jim Crow, despite being in the North, so that helped with the consciousness as well. But now we have our young people and others who say race doesn't matter to them. It's gratifying. It's gratifying that there are young people who say sexual orientation doesn't matter to them either. But the thing is that when nothing matters to you, you lose historical grounding.

Guy-Sheftall: That's why the *Meridians* collection of essays will be so important, because I don't think I've ever been to a gathering in which Harriet Tubman was spoken about in these complex, nuanced ways. And then it means that we can use these materials in classrooms. I still think we need a film.

Giddings: You know, your comments remind me that contemporarily we haven't been very good at connecting history to our lives, as you describe regarding your great-grandparents and grandparents. We lose these connections with not only them but [with] what is happening now. For example, one of the things I mentioned in our organizing a conference on human trafficking at Smith College was that the Trafficking Victim Protection Act of 2000 is based on the Thirteenth Amendment, the anti-slavery amendment. And of course the abolitionists, such as Tubman, are responsible for that, despite what is portrayed in the Lincoln movie.

Guy-Sheftall: I think we have to talk about Harriet Tubman in her complexity. I really like talking about her marital life and her eighteen-year period as a single person. I was also thinking about Anna Julia Cooper. There is also Ida B. Wells. I think we need to talk about their political activism, and we need to talk about their courageousness and struggles, but we also need to talk about their everyday lives and the choices that they made. That they were transgressing respected gender norms and the institution of marriage and other racial norms. I think that's one of the ways that we can have students, younger folk, not believe that these women have nothing in common with them. You know: their financial difficulties. I always think about Ida B. Wells liking to shop but never having enough money, these kinds of things. I think there is a way in which these iconic figures can come alive. I think about Coretta Scott King, whom I'm trying to rescue from *widowdom* in my scholarship. These iconic black women who just seem to be people who have nothing to do with me. . . .

Giddings: One thing that I liked about the conference, that Janell and the rest of you organized so well in terms of topics to explore, was the idea of talking more about situating Tubman in women's history and how many of the presenters have worked on curricula and syllabi for women's studies and for particular classes. That's one thing about this conference that makes me think about Harriet Tubman differently within the context of a syllabus and an anthology.

Guy-Sheftall: One thing we were saying over lunch is that not only is Harriet Tubman not included in women's studies syllabi but neither are people like Anna Julia Cooper or Ida Wells-Barnett. So there are these people, these extremely important influential black women, who were activists and who produced theory, who are absent from women's studies syllabi. Part of it, I think, is because there is so much emphasis on contemporary women of color and theorizing in women's studies, so the question I would like to raise is: what would women's studies look like if these women were at the center of what it is we do when we think about women's studies? It would totally disrupt notions of "first wave," "second wave;" it would totally disrupt notions of feminist theorizing. And I should also say that these women are not in African American studies either, generally speaking. So there are two interventions that we need to make, and I don't really know where to begin. Most of those women's studies textbooks focus almost entirely on the contemporary period, and I don't know why even Ida B. Wells, for example, who for me is one quintessential example of early intersectional theory, doesn't appear in these textbooks.

Smith: The fact that they are excluded [has to do with talking] about race and class and gender simultaneously, and obviously that eludes people's capacity even to this day. I'm shaking my head because of the fact that, back in the 1970s, I saw fit to work on a book, whose title I also chose, which is *All the Women Are White, All the Blacks Are Men, but Some of Us Are Brave: Black Women's Studies.* Yet Beverly, who is a practitioner of black women's studies right now, or Paula too, they're saying that it's still the same old, same old.

We fall through the cracks in both of those disciplines. And for me, Beverly being at Spelman at the Women's Research Center, if Beverly thinks this is what's going on, then, oh my goodness, we are lost! Because that's the epicenter. Spelman is the epicenter of organized black women's studies scholarship and practice, and it is happening there. But the thing is that you can't create a field on one campus, you can't keep a field of study healthy on one campus.

. . . I was particularly happy a couple of years ago when we went to a symposium at the University of Alabama in Tuscaloosa about black women public intellectuals, and Brittney Cooper was there, as was our younger sister from North Carolina, Alexis Pauline Gumbs. There are definitely people in younger generations who are keeping this going and who are creating more opportunities for truth-telling and for exposing our generation to what actually is the case, but that silence in conventional women's studies or mainstream women's studies teaching and curriculum and research regarding it just shows that race is a roadblock. It really is.

Giddings: What would Harriet think of President Obama? *(Audience laughs excitedly)*

Smith: Well, just for telling what would Harriet Tubman think, I think about what would my dear aunt would think, who raised my sister and me. She died in 1971. My mother died when I was young, so I didn't get to think of what would *she* think, because she was gone so early in my life. But I do think of my aunt, and I think about what she would think about everything, you know, computers, cellphones. I think the first thing is they would want to be pinched, like is this real? And then they—well, Harriet, and probably other people I just mentioned—they would really interrogate what it meant. I don't think they would take it for granted.

If we told her that President Obama is the president, she would want to know how and why that happened, and she would also want to know how my people are doing, what's the state of racism in this country and white supremacy in the present time? Did his being elected president, twice, keep a white man, all white men, from slapping a black lady on an airplane as happened a few weeks ago? Did he keep, and I won't say her name because I will butcher it, but did it keep Ms. Wallis,[3] the young girl who was in *Beasts of the Southern Wild,* did it keep her from being called the C word? No, it did not. So, the thing is that those people, generations past, first they would want to know is this real? And then when it's been established that it had actually occurred, they would be interrogating where we are. We are living in an incredibly historic time to have our first African American president, first president of African origin; his African origins are actually in Africa. But be that as it may, things are not all solved yet. It is the question that they would ask, and it is a question that we should all ask.

Guy-Sheftall: You know, I don't want to call somebody's name but after the very famous episode by the NAACP, where a certain black woman was fired,[4] a group of us were having dinner with her afterwards and I think Harriet would be on the same page as us. I think Harriet would say to President Obama: "Come to my house and let me give you a lesson in the deep structural, persistent, and systematic aspects of slavery's aftermath, and that without persistent struggle and naming of racism over and over and over again, it is not likely to go away." I think she would say: "We are very happy that you are in the White House; we don't know how you got there, and we don't know if this will ever happen again, but while you are there, we really want you to talk about race." I think she would say that to him, and she would probably say, "I know that's going to be hard, but now that you've been re-elected you can do a little better." I think she would say, "This thing called racism is so toxic and so pervasive, it has to be struggled against, over and over and over again."

Giddings: She might ask him, "What do you think freedom really means? I dragged you up here . . . What have you done for freedom?"

Smith: And she wouldn't just be asking about that relationship with President Obama, she'd be asking about that relationship to the state of our life in black and brown communities at the present day. Particularly around violence and particularly around how it's unfolding. I represent Arbor Hill on the Common Council, and that is one of our central, poor-people-of-color communities in Albany; Arbor Hill is like a stand-in, like Harlem is a stand-in. I always say what's going on today in Arbor Hill is the legacy of slavery. It's like how do you know what present repercussions of slavery are? You look at Arbor Hill and other communities like that: with the disinvestment and economic exploitation and lack of economic opportunities, to educational failure. I am not talking about individual failure; I am talking about how our educational system is failing our children.

All of those things are the legacy of slavery. She would also, and we would also, want to know about them. And what is it about black men killing each other and sometimes killing young women in the crossfire? What is that about? Because even for someone like me, such violence doesn't make sense at all, because when I was growing up, and I am not saying black people didn't kill each other, but it was not pandemic. I don't know if any of you've heard of *This American Life* that recently did a couple of [radio] shows, about these high schools in Chicago where at least a dozen black children were killed within one year. The way you get into a gang there is not because you make a conscious decision to be in a gang; but if you live in a certain place you are in the X gang, if you live in another place you are in Y gang, you don't have a choice. You are in a gang by the definition of the territory that you inhabit.

In Albany, we have people who look like each other, who are actually much related to each other by blood, but because they live on different sides of a neighborhood, also known as a city, they are at each other's throats!

The last thing I wanted to say about this situation, listening to that *American Life* piece about Chicago, I think of what many people usually do. I am thinking, where are the adults? The children are running the neighborhood!

The children are determining what goes on at that neighborhood. The adults have stepped back because obviously they are not armed or aren't as heavily armed as the young people. So the young people with the firepower have decided what goes on in communities for everybody, including their elders. There is something wrong with that.

Guy-Sheftall: I think [Harriet] would be absolutely appalled. I was talking here last night, and I mentioned an article that I've never forgotten from *Newsweek* in 1992 called "Losing Ground," in which a journalist was in an urban neighborhood and asked a group of young black folk, "What do you hope for yourself next year?" Many of them said, "I hope to just be alive next year." That is astounding! They do not mean that white people are going to be killing them, which is what Harriet Tubman would have imagined; what they meant was that "I am likely to be killed in my neighborhood by intraracial violence." I think Harriet would be appalled to come and see that a lot of the violence that we're dealing with is intraracial violence.

Giddings: They gave cocaine to slaves. Aren't we still doing that? I think I'll mention two things that have struck me about the presentations today, and we can open it up to the audience, and I just had a comment of liking so much of thinking about Tubman transnationally; I thought it was really important. And I love this idea of pulling together and correlating being single and being a radical and doing revolutionary work. And it really is in alignment with plenty of the women, like Ida B. Wells does her work when she is single, Ella Baker of course, so do you want to comment on that?

Guy-Sheftall: Let me mention something [that happened when] we (Johnetta Cole and myself for *Gender Talk*) interviewed Dorothy Height, and one thing I'll never forget is that she said over and over again: "I am *Miss*, M-I-S-S, Dorothy Height!" She really reveled in her single status. She said, "Did you get that? *Miss* Dorothy Height!" And her main role model (Mary M. Bethune) was single for most of her life. I mean, she had a husband somewhere. But I'll never forget that: "*Miss* Dorothy Height!"

Smith: This is also a very interesting question to me as an out black lesbian, because that is another status that I don't know if it helps your activism or not, but it can cause some challenges and heartaches because of the ostracizing and demonizing that goes on within our communities. But the thing I'm thinking about, having just read the Ella Baker biography, Barbara Ransby makes a clear point that [Baker] never changed her name, and many of the people whom she worked with at the time, closely and politically, didn't know she was married. It was fascinating because even when she was with her husband, which was for some time, they didn't know her marital status. She didn't see that as relevant to what she was doing, and she kept her name at a time when virtually no one did. And I find this thing about single women and marital status to be very interesting, and one other thing that I assume that you may know about even more than I, is how Mary McLeod Bethune had been a battered woman. I just found that fascinating. So, those day-to-day things actually do make a difference, and yet here [Bethune] was, like the leader of the race.

Guy-Sheftall: There is also a speculation about the nature of the partnership that Mary McLeod Bethune was in, once her husband was out of the way, and it was because of the Eleanor Roosevelt connection. . . .

Smith: . . . exactly, you know, because they were *tight,* and Eleanor Roosevelt, as we know, had relationships with women. Thanks to Blanche Cook we know that, and [to] other historians as well, and so there is more than meets the eye.

Giddings: Any questions or comments? *(Many hands go up)*

Audience member: My name is Aishah Shahidah Simmons. I am a filmmaker and faculty [member] now at Temple University in women's studies, and I wanted to say that I hear you, Beverly, about how Harriet is one of the few people that we hear about, and at the same time I really believe that if she were a white woman, or even if she were a black man and she had done what she had done, it would be so much more significant in the history.

Guy-Sheftall: She was the only black woman who was heard of if you were my age; I had not even heard of Ida Wells-Barnett and so many others. Why only Harriet Tubman of all the black women who were doing incredible things? So I am not minimizing her, all I am saying is that I could name ten or fifteen black men of Negro History Month, some of whom did rise to the level of Harriet. But it was only Harriet, the token black woman, and I think it is problematic that was the case for many, many years. Sojourner Truth wasn't even mentioned. And the fact that her women's rights activism was left out, I think was also problematic.

Smith: I just want to say one thing. I watched an abolitionist series on PBS, and I only saw episodes two and three, and I don't think Harriet Tubman was mentioned in that. They made Frederick Douglass the pivotal point for that. They had a few others, and Harriet Beecher Stowe. I almost lost my mind! Once when I was teaching African American writers, I thought, well let me teach *Uncle Tom's Cabin* in contrast to Jubilee by Margaret Walker, and I almost lost my mind. It was what it was. You see where I'm going . . . people get erased and excluded.

Audience member: I am a doctoral student from the School of Social Welfare. My question is in regard to what Harriet would do with the connection between the prison-industrial complex and race and the notion that it's the new slavery, which is explained in Michelle Alexander's *The New Jim Crow*. And I hear of the Underground Railroad and how it helped so many people escape slavery, and I am wondering how it relates to the issue of black men and black women being the fastest-growing population being imprisoned. What would she say about that, what type of Underground Railroad would she construct for the purposes of getting people out of this new modern slavery?

Smith: I think that those who are engaged and immersed and committed to the struggle, as you are, are involved in transforming or eradicating that prison-industrial complex; that is work Angela Davis started a couple of decades ago. *The New Jim Crow* is the latest lens into how pervasive it is, how evil it is, and how incredibly bizarre it is. I mean, the United States' incarceration rate is the highest in the entire world because of the legacy of white supremacy and genocide and imperialism.

But what [Harriet] would say is that we need to advocate for the abolition of prisons, not just the improvement of prisons, or having fewer people enter prison.

Audience member: My question, when I look at the women on this panel and I followed all your work as a young undergraduate, is when I think about the "Big Six"[5] and how we still fail to mention Miss Dorothy Irene Height. President Obama had his first Black History month panel on February 19 [2013]. He invited four historians, and I was one of them. (He would not allow the event to be videotaped; he said if you videotape it, I have to check all the papers.) We had to send in our answers to the questions in advance; he was concerned about how we were going to frame his administration around this discussion on race. I mean, I was happy to be there, but my hands were tied, my mouth had duct tape over it, and I could not even talk about the seriousness of this issue. So when I think about Harriet Tubman talking to President Obama, it would be in a closed room with no windows, a private conversation that he wouldn't even speak about. I guess we are back to the beginning of the struggle in so many ways. What would Harriet do when she looks out over what is happening? How do you change this?

Giddings: Thank you for reminding us of what the question is! What strikes me as you were speaking is that what she would do is almost unimaginable. Because she'd be helping people escape from prison. It is just beyond what we can imagine. So when you really think about what radicals do, what determined people do, what people with clarity do, and she did things physically as well. . . it really is interesting that we started thinking about what she would *think* instead of what she would *do*.

Guy-Sheftall: . . . I think it would be impossible for Harriet Tubman to imagine that there would be contemporary black people who don't get racism. She would be sitting somewhere, like many of us sit, and would just be confused, literally be confused by Condoleezza Rice or lots of people . . .

Audience member: Clarence Thomas? *(general laughter)*

Guy-Sheftall: Yeah! So, there is a world we are inhabiting right now that we were not prepared for. You cannot make any assumptions about anyone anymore based on their skin color, based on their class, based on their gender. You can't make those assumptions, so I think Harriet would be bewildered and would be deeply trying to understand what happened. On the other hand, I think she'd be trying to figure out what to do, but it's hard. It is hard to figure out what to do when you are sitting around a group of black folk, and they tell you that racism is no longer a problem. And you sit there, and you want to, I don't even know what you want to do, you just want to do something! You are immobilized.

Janell Hobson: In our time, the prison-industrial complex is our modern slavery. But I think if we're going to understand how someone like Harriet Tubman freed slaves from that system, we have to think of her in a more complex way, in terms of what she faced. What were her challenges? She had to motivate slaves! She had to motivate them to leave the plantation. I think this is what we're going to have to deal with in our own time, which is, some people don't get racism, just like those slaves who had to keep going under the barrel of a gun. I think we have to deal with the fact that not everybody is prepared for liberation and resistance.

Smith: What I would like to suggest is, do not assume that Harriet is not among us at this time. I mean, of course, she is someone who is for the ages, whose actual life, legacy, and reputation are transcendent, but I still assume that Harriet is among us at this time. When you said that if Harriet were alive she'd be leading people out of prison, I was thinking that when I went to Cuba, I met Assata Shakur.6 Somebody got her out. That is not the usual path for people being released from prison. I've been very involved with New Yorkers for Alternatives to the Death Penalty, and our objectives have repercussions for the freedom of black and brown people throughout the country, because we are primarily [concerned with] who is on death row in the United States.

So, that is getting people out of prisons, you know? And what is another way to get people out of prison? Never having them go in! So, I always say that my favorite way of dealing with the issue of violence in my community is—although I've been very involved in bringing the Chicago cease-fire to Albany, and with SNUG, which is "guns" spelled backwards—but I always say that my favorite way to do violence-prevention is to get these children out of secondary school, to get them to graduate high school then college, because there's a correlation between academic success and not being involved in violent criminal activity. Speaking to the police department, as I often do as a member of the Common Council, also as Chair of the Public Safety Commission of the City of Albany, I talk to the police all the time, which blows my mind—given my political history. But it's cool, it's fine, and sometimes when I talk to police, sometimes I get called about a crime. So I ask them, "Did this young person graduate from high school?" And they have information they can tell me, and the answer is always no. Virtually always no, they did not graduate. So, as I said, there's more than one way to get people, keep people out of prisons. All people who are working on that prison-industrial complex, they are in that tradition. Again, I say, do not presume that Harriet is not among you.

Audience Member: I'm Farah Tanis from Black Women's Blueprint. In other countries, when folks want to link what has happened in the past—unresolved human rights violations and atrocities—and link it to the present day (multigenerational effects), they use, for example, truth commissions. Within that particular kind of human-rights model, we could use the approach of a truth commission to talk about slavery and all those things that happened during slavery—like cocaine, which I had no idea about, how slaves were given cocaine—or to talk about and to link that, for example, to the prison-industrial complex. Or to link violence against women, and the rape and the ownership of women's bodies, to the high rates of sexual assault and domestic violence that still exist in the community. So, through a truth commission, what is really involved is some research. And we'd be looking at slave narratives, and we'd be looking at those today. And then you take those to the international community to show that there's been no change. And in fact, to some degree, some of these problems have gotten worse. And there is a need for the international community to really start looking at the United States and start holding the United States accountable for the continuation of slavery on various levels and manifestations. So yeah, it is possible . . . it is possible!

Giddings: Who is going to have the moral authority to make certain kinds of decisions? Even though I think that one should never give up on those things because it is what's needed . . . reparations.

Audience Member: Currently in the United States there is a series of World Courts of Women, the first one already happened in Oakland. It is around poverty as a crime against the human rights of United States citizens and other people in this country, and in the next eight months, one is going to be in Detroit, one in Philadelphia—October 18 and 20 of this year [2013]. They are councils of people who share their stories of resistance and struggle in front of an international panel of jurors who then make recommendations to the international community about holding the United States government accountable for crimes against economic human rights of the poor. The leadership is primarily, though not entirely, women of color. Evelyn Scott organized the one in Oakland.

Guy-Sheftall: The tribunals with respect to Palestine are another model. They are really compelling in that regard. I would just add getting back to a question that was raised: a couple of years ago I asked my students, what would they be prepared to die for? And number two, I asked them: what was the thing in life that they got the most pleasure out of? And the answers to those two questions almost sent me to my bed! The answer to the second question overwhelmingly was sleep: what is the thing that you most enjoy doing in life? Sleeping!

Audience: *(outraged voices in unison)* Wow!

Guy-Sheftall: And the question, what are you prepared to die for, having talked about some of these women, that was just a question they could not answer, just no answer.

Audience member: So what would Harriet say to them? Or do to them?! *(Audience laughter)*

Guy-Sheftall: I think Harriet would be in the same position that people like me are in in those classes. I think Harriet would . . . I leave my class, my almost three-hour class on Wednesday night and go to my office, and I have to do some serious reflection about what kind of pedagogical strategies and what kind of interventions can we make? And this is a feminist classroom! . . . This is a radical feminist classroom. This is not teaching Composition 101, which is what I used to teach. And it is becoming increasingly hard, and I'm not the only one who is saying this. It is becoming increasingly hard to teach feminist politics in our classrooms. The resistance is huge. So, I would say that Harriet would be like many of us—just really feeling a generational gap. The generational gap—I mean, we showed some of those horrendous [hip-hop music] videos in class—and our students said they didn't see anything problematic about them. So, all I know is that we have a lot of work to do. I don't know that I have all the answers, but I do believe that the Ida B. Wellses of the world, the Anna Julia Coopers, the Harriet Tubmans—whether they are present or past—they would just be struggling, really struggling to try to figure out how we can connect this generation with not just the past, but a present reality.

Giddings: And a future!

Guy-Sheftall: And a future.

NOTES

1. Janell Hobson is indebted to the meticulous work of her women's studies MA students at the University at Albany, who recorded and transcribed the conversation for this session: Elmira Alihosseini, Mahamadou Bagayoko, and Sara Querbes (edited by Janell Hobson, Beverly Guy-Sheftall, and Paula Giddings).

2. *Ida B. Wells: A Passion for Justice* (Dir. William Greaves, 1989, distributed by California Newsreel).

3. This is in reference to Quvenzhané Wallis, who was mentioned in a crude joke that appeared on the Twitter feed of the satirical publication *The Onion*, the night that she was honored as a nominee at the Academy Awards on February 24, 2013.

4. This is an allusion to Shirley Sherrod, who was embroiled in controversy when working in Obama's administration, which resulted in her unfair firing when targeted by conservative critics and the NAACP during a debate over racism.

5. A reference to the six men who were recognized as the leaders of the Civil Rights Movement: Dr. Martin Luther King, Jr., A. Philip Randolph, John Lewis, James L. Farmer, Jr., Roy Wilkins, and Whitney Young.

6. Assata Shakur (formerly Joanne Chesimard), a member of the Black Panther Party, was arrested, convicted, and imprisoned for the 1973 murder of a New Jersey state trooper. She later escaped from prison in 1979 and was granted asylum in Cuba, where she currently resides. She has received iconic status among the hip-hop generation, partly for her role as the aunt and godmother of the late rapper Tupac Shakur. She recently became the first woman to appear on the FBI's list for "Most Wanted Terrorists."

38. Feminist Freedom Warriors: (Linda E. Carty and Chandra Talpade Mohanty in conversation with Beverly Guy-Sheftall)

(2015)

CTM: We're talking to Beverly Guy-Sheftall on Sunday, June 7, in New York City. So, Beverly, you know we're talking to a lot of sisters who have actually been involved in feminist work for decades and you are one of our closest sisters here. Someone we do a lot of serious work with and a lot of playing with and so how about—let's start with you telling us a little bit about how you came to do the kind of feminist work that you do now, so at all levels, right. Personal—any kind of stories you want to tell, personal, political, intellectual, that have brought you to the scholarly, activist, institutional work that you've been doing for so many years.

BGS: Okay, hmm. Let me see if I can have a coherent narrative about my journey to feminist-scholar activism. If I had to locate a moment to begin with, it probably would be when I left Spelman College in 1966 as an undergraduate. I was an English major. Never had had any, of course, women's studies courses. I ended up going to Wellesley College for a year, a fifth year, and I ended up taking a course from Professor Patricia Speck called Women in Drama—and while I don't think it was a feminist course, it was the first women's studies course that I had. So, I think that taking that women's studies course, even though it was located in the English Department and it was a pretty traditional English course, it marked for me the absences and silences in my own training as an undergraduate English major. I left Wellesley and came to Atlanta University, came back to Atlanta to do a master's degree in English and, of course, I had no women's studies courses and I think I might have had one African American literature course, but I ended up—and I think it was the impact of having taken that Women in Drama course—I ended up deciding that I wanted to do a master's thesis on Faulkner's treatment of women in his major novels. Now this is 1969. There is no coursework, no mentoring, no professors, but I decided I was going to do this master's thesis. Now, by this time I'm beginning to read feminist literary criticism on my own. Feminist literary criticism was beginning to emerge, not within the context of women's studies programs, so I drew on the embryonic feminist literary criticism that was coming out and also the black aesthetic literary criticism, so at this point I'm a pretty focused literary scholar. Not very interdisciplinary, I don't think at that point. But doing the thesis on Faulkner's treatment of women in his major novels—I realize this now later—I'm beginning to do intersectional analysis by looking at race, class, and gender, though I'm not using that language.

CTM: Language, right.

BGS: But I'm looking at how a major Southern canonical white male figure deals with issues of race, deals with issues of gender, and deals with issues of class. So if I had to mark the moment it would be writing that thesis on Faulkner's treatment of women in his major novels, and I reread that thesis within the year and I was surprised.

CTM: Really?

BGS: I never got it published, I never did anything with it, which I should have, but I was surprised at what I was able to do in 1969 with no—

CTM: No mentoring, no community.

BGS: No mentoring, no formal, but just sitting with myself, reading feminist literary criticism and black literary criticism.

CTM: Yeah.

LEC: Wow, that's incredible.

CTM: But doesn't that suggest that whatever your frame was there was something that came before that?

BGS: Yeah, and I think my frame was absolutely shaped by my having grown up in the South and having been shaped by issues of race, gender, and class. And having been, sort of, located in the Civil Rights Movement, not Women's Movement, and also, I think having already been—though I didn't realize it at the time—having already been socialized by a feminist mother. I think that was critical, that is, my own personal relationship with my mother whose messages were feminist: if you get pregnant, I'll take you to get an abortion—in the '60s.

CTM: All the advice about boys and men, which I remember.

BGS: Very explicit; men are like buses—you know.

LEC: I like that one—

BGS: *[Laughter]* There's always another one coming—*[laughter]* so you don't need to fret, they are in huge supply. And don't be one of those women who just wants a pair of pants. *[Laughter]* That was, of course, heteronormative and all of that, but it was really—

CTM: Yeah and this—but we're talking this in the '50s

BGS: This is the '50s.

CTM: This is the '50s, exactly.

BGS: This is the '50s.

LEC: She was a feminist.

BGS: Also, she had left my father. This is the other thing. She had left my father when we were in the eighth grade. Only person in my family who ever disrupted a marriage. Left my father, unbeknownst to us and him, except on the day that we came home from school and our furniture's gone...and she's, we moved around the corner to my grandparents'. So, I already probably had that, but the intellectual, academic journey, I think, began with me writing that thesis. Should I keep going?

CTM: Yeah!

LEC: Mm-hmm.

BGS: Then I'm teaching—I finally come to the English department at Spelman in 1971, get back to Atlanta. And at this point I'm not even really trying to craft a career. I mean I'm married. Butch decides to go to law school at Emory, so I end up at Spelman because I needed a job, and within a few years I began to realize that my students didn't seem to know any black women intellectuals, didn't know any black women writers. This would've been around 1971. So long back—it's 1971—

CTM: Alright, so 1971—

BGS: So '71, I'm at Spelman, I'm in the English department, I'm teaching five

English courses, ooh—freshman English, the British—oh—terrible stuff.

CTM: Yeah.

BGS: Anyway, after a few years it's occurring to me that our students would be normal. Don't know anything about a black female literary tradition, don't know anything about black female intellectuals. They may have heard of Harriet Tubman. They may have heard of Sojourner Truth. So, a colleague and I, Roseann Bell, decided that we're going to publish this book. Now, mind you, I haven't even been to graduate school yet. I mean I have a master's but I haven't been to a doctoral program. Nor has she. We are untenured, junior faculty members in a very traditional, even somewhat hostile English department to what it is we want to do. The two of us decided, okay let's publish a book. We know nothing about publishing. So, this is what we decided to do—that we're going to publish this book that ended up being called *Sturdy Black Bridges: Visions of Black Women in Literature,* which was the first—amazingly—first anthology of black women's literature. In some kind of way, we ended up finding Marie Brown, who was an early black woman editor; at Doubleday, she was. And she shepherded this project through.

One of the most important things that I did during that process was to interview Toni Cade Bambara. We decided among many other things that in addition to having scholarly essays we would have interviews. I—very young, very shy, which people won't believe...a very shy, very reluctant, contacted Toni Cade and asked her if I could come and interview her. She said yes, so I trotted to Toni Cade's house with my little cassette recorder, which I didn't even know how to use. I had never used a cassette recorder... I had never even done an interview.

But I had been very much impacted by *The Black Woman* which came out in 1970. So this was four years later, 1974. So, I tried it there and we had one of the most extraordinary afternoons that I think I've experienced. And so that's, you know, when I think I really began to say to myself, okay, Beverly, you're going to do black feminist studies. And it was the impact of reading Toni Cade and talking to her, and that interview is really an amazing interview and it's been reprinted in a new work on Toni Cade. So, now I'm beginning to move away from literature and being much more interested in what we would now call black feminist studies...interested in essays, interested in nonfiction, and interested in people like Toni, who are also activists. I think the impact of Toni Cade was key. Then I decide, okay, Beverly, you don't want to go and get a

PhD in English. You want to go and get a doctorate in American Studies so you can do your women's studies and African American Studies. I go to Emory in the ILA, the Institute for Liberal Arts, which is a very, sort of, I would say progressive graduate space. And I take my first formal women's studies course, which is unusual for women and scholars in our cohort, to have actually taken a women's studies course as a graduate student.

LEC: As a PhD student.

BGS: As a PhD student. I took the first women's studies graduate course that was offered at Emory and it was offered by—really, an adjunct. She was the wife of a professor there. And so then I really decided I'm doing women's studies, I'm doing Black Feminist Studies and so on and I end up doing that dissertation on attitudes towards black women from 1880 to 1920. And then they—Elizabeth Fox-Genovese of all people, before I finished the PhD, asked if I would teach part-time in their graduate women's studies program. So, I started teaching graduate...I'm only thinking about this now...I started teaching graduate women's studies courses before I'm teaching undergraduate women's studies courses. I designed two courses. African American Women's History and African American Feminist Thought, out of which *Words of Fire* emerged. So that—Elizabeth asking me to teach those graduate courses—this would have been in the '80s...had a huge impact on my...on the kind of work that I would do...the kind of anthologizing work I would do and the kind of activist work I would do. So, that's the '80s. This is actually before I founded the Women's Center in 1981. So, by then I'm very clear about—still no PhD, no tenure, junior professor and—but I've been teaching graduate courses because there was nobody else to teach them. It was just Bessie Fox-Genovese—and this is before she abandoned feminism—and me.

CTM: Right, right.

LEC: Well, that's quite an unusual beginning and trajectory.

BGS: So I come to women's studies and come to feminism in very...one of the things that I say is that, I didn't come to it as a reaction to white women at all. I came to it at Atlanta University working on a master's thesis. I didn't come to it around white people. I came to feminism, academic feminism, in a black graduate space even though I was the only one doing it. And then, even in the university space, I wasn't navigating quietness. You know, ILA Emory

University Professor Elizabeth Fox Genovese says, can you teach and I said okay, there was no—

CTM: Yeah, you weren't struggling to do it.

BGS: No, I wasn't struggling.

LEC: That's really, you know, like black feminist praxis. Like you came to this through a kind of activism at the beginning, your mother is an organic feminist, I mean it was like just a natural sort of progression.

BGS: In familiar space, that is in black spaces and even in progressive sort of, a progressive space. Not an English department but in that Institute for Liberal Arts.

LEC: And through a lived space of self-empowerment.

BGS: Yes, and also coming to it because I was wanting to have my students have an experience of black women's intellectual traditions. So that was my motivation in terms of the publishing.

CTM: And then you—your first job was not Spelman?

BGS: No, first job was at Alabama State for two years.

CTM: Okay and that was after the PhD?

BGS: No, that was—my first job was—and you could do that then, you could get a job, a college teaching job with a masters' degree in 1969. So two years at Alabama State and then I came to Spelman in 1971, sort of serendipitously only because Butch, the person I was married to, ended up going to—

CTM: In Atlanta. At Clark, Atlanta.

BGS: No, Emory. Emory Law School. So I just went over to Spelman and said I need a job in the English department. And so they said well, we have these remedial English classes that we are teaching, and that's what I started. I started teaching remedial English just to get a job.

CTM: Okay, right.

LEC: Yeah, with that kind of unique beginning and that kind of framing that you were laying out for us that has so much of organic feminism in it as a black woman with a feminist mother and that kind of thinking, with no one mapping this path for you, or shepherding you through it or being your mentor—you know you just forge ahead—how do you see that work having impacted young women feminists that you know, as students? Knowing your scholarship now, how do you think it has impacted young feminists, in your imaginary?

BGS: Okay yeah. So let me say that probably the best decision that I made along these lines was leaving the English department, abandoning the English department, running away from the English department, becoming a refugee from the English department and founding the Women's Center in 1981. By now, it's very clear that I'm imagining that I want to create a radical black feminist space at Spelman that's not just tied to a women's studies major or minor, though that was part of it. And I'm very much impacted by visiting those women's research centers in New England. So by now the women's movement, the academic women's movement is kind of alive and well and I go to one of the main ones, which was at Wellesley College and I had been to Wellesley. Wellesley was the first one I went to and I came across Pat Bell-Scott who was working at the Wellesley Women's Resource Center and was of course one of the co-editors of *But Some of Us Are Brave*. I went and interviewed...I'm just now remembering this...I went and interviewed Barbara Smith who was the other co-editor, teaching part time at—still I think the English Department at Emerson College. So my visit to New England and coming into contact with black women who were in these women's spaces said to me okay there's no HBCU that has a women's studies program, there's no HBCU that has a women's center so that's what you really want to do. And you're interested in not just a women's studies program, but you're interested in research. And we founded *SAGE: A Scholarly Journal on Black Women* two years later, Pat Bell-Scott and I. But you're also interested in sort of bridging the divide between community and Spelman because there had been very little of that. So community outreach was important and I imagine community outreach to be global, somehow.

It was becoming clear that if you had a center, if you had an institute, you could write grants and get money, which you can't do as a regular faculty member. The first grant we had was from the Mai Foundation, and we would come to receive really important grants from the Ford Foundation, and this was because I became a member of the National Council for Research on Women and came in contact with those folk who were working at Ford and who were getting Ford grants. So that space, that Women's Center space I think enabled us to create not just an academic, intellectual space but an activist space.

And I think that the things that we attached to the Center, the Toni Cade Bambara Scholar Activist Collective and a whole range of black feminist organizations, have had a tremendous impact on students because they take the courses, you know, they begin to...initially they weren't taking the courses. I mean, I might have had five students in my women's studies class.

LEC: Wow.

CTM: But when are you talking? Are you talking early '80s now.

BGS: Early '80s, so '81. So we started the center in '81 and I started teaching Intro to...we crafted the minor immediately because it was just me teaching Intro and Feminist Theory and then they could take three other courses somewhere else and most of them were in the English department or history. We started that minor in 1981 and then over time we added the activist component to it and hiring Bahati (Kuumba) was probably critical to the activist part. So that space has had a huge impact on the development of a sort of new generation of black scholar-activist-feminists who explicitly self-identify as that and who know that that's what they're doing.

CTM: Yeah. So there's a whole...there are two or three generations that have gone through—

BGS: Two or three generations, that's right. And this commencement we had the largest number of women's studies majors that we graduated, which was twenty.

LEC: Right, in 2015.

BGS: In 2015, so yeah.

LEC: Who have been trained to understand that academic feminism is also connected to a community engagement commitment. So unique.

BGS: And ironically this year we had for the first time both the salutatorian and the valedictorian who graduated as women's studies majors.

CTM: Yeah, I saw that.

BGS: And who are also activists. And I think that, you know, were our program not the way it was, someone like Banah who came there as a—came from an activist family in Syria even as she grew up in Arkansas, she found a home in a very activist and intellectually stimulating space around feminism.

CTM: I think what's interesting also is that when you created a major at Spelman first you called it comparative women's studies, right? And you are one of the few people I know who actually does black feminist studies with a global reach, right? So why do you think that's the case? It's almost like you do transnational black feminist studies.

BGS: Let me tell you why that was. When I was teaching graduate students at Emory, when I was teaching PhD students at Emory, they asked me to teach a global feminist course and I taught a third world feminist course. It's quite possible that had I not been teaching graduate students many of whom were South Asian...so I devised that third world feminisms course but I decided that that was too big and then I started teaching global black feminisms at Emory. And I think that that shaped—that is probably what shaped my thinking about global stuff. It was those students saying can you teach something in addition to African American? And then the global black feminisms, which was really broad, so I think that that's the answer.

LEC: This is truly incredible to me because you won't remember this but in 1988 I came to Spelman and I talked to you—'89—talked to you about going to teach a third world feminism course at University of Toronto.

CTM: Yeah.

BGS: I do.

LEC: When I was getting that job there and I said I'm developing this—you remember that?

BGS: Yes, I do. Did I share the syllabus?

LEC: You shared the syllabus with me.

CTM: Yeah.

BGS: And that probably was an early—

LEC: Very early.

BGS: Very early.

LEC: You said I'm trying this out.

BGS: And I was teaching myself. And I was also having to teach myself—I mean I'm literate but I didn't know what structural adjustment was. I mean I didn't know any of that.

CTM: Right, of course.

BGS: So.

LEC: And I was so excited by it because when I saw the syllabus I said yeah, these are the things exactly that I know how to do, because here she was a literary scholar trying this out—

CTM: Trying this out—

BGS: And I was very honest with the students. I said I'm way away from my—training—

CTM: Comfort zone, yeah.

LEC: Unbelievable.

CTM: But the other thing is—so when did we meet?

BGS: We met when you were at Oberlin before Hamilton.

CTM: It was around exactly that time.

BGS: What year was that?

CTM: It's around the same year...when did I move—I think I moved to Oberlin in—the Audre commencement was '89!

BGS: Okay.

CTM: So I had been there two years then I think. '87 I moved to Oberlin.

BGS: So all of these things were happening.

LEC: Happening at the same time.

CTM: Yeah.

BGS: It was—

CTM: Late '80s it was for sure.

BGS: It was those graduate students at Emory I'm sure that pushed—said can you do this and I said, well, I can try.

CTM: But you could have done it and you could not have taken it seriously. I mean I think also what's important is the commitment in terms of certain decisions about what forms of knowledge really are important and why the connections are important.

BGS: The other thing I have to say that I think was connected to that: I had my first really impactful cross-cultural experience when I went to India in 1971. I mean '73. So two years after I get to Spelman, there's a study travel tour and I go to India for three months. My project is Indian women writers and so when I came back I incorporated my Indian women writers—so I would say that probably made me more open for the students to say can you come and teach third world feminism because I've had a little bit of cross-cultural experience. So that trip was—

LEC: Because I remember you telling me that you're feeling this out, that I'm feeling my way through this, don't know a thing about structural adjustment and economics. And we talked about structural adjustment and the IMF and what it's doing and that it has these policies that are so, you know, regular everywhere it goes. And I remember thinking, she says she doesn't know anything?

BGS: No I did but you know—now I'll tell you the other thing I think. The person I was married to was an economist, so he would say, you know, this stuff is not that complicated. He said I could give you just enough stuff, basic stuff for you to go in there and not embarrass yourself.

CTM: Right, that's important.

BGS: So I was accustomed to talking to an economist for a long time, even though half the time I didn't know what he was talking about.
[Laughter]

LEC: This is truly...this is really interesting. What would you say, Beverly, are some of the challenges then given this kind of history and this development? What are some of the challenges you encounter having come to doing this kind of work?

BGS: Ooh, I would say the first challenge was hostility on the part of African American scholars to feminism and to having a very explicit, loud advocacy around LGBTQ issues. I mean, one of the things that I was recalling recently was going to an Institute of the Black World gathering at which Barbara Smith, Pat Bell-Scott, and I were on a panel and they stopped us halfway through and said, "Are you all lesbians?"

CTM: Uh-oh.

BGS: Oh yeah.

LEC: When you say recent—when?

BGS: No, I was talking about it recently. I had remembered it.

LEC: Yeah, yeah.

BGS: So huge hostility to naming yourself a feminist and being in the company of out black lesbians. I mean it was a huge hostility

LEC: Yeah, we did talk about that before.

BGS: Oh, and then one of the worst experiences that I have ever had, that we have ever had: we wrote a little proposal to do a faculty development workshop on black feminist studies. This is Pat Bell-Scott, Gloria Hull, Barbara Smith, and me. It was for black faculty at HBCUs, and we invited them there for a week and people were so hostile. We had to—the workshop had to be disbanded. They accused us—

CTM: When was this?

BGS: This was 1980—

CTM: So it was in the '80s.

BGS: It was in the '80s. They accused us of trying to convert them to lesbianism. It was in the aftermath of that that Pat and I decided we would do

SAGE: A Scholarly Journal on Black Women. So huge hostility. Initially, the hostility was mostly from nationalist and anti-feminist African American women and men. Huge challenge. And then the students early on didn't want to take our courses. You know they would come and say, I'm not a feminist, I hate feminism but I'm going to take this course and blah, blah, blah. So initially I would say that was the biggest challenge. Just constantly having to explain why you're doing women's studies.

CTM: Ok, others? Other challenges? Has that remained the same? Has that shifted?

BGS: I think it has shifted. I think in the last decade there's not as much hostility to—I mean you can say you're a black feminist without people, uh—

CTM: Yeah.

LEC: But some of it is like the new and old racism.

BGS: Yeah, that's right. That's right.

LEC: Old was *du jour* but now—so it's there but—

CTM: It's in a different guise.

LEC: You know better than to say it.

CTM: Yeah. Yeah, yeah, yeah, yeah.

BGS: I think the other challenge which I think I've managed to avoid is burn out. Just sheer—when I think about just the huge number of things we took on. You know, activism, students, traveling. You know, going to all those international conferences, you know, Kenya, Beijing, constantly trying to be places, it's draining. So I think that's a huge challenge, figuring out how to conserve your energy. The thirteen years that we did *SAGE*—this was on top of regular jobs, and for us regular jobs were 4-4 then 3-3—and sustain that journal for thirteen years with no—very little, institutional support even though Johnetta was there. I mean I would literally go through the mailbox every day and process subscriptions at night at home, for thirteen years. Every day I'm doing that. No clerical support. That was really draining, doing the journal on top of doing the women's center on top of teaching on top of teaching graduate students at Emory for over a decade, with PhD students and exams.

CTM: Right.

BGS: *[Laughter]*

LEC: You know it still amazes us, right? We know your schedule even today, even now and it still amazes us. So one thing I always wanted to ask you, how do you avoid suffering burnout? I know you love, absolutely love what you do. I know that part of it is energizing and empowering. We understand all that. How do you avoid the burnout, Beverly? Because we have seen—it's taken out sisters.

BGS: You know what I think? I think that I have lots of outlets and shopping is one of them.

CTM: Yeah, I was going to say, she shops!

LEC: We know that.

BGS: Friendship, you know. Spending time with friends, eating at restaurants.

LEC: Pleasures.

BGS: The other thing that I just have to say. I have a very unstressful personal life. You know, if you don't have a partner—

LEC: I can relate on it.

BGS: Children. Unfortunately, parents who—my mother died when I was in my thirties so I don't have nuclear family responsibilities. I have almost no caretaking responsibilities so that when I come home, it's just me. I think that's huge. I don't think I could have crafted the life I have if I had all these other things. If I had lived in a city where I had relatives, you know, if I had a stressful personal relationship, marriage partnership or whatever, I think it would've been very, very hard. So I am very free to—

CTM: To shop, go out, to have vacations with friends.

BGS: To not go to the grocery store for a week. You know, just imagine. People come to my house and say you don't have any groceries. I say no, but I can get some!

CTM: Yeah.

LEC: Yeah, but it's true. Not having to be a caregiver is a major...

BGS: Probably the most caregiving I do is long-distance with my sister and students.

CTM: I think you do a lot of that stuff with students actually.

BGS: Yeah.

CTM: Yeah, you do a lot of that stuff with students.

BGS: I think otherwise I would really be burned out.

CTM: Don't you think some of that also has to do with having a real conviction in the work that you are doing?

BGS: But I don't know that I'm conscious of that.

LEC: But that's there and people who know you can see it and feel it.

BGS: I don't—but you know what I don't—it must be there but it's not—

CTM: It's not on the surface for you.

LEC: You see it's seamless because it is so integrated into your life.

BGS: Like when we said we're going to do this journal, okay? I had no idea what that meant.

LEC: What or how.

CTM: Yeah.

BGS: And so you know you say, okay, I've got this journal to do and you just sort of do it. Or like the anthology. I mean, if we had known...if we had known—

CTM: Yeah, I know...how difficult it's going to be. All the things many of us have done at certain moments, which were risky, but we didn't have any clue what that meant so you did it, because you weren't cautious and also no one else was doing it.

BGS: That's true.

CTM: I mean some of this is also groundbreaking stuff because...and if no one else has done it no one is saying to you don't do this also, because this is—

BGS: And also—I won't call a name but—also just having to sort of ignore people's little cruelties, like the first issue—which was really a strong one—the first issue of *SAGE,* a very well-known black woman literary critic, there was one page that had a typo on it. She Xeroxed those pages and passed them around.

CTM: Aye yai yai yai yai, this is the academy for you.

BGS: And you just have to park that somewhere. Because otherwise you'll be...you'll just be, you know, sad all the time. *[Laughter]*

CTM: But also, I think, but that's also part of how you create solidarities with people is that there are certain things you park.

BGS: That's right, that you just park.

CTM:: If you don't park them, forget it.

BGS: Oh yeah. And I think we've parked a lot. You know, when I think of the women that we...because of our work regularly have to interact with, a lot of that's complicated.

CTM: Yeah, absolutely.

LEC: Gotta do a lot of parking.

CTM: Yeah, yeah.

BGS: Hmmmmm.

CTM: So what about—okay, so given this history of the sort of collaborations that you've had constantly---collaborations with, you know, lots of different sets of women and feminists in not just places, but walks of life---what do you see as the best way forward for feminists working across all our racial, class, etc. differences?

BGS: I do think we have to really make an effort to do more cross-class collaborations, okay. And I had sort of lost that actually. My most cross-class collaboration was with the Black Women's Health Project for years. I mean those were grassroots women not mostly academics. It was difficult. I do less of that now. So I think that we, that it's quite possible to lose that if you don't make an effort. You can just mostly be around academic feminists.

I think you have to connect to certain kinds of organizations, like Project South. What I'm finding over time, with priorities, certain things just fall away and that has sort of fallen away. You know, when the Black Women's Health Project sort of left Atlanta and Byllye Avery left Atlanta, I wasn't as motivated because those were also about relationships.

CTM: Right. But say in general... so this is particularly what emerges for you in your narrative and location, but if you were to be asked in general, what are the kinds of things feminists need to be paying attention to, or working on, or strategizing about, to build solidarity right now, at this completely neoliberal time where there are divisions that are even being put in place but which are not visible to us sometimes? And a commodification of particular groups of people, the celebrity culture, I mean there's a whole bunch of stuff that is so much a part of our everyday lives.

BGS: Let me tell you what I also think. I don't know if you all have read the *New York Times* article about the fissures between trans* feminists, trans and—that's a huge one.

LEC: Big thing, big thing.

BGS: Big one. I'm not convinced anymore that it's possible to do effective healthy collaborations across all kinds of difference.

CTM: Okay, interesting.

BGS: I mean when I go to spaces and trans* feminists are saying I can't use the word "woman," I just, I'm not likely to go there. And I'm not likely to spend a lot of my time trying to figure out how to bridge that.
[Laughter]

CTM: So I guess the question then becomes how are we defining radical feminist praxis and what our vision is that then allows us to cross certain kinds of borders and build solidarity.

LEC: And build solidarity and still challenge neoliberalism. Some of these fads are not challenging it.

BGS: And I also think, the other thing that I really think—I think that we've gotten further and further away from grassroots women. And I think that you're not going to form very many solidarities with them if you're just constantly talking about trans* issues, or you can't use the word woman or...you know, at one of the sessions yesterday, the Black Arts Initiative session, a young man did a wonderful talk on trans* or queer readings of whatever. I mean it was brilliant, but a black woman raised her hand—she's an academic—and she said I don't understand anything you just got through saying. I'm not even sure that she even realized he was trans* and when he said top surgery, I mean, you know, it was clear that she was, it was like—

LEC: It was foreign to her.

BGS: It was totally foreign. I think that these disconnects are actually huge between even young folk who are trained in academic spaces, academic, highly theoretical, feminist spaces. I don't know that they have the language to talk to those women in the Black Women's Health Project. And I think that that's really critical. I don't see that happening very much. I would say that it is possible to even be a radical feminist of color and have very little contact with the grassroots women. And I think that's really bothersome. And I also remember how difficult it was when we were trying to do this work with the Black Women's Health Project. They did not want to come to Spelman's campus even though we were all black women.

CTM: Right.

LEC: I knew a bit about that, yeah.

BGS: They felt alienated from the Spelman campus. They felt like sometimes they didn't know who we were talking about. So, I think that we need to look for some examples of the way that works across class. I don't see a lot of it happening.

CTM: Between academics and women who are non-academic, but who are doing various forms of organizing or agitation for justice.

BGS: That's right. I mean I look at the Black Lives Matter movement, I mean the Black Lives Matter mobilization, and you know they are very impatient and frustrated with the older civil rights establishment. It's been very hard for them to create solidarities, and of course they have the gender split up in there, you know with the younger men basically—so, you know—I don't know. But I will also have to say like right now, one of my biggest frustrations is with younger black feminists who keep wanting me to bleed to Beyoncé as a feminist. *[Laughs]*. I mean this is huge. And it's the question that I get the most when I go around on college campuses among young black feminists. What do you think about Beyoncé? Do you think she's a feminist? And I want to say, "What!" I mean I've spent a lot of—I don't want to talk about Beyoncé!

LEC: I get that in class. I get that in classes. I go straight to the material conditions of people's lives and force them to answer the questions.

CTM: Mm-hmm,

LEC: And they can't answer the questions.

BGS: So even those solidarities—that is a huge generational split. And I'm not talking about now college students, but I'm talking about the generation split in terms of the Janelles and the pleasure feminists, I don't see them having any interest in grassroots women of color issues. They are very focused on popular culture, image, you know, all of that. So I don't even know how, I don't even know how—I'm challenged by appealing to my own students around feminism because they've been socialized to believe that it can mean whatever it is that you want it to mean.

CTM: Yeah, absolutely.

LEC: Do you think that—you know, I think we're all experiencing something similar, yeah? And as I'm listening, I'm thinking, it takes me right back to where you started with, the grassroots, the connection to grassroots women. And so many of us are working within and in grassroots organizations still and so you just find like little isolated pockets. You're doing this kind of work and you're trying to teach this kind of work but you feel the exact same thing that it's not happening across the borders in terms of feminism and where we want to see it going, no? Do you think that has something to do with feminism in the academy having lost its way around class?

BGS: I do. I really do think it's lost its way around class.

LEC: Not dealing with class.

CTM: But more than that, too, it may be that feminism in the academy no longer believes or most interdisciplinary feminist scholarship does not pay attention to political economy anymore. I think that that is—which is not true in the global South, but it is true here.

BGS: I think so, I think so, I think so!

LEC: Yeah, political economy is completely missing so class is something so—

CTM: Is out.

LEC: And class is the core, you know, so—

BGS: So there is an ability to deal to some extent with race but class is very hard.

CTM: Right. So if you were to be asked—if you were dreaming about what it is you want to see happen in the future to transform women's lives, what are the things that come to mind to you?

BGS: Yeah, so the poverty issue is huge. I mean, the lack of access to resources, inability to just make certain kinds of choices and I'm not now talking about necessarily even women in, let's say, public housing. I mean I even think about women who have a huge amount of debt from college and graduate school in an adjunct professor position.

CTM: Right.

LEC: Or three or four of them.

BGS: Yes, and when I hear them talking—no prospect for a stable tenure-track job with benefits. So what does that mean? So what does that mean? We're not even talking about a high school graduate. We're talking about highly educated women who cannot make ends meet and who don't have health insurance and who sometimes are forced to make really difficult choices about the partnerships that they, you know, get into. So I worry. And I don't see that women's studies is—

CTM: A place where that's being addressed.

BGS: No, you know there's a big movement about adjuncts, but women's studies is not—

CTM: Spearheading it or any of that stuff.

BGS: No. I would say that what I see happening is that highly privileged senior women's studies people are moving into administration.

CTM: Yeah.

BGS: Becoming deans, provosts, college presidents. And they don't even talk about adjuncts.

CTM: No.

LEC: That brings up the old critique of feminism, no? That it's been good assisting careers for those women, the same class of women. Very good for them. And some of that even in the global South. That where—places where feminists, academic feminists in particular don't have any relationship with grassroots women's organizations or structures and you talk to those women and they'll say—

BGS: Or even staff. Or even staff. That's the other thing. Even staff on college campuses. None.

LEC: No relationships, no new relationships.

BGS: I mean Levi was appalled at those status of women reports that they do at Johns Hopkins. They don't even look at the supports. They just look at the professionals. The majority of women at John Hopkins are support staff and they're not even in the report. And they just look at him like, oh ...

CTM: Right, right.

BGS: And even when I think about the support staff at Spelman, they're rreduced now from twelve-month to ten-month contracts which is a substantial cut in yearly salary. You know, my secretary makes $28,000. Most of them are single with children. There are days that they have to carpool because they run out of money to buy gas. So I don't have to go out to public housing. I could just listen to those women on Spelman's campus and know, you know—we try to do a—what is it—what's the wage, what's that project on campuses? We tried to do that on Spelman's campuses; it got shut down. And even the women admit...I mean we're talking about a women's college, a black women's college. The women administrators there are not caring about those women.

LEC: Yeah it's something about...

BGS: Fair Wage.

LEC: Fair Wage Project, yeah.

BGS: And you can't get most faculty on these campuses to care about...

LEC: Including feminist faculty.

BGS: Including feminist faculty, to care about the low wages of—so we don't even need to go out, we could just stay on these campuses. And also, there's—we've tried—there's very little solidarity between staff and faculty.

CTM: Oh yeah.

LEC: It's startling. It's startling.

CTM: Yeah, yeah. No, that's true. So what is the future for feminism then, Beverly?

BGS: Well, I think feminism has—I think the impact that feminism has on young men, I mean, young men and young women who come into these classes is huge. I don't think it's made its way to K-12, which people like Peggy McIntosh tried to do. I mean, I don't know if private schools have women's studies courses. So we know that it has an impact on college students, young college students. I don't think it has an impact on the situation of women who work in most spaces.

CTM: Right. So—that's the big challenge. Right?

LEC: It's so true. We have the thing about adjuncts and staff at SU, and it's a big thing to organize outside of women's studies. It's not there. It's not related to them.

BGS: Mm-hmm.

CTM: When women's studies was first started and it was not an academic field, it was much more about committees for women on campus. At those moments, I think there was more of a sense of cross-class space. And I think that was the case in a lot of spaces in the beginning, which were all white feminist beginnings, more or less, right? I mean what's interesting about it then is it suggests that we have been attentive to race and sexuality in ways that have completely invisibilized class—

LEC: Eclipsed class.

CTM: Eclipsed class altogether.

BGS: That is the case.

CTM: And so there are some people who talk in smart ways about all these things but a lot of times, because of the sort of development of the field into more and more theoretical and abstract paradigms of scholarship, you know there is a way in which we end up talking to each other about certain kinds of things. And those issues have been very complexly and interestingly dealt with but it's like the whole material basis has—

LEC: Collapsed.

CTM: Has collapsed or fallen out.

LEC: It's like you say, no political economy taking place, no political economy is taking place, no political economy analysis is taking place. All these separate identities and stuff, this has to be the foundation of it—political economy. How do we talk about sexualities and the multiplicity of changes and levels and differences—that I now have a particular gender pronoun or no gender pronoun—without understanding the foundation of political economy?

CTM: Okay, people, I think we're going to stop. Thank you so much!

BGS: Ok!

39. | *Auburn Avenue* Interview **(2016)**

AA: What does it feel like to have such a pivotal role in the history of Black feminism?

BGS: *[Laughs]* Oh my goodness. When I first got involved in Black feminism, it was a pretty demonized concept in the African American community. I constantly had to justify or explain why I was calling myself a feminist. People would say it's anti-male, it's divisive, and that Black women didn't really need feminism. It was pretty difficult space to constantly claim, though I constantly claimed it. What makes me pleased over these 40 years is that I don't have to constantly justify why I am a Black feminist. I see loads of young Black women *and men* taking Women's Studies courses, getting involved in progressive feminist struggles, and speaking out against misogynist images in popular culture, speaking about violence against Black women—I'm speaking specifically about the Say Her Name movement. At this point in my career, I feel happy about the way feminism has been embraced.

AA: Take us back to the 1960s... how was your experience as a college student and young Black woman, then?

BGS: Back in the 1960s, I was a student at Spelman. Even though there was clearly sexism on college campuses and sexism in the beginning racial struggles, our attention was focused on race. As a college student I wasn't thinking so much about gender issues, even though I was very aware that there were huge differences between the way students at Spelman and students at Morehouse were treated in terms of freedom to move about. I was aware of rigid curfews and a dress code at Spelman, not in place at Morehouse. I didn't have a feminist framework in which to view it.

AA: In intellectual and educational spaces, was there ever a time when you found it difficult to say exactly what you wanted to say?

BGS: Not much. I did experience the consequences of being open about my political thoughts. However, there are a lot of taboo subjects in Black communities. Sexuality is one. In gender politics, especially with respect to Black men and women, there are taboo subjects. Probably one of the most difficult moments around this issue was the Clarence Thomas and Anita Hill situation in 1991. Speaking out in favor of Anita Hill was, surprisingly, a controversial stance to take. Very few Black folk spoke out against Clarence Thomas. Speaking out against sexual assault in the Black community is still difficult.

AA: Has the American society become more aware of its inadequacies in recognizing and dealing with the issue of equality for women, particularly Black women?

BGS: Sometimes I say "yes" and other times I say "no." It's sort of a conundrum. It depends on where you are and who the audiences are. If you look at national polls, many white people would like to believe that race and gender are no longer issues. If you did polls in Black communities and asked them which of us was having the most difficulties—Black men or Black women—they would say Black men. I would say the particular plight of Black women, vis-a-vis race, is still invisible to most people including some Black women. A good example of that fact is that we had to have a movement called Say Her Name to say that Black women are also victims of police violence.

AA: What is your opinion of the modern-day Black liberation movement that is currently taking place?

BGS: Sometimes I don't know where it is. It seems to be fractured and not as public or visible as I would like for it to be. It seems to be off the radar for the media. If I think about the 1960s, 70s or 80s, sometimes it can be frustrating in terms of the lack of visibility.

AA: How important are writers in these types of movements?

BGS: Writers are as important today, but I don't think they have the same level of influence. I think social media have eclipsed the importance of writers. I don't know if people even read the newspaper like they used to. People used to read *Crisis* magazine and Black magazines that dealt with political issues. There is a young generation of people that doesn't engage print media.

AA: With regard to LGBTQ rights, what is your opinion on admitting transgender students at same-gender institutions?

BGS: I am in favor of admitting transgender students to same-sex institutions. However, I would quickly add that our colleges and universities must do a lot of work on our campuses with respect to raising consciousness about the issue. They need to make sure that transgender students are not discriminated against once they get there and that there are safe spaces.

AA: Can you talk a little about the Toni Cade Bambara Scholars/Writers/ Activists Program at Spelman College?

BGS: The program, that's now in its 16th year, is one of the most important scholar-activist spaces on campus. It is one of the spaces in which students can develop activist and leadership skills. It is the only annual conference that students conceptualize and organize, and it reaches out to communities outside of Spelman. We recognize Toni Cade Bambara's birthday in March; however, during the year on every Friday, the Toni Cade Bambara collective meets in the Women's Center. We host speakers and activities on campus and the conference is a culminating activity. We are one of the few HBCUs that annually recognizes a radical, Black feminist writer.

AA: What is the future of Black feminism? What, in your opinion, are the next steps?

BGS: I thought I would never be saying this, but I think Black feminism is strong. I just came back from the Black Feminist Think Tank in Michigan. It is a group of mostly young Black feminist scholars that are committed to the think tank collective. We're producing really important books and working on important projects. I guess I'm pretty convinced that Black feminism will live on college campuses. I'm more concerned if Black feminism is confined to the academy. I wish that we could get Black girls and boys involved before they get to college, when they are in high school. If I had my wish list, number one would be figuring out how to take Black feminism to communities that are not necessarily university communities.

AA: Considering your past work and contributions to the field, do you have any regrets?

BGS: I wish I had been louder and more radical. There were times when I sort of retreated because I got exhausted. I wish I had been more "in your face,"' particularly at Black colleges.

40. Honoring Beverly Guy-Sheftall, by Moya Bailey (2018)

What follows below are my remarks at the 2018 National Women's Studies Association Conference honoring the work of Beverly Guy-Sheftall.

It is my great honor to say a few words about the incomparable Beverly Guy-Sheftall. To give her her flowers while she is here. Who would have thought a shy girl from Memphis, Tennessee, would become a world-renowned educational freedom fighter by working on gender justice at Spelman College? As a first-year student from little bitty Fayetteville, Arkansas, I was floored when Dr. Guy-Sheftall told my entering class about Sarah Baartman's experiences as a human exhibit in Europe, the way her body was examined in life and death under the cloak of objective science but which was in reality reflective of scientific racism and sexism. In my first week at Spelman, before I'd even attended a class, Dr. Guy-Sheftall had blown my mind! After that moment, I knew I wanted to take every class I could with her. At some point she revealed one of my favorite stories about her childhood. Her mother insisted that she did not need to take home economics. Beverly's mother knew that her daughter had other work to do and other skills to learn. Her mother's nurturing of her intellect allowed her to become the venerable scholar she is today, and her mother's actions also account for Beverly's rarely if ever used oven.

Who has time to cook when you are growing a field of scholarship?

In typical Gemini fashion, Beverly is doing all the things all the time. If you ever send Beverly an email, don't be surprised if you get a response at 2:30 am. A prolific night owl, Beverly will answer your email while in between books she's reading and finishing that day. Her nightly productivity has resulted in multiple collaborative texts, the development and flourishing of the Spelman College Women's Research and Resource Center, and her latest venture with the Mellon Foundation, a Gender and Sexuality Institute dedicated to addressing the violence disproportionately experienced by Black women and girls.

Who has time to sleep when you are remaking institutions?

No one has a more eclectic sense of style or a more pithy set of one liners. Beverly does not dabble in shade. Beverly reads. And her reads are legendary. Some of you were there, in 2004, when Beverly said, at the Chicago hip hop feminism conference organized by Cathy Cohen, that it was ludicrous to compare Madonna's self-fashioned and commercialized eroticism to the exploitation of Black women dancers in rap videos. Beverly said it so simply, "You can't compare exploitation to the whorification of white women."

Who has time for propriety when you are telling the truth?

Beverly set the stage for me to be in that room, at that conference, and hear that comment. It was in her Feminist Theory class that the so-called Nelly protest was born that launched me, Leana Cabral, and Spelman into the national spotlight. How could Spelman, a historically Black women's institution, host the rapper Nelly on campus for a bone marrow registration drive after he depicted Black women as objects in his music and videos? Beverly gave us the time to process, in class, our conflicted feelings about his video "Tip Drill" and his impending visit to campus. She thought our voices mattered, and she gave us the space to work it out. Our meek interest in writing a letter blossomed, with her encouragement, to naming Nelly the Misogynist of the Month, which distressed him so much he elected not to come to campus at all. The national attention that Nelly's bowing out garnered led to the invitation to the hip hop feminism conference, where I got my first honorarium check, and got to see Beverly's brilliance in action.

Who has time for the theory vs. activism debate when your classroom is a spaceship for praxis?

The resulting media attention raised Beverly's star as well, but she has remained committed to Spelman despite its sometime ambivalent relationship to her. She could be at any institution, but she remains dedicated to the students of Spelman College, teaching and mentoring new generations of Black feminists who will be in every sector of society, even some we haven't thought of yet.

Who has time for the Ivy league or PWIs when you can make a choice to change the world?

We've done this here before, but if you have ever taken a class with Beverly, heard or read her words and been moved, stand up.

Beverly, look around. This is the profound power of your scholarship in a discipline forged out of necessity for something different. You have inspired generations of Black feminists and feminists writ large. I hope you can feel your impact because we continue to feel yours.

Index

A

Ableism, xxii
Abolitionism, 27, 28
Abortion, 10, 28, 42
Abrams, Stacey, 198
Abzug, Bella, 253, 263
Academic politics, 98
Academic success, 341
Activism, xxi, 27, 30, 37, 39, 45, 53, 64, 66, 70, 74, 86, 128, 132, 174, 227, 237, 249, 252, 256, 293, 327, 328, 330
Adair, Thelma Davidson, 147
Adjunct faculty, 364, 365, 366
Affirmative action, 307, 308
Afric-American Intelligence Society, 29
Africa, 11, 38, 45, 62-69, 71, 96, 120, 122, 123, 158, 159
African American art, x, 224, 232, 236
African American feminist thought/tradition, xxii, 27, 63, 65, 114, 305, 306
African American intellectual history, 110, 112
African American Studies, 87, 172, 297, 301, 303, 304, 307, 334, 349
African American Women in Defense of Ourselves, 47
African art, 229, 240
African diaspora, 62, 66, 95, 120-127, 158, 171, 172, 298, 304, 309
African Diaspora studies, 120-127, 171, 172, 309
African feminism, 62, 63, 64, 66, 124
African feminist discourse, 62-69, 125
African feminist politics, 66
African feminist scholarship, 65, 123
African feminist thought, 63, 65
African women, 28, 62, 63, 64, 65, 66, 94, 121, 122, 123, 125, 228, 229, 297, 306
  Liberation narratives, 228
Africana Studies, 86
Africana Women's Studies, Atlanta University, 7
Afro-American, 319
Afro-Hispanic, 319
Afro-Hispanic writers, 96
Afrocentric, 18
Afrocentric feminism, 72, 124
Afrofemcentric elements, 244
Agbor-Tabi, Peter, 286-288
Agnes Scott College, 7, 18
Aidoo, Ama Ata, 62
Alabama State University, ix, 7, 203, 282, 291, 350
Alexander, M. Jacqui, 117, 176
Alexander, Michelle, 339
Algeria, 309
Allen, Leon, 258
Ali, Shaharazad, 22, 44, 59
All Black Lives Matter, 170
Amadiume, Ife, 121, 122
American Anti-Slavery Society, 29, 31
American Woman Suffrage Association (AWSA), 32
Amos, Emma, 224, 226, 231, 232
Anderson, Jervis, 55
Andrews, Lucie Clay, 147
Angelou, Maya, 237, 245
Anthony, Susan B., 32
Anti-apartheid, 249
Anti-Black violence, 202
Anti-Blackness, xxii,
Anti-feminism, 357
Anti-war/peace, 249, 259
Apartheid, 4, 10, 13, 233, 249, 253
Apuzzo, Virginia, 253
Arcus Foundation, 168, 170, 171, 172, 176, 194
Area Studies, 115, 156
Artists, 224-235
Ashbaugh, Carolyn, 107
Asexual, 330
Asia, 11, 38, 71, 123, 253
Asian-Hispanic, 319
Association of Black Women Historians, 120
Atlanta University, ix, 7, 185, 203, 297, 345, 349
  Africana Women's Studies, 7
Atlanta University Center, 7, 111, 171, 185, 206
  Zami Salon, 171
Audre Lorde Papers
  Audre Lorde Project (Phase I and II), 168, 169, 70, 171, 172, 174, 175, 176, 179, 194
  Arcus Foundation, 168, 170, 171, 172, 176, 194
  LGBT Program, 170
  Spelman Archives, 169
Avery, Byllye, 12, 361
Awkward, Michael, 72, 73

B

Baartman, Sarah, 371
Badran, Margot, 117
Bagley, Edythe Scott, 249
Baker, Ella, 331, 337, 338
Baker-Fletcher, Karen, 85, 86
Baldwin, James, 110, 179, 306
Ballot, xx, 31, 32, 54
Bambara, Toni Cade, x, xi, xxi, xxiii, 41, 46, 52, 71, 72, 78, 101, 110, 132, 226, 228, 279-280, 291, 309-322, 348, 352, 370
Banks, Brenda, 172
Baraka, Amiri, 110, 113
Barber-Scotia College, 146
Barkley-Brown, Elsa, 95, 97, 303
Barrow, Nita, 3
Basu, Amrita, 117
Bates, Daisy, 41, 55
  Little Rock's Central High School, 55
Battering, 23, 28
Baxter, Vivian, 245
Beale, Frances, xx, 42
Bearden, Romare, 226, 236, 241
Beasley, Phoebe, 241
Beauty parlors, 315
Bell, Rosann P., ix, x, 8, 82, 103, 111, 279, 291, 309, 310, 348
Bell-Scott, Patricia, x, 10, 45, 93, 97, 104, 108, 145, 205, 356, 359, 360
  National Endowment for the Humanities, 11
  SAGE: A Scholarly Journal on Black
Women, 10, 45, 94, 108, 120, 351, 357
  Wellesley College Center for Research on
Women, 7, 9, 10, 102, 203, 283, 345, 351
Bennett College, 145-155, 175, 185
  Educational opportunities, 145-155
  Player, Willa, 145, 148
Bethune, Mary McLeod, 104, 337, 338
Beyoncé, 363
Bhan, Esme, 86
Bibliographical essay, 151-155
Biggers, John, 241
Billops, Camille, 232
Biological sex, 121
Birth control, 38, 39, 179, 194, 263
Bitch stereotype/myth, xxi, 41, 220, 310, 316, 320
Black arts movement, 224, 231, 316, 317
Black Britain, 66, 123
Black communist women, xi
Black culture, 54, 101, 323
Black empowerment, 71, 97, 112, 135
Black Entertainment Television (BET), 56
Black eroticism, 244
Black families, 59, 60
Black feminism, 27-90, 130, 131, 134, 136, 204, 224, 233, 304, 307, 323-326, 368, 370
Black feminist critique, 224
Black feminist discourse, 40, 72, 75, 82, 116, 292
Black feminist forefathers, 70-81
Black feminist foremothers, xix, 309-322
Black feminist intellectual tradition, xi, 46, 82, 84, 85, 110-113, 114, 131, 132, 270, 334, 347, 348, 350
Black feminist lesbian manifesto, 2, 43
Black feminist perspective, 10, 45, 94, 130, 134, 135, 136, 138
Black feminist practitioners/therapists, 130, 134
Black feminist studies, x, xi, 82-90, 172, 206, 323, 348, 349, 353, 356
Black Feminist therapy, 128-141
Black feminist theory, 27, 45, 84, 87, 116, 138, 309, 334, 350
Black feminist thought, xi, xxv, 27, 31, 45, 84, 85, 131-138, 323, 324, 325, 329
Black feminist visionaries, 86
Black feminist/women writing, 8, 44, 57, 58, 82, 95, 97, 102, 103, 104, 110, 134, 204, 270, 279, 280, 291, 304, 309, 312, 317, 321, 323, 347
Black feminists, xix, xxv, 35, 37, 38, 41, 42, 44, 45, 46, 47, 51, 54, 56, 58, 60, 104, 124, 172, 206, 227, 228, 244, 263, 292, 306, 311, 312, 324, 325, 327, 330, 362, 372, 373
Black is Beautiful, 244
Black LGBT issues, 171, 172
Black liberation struggles, 38, 43, 56, 58, 131, 228, 369
Black Lives Matter, 170, 362
Black literary tradition, 110, 348
Black male artists, 236
Black male bashing, 43, 44, 56, 57, 59
Black male discourse, 52, 85
Male/female relationships, 10, 44, 54, 55, 57, 58, 112
Black male feminism, 72, 278, 324
Black male-on-male homicide, 58, 60

Black male sexism, 35, 42, 56
Black male suffrage, 54
Black male writers, 110
Black matriarch, 41, 104
Black masculinities, 70, 71, 307
Black media/press, 58
Black men, 38, 104, 70-81, 105, 132, 293, 306, 307, 319
Black mother-daughter relationships, 245
Black nationalist thought, 53, 59, 60, 311, 320
Black neo-conservatives, 112
Black Panther Party, 41, 53
Black political history, 70
Black Power ideology, 53
Black scholar-activist feminists, 352, 363
Black spirit, 318
Black Studies, 36, 82, 93-141, 162, 179, 181, 307, 323
Black theology, 96
Black women artists, 224-248
Black women literary scholars, 323
Black Women's Health Conference, 12
Black women's club movement, 33, 36, 83, 84
Black Women's Health Project, 45, 98, 360, 361, 362
Black women's higher education, 145-155
Black women's liberation, 27, 31, 35, 36, 38, 40, 41, 43, 57, 279
Black women's political development, 37
Black women's resistance, 227, 230
Black Women's Studies, 6, 7, 8, 9, 93-141, 148, 178, 297-308, 309, 348
  Institutionalization of, 302, 303
  Master's/PhD programs, 114
Black women's union, 319, 321
Black women's victimhood, 300
Boas, Louise Shutz, 145
Bodily integrity, 66
Body politics, 60, 158
Boseman, Chadwick, 198
Brazil, 66, 97, 123
Brewer, Rosalind, 198
Britain, 157
Brooks, Gwendolyn, xi, 211-223
  Female ghetto dwellers, 215, 219
  Poverty, 212, 214
  Urban poems, 217
Brown, Dorothy, 147
Brown, Elaine, 53
Brown, Hallie Quinn, 84
Brown, Kay, 227
Brown, Malcolm, 236, 241
Brown, Marie, 348
Brown, Tony, 57
Browne, Vivian, 232
Bryant College, 12
Buchanan, Beverly, 231
Burkett, Randall, 277
Burnett, Myra, 95, 96
Burnout, 357, 358
Burrill, Mary, 39
Burroughs, Nannie Helen, 35, 36
Bush, George, 46, 261
Bush, Sandra "Mama", 244, 245, 246
Busia, Abene, 117
Butler, Selena Sloan, 13, 146
Byrd, Rudolph P., x, 70, 168, 169, 172, 277-278, 284

C

Cabral, Amilcar, 206, 207
Cabral, Leana, 206, 207, 372
Cadbury, Henry, 251
Canada, 66, 123, 157
Cannon, Katie, 46
Capitalism, 38, 112, 272, 312
Carbardo, Devon, 254
Carby, Hazel, 45, 84
Caribbean, 37, 62, 66, 96, 123, 158, 304
Carmichael, Stokely, 113
Carter, Barbara,
  Spelman College, 11, 299
Carter, Mandy, 254, 255
Cary, Mary Shadd, 32
Casey-Hayford, Adelaide, 36
Catlett, Elizabeth, 224, 225, 228, 229, 231, 232, 233, 236-242, 244
Chafe, William, 105
Chase-Riboud, Barbara, 227, 243
Chavez, Cesar, 259
Chicana women, 311, 319
Chile, 157
China, 38
Chisholm, Shirley, 41, 42, 226, 227,
Chrisman, Robert, 44
Christian, Barbara, 44, 45, 82
Christian relationships, 190, 191

Civil Rights Movement, 49, 53, 225, 264, 332, 346
Civil strife, 66
Clark, Septima, 41
Clark University, 7, 114, 116
Clark Atlanta University, 110, 111, 119, 175, 176, 203
Clarke, Cheryl, 243
Class, 120, 121, 130, 132, 133, 134, 135, 138, 156, 178, 181, 205, 224, 238, 254, 273, 305, 334, 340, 346, 363, 364, 367
Class bias, 98, 263
Class exploitation, 16
Classism, xxii, 17, 51, 60, 111, 128, 134, 136
Cleage, Pearl, xix, 95
Cleaver, Kathleen, 41
Clifton, Lucille, 316
Clinical trials, 132
Clinton, Bill, 47, 48, 290
Cohen, Beverly, 372
Cole, Johnnetta Betsch, x, xi, xix, 17, 18, 47, 51-61, 97, 162, 168, 169, 172, 173, 204, 205, 277, 280, 299, 337
Coleman, Julia F., 36
Collins, Patricia Hill, 45, 132, 323
Colonialism, 62, 64, 87, 123
Columbus, Christopher, 16
Combahee River Collective, 42, 64, 229, 244, 263, 272, 328, 329, 330, 331
Committees of Seven, 36
Common, 198
Communist Party, 47
Community outreach, 6, 11,12, 351
Consciousness raising, 129, 135, 203
Cook, Blanche, 338
Cooke, Miriam, 117
Cooper, Anna Julia, xx, xxiii, 13, 34, 35, 36, 38, 40, 45, 46, 51, 52, 82-90, 101, 111, 112, 113, 132, 227, 264, 333, 343
Cooper, Brittney, 334
Coppin, Fannie Jackson, 84
Cothren, Lynn, 256, 257
Cott, Nancy, 106
COVID-19, 198-202, 292
Crenshaw, Taryn, 176
Creque-Harris, Leah, 95
Cross-class collaborations, 360, 361
Cross-cultural perspective, 6, 7, 10, 11, 94, 115, 116, 122, 133, 307, 355
Cruelty, 293
Cruse, Harold, 110-113
Cuba, 291, 319, 341
Cudjoe, Selwyn, 98
Cultural interventions, 136
Cultural literacy, 19, 133,
Cultural sensitivity, 133, 136, 158
Culture, 254
Curriculum development/syllabi, 6, 7, 10, 12, 13, 17, 18, 93, 94, 95, 96, 114-119, 148, 156, 157, 159, 162, 163, 178, 179, 180, 184, 203, 204, 297, 298, 299, 302, 304, 333, 334, 354

D

Dailey, Jr., Maceo, 98
Date rape, 23
Davies, Carole Boyce, 63, 96, 97
Davis, Angela, xix, xx, 44, 45, 47, 53, 58, 113, 205, 228, 249, 272, 273, 339
D'Emilio, John, 254
DeCosta-Willis, Miriam, 96
Delta Sigma Theta Sorority, 13
De Veaux, Alexis, 169, 325
Digital divide, 202
Dillard University, 175, 176, 177, 199, 238
Disability, 178, 187, 253
Discrimination, 39, 129, 130, 147, 175, 186, 187, 188, 190, 190, 193, 249, 257, 308
Disease, 62
Diversity, 28, 96, 104, 116, 131, 138, 173, 174, 177, 178, 182, 189, 190, 193, 220, 260
Django Unchained, 332
Domestic workers, 40
Double jeopardy, 34, 42
Douglass, Frederick, 13, 30, 31, 32, 54, 70, 74-75, 78, 113, 293, 330, 339
DuBois, W. E. B., 13, 39, 36, 74-78, 83, 84, 85, 86, 110, 113, 195
Duke University/University of North Carolina Women's Studies Research Center, 13
Durden, Frances Collier, 102
Dwelle, Georgia Rooks, 147
Dyson, Michael, 52

E

Early, Sarah J., 84
Economic exploitation, 28, 40, 42, 131, 336

Economic resources, 131
Edelman, Marian Wright, 147
Ellison, Ralph, x, 110, 211
Elmore, Ronn, 59
Emancipation, 328
Emerson College, 351
Emory University, xxvii, 8, 9, 114, 116, 172, 203, 277, 278, 329, 347, 349, 350, 353, 355, 357
Empowerment, 29, 32, 33, 46, 65, 71, 93, 97, 112, 128, 132, 133, 135, 136, 158, 186, 193, 225, 350
Endangered Black male, 58
Endesha, Giza Daniels, 232
England, 157
Eroticism, 244
Equality, 3, 28, 34, 35, 37, 40, 44, 48, 70, 72, 103, 128, 129, 131, 157, 158, 173, 174, 175, 176, 185, 186, 225, 252, 311, 369
Ethnic minority health, 132
Ethnic Studies, ix, xxiii, 115, 156
Ethnicity, 3, 17, 19, 115, 123, 178, 186, 233, 273
Ethnocentrism, 122, 123
Euro-American women, 311
Eurocentric male models, 17
Eurocentric values, 15
Europe, 125
European women, 158
Evans, Mari, 95, 205

F

Facebook, 192
Faculty governance, 161-167, 204
Family separation, 28
Family values, 47,
Fanon, Frantz, 207
Farm workers, 258, 259
Farmer, James, 55
Fauntroy, Walter, 253
Fauset, Jessie, 112
Feinberg, Leslie, 169, 171
Female circumcision, 63, 66
Female socialization, 128
Feminism, xx, xxvii, 23, 117, 134, 262, 272, 279, 300, 301, 307, 309, 310, 363, 365, 366
Feminism tout court, xxv
Feminist art movement, 224, 231
Feminist discourse, 3, 30, 40, 45, 46, 47, 62-69, 72, 82, 116, 117, 124, 125, 273, 292
Feminist forefathers, 70-81
Feminist ideology, 44, 48
Feminist lesbian bitches, xxi
Feminist literary criticism, 103, 110, 345, 346
Feminist-pan-Africanist views, 36, 37,
Feminist political philosophies/analysis, 128
Feminist resistance, 64
Feminist studies, x, xi, 82-90, 172, 206, 304, 305, 323, 348, 349, 353, 356
Feminist theory, xi, xx, 8, 27, 45, 62, 65, 84, 86, 87, 104, 114, 116, 117, 121, 125, 138, 206, 270, 273, 279, 309, 310, 352, 372
Feminist therapy, 128-141
Feminist vision, 38
Feminist warrior, 319
Fifteenth Amendment, 54
First Lady of the Civil Rights Movement, Coretta Scott King, 250
Fisk University, 175
Floyd, George, 199, 202
Forced marriage, 63
Ford Foundation, 7, 93, 94, 114, 156, 171, 178, 299, 351
Foreman, Matt, 254, 255
Forum '85, 3-5
Foster, Frances Smith, x
Fox-Genovese, Elizabeth, 349, 350
Franklin, Eleanor Ison, 147
Frazier, E. Franklin, 110
Freedom fighter, 263
Fund for Improvement of Postsecondary Education (FIPSE), 7

G

Gabel, Leona C., 83
Gachukia, Eddah, 3
Garner, Margaret, 29
Garrison, William Lloyd, 251
Garvey, Amy Ashwood, 37
Garvey, Amy Jacques, xx, 37, 38, 113, 227
Garvey, Marcus, 37, 39, 113
Gates, Jr., Henry Louis, 84
Gault, Charlayne Hunter, 289
Gay rights, 173, 250, 253-258, 264
Gay sexuality, 60
Gebre-Hewitt, Judy, 329
Gender equity, 271
Gender identity/equality, 3, 28, 34, 44, 48, 51,

131, 157,183, 186, 187, 188, 211
Gender issues, xii, 17, 27, 34, 52, 53, 60, 64, 66, 70, 105, 112, 114, 116, 117, 120, 121, 122, 124, 125, 128, 130, 133, 134, 135, 138, 156, 157, 158, 178-181, 183, 185, 186, 187, 190, 203, 204, 205, 224, 225, 228, 230, 238, 254, 298, 304-307, 325, 334, 340, 346, 368, 369
Gender oppression, 37, 62, 64, 75, 78, 128 ,131, 132, 308,
Gender politics, 206, 368
Gender privilege, 60
Gender-progressive forefathers, 70-81
Gender roles, 60, 129, 134, 135, 136, 156, 225, 312
Gender studies, 176, 304, 305
Genocide, 293, 339
Geographical regions, 121
Georgia State University, 171
Ghana, 309
Giddings, Paula, 44, 45, 52, 53, 83, 95, 111, 205, 228, 324, 327-344
Giles, Harriet, 146
Gilkes, Cheryl, 46
Glave, Thomas, 171
Global economy, 158
Global feminisms, 114, 118, 124, 157, 353
Global majority groups, xix
Global women's movements, 66, 280, 310
Global outreach, 351
Global perspective, 19, 114
Gouma-Peterson, Thalia, 232
Grant, Jacquelyn, 46, 95, 96
Grassroots women, 362, 363, 365
Grimke, Angelina Weld, 39
Guatemala, 309
Guinier, Lani, 47
Gumbs, Alexis Pauline, 334
Guy, Ernestine Varnado, xii, 8-9, 14, 271, 272, 346, 347, 351, 359, 371
Guy, Jr., Walter P., xii
Guy, Carmella, 281
Guy, Francine, 281
Guy-Sheftall, Beverly, 95, 103, 117, 132, 156, 168, 172, 203-207, 281, 308, 323-326, 327-344, 345-367, 368-370, 371-373
  Gender and Sexuality Institute, 371
  Mellon Foundation, 371
  Visionary statement, 308

H

Haley, Alex, x
Hamer, Fannie Lou, 41, 310, 330, 331
Hammonds, Evelynn M., 156, 297-308
Hanh, Thich Nhat, 262
Hansberry, Lorraine, xi, xx, 110, 112, 249, 264, 273, 291
Hare, Julia, 22, 43, 56
Hare, Nathan, 22, 43, 56
Harley, Sharon, 83, 102, 120
Harper, Frances E. W., 13, 27, 32, 54, 84, 113, 229
Hatch, James, 232
Hatch-Billops Collection, 232
Hate crimes, 182, 183, 192, 193, 260
Hayward, Dave, 258
HBCUs, xii, 161-167, 194, 195, 198-202, 297, 351, 370
  COVID-19, 198-202
  Curricular issues, 178-181
  LGBT issues, 170-197, 356
  Shared governance, 161-167
  Women studies, 297-308
Healing, 78, 135, 138, 246, 292, 294, 318
Health care, 12, 43, 45, 158, 193
Hedgeman, Anna Arnold, 40, 41, 55
Hegemonic Black nationalist discourse, 71
Hegemony, 66, 84, 123, 125
Height, Dorothy Irene, 337, 339
Herring, James, 237
Herzog, Melanie, 239
Heteronormativity, 170, 171, 179, 180, 188, 347
Heteropatriarchy, 206, 323
Heterosexism, 28, 42, 51, 60, 65, 70, 71, 128, 131, 136, 171, 185, 191, 192, 312
Heterosexist texts, 59, 122
Heterosexual, 15, 191, 263
  Students, 181-187, 192
Heterosexual morality, 179
Higher education, 145-155
Higher education career advancement, 48
Hill, Anita, xxv, 21-24, 46, 47, 53, 56, 59, 205, 278, 306, 368
Hill, Grant, 236, 239, 240, 241
Hilliard, David, 245
Hine, Darlene Clark, 54, 228
Hip-hop music, 343, 372
HIV/AIDS, 65, 66, 112, 188, 190, 191, 194, 206, 256

Hobson, Janell, 327-344
Holistic healing systems, 318
Holmes, Hamilton, 289
Holmes, Linda Janet, 279, 280
Holocaust, 13
Homophobia, xxii, 43, 57, 58, 71, 98, 112, 131, 132, 134, 168, 171, 173, 176, 180, 183, 184, 185, 191, 194, 206, 254, 255, 256, 260, 325
Homosexuality, 71, 180, 184, 253
hooks, bell (Gloria Watkins), xix, xxi, 15, 18, 44, 45, 46, 48, 52, 58, 60, 103, 104, 111, 132 168, 228, 231, 232, 270-274, 279, 310, 324
Hooks, Benjamin, 253
Hope, Eugenia Burns, 106
Housing, 28, 131
Howard University, 173, 174, 175, 185, 186, 198, 237, 283, 298, 302
Hughes, Langston, 315
Hull, Gloria, x, 44, 45, 205, 356
Human rights, 56, 82, 83, 128, 158, 176, 186, 197, 249, 250, 251, 253, 254, 256, 258, 259, 260, 261, 264, 341, 342
Human Trafficking, 333
Hurston, Zora Neale, x, 13, 82, 102, 111, 174, 292, 315, 316
Hurt, Byron, 206
Huston-Tillotson University, 146
Hutchinson, Louise Daniel, 83
Hutchinson, Earl Ofari, 59
Hypermasculine constructions/form, 60, 330

I

Identity politics, 301
Ideology, 158
Igbo women, 121, 122
Illiteracy, 62
Imperialism, 28, 37, 45, 84, 87, 131, 272, 339
Incest, 10, 23, 293
Inclusion, 158
Inda-Hispanic, 319
India, 11, 38, 355
Indigenous women, xx, 66, 117, 125
Infanticide, 29
International perspectives, 96
International scholarship, 156
International studies programs, 156
Internationalist, 280, 311, 320
Intersectionality, 82, 84, 93, 115, 120, 346
Intra-racial patriarchies, xxv
Involuntary breeding, 28
Iraq, 259

J

Jackson, Jesse, 198
Jackson, Mae, x
Jackson, Samuel L., 198
Jackson, Yvonne, 165
Jacobs, Harriet, 28, 228
Jamaica, 157
James, Stanlie M., x, 117
Jeanmarie, Redvers, 255
Jim Crow south, ix, 282, 290,
Johnson, James Weldon, 277
Johnson, Karen, 86
Johnson, Poppy, 227, 243
Johnson, Kendra, 173
Johnson, Winston, 250, 257, 258
Johnson-Odim, Cheryl, 117
Jolly, Margaret, 116
Jones, Claudia, xi, 39, 40, 264
Jones, Lois Mailou, 237
Jones, Rufus, 251
Jordan, Barbara, 249
Jordan, June, 44, 264
Joseph, Gloria I., 44, 168
Junior/Senior faculty, 161-167

K

K-12 classroom, 331, 332, 341, 366
Kahle, Frida, 246
Keller, Frances Richardson, 86
Keller, Yelena, 245, 246
Kennedy, Flo, 42, 226
Kennesaw College, 7
Kent, George, 215
Kenya, 14
  Nairobi, 3-5, 6
Kenyatta, Margaret, 3
Kerry, John, 261
Kimbrough, Walter, 199
King, Coretta Scott, xi, 249-269, 289, 333
  Anti-apartheid activism, 249
  Anti-war/peace activism, 249, 259, 262, 263
  Farm workers, 258, 259
  First Lady of the Civil Rights Movement, 250

Human rights, 258, 259, 260
King Holiday, 249, 258, 263
LGBTQ activism, 249, 253, 259
Social Justice, 249
Women's advocacy, 249
King, Jr., Martin Luther, xi, 18, 41, 55, 57, 113, 170, 195, 198, 283, 289, 293
Kingston, Maxine Hona, xxvi
Kirby, Victoria Diane, 174, 186
Kuumba, Bahati, xxi, 352

L

LaForce, Thessaly, 245, 246
Latin America, 62, 225
Latinx, 198
Lee-Smith, Hughie, 241
Lemert, Charles, 86
Lerner, Gerda, 83, 101, 104, 227
Lesbian/Gay, 23, 121, 122, 168, 170-197, 356
Lesbian feminism, xxv, 131, 254
Lesbian sexuality, 60, 293
Lewis, Earl, 277
Lewis, John, 55
Lewis, Samella, 237
LGBT, 170-197, 249, 250, 253-258, 356, 369
LGBT Studies, 179-181
LGBTQ issues, xi
Gay faculty, 180, 184
Curricular issues, 178-181
Student life, 181-187
Lincoln, 328, 332, 333
Lippard, Lucy, 227, 232, 243
Literary criticism, 95, 110, 345, 346
Locke, Alain, 86, 110, 174
Lofton, Eloise, 316
Lomax, Michael, 175
Long, Michael G., 250, 253
Lopez, Yolanda M., 231
Lorde, Audre, xi, xxi, 21, 23, 44, 45, 51-61, 119, 122, 131, 168-169, 170, 171, 172, 175, 176, 179, 194, 205, 226, 243, 253, 264, 271, 273, 277, 280
Love, Gregory, 260
Lowery, Joseph, 253
Lynching, 13, 28, 76, 131, 237
Lyons, Henry, 54, 59

M

Madhubuti, Haki, ix,
Madonna, 372
Mai Foundation, 351
Major, Naima, 98
Malcolm X, 57, 293
Male chauvinism, 40
Mammy, 46, 132, 135, 320
Mandela, Nelson, 57
Manderson, Lenore, 116
Manley, Albert E. 289
Marable, Manning, 112
March on Washington, 40, 41, 55, 251, 253, 255
Marginalization, xxv, 55, 99, 124, 130, 171, 226, 228, 270, 292, 311, 324
Marshall, Paule, 8
Marshall, Thurgood, 23, 46, 198
Masculinist literary canon/bias, x, 112, 182
Masculinities, 115, 305
Mass media, 112
Massachusetts Institute of Technology (MIT), 47
Massiah, Louis, 280, 311, 312
Matiba, Kenneth, 3
Matriarch, 316
May, Vivian, 86, 87, 329
Mays, Benjamin Elijah, 73-74, 78
McDaniel, Hattie, 320
McDougald, Elise, 37
McDowell, Deborah, 103
McFadden, Patricia, xx, 65, 206
McIntosh, Peggy, 366
McKay, Nellie Y., 75, 76
McKinney, Gene, 59
McLaughlin, Andrée, 304
McMillan, Sean, 174
Media, xxii, 44, 56, 58, 112, 157, 192, 233, 237, 246, 255, 293, 325, 369, 372
Mellon Foundation, 371
Memphis State University
Center for Research on Women, 13
Men Against Violence, 18
Mendieta, Ana, 231
Mental health, 12, 128-141, 201
Michael, Jason, 256
Middle Passage, 13
Militarism, 259

Miller, Dene, 59
Million Man March, 58, 306
Milner, Ron, 320
Miner, Myrtilla, 145
Minor, James, 161, 163
Misogynist genre, xx, 23, 44, 59, 157, 206, 368, 372
Misogyny, xxii, xxvii, 43, 47, 56, 157, 169, 185, 312, 368
Miss Gladys types, 315
Miss Naomi types, 315
Mohanty, Chandra, xix, 117, 298
Momism pathology, 320
Montgomery, May, 290
Moore, Annie Mae, 15
Mora, Francisco, 238
Morality, 33, 86, 179
Morehouse College, xxi, 7, 18, 72, 73, 175, 176, 185, 260, 261, 368
Morgan State University, 175, 185
Morris, Robert, 227
Morrison, Toni, x, xxv, 8, 29, 41, 198, 226, 291, 312, 316, 323
Mott, Lucretia 30,
Multidisciplinary dialect, 94
Multiethnic/multicultural organizing, 319
Murray, Pauli, xix, 55, 228

N

National Association for the Advancement of Colored People (NAACP), 35, 39
National Association of Colored Women (NCCW), 34
National Association of Wage Earners, 36
National Baptist Convention, 35
National Black Women's Health Project, 45, 98
  Vital Signs, 45
National Black Women's Network, 12
National Council of Research on Women, 13
National Endowment for the Humanities, 11
National Federation of Afro-American Women, 33
National League of Colored Women, 34
National Organization for Women (NOW), 41
National Training School for Women and Girls, 35
National Urban League, 39
National Woman Suffrage Association (NWSA), 32
National Women's Studies Association, xxi, 324, 328
Nationality, 181
Neal, Marc Anthony, 325
Nelly protest, 205, 206, 372
Nelson, Jill, 52
Neo-Black Art Movement, 316, 317
Neocolonialism, 62
Neoliberalism, 361
Neonationalist rhetoric, 300
New England Woman's Suffrage Association, 34
New England Women's Club, 33
New Era Club, 33
Newcomer, Mabel, 145
Niebuhr, Reinhold, 251
Nigeria
  Igbo women, 121, 122
Nipper, Darlene, 174
Nkrumah, Kwame, 207
Nonacademics/nonactivists, 324
Non-Governmental Organization (NGO) Forum, 4, 158
Nonviolent resistance, 250
Non-Western women, 17, 18
North Carolina Central University, 175, 185
Norton, Eleanor Holmes, 42

O

Obama, Barack, 290, 325, 335, 336, 339, 340
Obama, Michelle, 325
O'Brien, John, 292
Ogundipe-Leslie, Molara, 64, 122, 123
Ohio State University, 117
Omolade, Barbara, 52
O'Neal, Wendi, 173
Oppositional world view, 15
Oppression, 28, 34, 35, 40, 44, 46, 51, 58, 62, 64, 75, 76, 78, 105, 128, 130, 131, 132, 134, 135, 136, 138, 170, 225, 238, 262, 263, 264, 292, 293, 300, 305, 306, 310, 311, 316, 319
Orozco, Jose Clemente, 237

P

Packard, Sophia, 146
Page, Cara, 171

Painter, Nell, 228
Palestine, xxi, xxii, 291, 342
Pan African Congress, 36
Pan African organizations, 53
Pan Africanist, xxiii, 36, 37, 123, 311, 320
Parker, Bettye J., ix, 82, 104
Parker, Pat, 131
Parks, Rosa, 41, 55
Parsons, Lucy, 107
Patriarchal African traditions, 63
Patriarchy, xxii, xxvi, 16, 23, 44, 54, 58, 60, 71, 72, 77, 78, 84, 104, 112, 128, 129, 130, 133, 134, 135, 272, 278, 300, 305, 306, 311, 312
Patterson, Orlando, 22, 52
Peace movement, 78, 259, 261
Pedagogical resources, 157
Pedagogical strategy, 17, 18, 94, 114, 181, 343
Petry, Ann, 211
Philander Smith College, 175
Phillips, Ivory Paul, 165, 166
Phillips, Layli, 171
Phillips, Mona, 96
Pindell, Howardena, 230, 231, 232
Player, Willa, 145, 148
Police brutality, 60
Political activism, 53, 29, 135, 333, 338, 345, 350, 357, 372
Political economy, 367
Political expediency, 170
Political institutions, 261
Political marginalization, 55, 86
Politicization, 128
Polygamy, 63
Porter, James, 237
Posey, Willi, 230
Poverty, 28, 60, 62, 76, 112, 131, 158, 159, 214, 260, 293, 342, 364
Powell, Kevin, 325
Powell, Richard, 240
Price, Aaron, 260
Price, Glenda, 156, 299
Prison-industrial complex, 339, 340, 341
Prison reform, 43
Profeminist activism, 70
Psychiatric symptoms, 135
Psychological distress/symptoms, 134, 135,
Psychosexual obsession, 320
Psychosocial stressors, 130, 133, 136, 137
Puerto Rican women, 227, 311, 319
Putnam, Glendora McIlwain, 147

Q

Queer theory, 116, 179
Quilts, 230

R

Race, 17, 60, 70, 105, 116, 120, 121, 125, 133, 134, 156, 178, 203, 205, 224, 228, 254, 273, 298, 300, 302, 305, 306, 307, 308, 319, 330, 332, 334, 339, 346, 364, 368, 369
Race/gender debate/messages, xii, 54, 60, 105, 106
Race loyalty/disloyalty, 56, 60, 311
Race regeneration, 51, 52
Race traitors, 51
Racial caste system, 105
Racial discrimination, 129, 238, 263
Racial equality, 157, 202
Racial/ethnic women, 123
Racial issues, 171, 172
Racial privilege, 4
Racial uplift, 35
Racialization, xxvi
Racism, 4, 15, 19, 28, 37, 40, 42, 43, 47, 51, 52, 60, 62, 78, 87, 104, 105, 111, 112, 128, 130, 131, 132, 136, 138, 231, 254, 256, 260, 284, 285, 293, 305, 306, 335, 336, 340, 371
Radical activism, 228, 264
Radical pedagogy, 17
Radical political work, 16
Ramphele, Mamphele, 305, 306
Randolph, A. Philip, 40, 55, 255
Randolph, Antonia, 173
Ransby, Barbara, 331, 337
Rap/Reggae music, 112, 157
Rape, 10, 23, 43, 60, 229
Read, Florence, 146
Reagan, Ronald, 47
Religion, 178, 307
Religious fundamentalisms, 66
Remond, Charles, 31
Reparations, 342
Reproductive freedom/rights, 38, 43, 66
Research processes, 97
Revolutionary feminism, 310
Revolutionary pedagogy, 15, 71, 78

Rice, Condoleezza, 340
Richardson, Bernard L., 175
Ringgold, Faith, 224, 226-230, 232, 243, 244
Rivera, Diego, 237
Robeson, Eslanda Goode, 113, 331
Robeson, Paul, 113
Robinson, Ruby Doris Smith, 41
Robnett, Belinda, 53
Rodgers, Carolyn, 316
Rodgers-Rose, LaFrances, 102
Role appropriate behavior, 314
Role identities, 135, 319
Roosevelt, Eleanor, 338
Ross, Susan J., 280
Roth, Moira, 231, 232
Royster, Beatrice Hom, 102
Royster, Jacqueline Jones, 11, 12
  Director of the Writing Center, 12
  SAGE: A Scholarly Journal on Black Women, 93, 108
Ruffin, Josephine St. Pierre, 13, 33, 34, 35
Rushing, Andrea Benton, 120
Russia, 38
Russo, Ann, 117
Rustin, Bayard, 55, 251, 253-256

S

Saar, Betye, 227, 231, 243
SAGE: A Scholarly Journal on Black Women, 10, 45, 94, 95, 108, 120, 351, 357, 359, 360
  Bell-Scott, Patricia, 10, 108, 351
  Guy-Sheftall, Beverly, 108
  Royster, Jacqueline Jones, 108
  Sims-Wood, Janet, 98, 108
Sage Women's Educational Press, 13
  Black mother/daughter relationships, 13, 45
Salem Massachusetts Female Antislavery Society, 29
Sales, Ruby, 168, 169, 174
Sanchez, Sonia, 113, 205
Sanders, Kimberly Wallace, 156
Sanger, Margaret, 38, 39
Sapphire, 320
Say Her Name movement, 368, 369
Schapiro, Miriam, 232
Science and technology, 45
Scott, Evelyn, 342
Scott, Joyce, 233
Scott, Obadiah, 252
Second-wave, xi, 48, 129, 131, 309, 331, 334
Senaca Falls, xx, 29, 30, 74
Senegal, 63, 64
Sex/gender binary, 121
Sex roles, 128
Sexism, 16, 19, 23, 28, 37, 40, 41, 42, 44, 46, 47, 51, 52, 56-60, 71, 78, 85, 103, 104, 105, 111, 128, 129, 131, 132, 136, 138, 256, 312, 325, 368, 371
Sexual autonomy, 39
Sexual exploitation, 28, 42, 47, 229
Sexual harassment, 23, 46, 183, 190
Sexual orientation/identity, 122, 130, 132, 135, 182, 183, 186, 187, 189, 190, 246, 319, 332
Sexual politics, 22, 43, 132
Sexual standards, 315
Sexuality, xii, 65, 66, 70, 116, 117, 121, 122, 125, 131, 134, 138, 168, 170, 171, 172, 178-181, 190, 204, 205, 224, 244, 254, 301, 302, 308, 325, 367, 368
Shange, Ntozake, 22, 43, 44, 56, 57, 324
Shahani, Leticia, 3
Shakur, Assata, 341
Shared governance, 161-167
Shepard, Matthew, 260
Simanga, Michael, ix
Simmons, Aishah Shahidah, xix, 338
Simmons, Ruth, 299
Simpson, O. J., 53, 54, 59
Sims, Lowery, 233
Sims-Wood, Janet, 98, 108
Siqueiros, David Alfaro, 237
Skeeter, Sharyn, 102
Slave men,
  Emasculation, 104
Slave narratives, 342
Slave resistance, 228
Slave women, 104
  Sexual exploitation, 104, 229
Slavery, 28, 44, 52, 104, 332, 335, 336, 339, 340, 342,
Sloan, Margaret, 42, 131
Slowe, Lucy Diggs, 174
Smith, Barbara, x, 42, 44, 45, 103, 131, 205, 228, 243, 291, 327-344, 351, 356
Smith, Karma Bene Bambara, 280
Smith, Maxine Atkins, 147
Smith, Charles Michael, 53
Social action/activism, 97, 128, 129, 135, 136, 263

Social equality, 129
Social gender, 121
Social identity, 129
Social justice, 66, 186, 263
Social media, 369
Social welfare activities, 106
Socialist, xxiii, 43, 280, 311, 320
Socialist Black feminist organization, 43
Solidarity, xxvii
South Africa, 4, 14, 66, 259, 305, 306
South America, 123
South Seas, 71
Southern Christian Leadership Conference, 41
Southern University, 175
Sowell, Thomas, 110
Speck, Patricia, 345
Spelman Archives, 13
  Audre Lorde Papers, 168, 169
Spelman College, ix, xx, xxvi, 4, 5, 93-100, 156, 161, 161-166, 168-169, 171, 173, 177, 178, 179, 198, 201, 203-207, 261, 277, 283, 285, 286, 287, 289, 290, 291, 297, 345, 347, 362, 365, 368, 371, 372,
  Black Women's Health Conference, 12
  Black Women's Studies, 7, 178, 299
  Black Women's Studies Faculty and Curriculum Project, 7
  Carter, Barbara, 11, 299
  Cole, Johnnetta B., x, xi, xix, 17, 18, 47, 97, 162, 168-169, 172, 173, 204, 205, 299
  Educational opportunities, 145-155
  Gender and Sexuality Institute, 371
  Giles, Harriet, 146
  LGBT issues, 173, 175, 179, 185
  Manley, Albert E., 289
  Mellon Foundation, 371
  Packard, Sophia, 146
  Price, Glenda, 156, 299
  Read, Florence, 146
  Simmons, Ruth, 299
  Stewart, Donald, 11, 147, 149, 204, 299
  Tatum, Beverly Daniel, 162, 165
  Toni Cade Bambara Scholars/Write/Activists Program, xxi, 370
  Women's Research and Resource Center, xx, 6-14, 93, 168-169, 170, 177, 178, 204, 205, 271, 280, 286, 291, 329, 334, 351, 371
  Women's Studies courses, 6-14, 301, 302, 303, 352
Spielberg, Steven, 22, 44, 57, 292
Spock, Benjamin, 262
Spousal abuse, 60
Springer, Kimberly, 53
Stanton, Elizabeth Cady, 30, 32, 74
Staples, Robert, 43, 57
Steady, Filomina Chioma, 45, 62, 102, 304
Steinem, Gloria, 253
Stereotypical images, 46, 47, 132, 134, 135, 230
Sterilization abuse, 28, 38, 42, 43, 131
Stevenson, Brenda, 228
Stewart, Donald,
  Spelman College president, 11, 147, 149, 204, 299
Stewart, Maria W., 27-30, 58, 83, 227
Stone, Lucy, 32, 34
Stowe, Harriet Beecher, 339
Strain, Tracy Heather, 291
Stress, 133, 136, 137, 139
Strobel, Margaret, 117
Student Nonviolent Coordinating Committee, 41, 53
Sub-Saharan Africa, 121
Suicide, 182, 183, 194
SUNY, Binghamton, 171
Superwoman, 136
Supreme Court, 23, 46, 53
Suffragists, 54
Syria, xix, xxii

T

Tang, Rosemarie, 117
Tanis, Farah, 341
Tatum, Beverly Daniel, 162, 165
Taylor, Breanna, 202
Terborg-Penn, Rosalyn, 83, 102, 120
Terrell, Mary Church, 13, 34, 35, 36, 83, 85, 104,
Terrorism, 328
Tesfagiorgis, Freida High, 224, 236, 244
Textbooks, 334
"The beloved community," 249-269
Therapeutic processes, 130
Theoharis, Jeanne, 250
Thiarn, Awa, 63
Third World feminism, 355
Third World women, xxiii, 3, 6, 11, 17, 41, 114, 117, 124, 156, 309, 310, 311, 319

Thomas, Clarence, xxv, 21-24, 46, 47, 53, 54, 56, 59, 306, 368
Thomas, Mickalene, 243-248
Thurman, Howard, 251
Tillet, Salamisha, 289, 294
Toni Cade Bambara Scholar Activist Writer's Collective, xxi, 280, 351, 370
Torres, Lourdes, 117
Townes, Emily, 46
Transformation, 15, 52, 64, 96, 114, 159, 162, 169, 178, 195, 203, 205, 206, 246, 261, 292, 299
Transnational feminism, 324, 337
Trauma, 138
True Womanhood, 85, 104
Truth, Sojourner, xx, xxi, 13, 27, 28, 31, 38, 42, 54, 77, 83, 104, 111, 227, 233, 338, 348
Truth-telling, xxvii, 60, 293, 334
Tubman, Harriet, xxi, 41, 42, 77, 104, 111, 227, 229, 233, 316, 327-344,
Tucker, C. Delores, 263
Tuskegee Institute, 36
Tyson, Mike, 53, 59

U

UN Decade for Women, 159
Underground Railroad, 229, 328, 329, 331, 339
United Kingdom, 123
United Nations Decade for Women Conference, 4, 6
Universal Negro Improvement Association (UNIA), 37, 38
University of Maryland, 117 ??
University of Medicine and Dentistry of New Jersey, 12
University of North Carolina, 13
Urban Black experience, 212

V

Vanderbilt Medical School, 283
Varnado, Willie Louis, 282
Vietnam, xxi, 259, 261, 262, 280, 309, 310, 319
Villard, Oswald Garrison, 251
Violence, xxvi, 10, 43, 48, 57, 66, 76, 78, 112, 157, 158, 182, 183, 184, 189, 192, 194, 251, 260, 293, 306, 324, 336, 337, 341, 368, 369
Visionary social theorist, 86
Vital Signs, 45

W

Wade-Gayles, Gloria, 103, 111
Walker, Alice, x, xix, xx, 8, 13, 22, 42, 44, 45, 46, 57, 82, 96, 102, 111, 124, 168, 170, 205, 226, 230, 243, 249, 261, 262, 263, 273, 277, 289-294, 312
Walker, Margaret, x, 112, 240, 339
Walker, Sheila, 96, 97
WalkingStick, Kay, 232
Wall, Cheryl, 230, 279
Wallace, Michele, 22, 43, 44, 56, 57, 227, 228, 324
War, 260, 293
Ward, Samuel Ringgold, 32
Washington, D.C., 83
Washington, Booker T., 113
Washington, Margaret Murray, 36
Washington, Mary Helen, 82, 84, 85, 102, 292, 317, 318
Washington, Sterling, 174
Watkins, Gloria (bell hooks), 271
Watkins, Jr., Levi., 198, 281-285, 287, 365
Watkins, Sr., Levi, xii, 271, 281
Watkins, Lillian Varnado, 281
Weems, Renita, 46
Welfare, 28, 131
Wellesley College, 7, 9, 10, 102, 203, 283, 345, 351
Wellesley College Center for Research on Women, 7, 351
Black Women's Studies Faculty and Curriculum Project, 7
Fund for Improvement of Secondary Education (FIPSE), 7
Wells, Aaron, 176
Wells, Ida B., 33, 84, 85, 106, 112, 113, 176, 237, 264, 331, 333, 334, 337, 338, 343,
Wells, James, 237
West Africa, xxii, 121, 249, 288
West Indies, 11
White, Deborah Gray, 45, 52, 228
White feminist discourse, 30, 41, 44, 56, 66, 122, 124, 125, 292, 309
White fiction, 320
White male artists, 227
White media, 44
White men, 97, 105, 271, 306, 335
White racism, 60
White suffragists, xx

White supremacy, xxii, 206, 251, 273, 312, 325, 335, 339
White women, 27, 31, 33, 105, 106, 129, 131, 133, 138, 158, 225, 227, 304, 307, 308, 311, 372
Racism of, 23, 40, 43, 44, 52, 87, 103, 231, 272, 273
White women's ideology, 44
White women's movement, 44, 103
Williams, John A., 320
Williams, Susan, 230
Winfrey, Oprah, 198
Wholley, JeShawna, 186
Wilkins, Roy, 55
Williams, Delores, 46
Williams, Fannie Barrier, 74, 83, 84
Wilson, William J., 110
Winfrey, Oprah, 326
Wisdom sharing, xxvii
Woman's Era Club, 34
Womanist, 46, 96, 124, 293
Womanism, 292
Womanist theologians, 46
Women's advocacy, 249
Women's art movement, 226
Women's Educational Equity Act (WEAA),10
Women's liberation movement, xi, 23, 30, 62, 83, 84, 262, 263, 271, 272, 293, 309, 310, 311, 319
Women's Research and Resource Center, xix, xx, xxi, xxiii, 6-14, 45, 93, 94, 108, 111, 148, 156, 168, 175-178, 204, 205, 271, 280, 286, 291, 328, 334, 351, 371
Arcus Foundation, 170, 178
Audre Lorde Project (Phase I and II), 171, 178
Charles Stewart Mott Foundation, 6, 93
Ford Foundation, 93, 94
Goals, 6
LGBT Program, 170
Mai Foundation, 351
Toni Cade Bambara Scholar Activist
Writer's Collection, xxi, 280, 351, 370
Women's rights, 28, 40, 41, 83, 263, 264, 330, 338
Women's Studies, x, 3, 4, 6-14, 58, 94, 95, 101-109, 114-119, 156, 178, 179, 181, 297-309, 334, 345, 349, 366
Master's/PhD programs, 114
Women's suffrage, 30, 31, 34, 54
Woodson, Carter G., 86, 110
Woody, Thomas, 145
Wright, Richard, 110, 211

X

Xavier University, 198
Xenophobic nationalisms, 158
Young, Andrew, 18, 198, 262
Young, Whitney, 55
Young Communist League, 39
Zami Salon, 171
Atlanta University Center, 171
Zinn, Howard, 289, 290
Zucker, Barbara, 230